Johann J. Hoffmann

A Japanese Grammar

Johann J. Hoffmann

A Japanese Grammar

ISBN/EAN: 9783741195327

Manufactured in Europe, USA, Canada, Australia, Japa

Cover: Foto ©Andreas Hilbeck / pixelio.de

Manufactured and distributed by brebook publishing software (www.brebook.com)

Johann J. Hoffmann

A Japanese Grammar

A
JAPANESE GRAMMAR.

BY

J. J. HOFFMANN, Phil. Doc.

MEMBER OF THE ROYAL ACADEMY OF SCIENCES, ETC. ETC.

PUBLISHED BY COMMAND OF

HIS MAJESTY'S MINISTER FOR COLONIAL AFFAIRS.

PRINTED BY A. W. SYTHOFF
WITH THE GOVERNMENT CHINESE AND JAPANESE TYPES.
LEIDEN 1868.

SOLD BY
E. J. BRILL AND A. W. SYTHOFF.

TO

HIS EXCELLENCY THE RIGHT HONORABLE

J. J. ROCHUSSEN
L. L. D.

MINISTER OF STATE, LATE GOVERNOR OF DUTCH EAST INDIA, LATE MINISTER FOR THE
DEPARTMENT OF THE COLONIES

IN GRATITUDE FOR THE LIBERAL AND ENLIGHTENED MANNER IN WHICH HE HAS PATRONIZED
THE STUDY OF THE CHINESE AND JAPANESE LANGUAGES AND LITERATURE

THIS WORK IS VERY RESPECTFULLY INSCRIBED

BY HIS EXCELLENCY'S MOST OBEDIANT SERVANT

THE AUTHOR

PREFACE.

The Grammar of the Japanese language, which accompanied with this Preface, is simultaneously published in the English and in the Dutch languages, is an original work, not a remodelling or an imitation of any other works of that stamp at present existing. As the result of a many years' study of the Japanese literature, it describes the written or book language, as it really exists in its ancient, as well as in its modern forms.

It also contains the author's own observations on the domain of the spoken language, which his intercourse with native Japanese in France, in England and especially in the Netherlands has afforded him ample opportunities to make; opportunites, which have been the more valuable to him, in as much as that they brought him in contact with people belonging to the most civilized and the most learned, as well as with those of the inferior classes of Japanese society. Thence he derives the right, even though he has never actually tredden the soil of Japan, to embrace the spoken language in the range of his observations, and to treat it in connection with the written language.

The author is convinced that, all he has quoted from Japanese writings, whatever their character, is genuine: he relies upon it himself, and trusts that the experience of others, unprejudiced, will find that it is so.

With regard to the manner in which he has conceived the language, and in all its phenomena treated it analytically and synthetically, he believes it to be in consonance with the spirit of this language, simple and natural, and, — his daily experience confirms this, — thoroughly practical.

PREFACE.

This method of his, was made known in general outline ten years ago, when he published the *Proeve eener Japansche Spraakkunst* door Mr. J. H. DONKER CURTIUS, and the seal of approbation was affixed to it by the judgement of scholars, whereas Mr. S. R. BROWN, who, in 1863, published the very important contribution: *Colloquial Japanese or conversational sentences and dialogues in English and Japanese*, not only founded his *Introductory remarks on the Grammar*, on the Author's method, but with a few exceptions, followed it in its whole extent.

The Grammar, now published, to lay claim to completeness, ought to be followed by a treatise on the Syntax, the materials for which are prepared. It will be published as a separate work, and be of small compass.

By these aids, initiated in the treatment of the language, the student may, with profit, make use of the Japanese-Dutch-English Dictionary, for the publication of which the author has prepared all the materials necessary, and by so doing he will have at his disposal the most important means of access to the Japanese literature.

LEIDEN, May 1868. THE AUTHOR.

CONTENTS.

INTRODUCTION.

Page.
1. Connection of the Japanese with the Chinese language. — The necessity of uniting to the study of the Japanese, that of the Chinese language............................... 1.
2. On the writing of the Japanese............ 2.
3. Introduction of the written and the spoken languages of China into Japan.............. 3.
4. Application of the Chinese writing, to the writing of the Japanese language.......... 6.
5. The Japanese writing proper.
   a. The Katakana................................. 6.
   b. The Fira-gana................................ 7.
6. The Japanese phonetic system............. 7.
   A. Systematic arrangement of the 47 sounds, expressed by Chinese and Japanese Kana signs................................. 7.
   B. The Irova in Chinese characters, and in Katakana signs.......................... 9.
7. Repetition of syllables. — Stenographic signs. — Stops........................... 11.
8. Remarks on the Japanese system of sounds, and the expression of it with our letters.... 12.
9. Doubling of consonants by assimilation..... 18.
10. Accent and rhythm....................... 20.
11. The Japanese running-hand Fira-gana.

    a. The Irova in Fira-gana.......... 21.
    b. Synopsis of the Fira-gana characters most in use................................. 22.
12. Written, or book language.................. 29.
    A. Exclusively Chinese.................... 29.
       Chinese dialects in Japan............... 30.
       Chinese text with Japanese translation... 32.
    B. Books written in the Japanese language. 34.
    C. Style. a. Old Japanese................. 38.
             b. New Japanese................. 38.
13. Language spoken. — General conversational language and dialects..................... 39.
    Epistolary style......................... 42.
14. On the parts of speech.................... 43.
15. Glance at the arrangement and connection of words in Japanese......................... 44.

ETYMOLOGY, NATURE AND INFLECTION OF WORDS.

CHAPTER I.

NOUNS.

§ 1. The root................................. 49.
§ 2. Radical or primitive word................ 49.
§ 3. Radical in composition................... 49.

CONTENTS.

	Page
A. Coördination	50
B. Subordination	50
I. Genitive subordination	50
II. Objective subordination	
1. direct	50
2. indirect	50
III. The radical form, as definition before adjectives	50
Emphonic modification	50
§ 4. Gender	51
A. Gender logically included in particular nouns	51
B. 1. Gender indicated by the particles *O* and *Me*	51
2. Gender expressed by *Oso* and *Mesu*	52
3. By *Ko* and *Me*, old-Japanese *Ki* and *Mi*	52
C. Application of the ideas of male and female to objects without sex	52
D. Chinese expressions for the distinction of sex	52
§ 5. Number	53
A. Singular	53
B. I. Plural expressed by repetition of the noun	54
II. Plural expressed by nouns used adjectively which signify a quantity, generality	55
1. Japanese forms	55
2. Chinese forms	56
III. The plural expressed by collective words, as *Ra*, *Tomo* (*domo*), *Gata*, *Bara*, *Nami*, *Tatsi*, *Siu*, *Goto* and *Nado*, used as suffixes	56
IV. Plural expressed by adverbs, which unite the idea of multitude to the predicate verb, *Mina*, *Nokorazu*, *Kotogotoku*	59
§ 6. Isolating of the noun by the suffix *ra*, *ro*; *y*, *wo*; *si*, &c.	60
§ 7. Declension	61
I. Nominative, Vocative	61
II. Accusative	62
III. Genitive	63

	Page
1. *Ga*, as index of the subject	64
2. Genitive suffixes *No*, *Na* and *Tsu*	66
IV. Dative and Terminative. The suffix *Ye* (*ye*)	67
The suffix *Ni*, as sign of the	
a. Dative or Ablative	68
b. Local	68
c. Modal	68
d. Causal and Instrumental	69
e. Dative of the person	69
f. Dative of the thing	69
g. Terminative	70
V. *To*, *Nite*, *De*	70
VI. Ablative, characterised by *Yori* or by *Kara*	71

CHAPTER II.

PRONOUNS.

	Page
§ 8. I. Qualifying nouns, which serve as pronouns	74
A. For "I"	74
B. For the person spoken to	75
Particular names of persons relative to distinguish the person concerned	77
II. Pronouns proper, formed from the adverbs of place *Wa*, *A*, *Ka*, *Ko*, *Yo*, *So*, *Do* (*Do*), *idem*	78
a. Immediate compounds with *N'a*	80
b. Immediate compounds of the other adverbs of place with *Ko* (*ku*), *Tsi*, *Tsira* and *Tsutsi*	80
c. *Da-ye*, *Wa-ga*	82
d. Pronouns possessive, formed from radical words indicating place, by suffixing *No*	83
e. Substantive pronouns, formed from adverbs of place, by suffixing *Re*	84
1) *Ware*, 2) *Are*, *Ore*, 3) *Kare*, 4) *Nare*	86
5) *Sore*, *()*	87
7) *Tare* (*Dare*), *Tore* (*Dore*), *idem*	88
III. Determinative and reflective pronouns	89

CONTENTS.

	Page.
A. 1. *Onore*, *omoi-dokoro*	89.
2. *Mi*, *Midzukara*, *Waga-mi*	89.
B. Expressions borrowed from the Chinese: 1. *Zio*, 2. *Zi-sin*, 3. *Zi-bun*, 4. *Zi-ovo*	93.
IV. Expression of reciprocity: *Tagai ni*, &.	94.
V. Pronouns indefinite: *Hito*, *Are-fto*, *Mo-no*. — *Dare mo* and *Nani mo* followed by a verb negative	95.
VI. Relative pronoun *Tokoro*	97.
VII. Interrogative pronouns derived from *Fa* or *To*, vulgo *Da* or *Do*	97.
1. *Nani*, what?	99.
2. *Ika*, how?	101.
Interrogative pronouns with the suffix, *mo*	102.
VIII. Arrangement of the personal pronouns in the conversational language	102.

CHAPTER III.

THE ADJECTIVE.

§ 2. Distinction between the adjective and possessive forms	110.
I. The adjective in the written language.	
A. Joined to a same substantive	105.
B. Adjectives in *Ki*.	
1. a. *Ki*, termination of the adjective, used as attribution	105.
b. Adjectives in *ki*, used as nouns concrete	106.
2. The termination *ku*, an adverbial form. The same, inclosed by the suffix *wa*	106.
3. a. *Si*, form of the adjective, as predicate	106.
b. As such, superceded by *Kari*	107.
4. *Sa*, forming nouns abstract	107.
5. List of adjectives in *Si*	107.
6. Examples showing the use of the forms cited	110.
II. The adjective according to the spoken language	110.

	Page.
Examples, showing the use of the forms	112.
Derivative adjectives	
§ 10. Adjectives in *baru* and *garu*	112.
§ 11. " " *siru*	114.
§ 12. " " *mira*, *na* and *kiru*	114.
§ 13. Derivative adjectives in *ka*	116.
§ 14. " " *yaka*	117.
§ 15. " " *biki* or *baki*	116.
§ 16. " " *sisi*	118.
§ 17. " " *bi-sisi*	124.
§ 18. " " *ra-sisi*	122.
§ 19. " " *beki*	127.
§ 20. " " *mabi*	127.
§ 21. Adjectives with the negative prefix *Na*, or the Chinese *Fa*	124.
§ 22. Adjectives with a previous definition	129.
§ 23. Definition of adjectives by adverbs, which denote the presence of a quality in full degree	130.
§ 24. Definition of adjectives by adverbs, which denote the presence of a quality in a higher degree. Absolute comparative	130.
§ 25. The relative or real comparative.	
1. Attribution of a quality in equal degree	131.
2. Attribution of a quality in a higher degree	132.
§ 26. The absolute superlative	124.
§ 27. The relative superlative	134.
§ 28. Expression of the excess of a quality	126.

CHAPTER IV

NUMERALS.

§ 29. The ancient Japanese cardinal numbers	137.
§ 30. The Chinese cardinal numbers	141.
§ 31. The ordinal numerals	142.
§ 32. The iterative numerals	142.
§ 33. The doubling or multiplying numerals	144.
§ 34. The sort numbers	144.
§ 35. The distributive numbers	145.
§ 36. The fractional, or broken numbers	146.

CONTENTS.

	Page
§ 37. Numeral substantives	147
I. Japanese numeratives	149
II. Chinese numeratives	152

Notation of time.

§ 38. Enumeration of years	154
§ 39. Chronological notation of years	155
1. after the cycle	155
2. after the years of governments	156
§ 40. Enumeration of years by year-names	157
§ 41. Division of the solar year	158
§ 42. Enumeration of months	159
§ 43. Enumeration of the days	160
§ 44. Notation of hours	162

Measures, weights and coins.

§ 45. Measures of length	166
§ 46. Superficial measures	168
§ 47. Measures of capacity	168
§ 48. Weights	169
§ 49. Iron, copper and bronze coins	171
§ 50. Silver coins	171
§ 51. Gold coins	172

CHAPTER V

ADVERBS.

§ 52. I. Adverbs proper	172
II. Improper adverbs, or adverbial expressions	172

	Page
I. Nouns	172
2. Verbs in the gerund	175
Distribution of adverbs according to their signification	175
§ 53. Adverbs of quality	175
§ 54. " " degree	176
§ 55. " " circumstance	176
§ 56. " " place and space	177
§ 57. " " time	178
§ 58. " " manner	181
§ 59. " " connecting propositions	182
Alphabetical synopsis of the adverbs cited	183

CHAPTER VI

WORDS EXPRESSIVE OF RELATION.
(POSTPOSITIONS)

§ 60. Retrospect of the inflexions	185
§ 61. Distinction of the words expressive of relation	185
§ 62. Nouns, used as expressive of relation	186
§ 63. Verbs in the gerund, used as words expressive of relation	192
A. With a previous accusative	192
B. With a previous local, or dative	195
Alphabetical synopsis of the words expressive of relation (cited)	195

CONTENTS.

CHAPTER VII.

THE VERB.

	Page
§ 64. Voices of the verb	197
§ 65. Moods	197
§ 66. Tenses	198
§ 67. Person and Number	198
§ 68. The verbal root	198
§ 69. The Imperative mood	199
§ 70. Closing-form of the verb	200
§ 71. The substantive and attributive form	201
§ 72. Gerund.	
1. Origin of the form	202
2. Modifications introduced by the spoken language	203
Examples of the use of the gerund	205
§ 73. The verbal root in the Local (substantive form)	205
§ 74. The concessive form expressed by *mo* or *demo*	206
expressed by *domo* or *ridomô*	205
§ 75. The form of the Future	206
1. The simple Future	208
Etymology of this form	209
Examples of the use of the forms cited	211
The certain Future of the written language	212
II. The periphrastic Future.	
A. of the written language, formed by	
1. ... *aran*, *arauzu*, *ran*	212
2. ... *nuramu*, *naranu*, *naran*	212
3. ... *uzuran* — *ouzuran*	213
4. ... *zuran*	213
5. ... *mazi*	213
B. The periphrastic Future of the spoken language	214
§ 76. The suppositive form	215
§ 77. The continuative verbal form (*ari*, *iri*, *uri*, *ori*)	217
§ 78. I. ... *te ari*, ... *te eri*, ... *te iri*	218
II. ... *tari*, ... *teru*	219
Forms of the past tense.	
§ 79. ... *tari*, ... *taru*, ... *ta*	220
§ 80. ... *eri*, ... *rei*, ... *eru*, ... *reru*	220

	Page
§ 81. ... *ki*, ... *si*, ... *kon*	224
§ 82. ... *keri*, ... *keri*, ... *keru*, ... *kerun*	227
§ 83. ... *tari-ki*, ... *tari-si*, ... *tari-ken*, ... *te-ki*, ... *te-si*, ... *ten*	228
§ 84. [... *mi*] ... *tsu*, ... *nuru*; [... *nuri*] ... *nuru*, verbs, ... *naran*	229
§ 85. ... *tsu*, ... *tsuteru*, ... *tsuru*, n. chs. fut. en.	231
§ 86. Synopsis of the inflected forms	232
§ 87. Causative or Factive verbs in *si* or *se*	234
§ 88. Causative verbs in *sime*	239

The passive form.

	Page
§ 89. Its derivation and signification	240
1. Passive verbs of the first class	241
II. ... second ...	241
III. ... third ...	212
§ 90. On the government of the passive verb	213
Examples of the use of the passive forms	245

The negative form of the Japanese verb.

	Page
§ 91. 1. Theory of the Derivation	247
Examples of the formation of negative verbs	248
II. Inflection of the negative verbs	249
§ 92. Continuative form of the negative verb	250
§ 93. Form of the forbidding Imperative	251
§ 94. Forms of the negative preterit	252
§ 95. Forms of the negative future	253
Examples of the use of the negative forms	254

Verbs expressing the being, the becoming and the causing to be.

	Page
§ 96. *Ari*, n. to be	260
§ 97. *Ori*, n. to dwell	263
§ 98. *I, Ite, Iru*, to be in	264
§ 99. Conjugation of non-deflecting verbs in *i*	265
Synopsis of non-deflecting verbs in *i*	265
§ 100. 1. *Ni, Nite, Naru*, to be	266
II. *Nari*, n. to be	270
III. *Narie*, n. *eru*, *uru*, to become	271
IV. *Nashi*, *e*. to cause to be	273
§ 101. *Mashi*, n, I. to abide; 2. to be	274
§ 102. *Samurawi*, *Soraw*, *Soro*	276
§ 103. *Si*, a. *uru*, to do	278
1. Use of the root-form *si*	278

CONTENTS.

	Page
II. 5, acting as verb...	290
Synopsis of the conjugational forms of ai	291
Compounds with ai	292
III. On the government of ō'i, u, uru, to du	293
§ 104. Beni, Behi, Behu, may, can, shall.	291
I. Derivation and signification.	291
II. Inflectional forms of Beni	292
III. On the government of Beni	293
IV. 1. Yuliu'y'i, u, uru, to be able.	294
2. Aliauu)i, u, not to be able.	295
V. Ahite, Aete, daring	295
VI. Tsu-een tur'i, u, it should be...	296
§ 105. The desiderative verbs, formed by Ta, dulrum.	296
§ 106. Verbs expressing the leaving off of an action	297
I. formed by Nuhi	297
II. „ „ Yumi	298
III. „ „ Stumi	298
§ 107. The adverbial form of a verb	299
§ 108. The derivative form muri	300
§ 109. Nasi, Nahi, Nuhu, and to esü-it.	301
I. The root Na	301
II. Nasi, Δ Nui, there is not.	302
III. Nahi, Δ Nai, the adjective form.	303
IV. Nahu, the adverbial form	304
V. Verbs compounded with Nahu.	305
1. Nabù-ui, Nabu-se, 2. Nakeri,
3. Nakeri, 4. Nabù-usri.
Synopsis of the inflectional forms and derivatives of Nahi, hi, hu	307
Remarks on the compound verbs.
§ 110. I. Verbs compounded with substantives.	309
II. Verbs compounded with verbs.	309

APPENDIX.

Distinctive verbs and verbal forms expressive of courtesy.

§ 111. General observation	311
§ 112. The honorary passive form	312
§ 113. I. Tomeri, Δ Tomeh	314
II. Tomemori, Ubo-tomemori	315
§ 114. Mètsuri, to attend	316
Distinctive verbs expressing
§ 115. Bring. Pumberi, Musei.	317
§ 116. Using. S. Itasi, Ambasi.	318
§ 117. Saying, Showing. Mi, Mise, Hai-tro etc.	319
§ 118. Saying. Iri, Ii-masi, Nori-tamai, Odos, Kitase. Mousi.	320
§ 119. Giving. Age, Sasdye, Kudasaru, Tsubo, Tonlsime, Tuwise, I'gri	321
§ 120. Going and Coming. Moiri, Meirvro, Moirute, Meirusuru, Ide, Agari, Mubiri, Thibe-desubi	323

CHAPTER VIII.

CONJUNCTIONS.

§ 121. Classification of the Jap. conjunctions..	376

A. Coördinative conjunctions

§ 122. I. Copulative conjunctions	327
§ 123. II. Disjunctive conjunctions	329
§ 124. III. Adversative conjunctions	331
§ 125. IV. Conclusive conjunctions	334
§ 126. V. Explanatory conjunctions	336

B. Subordinative conjunctions.

§ 127. I. Conjunctions of place and time...	336
§ 128. II. Conjunctions of quality and manner.	338
§ 129. III. Conjunctions of causality.
a. Conjunctions of an actual cause.	339
b. Conjunctions of a possible cause (Conditional conjunctions).	341
§ 130. IV. Conjunctions of the purpose	343
§ 131. V. Conjunctions of concession	344
§ 132. The relative comparative of prepositions.	346
Alphabetical synopsis of the conjunctions treated.	348

INTRODUCTION.

1. CONNECTION OF THE JAPANESE WITH THE CHINESE LANGUAGE. — THE NECESSITY OF UNITING TO THE STUDY OF THE JAPANESE, THAT OF THE CHINESE LANGUAGE.

In its general character, it is true, the Japanese is cognate to the Mongolian and Mandju languages, but with regard to its development, it is quite original, and it has remained so notwithstanding the later admixture of Chinese words, since it rules these as a foreign element, and subjects them to its own construction.

In the Japanese language, as it is now spoken and written, two elements, the Japanese and Chinese alternate continually and, by so doing, form a mixed language which, in its formation, has followed the same course as, for instance, the English in which, the more lately adopted Romance element, which forms a woof only, in like manner, is governed grammatically by the Anglo-Saxon.

In the study of the Japanese language the distinction of the two elements, is of the greatest importance; and as the Chinese element is rooted in the Chinese language, both spoken and written, and thence is to be explained, the student of Japanese ought to know so much of the Chinese language, as shall enable him to read and understand a Chinese text.

The Japanese learns Chinese by means of his mother tongue, thus one, who

2   INTRODUCTION.

is not a Japanese and does not understand Japanese, but wishes to learn it, must make himself master of Chinese by another way; to do this, he will be obliged to make use of the resources which already exist in European languages.

Whoever supposes that he can learn the Japanese language without, at the same time, studying the Chinese will totally fail of attaining his object either theoretically or practically. Even let him be so far master of the language spoken, as to be able to converse fluently with the natives, the simplest communication from a Japanese functionary, the price-list of the tea-dealer, the tickets with which the haberdasher or mercer labels his parcels will remain unintelligible to him; because they contain Chinese, if, indeed, they are not wholly composed of Chinese. Thus, whoever wishes to learn Japanese thoroughly, by means of this grammar, is supposed to possess, in some degree, knowledge of the Chinese written language.

2. ON THE WRITING OF THE JAPANESE.

The Japanese write Chinese but have, at the same time, their own native writing derived from the Chinese and which they, in imitation of the Chinese, write in perpendicular columns which follow one another, from the right hand to the left. Our alphabet, for that purpose would have to be written thus:

I	E	A
J	F	B
K	G	C
etc.	H	D

If the words are written in a cross direction, they begin at the right hand, thus, I H G F E D C B A.

The circumstance, that the Japanese writing does not run in the same direction as ours, but crosses it, or takes an opposite course, causes difficulty as soon as we have to couple Japanese writing with our own. Since, the Japanese, adhering to the custom of writing their words under one another, have altered their perpendicular columns of letters to cross lines, which thus show ＜ ≡ ◡; to bring their form of writing into some agreement with ours, I have, till now, thought it best to follow their example and, like them, placed the Japanese letters at the side. Now, however, some Japanese philologists, whenever their writing is coupled with ours have, in conformity with it, adopted the plan of writing perpendicularly, and from left to right, I likewise have relinquished the manner formerly adopted, and now have, together with the Chinese, reduced the Japanese writing to the rule of ours, and applied to it the modification in the order of the signs already generally in use for the Chinese writing.

The Japanese running-hand, on the contrary, is too much confined to the columnar system to be susceptible of any modification in its direction.

3. INTRODUCTION OF THE WRITTEN AND SPOKEN LANGUAGE OF CHINA INTO JAPAN.

The first knowledge of Chinese-writing was carried to Japan by a prince of Corea in the year 284 of our era, and then, immediately after, the tutor to that prince, a Chinese, named *Wang Jin* (王仁), having been invited, the Japanese courtiers applied themselves to the study of the Chinese language and literature. According to the Japanese historians, *Wang Jin* was the first teacher of the Chinese language in Japan [1].

In the sixth century, the study of the Chinese language and system of writing first became generally spread, by the introduction of the doctrine of BUDDHA. Then every Japanese, in polished society, besides being instructed in his mother tongue, received instruction in Chinese also, consequently read Chinese books of morality, and aimed at being able to read and to write a letter in Chinese.

The original pronunciation of the Chinese, it is true, degenerated early and that to such a degree, that new dialects of it sprung up, which were no longer intelligible to the Chinese of the continent; but notwithstanding that the Japanese, on account of their knowledge of the Chinese writing, and their proficiency in the Chinese style remained able, by means of the Chinese writing to interchange ideas not only with Chinese, but with all the peoples of Asia that write Chinese. The Chinese written language has become the language of science in Japan. It, still, is such and will yet long remain such, notwithstanding the influence which the civilization of the West will more and more exert there. The

---

[1] This historical fact is mentioned in *Japan's Bezüge mit der Koreischen Halbinsel und mit China. Nach Japanischen Quellen* von J. HOFFMANN, Leyden, 1839, page 111.

INTRODUCTION.

Chinese written language is, though, the palladium of Japanese nationality, and the natural tie which will once unite the East against the West!

And, however slight be the influence till hitherto exerted on the Japanese language written as well as spoken, by the study of the Western languages and, to wit the Dutch, formerly the monopoly of the fraternity of interpreters and a few literary men, who used this knowledge as a bridge, over which the skill of the West was imported and spread over their country, by means of Chinese or Japanese translations, just as little will it be in future, even if the study of the Western languages should be ever so greatly extended, as the consequence, of Japan's being eventually opened to the trade of the world.

4. APPLICATION OF THE CHINESE WRITING, TO THE WRITING OF THE JAPANESE LANGUAGE.

When, after the introduction of the Chinese written and spoken language into their country, the Japanese adopted it to write their native language, which is not in the least cognate to the Chinese, instead of resolving the sound of the words into its simplest elements, and expressing them by signs, like our letters, they took the sound in its whole, and expressed it syllable for syllable by Chinese characters.

Every Chinese radical word, it is known, is expressed by a more or less composite monogram (character) which has its peculiar ideographic and phonetic value — its peculiar signification and pronunciation. To choose an instance, such is 千 the Chinese word for a thousand. The Chinese says *tsiën*, the Japanese pronounces it *sen*, and the Japanese word for a thousand is *tsi*.

The Japanese considers the peculiar pronunciation of every Chinese character, i. e. the Chinese monosyllable, modified by the Japanese accent, as its SOUND, and calls it *Koyé* or, by the Chinese name 音 *Yin*, which he pronounces *won*; the Japanese word, on the other hand, which expresses the MEANING of the Chinese character, is called by him its *Yomi*, i. e. the READING or MEANING for which he also uses the Chinese terms 訓 *Kun* and 讀 *Tóku* [1]). The 千, above

---

[1]) The distinction between *Koyé* en *Yomi* agrees with this, as it is made do by the compilers and publisher of the *Élémens de la Grammaire Japonaise par le P. RODRIGUEZ* in § 1 of that work, and it is, therefore, important to maintain the contents of his paragraph as quite correct against the misconception,

quoted, may thus stand as an ideographic character and whether pronounced by the Japanese as *sen* or translated by *tai*, or it is only used as a phonetic sign and expresses the syllable *sen* or the syllable *tai*. That, by such a confusion of *Koyô* en *Yomi*, the whole writing-system of this people rests on an unfirm basis is evident at a glance.

Departing from the principle, to write Japanese with the Chinese writing, and to express the Japanese words syllable by syllable, by means of Chinese characters, some hundreds of the Chinese characters most in use were pitched upon and used for phonetic signs, *Kána*.

[The Japanese word *Kána*, pronounced as *Kánna*, has arisen from *kari-* or *kari-na* by assimilation of the *r*, and means taken upon trust, or borrowed name, thus a phonetic sign without farther meaning, in distinction from *Ma-na* (眞名), a real name. The word *Kána* is generally expressed by the Chinese characters 假名, *kià ming*, borrowed name; the *Kána* sign is called 假名文字 *Kána-mónzi*, and the *Kána* writing 假名書, *Kána-gáki*.]

These phonetic signs, just as the Chinese writing generally, were at first written in full, either in the standard-form, or in a running hand, which is produced of itself, whenever a Chinese character, composed of several strokes, is written in one continuous pencil-stroke, and gives rather a sketch of it, than a full draught. Running hand forms for 由 are e. g. ゆ ゆ ゆ ゆ 由 ゆ ゆ ヰ.

The standard-form, written in full, commonly called 元字 *Sin-zi* or 正字 *Sizzi*, the real, proper character, also 楷書 *Kai-sio*, normal writing, and 行書 *Gyoo-sio*, text-hand, was used in the Japanese Chronicle 日本書記 *Yamáto-bumi* or *Nippon-sio ki* [1]), containing the oldest history of Japan, from 661 B. C. till 696 A. C. and published in 720 A. C. as manuscript in thirty parts.

The running-hand form was used in the old Japanese Bundle of Poems

---

on the ground of which, S. ALCOCK, pp. 9 and 10 of his *Elements of Japanese Grammar*, takes the field against HOFFMANN and his publisher. *Yomi*, nevertheless, means the same, as the Chinese word 訓 *Kun*, the *Koyo* of ALCOCK.

[1]) This work is written in Chinese, and was one of the principal sources in the elaboration of my treatise: *Japan's Bezüge mit der Koreischen Halbinsel und mit Schina*; published in VON SIEBOLD'S *Nippon-Archief*, 1839.

6   INTRODUCTION.

萬⎴葉⎴集⎴ *Man-yor-siu* or the Collection of the Ten Thousand Leaves, compiled about the middle of the eighth century.

The first *Kána*-form was, consequently, called *Yamáto-kána*¹) (大和假名), the other *Man-yoo-kána* (萬葉假名).

5. JAPANESE WRITING PROPER.

An abbreviation of the two forms of Chinese writing led to the formation of another writing which, in opposition to the Chinese character writing, was styled, as the writing of the Japanese Empire. 日本國之文字, *Nippon góka no mon-zi*.

a. The *Káta-kána*.

Abbreviation of the Chinese standard writing gave rise to the *Káta-kána gáki*. It was, originally, intended when placed side by side with the Chinese characters, to express in remarkably smaller writing either their sound (*koyé*), or their meaning (*yomi*), and was therefore denominated *Káta-kána-mon-zi* (片⎴假⎴名⎴ 文⎴字⎴), i. e. side-letter ²). According to the Japanese sources ³), the inventor of this writing is unknown, and the invention of it has been, incorrectly, attributed to the Japanese statesman, KIBI DAIZIN, who died in 757.

b. The *Fira-gána* ⁴).

The more or less abbreviated form of the Chinese running-hand or short hand (假⎴字⎴ *Soo-zi*) is called *Fira-gána-gáki* (平假名書) or the even letter-writing, or, according to another reading, *Firo-gána* (廣假名), i. e. broad letters, since they take up the whole breadth of the writing-column. It is the running hand in which official documents, as well as letters and by far the greatest number of Japanese books are written and printed, and thus must be distinguished as the popular writing, proper. It has the advantage

---

¹) *Yamáto*, contracted from *Yama ató*, behind the mountains, properly the name of the Province, to which the Mikado's court was removed in 710, is at the same time applied to the Japanese Empire. See *Wa-kun-sen*, under *Yamáto*, and the Japanese Encyclopedia, Vol 73, p. 4 verso.

²) The notion of some Japanese writers seems less correct, as by *Káta-kána* were meant half-letters.

³) The Japanese Encyclopedia *hon-sai-tsu-e*. Vol. 10, p. 35 v.

⁴) People say and write too *Fira-kana*, and *Hira-kana*.

INTRODUCTION. 7

over other forms of writing, that the letters of a word can be joined to one another.

6. ON THE JAPANESE PHONETIC SYSTEM.

The number of sounds or syllables in Japanese was first, fixed at 47 and that in imitation of the Brahmanical-writing (梵字 *Bon-zi*), which distinguishes 12 vowels and 35 consonants [1]. The fixing of the Japanese phonetic system is attributed to the Buddhist Priest KOU-BOO DAI-SI (弘法大師), who, in his 31st year, went to China in 804 A. C. to study more closely the doctrine and institutions of BUDDHA and who, during a stay of three years, acquired there, among other knowledge, that of the Brahmanical writing (Sanscrit) and the phonetic system, as it was understood by the Chinese Priesthood [2].

A. SYSTEMATIC ARRANGEMENT OF THE 47 SOUNDS, EXPRESSED BY CHINESE AND JAPANESE KANA-SIGNS.

The Japanese phonetic system with its Chinese and Japanese *Kána*-signs systematically arranged according to the organs of speech, by which the sounds are produced, is as follows:

1. Palatal sounds [¹]. 阿 ア, a. 伊 イ, i. 宇 ウ, u. 江 エ, e (ye). 追 オ, o.
2.   ,, 加 カ, ka. 幾 キ, ki. 久 ク, ku. 計 ケ, ke. 己 コ, ko.
3. Lingual sounds [²]. 左 サ, sa. 之 シ, si. 須 ス, su. 世 セ, se. 曾 ソ, so.
4.   ,, 多 タ, ta. 知 チ, ti (tsi). 津 ツ, tu (tsu). 天 テ, te. 止 ト, to.
5.   ,, 奈 ナ, na. 仁 ニ, ni. 奴 ヌ, nu. 禰 ネ, ne. 乃 ノ, no.

---

[1] The Japanese Encyclopedia *Setz-sei-dzu-e*. Vol. 15, p. 35 v.

[2] The way in which the Chinese translators have copied, syllabically only, by means of Chinese characters, the Sanscrit words in the Buddhist writings imported from India, is placed in a clear light by the work: *Méthode pour déchiffrer et transcrire les noms sanscrits qui se rencontrent dans les livres chinois, inventée et démontrée par* M. STANISLAS JULIEN. Paris 1859.

[¹] 喉音.   [²] 舌音.

6. Labial sounds	波 ハ, fa	比 ヒ, fi		不 フ, fu		邊 ヘ, fe		保 ホ, fo		
	(va)	(vi)		(vu)		(ve)		(vo)		
7.	末 マ, ma	美 ミ, mi		無 ム, mu		女 メ, me		毛 モ, mo		
8. Palatal sounds	也 ヤ, ya	為 イ, i		油 ユ, yu		惠 エ, ye		與 ヨ, yo		
9. Lingual sounds	良 ラ, ra	利 リ, ri		解 ル, ru		禮 レ, re		呂 ロ, ro		
10. Labial sounds	和 ワ, wa	伊井 ヰ, wi		宇 ウ, wu		江 ヱ, we		於 ヲ, wo		

We give this view from a Japanese source [1]), we must, however, remark that the Chinese signs of the sounds are not generally those, from which the Japanese *Káta-kána* sign placed next it, by way of abbreviation, is derived, for, properly, the *Káta-kána* sign

ア, a, answers to the Chinese character 安.
オ, o, " " " 於, vulgo 扵.
チ, tsi, " " " 千, a thousand, Jap. *tsi*.
ウ, ue, " " " 子, the cyclical sign for mouse, Jap. *ne*.
ハ, fa, " " " 半.
ミ, mi, " " " 三, three, Jap. *mi*.
ム, mu, " " " 牟.
メ, me, " " " 女, woman, Jap. *me*.
ル, ru, " " " 流.
ヰ, wi, " " " 井, well, Jap. *wi*.
ヱ, we, " " " 惠.
ヲ, wo, " " " 乎.

According to this system, some dictionaries, particularly those of the unmixed old Japanese language have been arranged.

1) 曾音.
*) *Wa-kan Setsi-yau* see also before, p. 38, 1. where the pronunciation of the Sanscrit phonetic system is given with Japanese *Káta-kána*.

INTRODUCTION.   9

This system of 47 sounds or syllables, however, and indeed with relation to the consonants, is incomplete. It is not sufficient to express all the sounds of the Japanese language. Therefore, to supply the defect, recourse has been had to a modification of some *Káta-kána* signs, and for that purpose points, or a small ring, have been placed next them. Thus is placed

opposite the row of sound: カ, キ, ク, ケ, コ   the modification ガ, ギ, グ, ゲ, ゴ
                           ka, ki, ku, ke, ko   ga, gi, gu, ge, go.

  "   "   サ, シ, ス, セ, ソ   "   ザ, ジ, ズ, ゼ, ゾ
                    sa, si, su, se, so   za, zi, zu, ze, zo.

  "   タ, チ, ツ, テ, ト   "   ダ, ヂ, ヅ, デ, ド
                    ta, tsi, tsu, te, to   da, dsi, dsu, de, do.

  "   ハ, ヒ, フ, ヘ, ホ   "   ┌ バ, ビ, ブ, ベ, ボ
                    fa, fi, fu, fe, fo   ba, bi, bu, be, bo.
                                                  └ パ, ピ, プ, ペ, ポ
                                                      pa, pi, pu, pe, po.

The sounds, thus modified, are called *Nigorreu koye'* (濁音), i. e. confused or impure sounds, the points used to indicate the modification *Nigori*, and the small ring *Maru*.

In the *Yamáto-* and *Man-yō-kána* the modified sounds are expressed by proper Chinese characters chosen for that purpose. While, to give an instance, the syllable *ka* is expressed by one or another of the characters, 加, 伽, 架, 嘉, 迦, 可, 河, 何, 荷, 河, 柯, 舸, 訶, 謌, 歌, 甘, 間, 箇, 个, to express the syllable *ga*, one of the characters 我, 偐, 峨, 餓, 魏, 雅 may be chosen.

B. THE IROVA IN CHINESE CHARACTERS AND IN KATA-KANA SIGNS.

To facilitate the learning of the Japanese sounds or syllables, they have been so arranged as to compose a couple of sentences, and as these begin with the word *Irová*, that name has been given to the Japanese alphabet. The composition of the *Iroré* is attributed to the Bonze. KOO-BOO DAISI, (who died in 834) already mentioned, the writing-form he used for it was, it is asserted, running-hand or *Firu-gána*.

10   INTRODUCTION.

THE IROYA.	TRANSLATION.	THE IROYA WITH CHINESE TRANSLATION.
Iro vá nivoveló tsirinuruwó.	Color and smell (love and enjoyment) vanish!	色匂散 有我世 ○
Wága-yó daré so tsúné narám.	In our world who (or what) will be enduring?	夢誰常
U-wi no óku-yama kévú koyéte,	If this day passes away into the deep bosom of its existence,	奥山今 不
Asakí yúmémísi, évi mó sédsú.	Then it was a faint vision; it does not even cause giddiness! (it leaves you cold).	酔 越

The *Katta-kána* signs of the *Iroví*, which stand in the place of our alphabet, and according to which the Japanese dictionaries are commonly arranged, are derived from Chinese characters, which are likewise used, and that by way of Capitals or large letters. They are:

伊 イ, i.	和 ワ, wa.	宇 ウ, u.	阿 ア, a.
呂 ロ, ro.	加 カ, ka.	*非 井, wi, yi.	薩 サ, sa.
半 ハ, fa (ha), va.	與 ヨ, yo.	乃 ノ, no.	幾 キ, ki.
仁 ニ, ni.	多 タ, ta.	於 オ, o.	*弓 ユ, yu.
保 ホ, fo (ho), vo.	亂 レ, re.	久 ク, ku.	*女 メ, me.
反 ヘ, fe (he), ve.	曾 ソ, so.	也 ヤ, ya.	*三 ミ, mi.
土 ト, to.	州 ツ, tu (tsu).	末 マ, ma.	之 シ, si.
*千 チ, ti, tsi.	*子 子, ne.	介 ケ, ke.	唐 ヱ, we, e.
利 リ, ri.	奈 ナ, na.	不 フ, fu.	比 ヒ, fi (hi), vi.
奴 ヌ, nu.	艮 ラ, ra.	已 コ, ko.	毛 モ, mo.
流 ル, ru.	牟 { ム, mu, m.	*江 エ, ye.	世 セ, se.
乎 ヲ, wo.	{ ン, n.	天 テ, te.	須 ス, su.

The characters marked * stand for ideographic signs, answering to the Japanese word *tsi* (a thousand), *ne* (mouse), *wi* (well), *ye* (bay), *yu* (bow), *me* (woman), and *mi* (three).

The sign ム, *mu*, which was also used in the old Japanese for the final sound *m* (at present *n*) has, in this quality, more lately acquired the sign ン, *n*, as a variation.

7. REPETITION OF SYLLABLES. — STOPS.

The repetition of a letter is expressed by ヽ, of di- or trisyllabic words by 〱; thus, for instance, 〻 stands for 各々, *yoyo*; 色〻 for 色々, *iro-iro*.

As stenographic signs for some Japanese words that frequently occur, in connection with the *Káta-kána*, the following are to be remarked:

コト for 事, *koto*, sake.   トモ for トモ, *tomo*.
トキ „ トキ, *toki*, time.   シテ „ シテ, *site*.
トキ „ 時, *toki*, time.   タマ „ タマ, *tama*.

Stops.

As stops, only the comma (ヽ) and the point (ｏ or .) occur in Japanese. The use of them, however, is left wholly to the option of the writer. Some use ･ also at the beginning of a new period, and thus begin that with a point, while others with the same object place a somewhat larger ring, ◯, or a △ there. The comma (ヽ) stands on the right of the letter (for instance ク҆), while the repetition sign is placed on the diameter of the column of letters (for in- instance ク҅, *kuku*).

The principle of separating the words from one another in writing is, for the most part, quite lost sight of in writing with the *Káta-kána*, and the *Kána* signs of a whole period are written at equal distances. The consequence of it is, that for an unpractised person, who is not already pretty well acquainted with the Japanese, it is very doubtful how he has to divide some fifty or a hundred successive *Kána* signs into words. With a view to perspicuity and not to require from the reader that he shall be already acquainted with the period which is offered him to read, to enable him to read and understand it, it is in the highest degree desirable that our method of separating the words should be applied to the Japanese, as it is done by us. If the method of separating word for word were adopted by the Japanese, it would be great step in the improvement of their writing-system.

12   INTRODUCTION.

8. REMARKS ON THE JAPANESE SYSTEM OF SOUNDS, AND THE EXPRESSION OF IT WITH OUR LETTERS.

To promote the unity necessary in the reduction of the Japanese to Roman characters, we have adopted the Universal or Standard alphabet, by ROBERT LEPSIUS. As this alphabet enables people of various nations to reduce to their own graphic system, the words of a foreign language, in a manner systematic, uniform, and intelligible to every one; and as it has been adopted by the principal philologists in all countries, as well as by the most influential Missionary Societies, its application to the Japanese language will be welcomed by every one who prizes a sound, uniform and, at the same time, very simple system of writing.

In reducing the Japanese text to Roman character the following signs borrowed from the Standard alphabet have been adopted.

a.   *a* open as heard in the Dutch *vader*; — English *father*, *art*; — Jap. ア.
i.   *i* pure as heard in the Dutch *ieder*; — Eng. *he*, *she*; — Jap. イ.
î.   *i* long; — Jap. 井.
ĭ.   *i* short.
u.   *u* pure, as *oe* heard in the Dutch, *goed*; — Eng. *oo* in *good*, *poor*, *o* in *lose*; — Jap. ウ. At the beginning of a word it is frequently pronounced with a soft labial aspiration, as *wu*.
ŭ.   short, silent *u*.
e.   *e* close, *e* as heard in the Dutch *bezig*, *meer*, *geven*; — Eng. *a* in *lace*, *nation*; — German *e* in *weh*; — Jap. エ.
ĕ.   *e* short.
ę.   *e* open as heard in the Dutch *berg*; — Eng. *a* in *hat*; — French *è* in *mère*, *être*; — German *Bär*, *fett*.
o.   *o* close as heard in the Dutch *jong*, *gehoor*; — Eng. *borne*; — German *Ton*; — Jap. オ.
ŏ.   *o* short.
ǫ.   a sound between *a* and *o*, leaning rather to the *a* than the *o*, as heard in the English *water*, *all* and *oa* in *broad*.
ǫ.   When the sound ǫ inclines rather to the *o* than *a*, it is expressed by *o*.
au. In the dialect of *Yedo* ア ウ (au) changes to *go*, because the *a*, for ease in rapid pronunciation, inclining to the *u* changes to *ǫ*, while the *u*, to approach more nearly the *a*, changes to *o*.

In some dialects of Western Japan, particularly that of Kiu-siu, *au* changes to *m*, and *arau* (ラ/ウ) is superseded by *arŏo* (ラ̆/ウ̆, ラ̄/ウ̄).

The etymology considered, however the written form *au* or *gu* is to be preferred.

ou.   Etymologically *ou* (オウ) in the dialect of Yedo sounds *ŏo*, being the hard open *o* heard in the Dutch loopen, German mond, followed by the *u* inclining towards the soft *o*. By some Japanese, this diphthong is also pronounced as *ŏo* and is written so, as well. On the etymological principle we write *ou*, in distinction from *au*, or *gu* [1]).

eu.   (エウ) is pronounced *io*.

k,   as in Dutch, German, and English. — カ, キ, ク, ケ, コ, = ka, ki, ku, ke, ko.

g.   In Western Japan, particularly in Kiu-siu, ガ, ギ, グ, ゲ, ゴ are pronounced as *ga, gi, gu, ge, go*, thus *g* as the medial of *k*, just as the *g* in the German gabe, French garçou, English gain, give, go.

In the dialects of Eastern Japan, on the other hand, particularly in that of Yedo, the *g* has the sound of the *ng* in the German lang, English singing, thus a really impure sound, by no means the medial of *k*; and the series ガ, ギ, グ, ゲ, ゴ, are pronounced *nga, ngi, ngu, nge, ngo* according to the Standard-alphabet ñа, ñi, ñu, ñe, ño.

Even might the pronunciation of Yedo deserve preference above that of the other dialects, still we think we ought to retain the *g* for the representation of the impure *g*, because this form of writing is as good as universally adopted, and also because the *n* does not appear with it, even in the Japanese writing. Therefore without wishing to dispute the freedom of others to write *wunga* for ワガ and *Nangasaki* for ナガサキ, because people in Yedo speak so, we adhere to our already adopted written form *waga* and *Nágasáki*, and say *winga* and *Nángasáki*.

The Dutch guttural *g* (gaan, geven), = γ of the Standard-alphabet is quite foreign to the Japanese organs of speech.

s.   *s* sharp, サ, シ, ス, セ, ソ, = *sa, si, su, se, so*. — *Si* and *su*, in the pro-

---

[1]) Léon Pagès, also has kept this distinction in view, and expresses ヅ by ô and ヅ by ô. — Dictionnaire Japonais-Français traduit du dictionnaire Japonais-Portugais composé par les missionaires de la compagnie de Jésus. Publié par Léon Pagès. Première livraison. 1862.

nunciation of Yédo have the sound of the German *schi*, *sche*, the English *she*, *shay*, and thus answer to the written forms *si*, *se* of the Standard-alphabet. Etymology, nevertheless, requires for ズ and セ the written form *si* and *se*, leaving *she* and *shay*, and sometimes also *se*, to the pronunciation.

s. soft *s* impure, being heard, in the dialect of Yédo, as a combination of *n* and *z* or also of *d* and *z*. ・・ ザ, ジ, ズ, ゼ, ゾ = *za, zi, zu, ze, zo* (nza, nzi, nzu, nze, nzo or dza, dzi, dzu, dze, dzo), consequently アラズ occurs as *arânza* or *arádza*.

š. Dutch *sj*, German *sch*, English *sh*, French *ch*. As pronounced at Yédo this consonant is distinguished as a palatal variety of *s* which, as such, ought to be represented by *š* of the Standard-alphabet.

The combination of this sound with *a*, *u*, *o*, so ša, šu, šo, is expressed by シャ, シュ, ショ (*siya, siyu, siyo*), which, is pronounced by some Japanese of Yédo, as *sya, syu, syo*, with a scarcely audible *y*, whereas from the mouths of some others, a sound is heard which inclines rather to *ša, šu, šo*. Since the first pronunciation lets the etymological value of these combinations appear, we think to give the preference to the written forms *siya, siyu, siyo*, leaving it to the reader to pronounce them *ša, šu, šo* or *sya, syu, syo*.

ž. The Dutch *zj*, French *j*, English *s* in mea-sure. the softer pronunciation of *š*. ジャ, ジュ, ジョ *ža, žu, žo*. For the sake of etymology, we write *ziya, ziyu, ziyo*.

t. タ, チ, ツ, テ, ト = *ta, tsi, tsu, te, to*. Properly, チ, ツ, *ti* en *tu* are etymological; but these combinations of sound are, at once, foreign to the Japanese organs of speech and are, whenever they have to be adopted from another language, expressed by ティ *tii* and トゥ *tou*. チ (*tsi*), commonly pronounced *thi* as in the English *cheer*.

d. ダ, ヂ, ヅ, デ, ド, *da, dzi, dzu, de, do*, according to the dialect of Yédo *nda, ndzi, ndzu, nde, ndo*. The Coreans express the impure Japanese *d* by ㄴ (*nt*.)

tš. The Dutch *tsj*, English *ch* in *chair*. チャ, チュ, チョ, etymologically *tsiya, tsiyu, tsiyo*, according to the Yédo pronunciation *tsya, tsyu, tsyo*, the *y* being scarcely audible. Some are heard to pronounce it *tša, tšu, tšo*.

dž. The Dutch *dzj*, English *g* in *George*, *j* in *judge*. ヂャ, ヂュ, ヂョ, etymologically *dziya, dziyu, dziyo*, according to the Yédo pronunciation *dzya, dzyu, dzyo*, in the mouths of some also *dža, džu, džo*.

n. ナ, ニ, ヌ, ネ, ノ, *na, ni, nu, ne, no*.

ン, n, final letter, serves as well for the dental, as the nasal final sound, which approaches the French faint n at the end of a syllable and is expressed by ng (ṅ of the Standard-alphabet).

Formerly, instead of the final letter ン, the Kana-sign ム, mu was used, and pronounced as a mute m. In Japanese words ン, stands for the faint nasal final sound ṅ, in Chinese words, on the contrary, for the clear dental final sound n as in our „man, dan."

In composition, the final sound n has a euphonic influence on the consonants following it and changes k, s, t and f into the impure sounds g, z, d, b, which are pronounced more or less like ng, nz, nd, nb. The combined sound nb, in pronunciation, changes to mb; Tanba (タンバ) is pronounced Tamba; Nanbok (ナンボク), Nambok; Kenbok (ケンボク), Kembok.

For the sake of unity in spelling, although in the dialect of Yedo it is pronounced as the French faint n, we retain for the final sound ン, the written form n, since long current, and continue to write Nippon, leaving it to the reader to pronounce it Nippong.

f (h). v. ハ、ヒ、フ、ヘ、ホ, fa, fi, fu, fe, fo or ha, hi, fu (not hu), he, ho. Originally the aspirated labial sound f, which has been retained in some dialects, in others, on the contrary, superseded by the soft h; a phenomenon which occurs in the Spanish also, in which the f of the Old-Spanish language has, in later times, passed into the soft aspirated h.

In the dialect of the old imperial city of Miyako, and its dependent provinces, the f is retained, and so far as we know, in Sanuki and Sendai, where commonly fána, fudó, fúrú, fíri, fokú, are heard. In the dialect of Yedo, on the contrary, the f has been quite driven out and there, hána, hitó, húrú (fu remains fu), hiri, hokú are said.

This distinction of the two sounds, according to fixed dialects, rests on communications made to us orally by Japanese.

That, in the language of Miyako, where Japanese is spoken the purest, as also in the dialect of Sanuki, the f occurs to the exclusion of h, I have been assured by a native of Yedo who has passed some years in Sanuki [1]), while another native of Yedo [2]) has mentioned to me the province of Sendai

---

[1]) ONO-DAYA AITAROO, merchandise, resident in the Netherlands since 1863.
[2]) ENOMOTO KAMADSIROO, an officer in the Japanese Navy, also resident in the Netherlands since 1869.

and the North-eastern part of Japan as districts, in which the *f*, to the
exclusion of *h*, is commonly in use.

In the middle, or at the end of a word, the *f* or *h* in the pronunciation,
passes over to *v* or a pure labial (not labio-dental) *w*, and even in writing
ワ (wa) supersedes ハ (va): カハ, キハ, クハ are heard *kawa*, *kiwa*, *kuwa*,
or also *kawa*, *kiwa*, *kuwa*, for which カワ, キワ, クワ, is written.

On the contrary the syllables ヒ, *ri*, フ, *ru*, ヘ, *re*, ホ, *ro*, whenever
a vowel precedes reject the aspirate, and アヒ is pronounced as *ai*, アフ
as *au* (*ou*), アヘ as *ae*, アホ as *ao*, イヒ as *ii*, イフ as *iu*, イヘ as
ie, オホ as *oo* etc.

The aspirated labial ヒ, *fi*, in ヒト, *fitó*, man, sounds like a *fai* or *fwi*
whistled with the mouth, and is easy to be pronounced. In the *Yédo hi*,
on the contrary, the *h* often occurs as a palatal aspirate, which, whenever
it is pressed through the closed teeth, forms a sound quite strange to European ears, which it is not possible to express with our letters. What former
travellers, GOLOWNIN, MEYLAN and others have said about this sound [1] is
now confirmed by our observation; and we have only to add that in the
mouths of some from *Yédo* the word ヒト (*fito* or *hito*, man) became
even *sto*.

Since for the syllables ハ, ヒ, ヘ, ホ two forms of writing have now
come into existence, in proportion as one or the other pronunciation is followed, one with *f*, the other with *h*, the question becomes important, which
of the two forms of spelling deserves the preference. If Japanese is to be
written according to the accent of *Yédo*, then, naturally, the *h* must be
adopted, just as, to let the dialect of Zeeland enjoy its rights, *Olland* and
oofd must be written for *Holland* and *hoofd*, or, not to do injustice to the
Berlin dialect, *Jabe*, *Jott* and *jut* must be written for *Gabe*, *Gott* and *gut*.
If, however the pronunciation most generally in vogue, with the exception

---

[1] „No European," says GOLOWNIN, „will succeed in pronouncing the Japanese word fa', fire." — It
is C. *fi*. — I have practised at it two years, but in vain. As the Japanese pronounced it, it seemed to
be *fi*, *hi*, *pi*, *ffi*, being pronounced through the teeth; however we might wring and twist our tongues
into every bend, the Japanese still stuck to their „*pai* right."" — *Begebenheiten des Capitans von der
Russisch-kaiserlichen Marine* GOLOWNIN, *in der Gefangenschaft bei den Japanern in den Jahren* 1811,
1812 und 1813 *Aus dem Russischen übersetzt von Dr.* C. J. SCHULTZ. 1819. Vol. II. p. 30

INTRODUCTION. 17

of *Yédo*, that of *Miyako* be preferred, then must the *h* be put aside and *f* adopted. We do the last, and that for the following reasons:

1. The Japanese philologers themselves have, at all times, characterized the consonant of their series of sounds ハ. ヒ. フ. ヘ. ホ as labial, and made it equivalent to the labials of the Sanscrit.

2. The Chinese *Kána* signs, fixed upon to represent this series of sounds, are all sounds which, after the Chinese pronunciation, begin with a *p* or an *f*, whereas the sharp aspirated *h* of the Chinese words, just as the *h* of the Sanscrit, is expressed by *k*, and カイ, *kai* is written and spoken for the Chinese *hai*.

3. In Japanese, as in Dutch and English, the sharp *f* between two vowels passes over into the soft *v* or *w*, and beside the older written form カハ, カヘ, カホ, for which we must write *kara*, *kwe*, *kwo*, that of カワ, カヱ, カヲ, *kawa*, *kwe*, *kwo*, has gradually come into vogue.

4. From the beginning Europeans, who had intercourse with the Japanese, generally wrote *f* and not *h*; thus the Portuguese missionaries, and their contemporary, FR. CARON (1636); also more lately, E. KAEMPFER (1691), P. THUNBERG (1775), J. TITSINGH [1]) (1780), and others. All wrote *Farima*, *Fanna*, *Firando*, *Fori*. In this century the *h* first appeared, because then Europeans came more frequently in contact with interpreters and natives of *Yédo*. If now we adopt the *h*, then will all connection with what was formerly done for the knowledge of the language, history and geography of Japan be broken off, a door opened for endless confusion, and for thousands of Japanese words we shall have a double spelling.

b, impure, from the sound arisen from the blending of *n* with *r*, which the Coreans, whenever they write Japanese words in their character, express by *mp* (떠). · バ. ビ. ブ. ベ. ボ, *ba*, *bi*, *bu*, *be*, *bo*.

p. パ. ピ. プ. ペ. ポ. *pa*, *pi*, *pu*, *pe*, *po*,

y. The Dutch *j*; — English *y* in *yard*; — French *y*. ヤ. ユ. エ. ヨ. *ya*, *yu*, *ye*, *yo*. The pronunciation of 井 is not fixed, and fluctuates between *wi*, *yi*, *ii*, and *i*.

r. Soft guttural *r*, just as the English *r* in *part*, *art*, *r* of the Standard-

---

[1]) In TITSINGH's *Bijzonderheden* whenever an *h* occurs in Japanese words, it has been placed there, from a mistake of either the writer, or compositor.

alphabet. ラ. リ. ル. レ. ロ. ra. ri. ru, re, ro. The Japanese r, comes from the root of the tongue, which is kept almost motionless. Our trilling dental r cannot be uttered by a thorough-bred Japanese of Yedo.

This is also the case with our *l*; this sound too is quite foreign to the Japanese mouth [*]. Instead of adopting a proper letter for the *l*, the Japanese, whenever they have had to reduce words of European languages to Japanese writing, have made the foreign *l* equivalent to the *r*, and have used their *r* for both sounds: a mistake, by which they subjected themselves to a perpetual mutation of the letters *r* and *l* when writing a foreign language, and induced our philologers to suppose that the Japanese *r* was an intermediate sound between *l* and *r* which, as it now appears, is not the case.

In combinations of sounds such as レン, ren, リウ, riu, リヤウ, riyau (ryoo), the guttural *r* so nearly approaches the lingual *d*, that, with the utmost attention, it remains doubtful, whether the *r* or the *d* is meant. This is to be remarked especially in words adopted from the Chinese, and which in that language begin with *l*, which becomes *r* in Japanese, such as *den* for *ren* (Chinese *lin*), *dyu* for *ryu* (Chinese *ling*, dragon), *dyoo-ri-nin* and *doo-sok* for *ryoo-ri-nin* and *roo-sok* (Chinese *liuh-li-nin*, cook, and *la tau*, wax-candle).

It is worthy of remark, that with the Chinese just the opposite takes place, that they can pronounce the *l* easily, but the *r* not at all.

w. The German pure labial *w*. ワ. ウ. ヲ. wa, wu, wo.

9. DOUBLING OF CONSONANTS BY ASSIMILATION.

If the letter ツ *tsu*, which is mostly pronounced as the *ts* mute, occurs in a compound word before a *k*, *s*, *t* or *p*, then, for the sake of euphony, it passes over to the latter sound, — it is assimilated.

---

[*] This has become quite evident to me, from the instruction in the Dutch language which several Japanese have received under my superintendence. After having first pronounced the *l* as the guttural *r*, they required long practice before being able to utter a sound, that in any degree resembled *l*.

SPALDING also, has observed that thorough-bred Japanese of Yedo, with whom he met, could not possibly pronounce his name. "They cannot say L," he adds, "they call it R. The word *glove*, which they call *grove*, is too much for them." — J. W. SPALDING, *The Japanese expedition*, Redfield, 1855, p. 235.

一ﾂ箇ｏ, itsu-ka	written,	is pronounced	ikkó (one).
一ﾂ斤ﾝ, itsu-kin	„	„	„	ikkin (one pound).
一ﾂ見ﾝ, itsu-ken	„	„	„	ikken (a glance).
一ﾂ國ｸ, itsu-koku	„	„	„	ikkok (a whole empire).
北ｸ京ﾝ, Fitsu-kin	„	„	„	Fokkin (Peking).
一ﾂ切, itsu-sai	„	„	„	issii (all).
一ﾂ所, itsu-syo	„	„	„	isso (one and the same place).
一ﾂ寸ﾝ, itsu-sun	„	„	„	issun (the tenth of a foot).
合ｯ戰ﾝ, katsu-sen	„	„	„	kassen (battle, fight).
一ﾂ錢ﾝ, itsu-sen	„	„	„	issen (one cent).
一ﾂ代, itsu-tai	„	„	„	ittai (a whole life).
以ﾃ, motsute	„	„	„	mótte (with).
旹ﾃ, kitsute	„	„	„	kátte (already).
貴ｷ, tatsutoki	„	„	„	tattoki (worshipful).
合ｯ羽, katsu-pa	„			káppa (overcoat),
日ﾂ本ﾝ, Nitsu-pon	„	„		Nippon (Japan).

The リ ri also before t is sometimes subject to assimilation; of アリタ arita, the pronunciation becomes atta, for which アッタ is written.

A rule to determine when, in pure Japanese words, the ッ shall retain its value, as in マツマエ Mátsu-máye, マツダイラ Mátsu-daira, where it is not thus assimilated, has not, so far as we know, yet been fixed. Certain it is, that the vowel of the syllable, which precedes a double consonant, is short, and that the doubling of the consonant is chiefly applied to compound words of Chinese origin, of which the first syllable contains a short vowel, which in some Chinese dialects is stopped by t, represented in Japanese words, by ッ.

Upon this principle the double consonants in words from foreign languages also are expressed in Japanese writing; in this case some place the ッ of the diameter a little to the right and write ッ for dutch „ridder" and ッ for „schip."

10. ON ACCENT AND RHYTHM.

In Japanese distinction is made between accented and unaccented syllables.

To the unaccented belong chiefly those ending in *i* or *u*, in which these sounds are scarcely heard at all, and that especially at the end of the words. Thus, e. g.:

ミタ, *mita* (beneath) sounds as *mta*.
ミィ, *mine* (let) sounds as *mne*.
シキ, *siki* (like) sounds as *ski*.
マシ, マス, マレシ, *musi*, *musu*, *musitu* sounds as *msi*, *msu*, *msitu*.
タツ, *tatsu* (dragon) sounds as *tts*.
ヨム, *yomu* (to read) sounds as *ym*.
ナル, *naru* (to be) sounds as *ndr*.
ツクリ, *tsukuri* (to make) sounds as *tskri*, etc.

The *i* has, moreover, the peculiarity, that as a final letter it is whispered.

As in Japanese the *i* and *u* mute have not ceased to be real elements of the words, and to be necessary to the distinguishing of them, they ought to be expressed in all philological writings. Even if ミチ (*mitsi*, way) and ミツ (*mitsu*, three) sound as *mits*, in our writing we must, because the Japanese do so in theirs, distinguish both words and write *mitsi* and *mitsu*, or characterize the weak vowels, as weak and mute by writing *mitsi* and *mitsu*. — The form of writing adopted by some, *mitsi* and *mitsu*, answers that purpose also.

The accented vowel is pronounced either long or short-close. Thus is, e. g. the *a* long in マツ, *mátsu* (pinetree), short-close サケ, *sáke* (strong drink).

The consonant, following a short-close vowel is often doubled in pronunciation, though not in writing. Thus, e. g. ハナ, *fána* (flower) sounds as *fánna*; アサ, *ása* (the morning) as *ássa*; サケ, *sáke* (strong drink) as *sákke*.

Since, with regard to the correct indication of the quantity of the syllables, the Japanese graphic system is defective, it behoves us to keep it in view the more carefully, because the accentuation, provided it be based on the pronunciation of Japanese, is an indispensable help in the acquiring of a correct pronunciation.

Hitherto the only European, who has paid attention to the accent of Japanese words, and expressed it after a fixed principle, was E. KAEMPFER. From his manner of writing it might be gathered, that ツヤ, dragon, and マツ, pine-tree, are pronounced as *tats* and *máts*, thus with an a long, ヤマ, ヒトト and ヰチバナ as *yámama*, *mindto* and *tatsbánna*. Later travellers, who have visited Japan and written books about it, have been either unable or unwilling to follow his example, and thereby have left their readers in uncertainty with regard to the rhythm of Japanese. Only recently, since the arrival of natives of Japan in Europe, have our linguists had the opportunity to hear Japanese spoken by Japanese, and so to become acquainted with the rhythm peculiar to that language. Availing ourselves of this opportunity, we have already been able to publish the reading of a Japanese text [1] supplied with a continuous accentuation.

If we cast a hasty glance over what has previously been said, with regard to the Japanese phonetic system, the writing, the pronunciation, it will appear most clearly, that the Japanese phonetic system is very defective. It does not satisfy the requirement of being able, with it, to write the Japanese language itself, as it is spoken, let alone the possibility of its being applied to foreign languages. The Japanese, with all their attempts to write Dutch, French or English, after their *Kana*-system, have been able to effect nothing else, than caricatures of those languages.

From their defective syllabic-writing are the Japanese behind not only the Western nations, but other Asiatic peoples also, and even the Coreans, their neighbors who rejoice in the possession of an original, and simple character-writing, not borrowed from the Chinese. With regard to the writing of foreign languages, the Chinese alone are worse off.

The intricate, often equivocal writing with which Japanese is written, occasions more difficulty for those, who have not grown up with it, than the study of the language itself, witness the Japanese running-hand, whose turn comes next.

---

[1] *The Grand Study (Ta Hio or Dai-gaku)*. Part I, *The Chinese text with an interlineary Japanese version*. Part II, *Reading of the Japanese text in Roman character*, by J. HOFFMANN. Leiden, 1864.

II. THE JAPANESE RUNNING-HAND FIRA-GANA.

a. The *Irovi* in *Fira-gána.*

The *Irovi* in *Fira-gána*-writing, as it is learned in schools and, in connection with Chinese running-hand, is generally in use, consists of the following signs, which are derived by abbreviation from the Chinese characters placed next them.

以	い. I	和	わ. wa	宇	う. u	安	あ. a
呂	ろ. ro	加	か. ka	為	ゐ. wi	左	さ. sa
波	は. fa (ha), va	與	よ. yo	乃	の. no	幾	き. ki
仁	に. ni	太	た. ta	於	お. o	由	ゆ. yu
保	ほ. fo (ho), vo	礼	れ. re	久	く. ku	女	め. me
反	へ. fe (he), ve	甘	ろ. so	也	や. ya	美	み. mi
止	と. to	門	つ. tsu	末	ま. ma	之	し. si
知	ち. tsi	袮	ね. ne	計	け. ke	惠	ゑ. e
利	り. ri	奈	な. na	不	ふ. fu	比	ひ. fi (hi), vi
奴	ぬ. nu	良	ら. ra	己	こ. ko	毛	も. mo
留	る. ru	武	む. mu	江	え. ye	世	せ. se
遠	を. wo.		(ん ... n.)	天	て. te.	寸	す. su.

b. Synopsis of the *Fira-gána*-characters most in use.

Were the *Fira-gána*-writing confined to the 47 or 48 signs cited, it would not, with a slight exercise in writing with the pencil, be more difficult to learn, than the *Káta-kána*. But the desire for variety, change and ornament, has rendered this writing so abundantly rich, that to make learning to read *Fira-gána* texts possible, a synopsis of these signs has become an absolute necessity.

With the synopsis, we give at once the Chinese character to which each sign owes its origin.

INTRODUCTION.

SYNOPSIS OF THE JAPANESE HIRA-GANA.

A. 安 あ あ あ あ あ   KA. 加 か か か カ
   阿 ふ ふ ふ   可 う う う う う

I. 似 ら ら いら いい   KI. 幾 き き き
                            支 支 支
                            起 兆 兆 兆 兆
                            義 義 き む む

U. 于 う   KU. 久 久 ム く く
   宇   具 ク ク ク ク

E. 惠 え え え   KE. 計 け け け
   衛 衛   化 代 化 化 化 化
                              希 希 希 希 希
                              遣 を を を を

O. 於 於 於 於 於   KO. 巳 こ こ て て て
   於 於 於   古 古 古 古 古

SA. 佐 ...
SHI. 志 之
SU. 須 ...
SE. 世 せ ...
SO. 曽 ...

TA. 太 た な と
TSI. 知 ... 地 代
TSU. 洲 川 ...
TE. 天 て て て
TO. 止 と と と

INTRODUCTION.

NA. 奈 な な な た ち た
    南 ち ふ ふ ふ ふ ち
       ち
    那 那 那 奶 机 机 m

NI. 仁 に に に ル ん
    尓 尔 尔 尔 尔 子 了
    丹 丙 丙 尓
    耳 牛 千 刋 ろ ろ ち

NU. 奴 ぬ ぬ ぬ ぬ ぬ
    ね
... n ム ム

NE. 称 ね ね ぬ ね ね ね
    祢 祢 祢 袮 祢 [古]
    子 子 子
    年 年 年 年

NO. 乃 乃 乃 の の
    野 祀 祀 祀
    農 ゑ 禹 秀 禹 荗
    能 能 能 能 能 能

FA. 波 波 は は 波 は に
    八 八 八 ᆢ
    者 者 る る そ そ そ
    そ そ そ そ そ
    婆 娑 娑 娑 娑 娑
    娑 娑 そ

FI. 飛 飛 つ ろ 蛋
    比 比 ひ ひ

FU. 不 不 不 ふ ふ 上
    布 布 布 布 布 布

FE. 反 (へ) へ へ へ
    部 部 部 部 部

FO. 保 保 任 保 保 保
    本 本 本 不 不

MA. 末 ま ま ま 可
万 乃 る 万
滿 波 波 佐 両 毎 勾
勾 为

MI. 三 ミ 三
美 㚑 み み み 出
見 乄 尺 尺

MU. 武 む む む
無
䏍 郱 苯

ME. 女 め め め め め
み
兎 父 乆 乂

MO. 毛 も も も 毛 巨 も
す カ カ カ チ 㐄
母 舟 あ

YA. 也 や や ア
屋 𢁅 㐂

YU. 由 ゆ ゆ ゆ ゆ 由
田 少 中
遊 拹

YE. 江 汇 に
衣 え

YO. 與 与 よ よ よ
ら と ある

RA.	良 ら ら ら ら ら ら	WA.	和 わ わ わ わ わ
	羅 艻 艻		わ わ わ わ
	楽 楽 楽 楽		王 己 己 己 己

RI.	利 利 わ わ り り り	WI.	為 ゐ ゐ ゐ ゐ ゐ
	り り り り り ろ ろ		井 升 为
	梨 来		
	里 己 己 工		

RU. 留 ゐ る る る
　　 果 子 子 子
　　 流 流 流 流 流 流
　　 類 乱 乱 乱

RE. 礼 를 를 를 를 를 를
　　 禮 袮 袮 袮 袮
　　 乱 れ れ れ れ れ

RO. 呂 ろ ろ
　　 路 海 汤

WO. 遠 袁 を を を
　　 越 残 残 13
　　 平 安 之 す

INTRODUCTION.

The synopsis of Japanese running-hand characters, given on the preceding pages, collected by ourselves in reading Japanese books and manuscripts, is deserving of remark on account of its correctness. As we appreciated its being submitted to the criticism of a clever Japanese, we, some years ago, sent a few proof impressions, to a respected friend in Japan [1], on whose invitation Mr. MATS MOTO was so kind as to undertake the revision and correction of one of them. This impression being returned to us, we were enabled to submit our synopsis to a strict revision, and if we have given it a place here, it is with the conviction that it will be a faithful guide in the deciphering of Hira-gána texts.

To become familiar with this writing, the Chinese character should be taken for basis, and attempts made at learning to write with a pencil the more and more sketchy Hira-gána forms derived from it. By following this practical way, the student will most quickly become so conversant with this writing, as to be able to read without hesitation a text written in it, provided the printing of it be not too bad.

In the Hira-gána writing the letters are more or less obviously attached to one another. The way in which this is done will be best learned by copying some Japanese texts [2], in which it will at once be discovered, that some peculiarities in the manner of attaching them are only the natural results of a quick handling of the pencil.

The stops (°), and the sign ·, by which in the Káta-kána the change from pure to impure sounds is indicated, are used in the Hira-gána also, e. g. ガ ga, グ gu, ヂ dei, ヅ dzu, バ ba, ブ bu, etc.

The point, which in the Káta-kána, placed under a letter shows that it is repeated, in the Hira-gána runs together with the letter into one stroke. Opposed to キ kiki and タ tada, are the Hira-gána forms ξ and ξ.

The repetition of two or three syllables is shown by 〱.

---

[1] W J. C. BUIJSEN VAN RATTENBURG, Knight, Commander of the Naval-detachment in Japan in 1857, 1858 and 1859.

[2] The Japanese Treaties, concluded at Yedo in 1855 with the Netherlands, Russia, Great-Britain, the United States and France. Fac-simile of the Japanese text. The Hague, MARTINUS NIJHOFF 1863.

As stenographic abbreviations come under notice

あ, ぁ for 事 koto (sake).　　方, 方 for 自 yori.
と ̀ - と̀, と̀ koto.　　　　　せ, せ - 共 tomo.
ど, ど - ど goto.　　　　　　ㇾ - 也 nari.

12. WRITTEN OR BOOK LANGUAGE.

Books among the Japanese are written either in the Chinese, or in the Japanese language.

A. Exclusively Chinese are scientific works, intended for literate persons, who make use of the Chinese written language, just as formerly our learned men did of Latin. To this class of books belong, among others, the oldest Chronicle of Japan (*Yamato-bumi* or *Nippon-ki*), in which the pure Japanese words, such as the names of persons and places, are expressed phonetically with Chinese characters, the Japanese Encyclopedia *Wa-Kon san-sai dzu-e*, the Chronicle *Wa-Kan nen-kei*, the Japanese Government-Almanac, etc., while furnishing the books, which are written for the general public and in Japanese, with at least a Preface in Chinese, is still considered to be in good taste.

Among the pure Chinese texts must also be reckoned the Chinese translations of Buddhist works, originally written in Sanscrit, which translations, chiefly imported from China, are hummed by Japanese Bonzes in a peculiar Chinese dialect.

That a Chinese text can be read aloud with a Chinese pronunciation (*koye*) by literate Japanese is a matter of course, for, with the Chinese character, they become acquainted with its pronunciation also, and this according to certain dialects; but that whole sentences, when read aloud, according to the pronunciation of the characters, are intelligible to listeners, we have constantly doubted and now, upon the authority of a learned Japanese [1], dare deny. The Chinese text with its ideographic signs is there, to be apprehended according to its contents and, for the Japanese, the translation into his mother tongue is included in this apprehension. The apprehension and translation of a Chinese

---

[1] Mr. TSUBA SIN-ITSI-RAU.

text is therefore very justly called its reading (*yomi*) or *Wa-kun* (和訓), the reading in Japanese.

Respecting the Chinese dialects, which have been here mentioned, the following ought to be added.

In Japan the pronunciation of three dialects of the Chinese written language have been adopted, which are called after the Chinese dynasties 漢 *Hán*, 吳 *U* and 唐 *T'áng* (in the Japanese pronunciation *Kan*, *Go* and *Too*), *Kan-won* (漢音), *Go-won* (吳音) and *Too-in* (唐音) or *Kara-koto*, i. e. dialect of *Hán*, *U* and *T'áng*.

The dynasty of *Hán*, which had its seat in the country of *Ho-nan-fu*, thus on the borders of the *Hoang-ho*, flourished from 202 B. C. till 220 A. C. The dynasty of *U*, settled on the *Yang-tse-kiang*, where at present *Nan-king* is situated, existed from 222 till 280 A. C. The dominion of the dynasty of *T'áng* embraced the period between 618 and 906.

If with the Japanese it be accepted, that the said dialects were not local dialects existing next one another, but changes which the Chinese language has undergone in the lapse of ages, then the introduction and continued existence of those dialects in Japan would not be without importance in the knowledge of the old Chinese language. But since, with the defective Japanese *Kána*-writing, it is impossible to represent any Chinese dialect faithfully, those dialects too, that have wandered to Japan lose all historical value, and we therefore confine ourselves to the question of their introduction into Japan, and the use to which they have been applied.

On the first point the Japanese works at our command do not shed sufficient light. As the first teacher of the *Kan-won*, 表佰公 *Piao Sin-kung*, a scholar from the country of *Hán* is mentioned, with the addition, that he came to *Fakáta* in the country of *Tsikuzen*; but the time at which this happened we do not find recorded. Such also is the case with the introduction of the *Go-won*, which is attributed to 金禮信 *Kin Li-sin* and another Bonze from the country of *U*. As both had settled on the island of *Tsusima*, the *Go-won* was at first also called *Tsusima-won* (對馬音) or the *Tsusima*nian pronunciation [1].

With regard to the second point, it may be assumed as certain, that the

---

[1] The Japanese Encyclopaedia XV, 33 verso. — *Fak-bots-en* under *Kan-won* and *Go-won*.

Go-won was the dialect, in which the Bonzes read the Buddhist writings, imported from China, and that it still, with a few exceptions, is in vogue among them, whereas the *Kan-won*, the use of which was, in virtue of an edict published by the *Mikado* as early as 792, made obligatory in the study of the Chinese language [1], prevailed in the domain of science, and penetrated into the whole profane literature.

In the Chinese-Japanese dictionaries the pronunciation of each word is found, given in both dialects and that, first in *Kan-won*, and then in *Go-won*. In the instances 音 or 音 and 明 or 明, and are placed as *Kan-won*, and as *Go-won*.

The dialect of *T'âng* (*Too-in*), as it has been fixed by means of the *Kana*-writing approaches more nearly the ordinary Chinese official language (*K'wan-hoa*), than the two other dialects, but is just as unintelligible as they, to a Chinese. This dialect is found mostly in works about China, used in the description of the names of places, and it is also said to be used by the monastic order of the „Five hills or convents" (五山 *Go-san*) at *Miyako*.

We close this digression on the three dialects with a quotation of the specimen by which the difference is shown in the Japanese Encyclopedia.

Ka-kun. Too-in.		Kan-won & Go-won.		Ka-kun. Too-in.		○	Kan-won. Go-won.
		又				假	
		云				令	
		物				二	
		字				音	
		猶				如	
		子				兄	
		孫				弟	

Japanese translation: *Tatoeba Fitatsu kuwa mi otōto no gotoku. Mata iwaku, fhiki no nina ko mogomo gotoshi*, i. e. The two dialects, to me as example, are like brothers. It is also said: The a-manner, or finals are like sons and grandsons.

[1] *Wa-wen lei oder Geschichtsblätter van Japan, aus dem Originale übersetzt von J.* HOFFMANN

Chinese text with Japanese translation.

In Chinese there are books written, which contain a complete Japanese translation at the side of the text.

There are also some, in which the Japanese translation is incomplete, and only here and there words or fragments of words are explained. In this case are found either only the principal ideas translated, or merely the terminational inflections given. It is supposed here, that the Japanese reader knows the signification of the Chinese character and the word corresponding to it in his mother tongue, or not being acquainted with it, he resorts to a Chinese-Japanese dictionary, to supply all that, in which the translation is deficient.

Were the construction of the two languages alike, it would suffice simply to represent the signification of each Chinese character by a Japanese word placed at the side of it, and to read Japanese in the same order as Chinese. But there is one point, from which the two languages diverge; to wit, the Chinese verb has its objective (*complément, régime*), whether a simple noun or a substantive phrase objective, after it, the Japanese has it before. To give an instance, the Chinese construction requires one to say: „He reads a book; he desires to go home;" on the contrary, the Japanese: „He a book reads; he homewards to go desires."

Thus in the reading aloud of the Japanese translation of a Chinese sentence a transposition, a skipping over of the Japanese words is necessary, as often as the case in question occurs. This transposition is shown on the left-hand-side of the Chinese text — the right-hand one being occupied by the Japanese translation — by numbers or equivalent signs. This transposition of the words is called 逆ニ讀トス ル *Gekidoku-suru*, i. e. against (the order) in reading, or also *Kayeri*, turning back, and the transposition-signs *Kayeri-ten* or marks of going backwards.

These marks are

1) the hook ν, which indicates the transposition of two words following each other, as 以ヲ 曆ヲ *motte korewo* = *korewo motte* (thereby);

2) the Chinese ciphers -, =, = (1, 2, 3) when the translation of a character skips over two or more characters;

3) the signs 上, 中, 下 (above, in the middle, beneath), whenever the parts of a sentence, that have been already marked, must be again skipped over;

INTRODUCTION.

4) the cyclical signs 甲, 乙, 丙, for a further skipping over.

The ciphers and signs cited may occur in connection with the simple transposition-sign, thus: 二, 三, 亖, 上, 中, 下; 囗, 口, 囗.

A practical indication of the use of these signs will be found in our edition of the *Grand Study (To-Aic)*, a few lines of which are subjoined as a specimen of Chinese text with a complete as well as a fragmentary translation in Japanese.

CHINESE TEXT

1, with a complete translation in Japanese.   2, with a fragmentary translation in Japanese.

大學之道在明明德在親民在止於至善知止而后有定定而后能靜靜而后能安安而后能慮慮而后能得

大學之道在明明德在親民在止於至善知止而后有定定而后能靜靜而后能安安而后能慮慮而后能得

Reading of the translation in Japanese:

Dai-Gakŭ no mitsi vá méi tŏkŭ wo akiráká ni súru ni ári; tami wo aráta ni súru ni ári; si-zen ni todomárŭ ni ári.

Todomárŭkoto wo sitté, sikŭsité notsi sadamárŭkoto ári. Sadamátte, sikŭsité notsi yókŭ sidzŭká nári. Sidzŭká ni sité, sikŭsité notsi yókŭ yásŭsi. Yásŭsité, sikfusité notsi yúko ómonbakúrú. Omónbakátte, sikfusité notsi yúko u ¹).

If, as here, the Chinese text is in the standard form written in full, then the *Káta-kána* is used for the interlinear translation in Japanese, whereas the *Fira-gána* accompanies the Chinese running-hand.

B. Books written in the Japanese language.

In these, the national writing, whether *Fira-gána* or *Káta-kána*, forms the chain, in which a larger or smaller number of Chinese characters are inserted. In this style, the Chinese characters represent ideas, for which the reader, in case the meaning of the Chinese character has not been already expressed at the side of it in Japanese writing, must substitute Japanese words and connect them with the inflectional forms, which the writer has placed after the Chinese character. Here also the *Káta-kána* accompanies the Chinese standard-writing, and the *Fira-gána* the Chinese running hand. In this style the whole Japanese literature proper is written. A Japanese text without an admixture of Chinese ideographic signs, women's letters excepted, has never yet come under our notice.

To exemplify what has been said, we subjoin a few lines written in this style. In the one specimen the translation in Japanese will be found written next to each Chinese character, in the other it is left out; the latter happens chiefly in official documents.

期限コリ開ヘレ　外夊ニ載スル場所ヲ　〇長崎オヨビ箱館ノ港ノ　期限ヨリ開ヘレ　外夊ニ載スル所ヲノ　〇長崎オヨビ箱館ノ港ノ

¹) Translation. The way of the Grand Study consists in illustrating illustrious virtue, it consists in renovating the people, it consists in resting in the highest excellence.

The point where to rest being known, the object of pursuit is then determined; that being determined, a calm unperturbedness may be attained. To that there will succeed a tranquil repose. That being attained, there may be careful deliberation, and that deliberation will be followed by the attainment (of the desired end). — J. LEGGE, *Chinese classics.* Vol. I. 220.

Reading of the Japanese text.

Nagasáki oyóbi Hakodate no minâto no hoká, tsugini nósuru ba-siyo wo sa no ki-gen yori ákubesi [1]).

The frequent use made of Chinese ideographic signs in this style of writing has for consequence, that even people of the lower order are more or less acquainted with it and, appreciating a sort of knowledge, which pleads for a good education, make ample use of it. We possess written communications from Japanese work-people which, written in the prevalent epistolary style, contain more Chinese characters than Japanese letters.

It stands to reason that, to understand texts written in this style, in the first place, an acquaintance with the Japanese language is necessary, since the logical connection between the parts of the proposition and the ideas indicated by the Chinese characters is expressed in Japanese letters, thus in Japanese.

C. Style.

Just as every living language the Japanese too has, during the lapse of centuries, undergone change and had a gradual development, which is reflected in a literature of more than a thousand years. This is not the place to investigate those changes or to indicate specimens of different periods. We desire merely to direct attention to the difference which exists between the old and new Japanese language, written as well as printed.

a. Old Japanese.

The old language, *Furá-koto*, is an idiom free from foreign ingredients, that has been developed freely and independently in the isolated *Nippon*. Originally the language of the ancient Mikado-dynasty, that was settled in *Yamáto* 660 years B. C., and therefore also called *Yamáto-kotobá* or the language of *Yamáto*, this idiom had, with the political, intellectual and spiritual power of that dynasty obtained supremacy over the other dialects of the empire and was, for ages long, the general written language, expressed at one time in Chinese, and then again in Japanese writing; but when at last the power of this dynasty declined, and lost its direct influence in the government of the empire, this old language shared its fate: it was superseded by a new idiom, and supplanted in

---

[1]) That is: Besides the Ports of Nagasaki and Hakodate, the places mentioned beneath shall be opened at the following periods. — Art. 2 of the Netherlands-Japanese Treaty of the 18th August, 1858.

the political life, but by no means driven from the mouths of the people, or forgotten. As the vehicle of an extensive literature, and chiefly by the power of its poetry and of the old religion, this language has kept its stand, and is still held in respect, since the literature founded on it, as the expression of an ancient civilization, and as the witness of a past, glorious in the eyes of the nation, still finds its admirers; and the old service of *Kamis*, which still lives on among the people, is rooted in this language.

Considered from a philological point of view, the *Yamato-kotoba* is the mirror which reflects most faithfully the being of the Japanese language, the most exposes its organic structure, and sheds a clear light on the grammatical forms also of the new idiom, now become prevalent.

The student of the Japanese language, who is not satisfied with the mechanical learning of grammatical forms, but wishes to penetrate into the knowledge of their origin and being, must, in the etymological and grammatical treatment of that language, take the *Yamato-kotoba* for basis, following, in this respect, the example of the Japanese themselves who, to be able to lay any claim to literary proficiency, apply themselves to the study of their old language and read the old authors and poets, and sometimes even imitate their versification.

The Japanese literature is rich in works in the *Furu-koto*, but not less rich in philological resources, chiefly in dictionaries, in which the old or pure Japanese language is illustrated by citations of the sources. The principal sources are the works on mythology and history, the oldest of which are those which have been designated with the name of „the three records" (三 部 本 書 *San-bu fon-syo*).

1. „Original account of the old events of former times, 先代舊事本紀 *Sen-dai ku-zi fon-ki*," executed by SIYAU-TOK DAI-SI and Soga no MUMAKONO SUKUNE, by order of Mikado SUI-KO, in 10 volumes, beginning with the god-dynasties, and extending to 620 (the 20th year of the said Mikado).

2. The „Book of antiquity, *Furu-koto-bumi* or 古事記 *Ko-zi-ki*," written by Oho-ason YASU-MARO and presented to the Mikado GEN-MEI in 711 or 712, 3 volumes. It begins with the mythological times and reaches to 597 (the 5th year of the Mikado SUI-KO).

3. The „Japanese book, *Yamato-bumi* or 日本書紀 *Nippon syo-ki*," completed by TONERI NO SIN-WOO and Oho-ason YASU-MARO, in 720, in

20 volumes, beginning with the creation and ending with the year 697 [1]).

These works, executed before the introduction of the Japanese *Kata-kána*-writing, are, as appears from the copies, that we have of them, generally written with Chinese writing, partly ideographic, partly phonetic; at the side of which is found the reading in Japanese expressed with *Kata-kána*, but this is an addition of later time. As a specimen we here subjoin the first lines of the *Ko-zi-ki* (古事記 [2]).

○ 天 地 初 發 之 時,
於 高 天 原 成 神
名 天 之 御 中 主
神, 次 高 御 産 巣 日
神, 次 神 産 巣 日
神. 此 三 柱 神 者,
並 獨 神 成 坐 而,
隱 身 也.

Reading: *Ame tsutsi no fazime no toki taka-ma no fara ni nerimaseru kami no mi-na ua Ame no mi-naka-nusi no kami, tsugi ni Taka-mi-musúbi no kami, tsugi ni Kami-musúbi no kami, — Kono mi fasira no kami wa mina ftóri pam wirimashi, mi-mi wo kákusi-tamáriki.*

Translation: The three gods: Ame no mi-naka-nusi no kami, Taka-mi-musúbi no kami, and Kami-musúbi no kami, at the time of the creation of Heaven and Earth existed in the high expanse of heaven, were solitary gods and hid themselves.

As sources for obtaining acquaintance with the *Fúri-koto*, the topographical, physical and historical descriptions (風土記 *Fuu-to-ki*) of Japan, collected as early as 713 come further under notice; the laws and precepts edited

---

[1]) Of this work I have made ample use in the elaboration of an historical treatise, which appeared in 1859 in VON SIEBOLD's „Nippon-Archiv" under the title of *Japan's Bezüge mit der Koreischen Halbinsel und mit China. Nach Japanischen Quellen bearbeitet*.

It might be expected, that the style, in which these annals are written, would be characterized by an adorned simplicity; but the opposite is the case. The oldest Japanese prose is completely subservient to courtly manners; it is verbose and diffuse, and any one, unless he is prostrated, like the authors themselves, with the divine worship, which they display towards the prince and his house, will discover but too soon that behind the richness of courtlike expressions lies hid — poverty of ideas.

in three different periods (三代格式 *San-dai kiku-siki*) of 820, 869 and 907; — Historical narratives and romances (物語 *Mono-gatari*); — collections of Lyric poems (歌 *utó*), as well as the Bundle of Ten thousand leaves; Epic poems and Melo-dramatic pieces (舞 *Mai*, or *mai*) etc.

As philological aids towards illustration of the *Füru-koto* deserving of mention are:

和名鈔 *Wa-mei-seo*, or explanation of Japanese names, collected by MINA-MOTONO SITAGAVU (源順), a famous poet, who died in 980, 20 volumes. There are editions of 1617, 1667 and 1831.

古訓梯 *Füru koto no hási*, or „Ladder to the old language." 1765.

雅言集覧 *Ga-gen siyu-ran* or *Miyabi-koto-atsumé*, „View of the correct language," by ISI-GAVA GA-SAI. 1812.

雅言仮字格 *Ga-gen ka-zi kaku*, „Standard of the correct language" in *Kána*-writing, by ITSI-OKA TAKE-FIKO. 1814.

倭訓栞 *Wa-gun no sicori*, or „Guide to the Japanese language," by TANI-GAVA SI SEI. 1830.

b. New Japanese.

Opposed to the *Füru-koto* is the New Japanese, as it has been in vogue since the 16th century, for the newest type of which the style may pass, in which the diplomatic documents of our time, particularly the treaties concluded with the Western Powers in 1855, are composed[1]).

The distinguishing characteristic of this style does not lie in the spelling, - for this, as the literature of this people, dating more than a thousand years ago, has undergone but few changes, — but in the analytic character, by which it forms an opposition to the antique-synthetic Japanese, and chiefly in the strong mixture of Chinese, or, properly, Japanized Chinese words, which, it is true, are governed by the Japanese element, but play so important a part in it, that this style has been, not with injustice, called the Sinico-Japanese.

Rising in the opinion of the Japanese, above the popular language proper, in dignity, conciseness and strength of expression, this style is more particularly a possession of the more civilized classes of society and, at one time more, at another less, impregnated with the foreign element, forms the book-language;

---

[1]) See p. 28, note 2.

as such, has penetrated to the lower classes of the people, and exercises its influence even on the polite conversational language and the epistolary style.

It follows, as a matter of course, that in our treatment of the Japanese language this style occupies a prominent place, and if at the same time we look back upon the old as well, it is but to be able, from a grammatical point of view, to illustrate the new as it requires.

13. LANGUAGE SPOKEN. — GENERAL CONVERSATIONAL LANGUAGE AND DIALECTS.

Almost each province of the Japanese Empire has its peculiar dialect, and the difference of dialect becomes greater, in proportion as the provinces are more distant from one another.

It is a fact confirmed by the testimony of different Japanese, whom we have questioned on the subject, that a native of the southern part of Japan and one from the northern cannot understand each other's dialect. The merchant or functionary passing from *Yédo* to *Nagasaki*, understands the dialect spoken there just as little as, on the other hand, a native of *Nagasaki* understands the language of the common people of *Yédo*.

The case is just the same with dialects of Japan, as with the many dialects, which, e. g., exist next one another in Germany. But as amidst those many dialects one general polite written and spoken language, — the High German, — has gained the ascendancy there, so in Japan also, (instead of the old *Yamato-kotoba*) a general polite spoken language has obtained admittance. It is the spoken language, at present in general use in *Miyako* and, with slight modification at *Yédo* also, but here it is spoken by the polite classes alone [1]. Since the influence of *Yédo* spreads to the most remote parts of the empire, and the instruction in the schools is everywhere given in that lan-

---

[1] In confirmation of this assertion, we here quote the very words of O. . K. . as we noted them down, where uttered „Miyako no stô ha-wen ro yomi-moto touri ni hanasi-mass; kera-nga-yuhei yoroisii' hotoma hahori gozarimas. Edds no hotoba wa, ti-nin wa yoroisii hotoba nite hânasi-mâsu," i. e. The inhabitants of Miyako speak as one reads in a book, and therefore have only good language. With regard to the language of Yédo, only the polite man speaks good language.

guage, every well-bred person in the provinces makes use of it in his intercourse with the educated, and leaves the local dialect to the lower classes of the people. To foreigners, who wish to get some knowledge of the spoken language whether at *Kanagawa* or at *Nagasaki*, it is not a matter of indifference to whom they apply for instruction. If they choose for language-master a servant taken from the street, he will sell them his patois for good Japanese, declares what really is good Japanese „not good," and, although it may not be his intention, gives them the means to afford Japanese functionaries -- amusement. As in every language, so in the Japanese also, the dialects have their unquestionable right to existence, and knowledge of them is of importance, as well for the daily intercourse with that portion of the population that do not rise above their dialect, as for comparative philology; but to intercourse with the well educated part of the nation, with whom the foreigner will certainly wish to place himself on a level, he gains admittance only by means of the general polite spoken language, and for this he must look about him. To take an instance, he will then use the word *watdkasi* for „I," just as the gentleman and merchant of *Yedo*, and not accept the porter's „*wataki* or *wasi*," or a servant-maid's „*wadsi*" or „*wudsi*" instead, or please himself with the *ataksa* from the district of *Yorikara*.

The ordinary conversational language differs from the book-language, both in respect of diction and pronunciation. If the book-language is succinct, and concise, the conversational is more circumstantial and diffuse; the natural consequence of the task laid on it of coming up to the rules of good-breeding, which prescribe the form of social intercourse in the different ranks of society.

These rules require from every one respectful politeness to his superiors, strict courtesy to his equals. From a people that, like the Japanese, has obtained among the Western nations the reputation of being the most civilized and most courteous on the earth [1], it is to be expected that its conversational language should express that character, and this is the case: the language familiarly spoken is a concatenation of courtly expressions and goes even so far, that a person, who has not been brought up with it, will not, to use the mildest expression, acquit it of exaggeration.

With regard to pronunciation, of which we have already spoken above (p. 21), the same phenomenon occurs as, among the Western languages, in the

---

[1] In 1865 the Netherlands became acquainted with some exceptions to this rule.

French: the pronunciation deviates from the written form, and this deviation arises partly from the original inadequacy of the Japanese phonetic system, which cannot possibly express all the existant combinations of sound, partly from the development of the language, in which the pronunciation has undergone many a change, whilst the once adopted, old orthography, with but slight modifications, has maintained its historical claim.

Specimens of the Japanese conversational style in the form of dialogues have only very lately reached us.

It is true, about forty years ago, a Japanese translation of Dutch dialogues found its way into a Museum in the Netherlands, and later a place in a book about Japan [1]), and every one who attached importance to the study of Japanese, in the supposition that that translation was also in the Japanese conversational style, had then to attach no small value to it; but, now that we have been able to become better acquainted with the familiar conversational style, it appears that people were misled: the translation of these dialogues is not written in the conversational, but in the book style, and therefore loses its supposed value.

The first specimen of the genuine conversational language that reached us was a pocket-work published at *Nagasaki* for the use of Japanese merchants, which we, with a view to the wants of the non-Japanese, recast and published in 1861 with the title of *Shopping-dialogues in Dutch, English and Japanese*. The Japanese it contains, is the pure conversational style in use among the tradespeople.

This specimen was in 1863 followed by *Familiar dialogues in Japanese with English and French translations for the use of students*; a contribution with which the names of B. ALCOCK and LÉON PAGÈS are connected.

Now the want of aids to oral intercourse with Japan is daily becoming more prominent, and as yet it is not to be expected, that the Japanese, who reluctantly see the attempt of the foreigner to become in any degree master of their language, will themselves coöperate therein and publish dialogues, from which the foreigner may draw profit, — it may be hoped, that for that very reason the zeal of such Europeans, as apply themselves more particularly to the study of language in Japan, or do so in their intercourse with Japanese out

---

[1]) *Bijdrage tot de kennis van het Japansche Rijk*, by VAN OVERMEER FISCHER. 1833.

of Japan, — for the Japanese language is not grown fast to the Japanese soil,
will succeed in collecting new series of dialogues and distinguishing in them the
more or less polite style of speaking, the correct and the incorrect manner of
expression.

Epistolary style.

The Japanese epistolary style (文の氏, *Bun sigyu*) is the conversational
language purified; it is equally subject to stamped forms, and is a model of
courtliness and deferential politeness. Knowledge of it is rendered easy, because
every popular encyclopedia contains a series of model letters, in which, the
difference in rank between the writer and the person to whom the letter is addressed being considered, the choice of words and expressions is defined.

14. ON THE PARTS OF SPEECH.

The Japanese have of old distributed the words of their language in three sorts:

1. The **Noun**, 名, **Na**, i. e. name (*nomen*). To this category belong besides
the noun substantive, the pronouns, the adjectives, the numerals, and the
exponents of relation, which last, placed as postpositions, do the office
of our so called prepositions, as well as, in part, of our conjunctions also.

2. The **Verb**, 詞, **Kotoba**, i. e. the word (*verbum*) by eminence, and considered as the living element of the sentence.

3. **Particles**, formal or constituent words, generally suffixes (*suffixa*), which
do the office of our terminational inflections (*casus*) such as the particles *te*, *ni*,
wo, *ni*, and therefore comprised under the name of *Tsukuwa* or *Tenius*.

Remark 1. By the written form 出ル葉 or 出葉, used
for the name *Tenius* by which the signification of „opening leaves" is attributed to the word, one must not be misled into the supposition, that
these particles might be actual shoots of words, or what are sometimes
called organic terminational inflections, and not suffixes. The form of
writing quoted is nothing else, than one of the frequently occurring re-
buses, in which, to arrive at the truth, the meaning of the characters
employed must be overlooked.

Remark 2. In one European Grammar [1] these particles are also called

---
[1] RODRIGUEZ, *Elem* § 67.

INTRODUCTION. 43

„*Sutegana*" and „*Wokiy*," names, which require a further illustration.

Sute-gana (捨テ假ケ名'), i. e. deserted, or foundling-letters (a foundling child is called *sute-go*) is the name given to the terminations of Japanese words expressed with Japanese *Kana*-writing between, or at the side of, Chinese characters, which words themselves are only indicated ideographically by Chinese characters [1]). The marks ノ *no* and ク *ku* in 孔子, *Kon-si NO notamawaKU* (= saying of Confucius), or ツ *tsu* in 思曰, *omoI'U* are thus foundling-letters that must be taken up in the translation.

Oki-si (置キ字ジ) — the written form *Wokiy* appears to be an error of impression — is said of those characters of a Chinese sentence which, in the translation into Japanese, must not be translated separately, but passed over, as 於 in 遊於山中, *San-trin-ni asobu* (= walking among the mountains). The *Oki-si* thus are characters to which, in translating into Japanese, the part of statists or mute players is assigned.

By more recent Japanese grammarians the name of 體ジ詞カ *Tai no kotoba* corporal or bodily word has been given to the noun, and that of 用ジ詞カ *Yon no kotoba* or effective word to the verb, whereas for the particles the name of *Tenivoa* has been retained.

If the Japanese grammarians confine themselves to the distinction of three classes of words, we, to be able to fix the logical and grammatical value of the words properly, must apply our grammatical categories, our distinction of the parts of speech to the Japanese language. Consequently we distinguish 1. Nouns, under which are included 2. Pronouns, 3. Adjectives, 4. Numerals, 5. Adverbs. 6. Verbs, 7. Suffixes (*postpositions*) simple, answering to our terminational inflections, and such as answer to our prepositions and conjunctions, 8. Interjections.

---

[1]) Compare p. 34

15. A GLANCE AT THE ARRANGEMENT AND CONNECTION OF WORDS IN JAPANESE.

The laws for the arrangement of words, which govern the Japanese syntax, also govern the formation of the words themselves, that is: the manner, in which that language, from its monosyllabic roots, has formed words, and from those existing words has formed, and is still forming new ones, is subject to the same laws, as the manner in which the elements of sentences standing in relation to one another are governed. A concise view of those laws should, therefore, precede the theory of the grammatical forms of words.

The Japanese construction of words is based on two principles, viz: that of *Predicative Apposition*, and that of *Subordination* or order of dependance.

A. Predicative Apposition.

The subject, if it is named, precedes, the predicate follows, the subject being mostly separated from the predicate by an isolating particle (ﾊ), whereas the predicate, in the absence of personal inflections of the verb, is not joined to the subject grammatically. As the subject too is left without a sign of the nominative, a congruency of predicate and subject properly so called does not exist.

B. Subordination.

Every modifying word precedes the word to which it belongs. — Application.

1. The attributive definition, be it a genitive, or adjective; is thus placed before the word to which it belongs.

    Thus *Fána-mi*, mountain-wood, *Móri-yáma*, wood-mountain; *Áme ga furu*, rain-fall, raining; *Natsume ame*, summer-rain; *Tsuyói ame*, heavy rain; *Yóku*, well; *Yóku wakári*, understanding well; *Hána-háda yoróshiku*, very well. Consequently the connectives answering to our *in*, *at*, *of*, *through*, *with*, *on*, *under*, *before*, *after*, *for*, *by* etc. etc. become suffixes to the word, which is their attributive definition. This takes place also with the *sena*, which is to be considered as the attributive definition of the inflection.

2. The verb is placed before the connective (*conjunctio*), because it is governed by it.

    Instead of "I go, because he goes," an expression is used answering to "he to go because I going am."

3. The adverb precedes the verb, and the subordinate or dependent proposition, in quality of adverbial definition, precedes the principal proposition.

    E. g. "The sun brightly shining is," instead of our "The sun is shining brightly."

INTRODUCTION.   15

4. The predicate is placed before the copula, because the meaning included in the predicate adds a definition to the copula (be, is).

E. g. „The flower in bloom is," for our „The flower is in blossom," or „the flower blooms."

5. The object direct, as well as the indirect, is placed before its verb; the substantive phrase objective is placed before the principal proposition governing.

Instead of „he sends a letter home; — he knows that I shall come," expressions are used answering to „he || home(wards) a letter sends; — he || I come shall that, knowing is."

6. The verb is placed before the auxiliary verb, whether it be affirmative or, in consequence of the blending with a negative element (= not), negative.

Instead of „he will go; I will not go;" expressions are used answering to „he go will, or he || (to) go willing is; I || (to) go willing not am."

7. The verb, by means of which a derivative verb is formed, has the root of this verb placed before it.

The saying: „I let him go," is rendered by an expression equal to „I him go let."

The interrogatives and certain exclamations (*interjections*), follow the word or proposition they characterize.

Instead of „Understand you? — Oh heavens!" we meet with expressions answering to „You understand eh? — Heavens, oh!"

When several definitions independent of one another belong to one predicate, then the less important precedes the more important: the definition of time is placed before the definition of place; the object indirect (Dative, Local, Instrumental, Ablative) before the object direct (Accusative).

Coördination.

In coördination of words, the last alone receives the characteristic of grammatical relationship, while the preceding ones are left undefined.

Thus if it be a series of nouns, which are linked together, the last only receives the terminational inflection, that refers to them all.

One saying: „The three lights of sun, moon and stars" gets the Japanese form of „sun, moon, stars or three lights." (日ジ月ゲ星セ之ノ三ミツ光クワウ Zit get sei-NO san book). —

In the saying: „Who has made heaven, earth, sea, mount, water, air, fire?" only the last of the nouns linked together gets the terminational inflection of the accusative, thus *Ten ga ame, tstuti, β, tstuki, midzu, kazi, β WO go-zdi-s nasareta?* — Both examples, corrected, have been taken from SODRIGURE *Elém.* § 88.

The case is just the same with propositions linked together, the verb only of the last proposition, in like manner, receiving the terminational inflection, while the verbs of the preceding propositions, left undefined, retain their radical form.

The Japanese and the Chinese order of words, with regard to the attributive definitions, agree, as in both these languages they precede the word to which they belong; but they differ from each other, in respect of the object (*complément*), which, as it has been shown on p. 32, in Japanese is placed before, in Chinese after the verb.

Might it be objected that in Chinese there are prepositions also such as 於, 于, 自, 由 etc. which have the word they govern placed after them, we must observe that, in our opinion, these prepositions are verbs, and therefore have the complement after them.

Inversion.

Inversion or transposed order of words plays an important part in Japanese. The Syntax will show, how it can step out of the monotonous march of the regular order of words, and without violating its laws, set off the principal elements and the definitions of a sentence rhetorically.

ETYMOLOGY, NATURE AND INFLECTION OF WORDS.

CHAPTER I.

NOUNS.

§ 1. The root is the monosyllabic element of a word. Roots are, e. g.

i, to go,   *kik*, to hear,
ki, to come,   *ag*, to ascend,
mi, to see,   *sag*, to descend,
tor, to take,   *tat*, to stand.

§ 2. The verbal form, on which derivative or inflectional suffixes are grafted, is called the RADICAL or PRIMITIVE WORD.

The Radicals are the names either of objects or qualities, or verbs, as:

Kára, river,   *Tůka*, high,   *Itári*, gone,   *Kíki*, hear,
Yáma, mountain,   *Fikí*, low,   *Kitári*, come,   *Age*, raise,
Kuni, land,   *Firo*, broad,   *Miye*, seem,   *Súge*, abate,
Miti, way,   *Nága*, long,   *Tóri*, hold,   *Tůte*, fix, place.

§ 3. The RADICAL IN COMPOSITION.

If a word in its radical form stands before a noun, then both words are either coördinate, or the first is to the second, as a definition, subordinate. In the latter case the rule is, that Japanese words are combined with Japanese, Chinese with Chinese.

CHAPTER I. NOUNS. COÖRDINATION. SUBORDINATION. § 3.

A. Coördination takes place in expressions as: *Ame-tsutsi*, heaven-earth; — *Fi-tsuki*, sun (and) moon; — *Kusa-ki*, plant (and) tree.

天〻地〻 *Ten-tsi*, heaven (and) earth; 日〻月〻 *Zit-get*, sun (and) moon; 國〻家〻 *Koku-ka*, country (and) people; 草〻木〻 *Syu-mok*, plant (and) tree.

B. Subordination.

I. Subordination by way of genitive or adjective definition takes place in compositions, as:

  Kawa-oso, river-otter; *Oso-gawa*, otter-river.
  Kawa-yeda, river-branch; *Yeda-gawa*, branch-river.
  Yama-mori, mountain-wold; *Mori-yima*, wold-mountain.
  Taka-ydma, high-mountain; *Yoko-hama*, cross-strand.
  Naga-saki, long-cape; *Firo-no*, large-field.

天〻神〻 *Ten-zin*, heavenly gods;
地〻神〻 *Tsi-zin*, earthly gods;
國〻人〻 *Koku-zin*, country-men, inhabitants;
國〻字〻 *Koku-zi*, country-writing, the *Kata-kana*.

II. The object direct or indirect, if taken in a general sense, is placed in its radical form before the verb [1]).

1. The radical form occurs as object direct (Accusative) in compounds as *Ana-tori*, the hole-digger; *Kawa-watari*, one who crosses a river; *Sund-tori*, sand-fetcher, sand-skipper; *Midsu-kimi*, water-filler; *Ama-terasu*, heaven-lighting.

2. The radical form occurs as object indirect in *Ama-kudóri*, (from) heaven descending; *Te-tori*, *asi-tori*, to seize (any one by the) hands, seize (by the) feet; *Me-gake*, (in the) eye hold; *Me-susi*, (with the) eye show, give a wink; *Ana-dori*, (in) holes catch.

III. The radical form as a definition before adjectives, e. g. *Te-haya*, = hand-quick, handy, dextrous; *Asi-faya*, = foot-quick, swift of foot, fleet; *Asi-taka*, = leg-high, high-legged; *O-naga*, = tail-long, long-tailed.

Remark. In composition rules of euphony are observed and bring about modifications of sound, as well with regard to vowels, as to consonants, whenever

---

[1]) Comp. H. STEINTHAL, *Charakteristik der hauptsächlichsten Typen des Sprachbaues*, p. 184, 185.

CHAPTER I. NOUNS. GENDER. § 4.   51

their meeting is embarrassing to the pronunciation. From *Asa + ake*, dawn, is formed *asáke*; from *Yáma + ósto*, = hill-behind, behind the hills, *Yamáto*; from *Tóyo + ura*, = rich-creek, the name of a place, *Toyúra*; from *Fö + isi*, = fire-stone, *fúsi*, star, etc.

As we must draw up the rules of euphony from the grammatical phenomena we shall, to be able to refer to them, insert the rules at the end of the Etymology.

GENDER.

§ 4. Grammatical gender does not exist. If the gender must be definitely expressed of objects in which a distinction of sex exists, then this distinction is made, either by means of particular words A. or as in English in which *male-servants* and *female-servants*, „*a he-animal*" and „*a she-animal*" are spoken of, by placing ヲ O, man, and メ Me, woman, as attributive before the word, B.

A. To the particular names belong: *Mi-kádo*, = the sublime port, the sovereign, king or emperor. *Ki-saki*, originally 妃 幸, *Kimi-saki*, princely fortune, the queen or empress; thence in the Mythology which, under the name of *Kámi*, *Kin*, = prince, chief, includes the gods, the expression *Kisaki-gámi*, i. e. higher being (*kimi*) that is consort (*kisaki*), to indicate a goddess, who is the consort of a god.

Tsitsi, knzo, father.	*Fava* (*haha*), irora, mother.
Mama-tsitsi, stepfather.	*Mama-fava*, stepmother.
O-dsi, uncle.	*O-ba*, aunt.
Ani, eldest brother.	*Ane*, eldest sister.
Tsitsi-tori, = father-bird, cock.	*Fava-tori*, = mother-bird, brood-hen.

B. 1. By the prefixes ヲ O and メ Me the sex is determined in

O-ri, oï, nephew.	*Me-ri, me-i*, niece.
O-ke-mono [1]), male-mammal.	*Me-ke-mono*, female-mammal.
O-usi, ox.	*Me-usi*, cow.
O-muma, stallion.	*Me-numá*, mare.
O-inu, dog.	*Me-inu*, bitch.

---

[1]) *Ke*, hair, hairy, *mono*, being.

CHAPTER I. NOUNS. GENDER. § 4.

O-inó-ko, boar.   Me-inó-ko, sow.
O-fitstsi, he-goat.   Me-fitstsi, she-goat.
O-sikā, stag.   Me-sikā, hind.
O-neko, he-cat.   Me-neko, she-cat.
O-kuzira, male-whale.   Me-kuzira, female-whale.

2. Instead of the radical form O and Me the genitive attributive Ono and Meno also occur.

Ono-ko, male-child.   Meno-ko, female-child, girl.
Ono-kami, a god.   Meno-kami, goddess.

Remark. When *Ono* and *Meno* are contracted to On and Men, then the pure sounds k, s, t if following, generally pass to the troubled g (n̄), z (nz), d (nd)[1].

From *ono* + *tori*, male-bird, becomes successively ヲンドリ ondori and ヲドリ odori (pronounce *ondori*); from *meno* + *tori*, female-bird, メンドリ mendori, and メドリ medori (pron. *mendori*); from *meno* + *saru*, female-monkey, メンザル menzaru and メザル mezaru (pron. *menzaru*); from *meno* + *tora*, female-tiger, メンドラ mendora and メドラ medora (pron. *mendora*); from *meno* + *kataki*, female-enemy, メンガタキ me-gataki (pron. *mengataki*).

3. There come under notice also Ko (子 [2]) and Me (女 [3]), lad and lass, with antecedent attributive definition.

Otó-ko[1]), lad, man.   Oto-mé, virgin, maid.
Musu-kó = begotten son, (my) son.   Musu-mé = begotten maid, (my) daughter.
Fikó, young nobleman.   Fimé, young lady.
Kana-yāma fikó no kami, the god of the ore-mountain.   Kana-yāma fimé no kami, the goddess of the ore-mountain.
Mi-koto, Sublimity, Highness.   Fimé-gami, goddess.
Ono mi-koto, His Highness.   Fimé no mi-koto, Her Highness.

The old-Japanese also has *ki* and *mi* instead of *ko* and *me*, probably with a view to the vocal-harmony; thence *Izana-ki* and *Izana-mi*, = male-goer to and fro, female-goer to and fro, name of the divine pair that first mingled carnally.

---

[1]) Comp. Introduction, p. 15, line 8.
[2]) *Oto*, old-Japanese for *ono*, genitive attributive of *o* (小), small, young.

CHAPTER 1. NOUNS. NUMBER. § 5.   53

C. The ideas of male and female are sometimes transferred to objects without sex, for the purpose of characterizing the one as big, strong, rough, the other as little, weak and mild, or to indicate other peculiarities of one or the other of the sexes; e. g. *O-matsu*, the masculine firtree, or *Kuró-matsu*, the black firtree [1]; *Me-matsu*, the feminine firtree, also *Aka-matsu*, the red pinetree [2].

Two islands being next each other, when they are of unequal size, are often denominated *O-sima*, man-island, and *Me-sima*, woman-island.

Me-ikusa, a female-army, means a weak army (= *Yowaki ikusa*); *me-nizi*, a female-rainbow, is the name of the faint by-rainbow. *Me-kawdra* or feminine-tile is the name given to flat tile (*jira-kawdra*), on which the rollshaped (*mdru-kawdra*), as the masculine tile (*O-kawdra*), rests.

D. The Chinese expressions, used in connection with Chinese names for female and male, are for quadrupeds 牝ヒ 牡ボ *jin* and *bo*; for birds 雌シ 雄ユ *si* and *yuu*, e. g. 牝ヒ 馬バ *jin-ba*, mare; 雄ユ 雉チ *yuu-tsi*, cock-pheasant.

NUMBER.

§ 5. The grammatical distinction of singular and plural is wanting. The noun used in its radical form expresses the idea generally and leaves it undetermined, whether the said object is to be adopted in the singular or plural.

Only when it is strictly necessary to make the general idea appear in a definite sense as something either singular or plural, such is expressed in one way or another.

A. In Japanese words the singular is expressed by the numeral ヒト *fitó*, one;

    Fitó yo, one night.   *Fitó kádo*, one corner.
     „ *tose*, one year.   „ *katamúri*, one clog.
     „ *tabi*, one time, once.   „ *fána*, one flower.

in Chinese words by 一ィ 箇ヲ, *ikka* or *ikkáno*, as

     一ィ 箇ヲ 所ショ, *ikka siyo*, one place;
     一ィ 箇ヲ ノ 地ヂ, *ikkáno tsi*, one piece of ground.

More amply, when treating of the numerals.

---
[1] *Pinus massoniana* LAMB.   [2] *Pinus densiflora* SIEB. et ZUC.

54   CHAPTER I. NOUNS. NUMBER. § 6.

B. The plural is expressed:

1. By a repetition of the noun, for so far as a distributive generality [1]) indicated by the repetition includes the idea of a plural. *Yáma*, hill; *Yáma-yáma*, every hill.

The number of such repetitions is determined by custom. In the pronunciation the accent lies on the first part of the compound, while the second occurs as a soft prolongation of the sound, and the consonant, with which it begins, undergoes a softening and becomes impure. Examples:

國 *kuni*, country, province;	國々 *kuni-guni*, each country, every province.
郡 *kokóri, kodri*, district;	郡々 *kokóri-gokóri*, every district.
村 *mura*, village;	村々 *murá-murá*, each village.
邑 *sato*, village;	邑々 *sato-zato*, each village.
町 *matsi*, ward, street;	町々 *matsi-matsi*, every ward.
家 *i hé, i é*, house, family;	家々 *i hé-i hé*, every house, each family.
戸 *fe, he*, door, family;	戸々 *fe-fe*, door for door, every family.
社 *yasiro*, chapel;	社々 *yasiro-yasiro*, every chapel.
山 *yáma*, hill, mountain;	山々 *yáma-yáma*, every hill or mountain.
處 *tokoro*, place;	處々 *tokóro-dokóro*, every place, everywhere.
隅 *sumi*, corner;	隅々 *sumi-zumi*, every corner.
間 *ma*, space, (place and time).	間々 *ma-ma*, every space, every time.
間 *ai*, space between;	間々 *ai-ai*, meanwhile.
橋 *fási, hási*, bridge;	橋々 *fási-básí*, every bridge.
己 *ono*, one;	各々 *onó-óno*, each.
人 *fito*, one, man;	人々 *fito-bito*, every one.

---

[1]) „Die Wiederholung der Substantivwörter bezeichnet nicht den Plural, auch nicht schlechthin Mehrheit, sondern distributive Allheit, die wir am besten durch „jeder" wiedergeben." — STEINTHAL, *Typen des Sprachbaues*, pag. 168.

親 ৳ oya, old;   親৳ ヤ | oya-oya, both parents.
役ヲ yáku, office;   役ヲ ヤ | yáku-yáku, every office.
世 ° yo, age, time of life;   世 ª ヤ 、 yo-yo, every age.
年と tosi, year;   年と ヤ | tosi-tosi, each year.
日 ヒ fi, day;   日 ヒ ヤ ˇ fi-bi, every day.
時 ト toki, time, hour;   時 ト ヤ | toki-doki, always, each hour.
色ぁ iro, 1) color, 2) sort;   色ぁ ヤ | iro-iro, every color or sort.
級ナ, 品ナ sina, 1) degree, rank, 品ト ヤ | sina-zina, every quality, every
   2) quality.   article.
種ュ siyu, sort;   種ュ ヤ | siyu-siyu, every sort.
樣さ sama, the look, the mien   樣さ ヤ | sama-sama no, of every form.
度ξ tabi, journey, turn;   度ξ ヤ | tabi-tabi, each turn.
藥ヶ kusuri, medicine;   藥ヶ ヤ | kusuri-gusuri, every medicine.
聲ェ koyi, sound;   聲ェ ヤ | koyi-goyi, each sound.

II. The plural is expressed by nouns used adjectively, which signify a quantity, generality.

1. In composition with Japanese words (yomi) are used:

多ヲノ, ohóku no, oókuno, many. Oóku no fitó, many people. Oóku no kane, much money, in opposition to sukósi no kane, little money.

大ヲ勢ヲノ, tai-sei no, in great power, in multitude. Tai-sei no fitó, people in multitude.

大ヲ壯ヲノ, tai-su no, tai-soo no, exceedingly.

澤ヲ山と, 沢ヲ山と,, táku-san no, abundant.

色ぁ ヤ ノ, iro-iro no, of every color or sort, of all sorts. Iro-iro no fána, all sorts of flowers. Iro-iro no yáku nin, functionaries of every rank.

品ト ヤ ノ, sina-sina no, of every quality.

樣さ ヤ ノ, sama-sama no, of all sorts. Sama-sama no wake, all the different judgements. Sama-sama no mono, things of all sorts.

數ヶ ヤ ノ, kasu-kasu no, numerous.

種ュ ヤ ノ, siyu-siyu no, ku-ku no, of every sort. Siyu-siyu no fitó, people of every sort.

一切ノ, is-sai no, all. 一切ノ眼生ノ, is-sai no sia-ziyou, all living beings.

Moro-moro no, all [from 双ゝ, moro, both]. Moro-moro no fitó, all people; moro-moro no mono, all things; moro-moro no tensai-rui, all sorts of earth. Taka moro-moro no tori wo kdzumu, the falcon plunders all birds.

2. In composition with Chinese words (koyé) are used:

数, sa, number, many.

数代, su-dai, many generations.
| 年, su-nen, many years.
| 月, su-get, many months.
| 日, su-sit, many days.
| 人, su-zin, many people.

数万, su-man, many tens of thousands.
| 千, su-sen, many thousands.
| 百人, su-byaku nin, many hundreds of men.

諸, siyo, every, all.

諸国, siyo-kóku, the countries.
| 方, siyo-fqu, the regions.
| 物, siyo-buts, the things.
| 人, siyo-nin, mankind, the people.
| 士, siyo-si, the warriors.

諸役, siyo-yáku, the functions.
| 說, siyo-setsi, the arguments.
| 藝, siyo-kei, the arts.
| 職, siyo-siyúku, every trade.
| 宗, siyo-siu, the sects.

III. The plural of a noun is also expressed by one or another suffix, which signifies a quantity or generality, and either must be considered as coördinate, as e. g. Co in I and Company for we, or with the preceding word forming a collective word, as e. g. man-kind for men. These suffixes are ra, domo, gara, bara, nami, tatsi, stu, gata, nado.

1. Ra (等) signifies a class of persons or things without any distinctive, e. g. Yátsukdre, subject or vassal; Yátsukdrerd (臣等), subject and class, all that belongs to the category of subjects, the subjects (or vassals).

Otóko, man; Otókord (男等), man and class, all that belongs to the category of man, men.

Fiyaku-siyou rá (百姓等), or Nou-min rá (農民等), country-people.

Ware, the I; *Warerd* (吾等), I and class, we. *Nandsi*, thou; *Naadsird* (汝等), you.

Kore, something that is here, this; *Korerd* (是等), this and class, such. *Korerd no nozomi*, such a desire, a desire of that nature¹). *Koto*, matter; *Korerd no koto*, such a matter. *Sono mono*, such a one; *Sono monord* (其者等), such a one and Cº., such persons²).

Migi (pronounce *mingi*), on the right, in a writing referring to what precedes. *Migird*, all that precedes, the aforesaid. 右ノ 等ノ 諸シ 入ノ 費ニ, *migird no siyo niu-fi*, the expenses of all the aforesaid³).

Atsi kotsi, there and here; *Atsira kotsira*, all that is included in there and here.

Koro Wani no kimi, *Kamo no kimi rd ga oya nari*, this is the father of the princes (princely houses) of *Wani* and *Kamo*.

Remark. If we are at liberty to consider *ra* as a coördinate word, and then again as a suffix that forms collective words, logic will require the first, seeing that such an expression as *I and Company* really answers to *we*, which is not the case with the expression *my company*, by which „I" may be excluded.

2. *Tomo*, *domo*, mate, fellow, companion, particularly in the spoken language, for persons and things.

Watdkusi no tomo, my mate or friend; *Watdkusi domo* (我共), I and mate, we; *Watdkusi domo no hon*, our book. *Ko*, child; *Ko-domo*, a mate who is a child, (my or his) child; *Ko-domo ra* or *Ko-domo domo*, (my or his) child and mate, (my or his) children. *Ke-rai*, attendant; *Ke-rai domo*, attendants, the suite of a prince. *Sono mono domo* (其ノ者ドモ), such persons⁴). *Ware*, I; *Ware domo*, we. *Mi*, I myself; *Mi domo*, we ourselves; *Mi domo ga kimi*, the prince of us ourselves, our own prince. *Ohikuno taka domo*, falcons in multitude. *Yebisu domo wo tairukesima*, he has the savages subjected. *Taka no na tomo wo siruru*, to give up the different names of the falcon. *Neko*, the cat; *Neko domo*, the cats. *Mumd*, horse; *Mumd domo*, horses.

3. *Gara*, series, row; division of objects distributed in classes.

Fito, man; *Fito-gara* (人品, 人柄), series of men. *Fito-gara no you ni*, after the manner of men. *Fi-gara* (日柄), series of days. *Koto*, matter; *Koto-*

---

¹) The Treaty between the Netherlands and Japan, concluded at Yedo, 18th August, 1858 Art. II, al. 18.
²) Ibid. Art. VI, al. 9.   ³) Ibid. VIII, 8.   ⁴) Ibid. VI, 10.

yara, series of matters. *Tomo* (友, 朋), fellow, mate; *Tomo-yara* (倫, 黨, 曹, 儕), a row of companions, a series or class (of men or brutes). *Wa ga-tomo-yara* (吾儕), the class of the I, we. *Nandsi ga tomo-yara* (爾曹), the class of you, you. *Nezumi no tomo-yara* (鼠之儕*)¹), the mouse-kind.

4. **Bara**, group.

Taki-bara (竹林), bamboo-wood. *Matsi-bara* (松林), firtree-wood, a group of firtrees. *Nandai-bara* (汝曹), your group, you. *Tomo-bara* (儕曹), they there without.

5. **Nami** (次), series.

Hi-nami, series of days. *Tsuki-nami*, series of months. *Se-ken-nami*, the common people. *Fito-nami*, the people. *Wa-nami* (吾儕), my series, we.

6. **Tatai** (等*)¹), row of persons who are, or may be, in an upright posture for, or at a given time, host.

Yaku-nin, functionary; *Yaku-nin-tatai* (役人等), row of functionaries, functionaries. *Kami*, god; *Kami-tatai* (神等), series of gods, gods. *Kono mi-fasimo-no Kami ra mina Watarari-agata ni masu Kami-tatai nari*, these three gods are a series of gods residing in the district of *Watarusi*. — *Kono futi fusira no kami ra minamoki-ni narimaseru Kami-tatai nari*, both the gods are gods sprung from the bed of the river. *Tomo*, fellow, friend; *Watakusi-no tomo-tatai*, my friends.

7. **Siu, siyu** (眾ジュ, シュ), *siu*, also *su*, in the written language 眾ジュ 中ュ, *siu-dayu*, company, circle of persons. *Samardi siu*, band of warriors, warriors. *Onago-siu*, circle of women.

Remark. Both expressions, *samardi-siu* and *onago-siu*, already given by COL-LADO as forms of the plural, are acknowledged by natives of *Yedo*, in answer to our personal inquiry, to be good Japanese, in colloquial style. Thus, when in the *Japanese Grammar* of 1861 (page 19, line 6 from the bottom) it is remarked: „HODDIGURZ speaks of a fourth (particle expressing the plural), *suo*, but this appears to be always a prefix. It has reference to number, but is not indicative, as alleged, of *rank*, while the other three (ラ, ト, ト, ド) undoubtedly are," it appears that there the difference between 數ス *su*, number,

---

¹) Jap. Encycl. 59, 5, v.
²) Instead of 等 occurs 達, but only as the phonetic representative of *tate*.

multitude (see page 56), and the 限り *kiri*, *tis*, used elliptically is not taken notice of.

8. **Gata**, pronounced *agata* = *no gata*, side of.

Mi-kata, the side or party of the Mikado. *Teki no kata*, the hostile party. To indicate the plural *gata* is used for high persons, and characterizes deep respect towards them.

Dai-miyau, = great name, nobleman; *Dai-miyau-gata* (大名方), the noblemen, the nobility. — *Tono sdma*, young nobleman; *Tono-sama-gata*, young noblemen. — *Te-mae-sdma*, you, Sir; *Te-mae-sama-gata*, you, Sirs or gentlemen. — *Ka-nai-sdma-gata*, the gentlemen house-mates, your family. — *Oko-gata*, your Highness's children, your children. — *Dzyo tsin gata* (女中方), women of quality, young gentlewomen.

9. **Nado**, from *nani-to*, *nando*, whatever, and so forth, and such (等, vulgo 抔, 夲). *Iye-nado*, house and so forth, house and such like, houses. — *Samurdi-nado*, warriors.

As the grammatical distinction of singular and plural is wanting, so the compound words, which express a plural, have no separate declension.

Remark. With a view to courtesy, which particularly dominates the spoken language, it is not a matter of indifference which of the words given, is used to indicate the plural. **Ra**, **domo** and **nado** refer directly to a class of persons or things and therefore are used when one speaks of his own or of subordinate people, or in general of objects, to which no importance is attached. — **Gara** and **bara** belong to the written language. — **Tatsi** implies respect, and **gata**, side, the highest respect, which is analogous to our „on the part of the King" for „from the King."

It is natural, that more or less elevated expressions, which from politeness are used to others, are not applied to oneself and one's own.

IV. The plural is also expressed by adverbs, as **Mina** (皆), together, **Nokorazu** (不残), without exception, and **Koto-gotoku** (悉), generally, which then precede the predicative verb to which they belong, for instance *Moto sino wa mina yorisii*, the article itself is together good, the articles themselves are all good. — *San-kan wokorizu mitsuki-mono wo tate-matsuru*, the three empires offer without exception tribute. — *Taue kotu-gotoku me wo idesi nari*, the seed shoots generally, all the seed shoots.

ISOLATING OF THE NOUN.

§ 6. The suffix ハ va, ワ wa, ヾ ba.

Every one, who for the first time hears a Japanese harangue, is struck by the continual repetition of the little word wa, which pronounced in a sharp and high tone and followed by a pause, breaks off the equable flow of words, in which the speaker then proceeds in his ordinary tone of speaking. On a hearer, not acquainted with the language, this little word with its resting point makes the impression, that the speaker would emphasize what he has just said, and separate it from what follows. And that impression is correct. Wa, ワ, in the book-language ハ, va, is an emphatic suffix or rather an interjection, intended to isolate some word or saying, and to separate it from what immediately follows. We do the same, when we raise the voice at some word and, after a pause, continue speaking in our ordinary tone.

Va or wa therefore is used, in the first place, to separate the subject from the predicate, as in *Tâma và yâma yóri ideti*, = the jewels || mountain out come (jewels come out of mountains); and it may not cause surprise when, on that account, it is understood as characteristic of the subject and consequently as the sign of the nominative, which, strictly considered, it is not. It is indeed joined to the subject, but not exclusively, and serves to isolate every other relation, every dependent case. The isolating power of va finds its equivalent in expressions like as to, with regard to, *quant à* Fr., *quoad, quod attinet ad*, Lat., *wat ... aangaat*, Dutch.

Whenever va isolates the subject, it answers to the Chinese 者 *tśè*, which has the signification of a „definite something" and passes for a relative pronoun. As a euphonic modification of va, ヾ ba also occurs.

The subject and the predicate are not always separated by va, but how necessary this separation sometimes is, appears from the instance quoted, which, with the omission of va, may also signify: „jewel-mountain from come," i. e. be produced from a jewel-mountain.

Examples: 獅レ子ンハ百ヲ獸ジノ長チナリ, *Sisi va fâku-ziu no teiyqu nari*, the lion is the head of all brutes, or: as to the lion, he is the head etc. — 牛ヲハ田ヲツ耕スル畜ナリ, *Usi va ta wo takayesu tiku nari*, as to the ox, he is a field-ploughing domestic animal. — 獺ハ水ス中ニスム, *Oso va sui-tśiu ni sumu*, the otter in (the) water lives.

CHAPTER I. NOUNS. DECLENSION. § 7.

DECLENSION.

§ 7. The **relations** of one noun to another word, or its cases, are expressed by suffixes, by particles (*Tenizora* or *Teniwoji*) [1]), which generally have a definite signification and, arranged according to our declension, are limited to the following.

Nominative (subject) and Vocative ...
Accusative (object direct) .... ヲ wo.
Genitive .... ガ ga (pronounced *nga*, *na*), among inexact writers often カ *ka*.
Qualitative Genitive .... ノ no, old-Japanese also ナ na and ツ tsu, originally tu.
Dative and Terminative .... ヘ ve, he or エ ye, e (wards).
Index of the relation of the Place, ニ ni (in, at), ト to (to).
Means and Instrument .... ニ ni, ヲ te.
ニテ nite, デ de (pron. *nde*).
Ablative .... ヨリ yori, カラ kara (out, from).

ヲ wo alone, which indicates an object direct is characterized as a real form of declension, the other inflections belong to the suffixes, that have their own signification. If, notwithstanding, they are here already cited and illustrated, it is for the behalf of those, who do not willingly dispense with the ordinary declensions.

Explanation.

I. NOMINATIVE. The primitive form of a noun is at the same time that of the nominative, which thus has no inflectional termination. In imitation of former grammarians the suffix ハ wa, vulgo ワ wa, has been considered as a characteristic of the Nominative, but as this suffix is merely an isolating particle, which may also be of use with other cases, it must not be longer considered as a definite characteristic of the Nominative (subject) [2]).

---

[1]) See Introduction, § 14. 2. pag. 48.
[2]) „Keine altaische Sprache hat einen Nominativ." H. STEINTHAL, *Characteristik der hauptsächlichsten Typen des Sprachbaues*, 1860, pag. 184.

VOCATIVE. The poet sometimes stretches or doubles the final sound of a noun, to make known, that his feelings are thereby affected, or that he invokes the object. This emphatic prolongation of sound, by which the vocal-harmony comes into play, belongs properly to the interjections, and has the same effect as our exclamation *O!* or *Oh!*

  Hána, flower; *hina a!* (花ナ 分ア) o flower! oh the flower!
  Tori, bird; *tori i!* (鳥ル 分イ) o bird!
  Mi, three; *mi i!* (三ェ 分イ).
  Yo, four; *yo o! yo wo!* (四ヲ 分ヲ).
  ... *u*; ... *u wo!*

An exclamation ヲ, *wo* occurs, e. g. in *Iro ra nirore to tsirinuru wó*, — the colour with the smell corruption o! i. e. oh! that the colour with the smell should vanish!

Besides, ヨ *yo*, just as in German: *Feuerio! Mordio!* is used as an emphatic suffix and, added to the simple root of a verb, strengthens the Imperative, e. g. *To wo aké yo*, open the door!

II. ACCUSATIVE. If the object direct of a transitive verb is indefinite, it is placed before the verb in the primitive form and the logical accent falls upon the verb, e. g. *Kusa kari*, = grass to mow. If the object is definite (Accusativus definitus), it is characterized by *wo* and at the same time is accentuated, e. g. *Kusá wó karu*, = grass (or the grass) to mow. If it is to be brought out with emphasis as the subject of conversation, then the accusative is isolated by the particle *ra* besides, and the form *wo va* is obtained, which for euphony passes over into *woba*, and is frequently pronounced *oba*.

Examples: *Tori-odósi ra tori kedamono wó odósu mono nári*, the scarecrow || is something that frightens birds and beasts. — *Uwó toru ami rá awo wó toru gu nari*, = the fish catching-net, is a fish catching-net. — *Midzu kumi*, water scooper. — *Ike no midzu wó kumu*, to scoop the water from a pond. — *Kefuri no noboru wó miru*, to see the mounting of the smoke. — *Kami ni nikumu tokoro o ba motte simo wó tsukjú koto nakáre* [1]), with that which people disapprove of in their chief, they must not charge their inferiors.

In the book on the Middle-Way (中肺 Cap. IX) after what a man may an-

---

[1]) *The Grand Study (Dai Gaku)*, X, 2.

dertake of what is great has been summed up, there follows an antithesis: „but he cannot keep the Middle-Way," which the Japanese translation very correctly expresses by 中ヲ斯ヲツバ不ス可ク能ズ也 *Tsiu-you wóba yó-kusu bikárizu*. It would have the same effect, if it were: „*Tsiu-you wa, kor' wo yokusu bikardzu* – but the Middle-Way — that can one not keep." The form *Tsiu-you* we cannot, it is plain, pass for an accusative. On the other hand the saying: „*Muma sira wo ba nawa nité kore wo shiiru*, = the horse and the ape — with a rope (one) binds them fast," contains an unnecessary repetition of the object, characterized as accusative. If the *wo ba* is preserved, the *kori wo* is superfluous; if the *kori wo* remains, *Muma sdru* ea must remain, the *wo* being superfluous.

The use of *wo* in *Kai-hen wo isi-kabe wo tsiku*, to build a wall on (or along) the seaside, deserves notice. — *Nippon no bu-nai wo riyo-kyu-suru men-giyo* (日本ノ部内ヲ旅行スル免許), permission to travel through the inland of Japan [1]). The Accusative employed here indicates a continuous motion which we express by means of *along, through*.

III. GENITIVE. 1. ガ゜ *ga*, nga, ńa (之), in pronunciation sharp toned, characteristic of the genitive relation, sets forth the object as something taken in a definite sense, and has the effect of *of the*. The genitive subordination by means of *ga* is considered disrespectful; thence the speaker applies it only to himself and to persons and things of which, having higher persons in view, he makes no case. One says, indeed, *Wáre gá* or *Watákusi ga*, – of the I, of me, and *Are gá*, of him; but *ga* is not used with those nouns and pronouns, with which respected persons are addressed or indicated [2]).

Examples. *Kore Misima-agata-nusi gá oya nari*, this is the progenitor of the bailiff of the district of Misima. — *Kono kami rá N. N. ra gá oya nari*, this god is the progenitor of the N. N.s.

Fitó minu Sukune gá kan-riki wo zo kan-zi keri, each admired Sukune's strength. —

---

[1]) *Netherlands and Japanese Treaty* I. al. 3.

[2]) This RODRIGUEZ also must have meant, when he, according to the French edition § 7, says: „*ga s'emploie comme pronom de la troisième personne, pour les inférieurs, et comme pronom de la première, par humilité.*" Let the misprint „comme pronom" be altered to „après" or „pour le pronom," and the agreement with our assertion will be found. A pronoun, *ga*, does not exist. The same mistake is met with in another Japanese Grammar of 1861 p. 16, where we read, *ga* *ga*, a sign of the genitive in *nouns*, is used as a pronoun in the third person for inferiors, and in the first person as a term of humility."

Kai-mon gá dake, the peak of the sea-port (*Kai-mon* is the name of the entrance to the bay between the provinces of *Oósmi* and *Sátsuma*).

Sagámi no Miura gá sáki, the cape of the *Sagámian Miura*, the cape of *Miura* in the province of *Sagámi*. — *Áme gá sitá* (天下), under the heavens, the sublunary world. — *Filó wo nai gá siro ni su*, to estimate others at the value of nothing, to consider others of no value. — *Káru*, being so, *Káru gá yuǘni*, = for the reason of the being so, on account of the state of affairs. — *Watákusi gá kimono*, the dress of me.

ガ Ga, no index of the subject.

The particle *ga* is also considered as an emphatic definite characteristic of the subject. Now the question arises, if a particle, which, as it most evidently appears from the instances cited, is an emphatic definitive characteristic of the genitive, can also be one of the nominative. The answer is negative. The cases, in which *ga* is considered as an emphatic nominative termination, are capable of a conception, which leaves to this particle its value of a characteristic of the genitive, and besides places in a clear light the reasons, why *ga* has that effect, which is ascribed to it as an emphatic characteristic of the subject. An instance will make this clear. Speaking of an undertaking the question is proposed: „Is there MONEY for it?" and which is answered by: „There IS money for it." Now in the question money is the subject, which after the Japanese arrangement, is placed first and, as a subject first brought into conversation, isolated by *ra* or *wa*. In the answer, on the contrary, the predicate „*there is*" logically has the greater weight, and the subject „money," as subordinate attributive definition, precedes the predicate, as genitive, emphatically characterized by *ga*. The answer: „*There is money*" changes to: „of money the presence (is)" [1]. The question sounds in Japanese: *Kane wa árimásiká?* the answer: *Kane gá árimásu.*

Another instance consisting of the words *fi*, day, and *kurétá*, become dark. To the question: *Fí wa kurétaki?* = the day (as to the day) || has become dark? i. e. has the day approached the end? as answer, follows: *Fí gá kurétá* = the day's having become dark is. i. e. the day has become dark [2].

---

[1] It must be kept in view that in Japanese no congruency, properly so called, of the predicative definition with the subject exists. See Introduction § 15 A. p. 46.

[2] This instance is taken from the Japansch en Hollandsch Woordenboek van den Vorst van *Nakats*, 1810, letter *fi*.

The *Shopping-Dialogues* are rich in instances, which plead for this conception. E. g. pp. 1 and 2:

The buyer. I have come to buy something. *Watakasi wa kai mono ni mairu.*
The seller. What will you buy? = *Nani wo O kai nasaru ka?*
The buyer. What is there? = *Nani ga ari-masuka?*
The seller. There are lacquered goods inlaid with mother of pearl = *Awo-gai mono ga ari-masu.*
The buyer. Are there any gold-lacquered goods? = *Maki-ye mono wa dri-maisaka?*
The seller. Yes, gold-lacquered goods are at hand = *Hei. Maki-ye mono ga drimasu.* —

Question: *O ko samagata wa ikaga de imasaru musuku?*, your children, how do they do? — Answer: *Suëno ko ga sugure mas'nu*[1]), the youngest child is not quite well.

Therefore is said rightly for „it snows:" *Yuki ga furu* or *furi-masu*, = of snow come down is, whereas *Yuki wa furu* = with respect to the snow, it is coming down, would be a definition which attributes „come down," the predicate, to the snow. The same is the case with *Hoki no fune ga tsuki-masta*[2]), there is another ship arrived, properly the arrival of another ship has happened, whereas *Hoka no fune wa tsuki-masta*, would signify: „another ship — is arrived," the subject now being „another ship" the idea to which the most importance is attached, and on which the attention is first fixed. The degrading of the subject to attributive genitive of the predicate is a phenomenon, that commonly occurs in the Altaic languages[3]), and in the Chinese also, plays an important part. Thus, to choose a classical expression, the saying 回 是 人 也 *Hoei wei zin ye*, means Hoei is (or was) a man, Japanese *K'wai va fito to nari*. Hoei is here the subject brought under consideration, of which something is said. On the contrary the saying of CONFUCIUS: 回 之 為 人 也 [4]), Japanese *K'wai ga fito to nari*, = Hoei's a man to be (is), lays the accent emphatically on the predicate „to be a man," which we might express by „Hoei was eminently a man."

---

[1]) Copied, with corrections, from R. ALCOCK, *Familiar dialogues*, pp. 1, 2.
[2]) S. BROWN, *Colloquial Japanese*, p. 1, n°. 6.
[3]) SCHOTT, Characteristik etc., p. 106.
[4]) *Tschung-yung*, Cap. VIII.

Still worthy of a place here, is B. Brown's remark in his *Colloquial Japanese*, pp. XXXIII and XXXIV, his opinion concerning the power of both particles being fully confirmed by our illustration.

„*Wa*, which is merely an isolative particle, serving to separate a word or clause, from the words that follow it, is not a sign of the nominative, though it frequently stands between the subject and its predicate... *Wa* is a sort of cincture around a collection of words, and serves to give definiteness to this group of words, distinguishing it from the other elements of the propositions. ... *Nga* or *ga* (ヶ) is used for the same purpose, except that it seems to be more emphatically definitive. — The difference between *wa* and *nga* is scarcely translatable, but is to be expressed by the tone of the speaker's voice, rather than by any corresponding word in English. The native ear at once perceives the difference, and a foreigner one acquires the use of these particles only by practice and much familiarity with the Japanese usage. The native teachers say that *wa* is a kind of cordon drawn around a word or words, as if to isolate it or them as a distinct subject of thought, and that *nga* is used when one or more objects are singled out, being present or conceived to be present, spoken of specifically. Thus, if a Japanese should say of a certain lot of tea: Here are the masters, his expression for the masters, would be *Midon wa*, i. e. the masters, as separated from the original packages, but, if a buyer, taking one of the samples should say he liked it, his expression would be *Kono midon ga ki ni irimas*'. The idea would then be, that that particular sample suited him." — Thus here a difference is made between *Mi-don wa* (properly *Te-hon wa*) *hoto ni arimasu*, samples are here at hand, and *Kono te-hon ga ki ni irimasu*, these samples please me.

2. **No**, ノ, cognate to *ni*, to be, is used for the attributive subordination of one substantive to another, and gives to the subordinated the character of an adjective. As the use of *ga* is limited by etiquette, no distinction of person is intended by *no*; it is used for high and low.

Examples: *Kousi no i-sigo* (孔子之遺書), a writing left by Kung tsĕ. — *Dai-gaku no mitsi* (大學之道), the way of the Grand Study. — *Ama no gara*, the river of heaven, the milky-way. — *Fosi no fikâri*, starlight. — *Tüsi no fózimé*, beginning of a year. — *Fúzimé no tosi*, a beginning year, New year. — *Kabe no fima*, a split in a wall. — *Nisiki no bousi*, cap of colored silk. — *Akagane no deru tokôro*, — of copper the birth place, i. e. the place whence copper comes. — *Watakusi no kimono*, my garment.

Remark. By way of elision the *o* of *no* is suppressed as in ヲンドリ *ondori*, for *ó no tori*, male bird; メンドリ *mendori* [1]), for *me no tori*, female bird.

That *no*, frequently, has still another particle (case) after it is the consequence of an ellipsis, e. g: 潮ヲ早ノ〃日ノ潮ト. 晩ノ〃日ノ汐ト.

Usiwo, tsitsi no wó douxirotu iri, kun' no wó yúuniro to iru [2]), tide, that of the morning is called the morning-tide, that of the evening the evening-tide. — *Kore*

---

[1]) Compare § 4, A. 8. Remark p. 52.   [2]) Jap. Encycl. 57, § verso.

wa amari tiisai; mo sukosi ookii no wo O mise ¹), this (case) is too small; let me see a larger one.

3. **Na,** ナ (abbreviation of *nâru*, „being"), old, and in the popular language, still used variation of *no*, in the mouths of the vulgar at Yedo *da* (ダ) also (pronounced *ndu*) ¹), which, however, is to be considered as a syncope of *de-âru*.

Simoxama na *koto* (鄙事), baseness, vulgarity, from *simo*, beneath, *sama*, manner, and *koto*, thing. — *Kora na-bakâri nari*, that is only a name. — *Na-bakâri* na *mono*, something (*mono*) that exists only in name. — *Kanna gawa*, for *kanemo gawa* (金川), metal-brook, or *kami no gawa* (神奈河), god's-river. — *Tai-zi da* (for *Tai-zi de-aru*) *koto wi gozarimasn*, there is nothing of consequence.

4. **Tsu,** ツ (津), old-Japanese characteristic of attributive relation, appears still only in old compounds, instead of *no*; sometimes, for the sake of euphony, after *m* or *n* it passes over to *dsu* (ヅ). The oldest records sometimes have, instead of ツ and ヅ, ス *su* and ズ *zu* also.

Examples. *Ama tsu kami*, = of heaven khan, heavenly god. — *Amatsu sora*, the expanse of heaven, the firmament. — *Amatsu miko*, the son of heaven (the Emperor). — *Ama tsu jitsuki*, the heavenly (imperial) crown. — *Kuni tsu kami*, the country god. — *Kuni tsu* or *kuni zu* (クニズ) ²) *mono*, country objects, country products. — *Ie tsu imo*, house-potato ³). — *Ira tsu kokoro*, prickle heart, shrewdness. — *Niwa tsu dori*, the court-bird, the cock. — *Aki*, 1. glitter, 2. autumn. — *Aki tsu musi*, the glittering insect (*Libellula*). *Aki tsu sima*, glittering islands (a name of Japan). — *Sita*, beneath, under. — *Sita tsu mitsi*, an underground way. — *Kibi tsu* ⁴) *takefuko*, the hero of *Kibi*.

Instead of 少 ヅ 子 ³ *otsuko*, bachelor, and 少 ヅ 女 ⁴ *otsume*, spinster, occur in old writings *otsko* and *otsme* also.

IV. DATIVE and TERMINATIVE. ヘ ve (he) or エ (江) ye, properly signifies side or direction, e. g.: *Yama no ye*, the mountainous side, the side of, the direction of (towards) the mountains. — *Yuku ye*, the side, by which one goes

---

¹) *Shopping-Dialogues*, p. 3.   ²) From oral communication by O. T. from Yedo.

³) In the *Nippuashi*, XXII, 80, both forms (ツ = ヅ and ツ = ス) occur alternately.

⁴) *Caladium esculentum*.

⁵) It sound more strange, that the writer of the Japanese Encyclopedia (75. 8. r) has thought it necessary to explain to this name the note: 津ノ 助ジ 爾ノ 與ト 之ノ 同 じ, *tsu va sipo-no*, *no to onaii*, i. e. *tsu*, an auxiliary word, the same as *no*.

away. — *Ma ye*, *ma yĕ*, vulgo *mai* = look-wards, i. e. forwards, before. *Ato re* or *ato ye*, = spur-side, backwards, behind.

As suffix *re* or *ye* answers in all respects to our *wards* and indicates the direction in which any thing proceeds, e. g. *Yédo-re* (or *Yédo-he*), Yedo-wards, as distinction from *Yédo ni*, in or at Yedo, *Yédo ni ôtĕ*, being in Yedo; *Yédo re no mitsi*, = Yedo-wards road, the road to Yedo. — *Nippon re no miyăke*, presents for Japan.

Examples: *Siyok'-motsu wŏ fitŏ ré okŭru*, to send victuals to others. — *Kari wa minđmi ré sŏritu*, the geese have gone away towards the south. — *Toróki kuni re yuka*, to go to distant countries. — *Ten-ki vŏ simo ré kudŭri*, *tsi-ki wŏ kami re no-bŏru*, the mists of the sky sink towards beneath (to the earth), the mists of the earth rise towards above. — *Moto re moŭŏru*, to return to the source. — *Kura-fune itsu mou (imou) Sugŭmi no Misŏrŏ ga sakive fru-tsiyaku-su*, a Chinese junk ran aground on the cape of *Misŏrŏ*, in the province of *Sugŭmi*.

Instances from the treaty between the Netherlands and Japan. Art. II, § 17. *Kŏku dai re juri-watasu*, to make known into every part of the realm. — II, 18. 軍ノ用ノ諸ノ物ハ日本ノ役所ノ外ヘ賣ベカラズ, *Gun-yoŭ no sigo-buts eu Nippon-yek'-siyo no fŏki re ura-bikarŭzu*, munitions of war may not be sold to any other than the Japanese government. — V, 1. *Olando-zin re (or ni) tuisi* (對ノ) *fuu wo* (法ヲ) *okiau*, to transgress the law against the Dutch. VI, 9. コンシュルヘ 申ノ達ヲス, to communicate to the Consul. V, 1. 各ノ方ヘ, in every direction, towards every side.

Ni (於, 于), with relation to, in general, points out the relation of an indirect object, is, therefore, used for the indication of the place at which, as well as of the direction towards the innermost part, or to the attainment of anything, and answers to our in, at, to, unto, by and by means of, according as the verb, to which it belongs, indicates that the place has been reached, or that the object makes movement towards it.

The relation expressed by **Ni** may be understood as:

a. Dative or Ablative, by which, in general, a collateral relation to the predicate verb is expressed. E. g. *Fitŏ ni taikiki mitsi*, a road, which with relation to people is near. *Fitŏ ni torŏki mitsi*, a road which with relation to (for) people, is remote. — *Fito ni sanŏrŭru*, separated from people. — *Kŏsi ko kuro ni fanarŭnu*, the silkworm does not remove from the foliage.

b. Local, to the question where or when. E. g. *Kono tokŏro ni*, at this place. — *Nusubitó tokóro-dokóro ni okóru*, robbers rise at every place (everywhere). — *Fi ga figíni ni nobóri, nisi ni iru*, the sun rises in the east, and goes in (down) in the west. — *Yédo ni kiyo-riu-suru yaku-nin*, functionaries residing in *Yédo*. — *Yáma ni iri ki wo kiru*, = to go into the mountains and chop wood. — *Funi ni noru*, to be load in a ship (to navigate). — *Yáma-gusa wo núwa ni touri, kasí ni sarōsu*, to hang up mountain-herbs on a rope and dry (them) in the air. — *Kaiko ni yumawi dekiru*, by (among) the silk worms exists sickness. — *Ion ni todokororu*, to stick fast in speaking. — *Kono tosi ni*, in this year. — *Firu ni*, at noon. — *Yuru ni*, in the evening. — *Firu-garo dsa ni ake, yúeubé ni sibómu*, the „face of noon" ¹) opens in the morning, and closes in the evening.

Ni va, the relation indicated by *ni* isolated by *va*. — *Nan-bu, Tsukúra-ben no tai-mei ni ro fuu-uei ohūsi*, among (*ni va*) the names of places (地 ⁺ 名 ⁼) of the country of *Nan-bu* and *Tsukúra* strange names are manifold.

Ni va sometimes elliptically changes in to **nva** (ン ハ). — *Aru tóki ni va* or *dru tokinva*, at any time.

c. Modal, to the question how. E. g. *Dai-si ni tatsi-tamaru*, he appears as (in the quality of) hereditary Prince. — *Ikâ ni*, vulgo *ikin'* (I ⁵ ヒ), how, in what manner. — *Iki-simuui*, in what (or which) manner. — *Saka-sama ni*, perversely. — *Koto ni*, particularly. — *Makóto ni*, in truth, indeed. — *Tada ni*, mere, only. — *Ooki ni*, often, very. — *Sumiyaka ni*, suddenly, quickly.

d. Casual and Instrumental, to the question of whom, by which or by what, with which, with what, although here also the original signification, with relation to, is preserved. E. g. *Ya ni atarôta*, struck with an arrow. — *Fitó ni damasarōta*, deceived by people (others). — *Dai-Min no mi ro fai-guu ni korite musumi taikó-dzukóen, Ti-Ming's* army, confounded by the defeat, does not approach.

e. Dative of the person, to the question to whom. E. g. *Oya ni niru*, with relation to the parents, to be like, to resemble the parents. — *Fitó ni tai su*, to stand opposite others. — *Fitó-ni mono wo ataeru* (pron. *atgura*), to concede or give anything to others.

f. Dative of the thing, to the question to what or to which, for which the suffix *to* is used also. E. g. *Kuró no mi wo tane ni* (or *tane tó*) *tóru*, to take mulberries for seed. — *Miiyu wo wáta ni tóru*, to use cocoons for wadding. —

---

¹) The flower of *Pharbitis Nil* Chois, or *Ipomoea Nil* Linn.

70   CHAPTER I. NOUNS. DECLENSION. § 7.

Yumi ni tsukuru ki, wood worked into bows. — *Wāra ed musiro ni oru bèsi, nāva ni ndra bèsi, fäki-mono ni tsukuru bèsi*, with regard to straw (*wara ni*), it can be woven into mats, it can be twisted into rope, it can be worked up into shoes. — *Nami kaze mo tsuvoyaka ni nari*, wind and waves become smoother. — *Asi wo kirite siyiku-mitasi ni tagen beni*, he will cut off his feet and give (them) for food.

g. Terminative, the direction whither, signifying to which (to what, to whom), provided the movement directed towards an object extends to within its limits or reach, distinguished from ·ヽ *ro* which properly answers rather to our wards. E. g. *Kaze wi nisi-kata ni kaodru*, - the wind changes to (veers towards) the west side. — *Yo wo fi ni tauys*, to continue the night to the day. — *Kaze yomite (yande) fune kisi ni tsúka*, the wind lulls and the ship comes to the shore. — *Fūkumi yori Nippon ni watáru*, he passes from Fakumi to Japan. — *Isi ni ndru*, to turn to stone.

V. To, ト, to, Dutch tot, ter, German zu, a particle that denotes the inherency of a substantive in a predicate verb, which expresses a becoming or a making to, in general a working, which has an object for its apposition. Of such sort are the verbs *nari*, to become; *nasi*, to make; *iru*, to be called, to name; *midoukuru*, to name; *miyu*, to seem; *kaku*, to write, etc. E. g. *Midsukāra torawarete-fitō to sari*, he becomes, of his own accord (to) a prisoner. - *Mājn wo wa-wata to nasu*, people make (work up) cocoons to silk wadding. — *N. ra tori to kwite tobiyuku*, N. changes himself to a bird and flies away. — *Fitō to iru*, to be called man; *Fitō to iru va* (by syncope *Fitō tó va*), that which is called man, the so called man.

Nite, ニテ, ニ デ, in the spoken language, passing into nde, for which デ (de) is written, characterises alike the Local and the Instrumental and is used, especially, when the predicate-verb does not follow it immediately, but is separated from it by the interposition of the subject or of the object direct. E. g. *Kono wto nite sivo faydsi*, = in this strait the tide is rapid. — *Kari-bási nite kara wo watáru*, to cross the river by means of a temporary bridge. — *Kome wo kdrausi nite kómakdai kuddku*, to stamp rice fine in a mortar. — *Kāwi nite kawiko wo ydsindeu*, to rear silk-worms with leaves. — *Tamago nite siyutu-zuru mono*, beings proceeding from eggs. — *Fūku-sai-kwika nite ro tuka wo Kutzin tō fen*, in the country of *Fūku-mi*, the hawk is called *Kutzin*. — *Iru kuni nite wo kaviko-ami wo tsukaeu nari*, in a certain country the silk-worm net is used. — *Moroyosi nite va*, in China. — 中 ³ 國 ² = デ ハ, in the Middleland. — *Kuni-yuni nite*, in each

CHAPTER I. NOUNS. DECLENSION. § 7. 71

country. — *Te nite*, with hands; *Te nite no si-kata*, gestures with hands. — *Fasi nite fasidmu*, to take hold of with eating-sticks.

De, デ, contraction of *ni + te* and pronounced as *nde*, characterizes alike the relation of *a*. the Local and *b*. the Instrumental is, however only peculiar to the easy, spoken and written styles. Examples:

a. Miyako de, at *Miyako*. — *Tsuki no mito de avu*, to meet under the moon (here below). — *Yamé no utsi de úru*, to meet with in a dream. — *Mumi no uye de ku-tamukeru*, to sit awry on horseback. — *Fana no uted de maySeu*, wander among flowers. — *Tsubame ga yanagi no fotori de maySeu*, the swallow roams around willows. — *Kusa naka de naku musi*, insects chirping in the grass. — *Musi ga kabe de ndka*, insects chirp on the wall. — *Ikka de dékimósu ká*, in how many days can it happen, is it possible?

b. Fude de kūku, to write with the pencil. — *Isi de gwa wo tsukuru*, to build a temple of (with) stone. — *Sono ne de wa kaye masínn* [1]), with (for) that price I do not sell it. — *Tsi wo tri de arúru*, to wash off blood with (or in) blood. — *Yotsu mumi de jikawera kurúma*, a waggon drawn with four horses.

Remark 1. The book language generally expresses the Instrumental by ... *wo motte* (以 ッ ... リ). and uses for „to wash off blood with blood," the expression 以 血, 洗 血: *Tsi wo motte tsi wo aroru*, = holding or using blood (with blood) to wash off blood.

Remark 2. For the explanation of expressions belonging to the book-language, in schools and school-books the spoken-language is used, and this, whenever *ni* occurs in the book-language as a characteristic of the Local or of the Instrumental, generally substitutes *de* for it.

VI. ABLATIVE. Yori, ヨリ and kara, カラ (由. 自. 従), out of, from, indicate a movement in a direction from a place, in opposition to ヘ, *ye*, towards, or マデ, *made*, to, till. If the point of departure is a period of time, or an action, then *yori* and *kara* answer to our *from..to, from, since; after, afterwards*.

Examples. *Firato yori Nagasaki made sun ziya fútsi ri dri*, from Firato to Nagasaki it is 38 *ri* (Japanese miles). — *Inisiê yori* (自 昔 ヘ), from old times. — *Fázimê yori*, from the beginning. — *Ima yori* (自 今), from now.

---

[1] Mepping Dialogues, p. 3.

國ニ=到リ着ケノ日ヒヨリ, *Kuni ni tou-tsiyaku no ji yori*, from the day of the arrival in the country¹). — *Fusi-yama ca Wan-zen ga take yori takasi*, = Fusi-mountain is out of the peak of the warm springs high, i. e. the Fusi-mountain is higher than the peak of the Wnzen. — *Kore wi sore-yori takaku drimden*²), = this from that out high is, i. e. this is higher, than that.

Yori, subordinated by means of *no* to another substantive: *Kono misaki wa oki yori no medte nari*, this cape is a mark (medte) out of sea.

Kara, indicating rather the direction, from which any thing comes³), as the German *her*, occurs in the written language seldom, and only in old compounds, as in *Oki kara*, out of sea, and is, rather, peculiar to the spoken language. *Kore kara* (由是), thence, also therefore, for that reason (= kore ni yotte). — *Sore kara*, so with. — 見ル本ニ切レガ有リマスカラ是ヲリ 卽ゴ覧ニナサレ, *Tchon-gire ga drimdsi kara, kore wo (ioran-nasare*⁴), since (kara) there are patterns at hand (irimasu), please see this. — *Age-nusu kara uke-tori-gaki wi kudasare*⁵), after (kara) delivery (agemasu) please, give a receipt. — *Kon-niti wa yohodo osii kara*⁶), *myya-niti kuhiri mawroo*, as (kara) to day it is too late (yohodo-osii), I will come back to morrow.

Remark. *Yori*, verb continuative, derived from *yi* (射), to shoot, from which, among others ya, arrow, and yumi, bow, derive. (*Kara* seems to belong to the root, ki, come). Preceded by a local ni, *yori* means to have its point of departure in: *Kore-ni yoreri*, from that flows forth. — *Kore ni yorite* or *yotte*, in consequence of, therefore.

---

¹) *The Treaty between the Netherlands and Japan*, I, § 3. ⁴) *Shopping-Dialogues*, p. 26.
²) 所從來也, *No-gan sinori, under Kara*.
³) *Shopping-Dialogues*, p. 28. ⁵) Ibid. p. 14. ⁶) Ibid. p. 41.

CHAPTER II.

PRONOUNS.

§ 8. The Pronouns in Japanese are:

I. Nouns which express a quality.

II. Pronouns demonstrative, which point out something, either a person or thing according to its relation to the speaker.

They are all subject to the ordinary declension, and with the genitive suffix, no, are used as pronouns possessive.

The distinction of three grammatical persons (I, Thou, He) has remained foreign to the Japanese language [1]. All the persons, that of the speaker (the I), as well as that to which or of which he speaks (Thou, He), are considered as contents of the proposition and thus, according to our peculiarity of language, in the third person, and etiquette, having in view the meaning of words expressive of quality, has to determine, which person, by one or another of these words is intended. Etiquette distinguishes only between the „I," and the „not-I," it abases the one, and exalts the other. Thus, it is the meaning, which in this sort of words comes first under notice, before the use, that etiquette makes of it, is indicated.

---

[1] Therefore, as it will be seen hereafter, the verb has no conjugational suffixes, which tend to the expression of this distinction.

74 CHAPTER II. QUALIFYING PRONOUNS. § 8.

With respect to the use of the qualifying pronouns especially, the written or book language and the conversational differ from each other.

I. Qualifying nouns, which are used as pronouns, are,

A. For the „I":

Yatsŭ-ko (奴ｺ), pron. Yakko, house-boy, valet, servant; belongs to the old written language. — Yatsŭ-kăre (僕ヲレ), valet, your servant.

Yatsŭ-bara (奴ﾉ儕ﾗ), the valets, we subjects.

The Chinese 愚 yu, Jap. gu, unintelligent, in compounds, as:

愚ﾉ人ﾆ gu-nin, the unintelligent man, I.

愚ﾉ者ﾉ gu-ša, the unintelligent.

愚ﾉ草ﾆ gu-sou, the unintelligent herb [1]), the „I" of the Bonzes.

愚ﾉ老ﾆ gu-ryo, the unintelligent old man.

愚ﾉ心ﾆ gu-sin, my heart.

B. For the person spoken to, THOU:

1. **Nandsi** (汝ｼ), formerly namadzi, originally na-mutsi, = having a name, name-having, name bearing, renowned, honoured; plural nandzira, nandziga-tomo-yara. It belongs to the written language and to the solemn style. Nobles, and literate persons address one another with Nandsi. 爾. 尔. 尔. 你.

Nandsi tomo ni namdzivō miru, the people look up to you together, or every one looks up to you. — Nandsi fitō ga me wo tsukete oru, you have attracted the eyes of the people.

2. **Imasi** (汝ｼ), shortened masi, = present, leaves it uncertain, whether a person speaks to his betters or inferiors. 麼下.

3. **Sama** (樣ﾏ. 㨾ﾏ. 枕ﾏ), vulgo San, = the look, appearance, shape, e. g. *Minatono sima yósi*, the shape of the harbour is beautiful, the harbour looks well, — was, originally, as a characteristic of modesty, applied by the speaker to himself; since the middle ages, however, conceded to a person beyond the speaker, it is now generally used as an expression of respect and at present answers to our „Sir, Mister." It is subjoined to nouns and pronouns.

4. **Kimi** (君ﾐ), Sir, Mister; **Kimi-sama** (君ﾐ 樣ﾏ), vulgo kimi-san honour, lordship. — *N. N. kimi-sama ye*, to Mr. N. N.

5. **Te-maye** (手ﾉ前ﾏ), vulgo Te-mai, Te-mee, at hand, indicates the per-

---

[1]) Corporal, only to vegetate from the example of the Lotusplant, but to make the spirit free, is the duty of the Buddhist's life; thence the clerical (Bonze) considers himself as an herb.

son spoken to. Plural *Te-máye-tatai*, vulgo *Te-mairé*, *Te-mae-tatsi*. *Te-máye-sáma*, vulgo *Te-mdye-sin*, the gentleman at hand (present), you, Sir; plur. *Te-mdye-sáma-gáta*.

On, O (御), Ki (貴), Son (尊), honorary adjectives, used in the conversational language and in the epistolary style as pronouns possessive, of the person, to whom or of whom spoken.

6. On, O (御, abbreviated 卨・欣・㐂・𢰏・𣓤・𣏾・𣏽), as given by Japanese authors, an abbreviation of 大, *óo*, *óonō*, great, sublime, answers to our „His or Her Highness" referring to a prince; it is, however, prefixed to the names of things or matters that have reference to any person in honour, and applied by the speaker to all beyond himself, for which he wishes to make his respect known. Thus the presence of *on* or *o* before substantives and verbs, makes known, without the help of another pronoun, that the things or matters have reference to a person beyond the speaker. As a Japanese element *on* or *o* is compounded with Japanese words. e. g. *O-Yédo*, the princely Yedo. — *O-kata*, the honoured side, Your honour. · · *O-mi*, the honoured body, Your-self — *O-me*, Your eye. — *O-me ni kakdri-mansyoo*, I shall appear before your eyes. — *O-na*, your name. · · *O-ide*, your rise. — *Yóku O-ide nasaré*, may your rise happen = be welcome! — *O-agári*, your rise. *O-agári nasaré*, = may your rise happen, come on! — *O-negái*, your wish. *O-negai-mdse*, may you wish, the common expression for „if you please." — *O-mise*, let me see! — *On-táddsuné*, your inquiry. — *On-bumi*, your letter, etc.

In old-Japanese the place of *On*, *O* is filled by **Mi**, thence *Mi-kado*, sublime port; *Mi-koto*, Highness; *Mi-yáma*, chief mountain.

7. 御 **Go**, the *koye* of *o*, is generally prefixed to Chinese words. It means „princely," but from politeness is also used towards other persons beyond the speaker.

御恩 *go-won*, your favour.　　　　　御覽 *go-ran*, your look.
御用 *go-you*, your use.　　　　　　御懇意 *go-kon-i*, your friendly
御書 *go-syo*, your writing.　　　　　　feelings.
御前 *go-sen*, before you, in your　　御相談 *go-syu-dan*, your con-
　　presence.　　　　　　　　　　　　versation.
御座 *go-za*, sublime seat.　　　　　御機嫌 *go ki-gen*, your dispo-
御免 *go-men*, your permission.　　　　sition.

76   CHAPTER II. QUALIFYING PRONOUNS. § 8.

8. O-máye, o-mas (御前), vulgo o-mái, from the honorary *o* and *ma-ye* or *ma-ev*, = look-wards, that is before, thus something that is present before the speaker, or as by him imagined present and honoured, = Your Honour. The lower classes of functionaries and small people call one another *omae* and *omae-sama, omaesan*.

Formerly by *O-mae* was meant the place before the prince; thence: *Omae ni mairu*, to step before the Emperor. Npr. II, 4, 1.

9. 貴 KI, noble, honourable, - „you" in genuine Chinese compounds, as:

貴國 *ki-koku*, your country.
貴府 *ki-fu*, your town.
貴縣 *ki-ken*, your district.
貴郡 *ki-gun*, your canton.
貴所 *ki-sho, ki-so*, your place, your Excellency.
貴宅 *ki-taku*, your house.
貴顏 *ki-gan*, your face.
貴面 *ki-men*, your countenance.
貴覽 *ki-ran*, your look.
貴翰 *ki-kan*, your pencil, your pen.
貴札 *ki-zat*, your letter.
貴書 *ki-myo, ki-so*, your writing.
貴命 *ki-mei*, your command.

貴意 *ki-i*, your will.
貴慮 *ki-riyo*, your care.
貴報 *ki-fgu, ki-foo*, your answer.
貴答 *ki-too*, your answer.
貴公 *ki-kvo, ki-koo-sama*, the noble Lord, your Lordship.
貴殿 *ki-den*, your Excellency. *Ki-den sama*.
貴邊 *ki-fen, ki-ken*, your side, your Excellency. *Ki-jen-sama*.
貴方 *ki-fgu, ki-hoo*, your side. *Ki-foo sama*.
貴樣 *ki-sama*, your Honour.

10. 尊 son, worshipful, reverend, - „your" in Chinese compounds, as:

尊君 *son-kun*, the worshipful gentleman, Sir.
尊公 *son-kou*, the worshipful gentleman, your father.
尊父 *son-fu*, the worshipful father, your father.
尊母 *son-bo*, your mother.

尊客 *son-kek*, the worshipful guest, my guest.
尊草 *son-sju*, the worshipful herb, you, Bonze.
尊體 *son-tai*, your body, your person.
尊骸 *son-gai*, your limbs.

CHAPTER II. QUALIFYING PRONOUNS. § 8.   77

尊ン容ヨ son-you, your appearance.
尊ン覌ヲン son-ran, your look.
尊ン方ヲン son-fqu, the worshipful side.
尊ン札サツ son-zat, your letter.
尊ン䟽ショ son-siyo, son-so, your writing.
尊ン簡カン son-kan, your letter.
尊ン翰カン son-kan, your pencil, your pen.

尊ン意イ son-i, your will.
尊ン慮リヨ son-riyo, your care.
尊ン答トウ son-too, your answer.
尊ン號ゴウ son-gyu, your title.
尊ン下カ son-ka, that which is below the worshipful; the „I" of the modest speaker.

In proportion as any thing belongs to the speaker or to a person beyond him, it is frequently mentioned under different denominations, to express modesty on the one side, and respectful politeness on the other. As much is presumed on this abundance of names, and ample use is made of them, we may not entirely overlook them here. They occur in popular books under the title of „Particular names of human relations" (人ジン倫リン之ノ異ヰ名メイ Zin-rin no i-miyou).

One's own father (我ガ父フ) is:

家カ父フ Ka-fu.
家カ君クン Ka-kun.
家カ大タイ人ジン Ka-tai-zin.

Another's father (人ニン之ノ父フ) is:

令レイ父フ Rei-fu.
厳ゲン君クン Gen-kun.
老ラウ大タイ人ジン Ryu-tui-zin.
尊ソン父フ Son-fu.

One's own mother (我ガ母ボ) is:

慈ジ母ボ Zi-bo.
家カ母ボ Ka-bo.
老ラウ母ボ Rqu-bo.

Another's mother (人ニン之ノ母ボ) is:

令レイ尊ソン Rei-son.
令レイ堂ダウ Rei-dqu.
北ホク堂ダウ Fuku-dyn.

One's own eldest brother (我ガ兄ケイ) is:

長チヤウ兄ケイ Taiyqu-kei.
家カ兄ケイ Ka-kei.
阿ア兄ケイ A-kei.

Another's eldest brother (人ニン之ノ兄ケイ) is:

令レイ兄ケイ Rei-kei.
雜ナン兄ケイ Nan-kei.
令レイ伯ハク Rei-fuku.
元ゲン芳ハウ Gen-fqu.
長チヤウ公コウ Taiyqu-kou.

One's own youngest brother
(我ガ弟ヲ) is:

家ヵ弟ヲ Ka-tei.
阿ア弟ヲ A-tei.
阿ア叔シュク A-syuk.
阿ア仲チウ A-tiu.
舍シャ弟ヲ Siya-tei.

Another's youngest brother
(人ノ之ノ弟ヲ) is:

令レイ弟ヲ Rei-tei.
貴キ弟ヲ Ki-tei.
難ナン弟ヲ Nan-tei.
令レイ仲チウ Rei-tiu.
淑シュク弟ヲ Siyuk-tei.

One's own son (我ガ子ヲ) is:

小セウ子ン Seo-si.
愚グ子ン Gu-si.
痴チ子ン Tsi-si.

Another's son (人ノ之ノ子ヲ) is:

國コク器キ Kok-ki.
令レイ子シ Rei-si.
秀シウ子ン Siu-si.
韓カン玉ギョク Han-giyok.
掌シャウ珠シユ Siyou siyu.

One's own wife (我ガ妻ヲ) is:

荊ケイ妻サイ Kei-sai.
賤セン妻サイ Sen-sai.
内ナイ助ヂョ Nai-tsuyo.
賤セン室シツ Sen-sits.

Another's wife (人ノ之ノ妻ヲ) is:

令レイ室シツ Rei-sits.
内ナイ子シ Nai-si.
内ナイ相シャウ Nai-siyou.
細サイ君クン Sai-kun.

One's own concubine (我ガ妾ヲ) is:

小セウ妾セフ Seo-seo.
荊ケイ妾セフ Kei-seo.
側ソク室シツ Siku-sits.

Another's concubine (人ノ之ノ妾ヲ) is:

令レイ可カ Rei-ka.
令レイ寵チョウ Rei-tsiyou.
盛セイ寵チョウ Sei-tsiyou.

One's own country and town
(我ガ國クニ郷サト) is:

山サン縣ケン San-ken.
賤セン里リ Sen-ri.
弊ヘイ里リ Hei-ri.
里リ閭ケン Ri-ken.
寒カン郷キョウ Kan-kiyou.

Another's country and town
(人ノ之ノ國クニ郷サト) is:

貴キ國コク Ki-koku.
仙セン(貴キ)府フ Sen-fu of Ki-fu.
貴キ縣ケン Ki-ken.
貴キ郡グン Ki-gun.
錦キン里リ Kin-ri.

CHAPTER II. QUALIFYING PRONOUNS. § 8.   70

One's own dwelling place
(我 居 處) is:

蝸 舍 *Kwa-siya.*
蝸 室 *Kwa-sits.*
矮 屋 *Wai-uku.*
孤 廬 *Tako-ro.*
寒 舍 *Kan-siya.*
菲 室 *Fou-sits.*

Another's dwelling place
(人之居處) is:

高 祐 *Kqu-iu.*
甲 第 *Kqu-tei.*
華 第 *Kwa-tei.*
闕 別 *Han-bqu.*
佳 室 *Ka-sits.*

One's own letter (我 狀) is:

寸 書 *Sun-kqu.*
手 蘭 *Siyu-kika.*
柔 尺 *Ziu-siki.*
尺 楮 *Seki-tuyo.*
愚 翰 *Gu-kan.*

Another's letter (人之狀) is:

朵 雲 *Da-un.*
蘇 翰 *Sqa-kan.*
芳 札 *Fqu-sai.*
綿 雲 *Siyun-un.*
華 翰 *Kwa-kan.*

II. Pronouns proper, which point out objects with distinction of the place they occupy in space. They are formed from adverbs of place. They are:

1. Wa (ワ), pointing to the centre of space, therefore to the person speaking, to his „I."

2. A (ア), anywhere, elsewhere, indicates a place not sufficiently known beyond the speaker.

3. Ka (カ), there, indicates a definite, more distant place.

4. Ko (コ), here, indicates a definite place in the neighborhood.

5. Yo (ヨ), yonder, indicates a place, which is beyond a place already defined, and serves to suggest the idea of other, Dutch *ander*, German *der andere*, *answere*.

6. So (ソ), so, indicates a place already mentioned or imagined as mentioned, and serves to form the reflective pronoun.

7. The interrogative elements Ta (又) or To (ト), vulgo Da (ダ) or Do (ド), and Itsu (イツ) or Idsu (イヅ), answering to *wh* in „who? which? what? where?" and to the Latin *qu* in „quis? quid?" — 又 and ト is the written form occurring in old books, that now, in accordance with the pronunciation of the people,

is more generally superseded by 父 and 卜 [1]). The first form may perhaps be attributed to the inaccuracy of writers and engravers.

a. To the immediate compounds with the root Wa (own, proper) belong:

Wa-nusi (吾 主), proper master, the master, the master of the workpeople.

Wa-dono (吾 殿), my or our master.

Wa-nami (吾 儕), the proper row, we.

Watákusi (我, 私), the „I." plural Watákusi-domo, we, among people of fashion, and in the familiar language the ordinary pronoun for the first person. It is commonly abbreviated to Watákusi or Watáku, and Watákusi ed to Watákusi, whereas the porter at Yédo says Wátski, Wási or Wési, and the servant-girl Watáki, Watki. Whoever does not wish to put himself on a footing with the last mentioned should, thus, use Watákusi.

About the meaning of tákusi, the second element of this compound, the Japanese etymologists keep silence; likewise, our question directly proposed on that subject always remained unanswered. Referred to our private judgement, we now recognize this word as the tóki (欲, vulgo 慾), greedy, desirous, in use in the popular language, adv. tóka, whence the verb tákusi to desire, to be greedy, is derived. Thus Wa-tákusi means self-love, egotism, and is tantamount to the ordinary Chinese compound 私慾, self-love, egotism.

b. The remaining adverbs of place enter into immediate composition with words as 1) Ko (處, 所), place, region, 2) Tsi (千), plural tsira (千ラ), way, tract, in the popular language also Tsutsi (ツ千), province, etc. These compounds indicate a place or places, and are, as nouns, declinable.

1) Compounds with Ko (處, 所):

Doko (何 處), what place? — Doko no tsurugizo, whence this sword? — Doko ni or Doko de, at which place? at what place? — Doko ri or Doko yi, towards which place? whither? — Doko ye yúku ka, where is it going? whither is it going?

Koko (此 處, 此 所, 爰, 茲), this place, here. — Koko ni or Koko de wakáru, herein lies the difference. Koko ni óité, herein.

soko (彼 處, 其 所), pron. also, such a place, the place of which is

---

[1]) Wa-gan siuvri, under Tsrn.

spoken, or the place of something, pointed out, serving formerly to indicate the person spoken to; plural *sokora* (其 ゜ 所 ゜ 等 ゜). — *Siko-moto*, for *dsoki-moto* = the seat there, serves as pronoun for the person spoken to: Thou, You. — *Soko-moto nani wo kerdsu zo?* in the spoken language: *Siko-moto ikaga (?) kurdsi nasdru*, how do you do? literally: how do you let (the time) go round, how do you wind round? — *Asoko*, pron. *dsko* - of some where the quarter, any where. — *Kasiki*, vulgo *ksiki* (彼 處), the place of there, that or yon place. — *Doko kasiko*, which quarter? — *Koko kdsuko ni*, at this and yon place, here and there yonder. — *Kono yama yori kasiko no yama ye utsuru*, to remove from this mountain to yonder mountain.

Yoko, because it means „cross" is superseded by Yoso (外 ゜, 遣 ゜), another place, elsewhere. — *Yoso ye utsuru*, to remove to elsewhere. — *Yoso ye ugokunu*, not to remove to elsewhere, i. e. to stay firm at (or in) one's place.

Idsüku (何 ゜ 處 ゜), old-Japanese *Idsuko*, which place? Some consider *ku* as an abbreviation of *kuni*, country, and consequently write 何 ゜ 国 ゜, which country? — *O kuni wa idzuku de gozarimasu*, your country -- which country is it? what is your country? — *Idsuku no futo zo*, from what country is the man? — *Idzuku ye*, whither? — *Idzuku ye nsi*, whithersoever, — to every-where. — *Idzuku yori kita zo*, whence has he come? — *Idzuku yori mo*, whencesoever, from every place whatever. — *Idsuku ni dru zo*, where is he? *Iye ni dru*, he is at home. — *Idzuku ni ki*, or *Idzukunki*, where? whither? [1]). — 牛 ゜ 何 ゜ ニ , 之 ヨ [1]), *Usi idzukunki yuku*, whither is the ox going?

Idsükunsö, イヅクンゾ, originally Idsuku ni so, イヅクニゾ, — old-Japanese Idsukonso, イヅコニゾ, from the elements, of which it is composed, has the meaning of „at what place? where?", answers nevertheless to our „on what ground? why?" also, and with this meaning is ranked with *Nan to site* and *Dousite* [3]). The force of *Idzukun zo* appears most plainly in the Japanese translation of the Chinese expression following:

知 ゛ 彼 ゛ / 之 ゛ 歟 ゛   *Kare idzukun zo kore wo siran?* [4]) he there on what ground (why) shall he know this?

The speaker's object here is, not to draw out an answer, but

---

[1]) See p. 68, line 8 from the bottom.   [3]) MENCIUS (LEGGE, *Chinese Classics*, Vol. II, p. 15).
[2]) See p. 85.   [4]) " " Vol. I. Book I. Pt. I. Ch. VII. § 7).

he will have it understood that he not only doubts the assertion, but even is convinced of the contrary: "one does not know it."

If the question proposed by *Idzukunzo* is affirmative, as in the instance quoted, the speaker has the negative contrary in view, if however it is negative, then the positive, as in the phrase:

未广広ゞ *Kau-miyga idzukun zo imáda firokarázu?* Why should his fame not
ゞ名ゞ be spread everywhere?
廣ゞ名ゞ
胡ゞ   The affirmative question 胡彡可彡乎, *Idzakunzó ka-*
ゞ   *narán?* — why shall that be possible? implies that the speaker is
convinced, that it is impossible; the negative form: *Idzukun zo kanarazdran?* — why shall that not be possible?, is a consequence of the conviction, that it must indeed be done.

The Chinese characters, which are used to represent *Idzukunzo* are 焉, 悪, 烏, 胡, 奚, 曷, 豈, 胡, 胡乎. Of the Japanese word only the termination *zo* is mostly found added. These characters have the force indicated only, when they occupy a place before the verb of the predicate; at the end of a sentence, where some occur likewise, they imply a direct question.

2) Compounds with **Tai** (道°, 地°), way, place.

Dotai, which place? where? — *Dotaira*, which places? — *Dotai ye*, whither? — *Dotaira ye mó*, whithersoever, to everywhere. *Dotaira kara mó mukái-áru*, to meet each other from whatever places it may be (from all sides).

Atai (外° 地°), *ataira*, elsewhere. — **Kotai** (此° 地°), here. — *Atai kotai* or *atai kotai*, *atai kotai to*, plural *ataira kotaira*, elsewhere and here, here and there.

Sotai (其° 方°), old—Jap., his place, plural *sotaira*, serves to indicate the person, of whom it is spoken. — *Sotaira kotaira*, those (the persons) there, and those here.

3) Compounds with **Tsutai**.

Do-tsutai, which place? — *Do-tsutai ye*, whither? — *Do-tsutai kara*, whence?

c. The adverbs of place **Ta** (vulgo **Da**) and **Wa** with the genitive possessive termination 力°, **ga** (pron. **nga**), which is mostly, but improperly, written 力, **ka**.

Tá ga, vulgo **Dá ga**, (pron. *Da-nga*), arisen, perhaps by syncope, from *Tarega* or *Iwrega*, whose. — *Ihi ga iyéka*, whose house (is this)? — *Ihi ga awarémi-koto argu* (or *aroo*), whose compassion will there be? who will have compassion?

CHAPTER II. PRONOUNS PROPER. § 8. II. 63

Wága, pron. *Wa-aga*, own, my or his own, according as the subject of discourse, to which *Waga* refers, is the speaker or another person, — for distinction from *Waka*, young. — *Wága kuni*, own country, my or his native country. — 我ノ朝ノ *Waga teô* (or *Waga tao*), own realm, my or his, our realm. — *Wága iyé*, also contracted *Wágiyé*, own house. — *Watákusi rá wága iyé yé kayéru*, I return home. — *Kare va wága iyé yé kayéru*, he returns home. — *Wága tsúmá*, one's own beloved, my wife. — *Wágí-moko*, old-Jap. for *Wágya imóko* (吾ノ妹ノ子ノ), my little wife. — *Wága ko* (吾ノ子ノ), own son. — *Wága-mi* (我ノ身ノ), own body, one's own person, my person, — the „I" in a woman's mouth. — *Wága tátai*, one's own station, we. — *Wága-tómo*, ours. — *Wága-tómo de sai*, they are not of ours. — *Wága tómo-gára*, one's own relations or clan, we. — *Wága mámá*, own authority, arbitrarily. — *Wága mamú si* (or *de*) *wó nái*, it is not arbitrary. — *Wága rikutsú wó tatéwa*, not to persist in one's perverse view. — *Wágá taméni*, for own behoof; I for my own sake, or he for his own sake. — *Ware sorí wo wógá monó ni sitá*, I have made that my own property. — *Kare sorí wó wóga mono ni sitá*, he has made it his own property, he has appropriated it. — *Waga mave ni*, = „before the I" of the subject of discourse, whether the speaker, or a being beyond him. — *Kaviko sono siki wó sardzu, wite, kuwá mo waga mave ni kitaréba, kivu*, the silkworm does not leave its mat, sitting still it eats, whenever food comes before it. — *Wága de ni*, with one's own hands.

In the old-Japanese, which used *A* for *Wa*, we meet with *Aga* for *Waga* also; thence *Aga-kimi* (我ノ君ノ), abbreviated *Agimi* and *Agi*, Sir. — *Aga fotoke* (吾ノ佛ノ), our Buddha. — *Ago* (吾ノ子ノ), abbreviated for *Aga-ko*, my son. — *Adzúma*, abbreviated for *Aga-tsuma*, my beloved, my husband (吾ノ夫ノ), my wife (吾ノ婦ノ).

d. Pronouns possessive.

By suffixing *no*, the adverbs of place become pronouns possessive; thus we have Ano, Kano, Kono, Yono, Sono, Dono, idzuno.

Anó fitó (アノヒト), after the Yédo pronunciation: *Anó kió* and *Anó stó*, a man of elsewhere, any one, he. — *Ano onna* (アノヲンナ), a woman of elsewhere, she. — *Ano fitó tatai, Ano fitó gata*, the men there, those people, they. — *Ano káta* (アノカタ), contracted *Anáta* (アナタ), the side of elsewhere, is used as a polite indication of the second person, thou (you); plural *Anáta gáta*. — *Anáta de wá gozáiri-masénu; watákusi si-sin ni itási-mánita*, = it is not you; I have done it myself.

Ada (アダ), pron. *Ada*, is used with the signification of other, opposed to *Ware*, I, *Mino*, own and *Midzukára*, self.

Kano kisi (カノキシ), the bank (or shore) yonder, the other world. — *Kano kata*, yon side. — *Kano fitó*, that man.

Kono yo (コノヨ), this world, this life. — *Kono toki*, this time, this hour. — *Kono kata*, this side, — with relation to time, since. — *Kono aida*, between there, meanwhile. — *Kono yaéni*, for this cause, therefore. — 此ヅ箇ヵ條ヅハ, these articles.

Yono (ヨノ), without, on the outside, other, with reference to something that has been already mentioned. — *Yono fitó* (他ヅ人ジ), another man, someone else; the same as *Fokéno fitó* (外ヅ人ジ) or *Bétsu zin* (別ヅ人ジ). — *Yono isyá*, another physician than he, of whom it is question. — *Sobéno isya*, an additional physician.

Sonó (其ヅ), his, its.

Ano fitó sono tokoro mdée yuki-tsukú, he arrives at his place, he reaches his object. — *Fitó bitó sono simidamú wo fadzsadzu*, each one misses not his aim, — no one misses his aim. — *Kun-si sono kurdí ni so-sité okonáfu, sono foká wó negaédzu*, the nobleman acts according to his station, what is beyond that, he does not long for. — *Sono mi*, his body, himself. — *Ayamatsi wó sono mi ni motomura béki*, men must seek for the fault in or with themselves. — *Sono toki*, or *sono setsú* (其ヅ時ξ, 其ヅ節ξ), its time, such a period, the period of the act that has just been mentioned, then, there. — *Sono fi* (當日), that day. — *Sono migíri* (其磯), that point of time. — *Sono fen* (其ヅ邊○, 其ヅ邊, 其ヅ辺), thereabouts. — *Sono nótsi* (其ヅ後ξ, 自ヅ後ξ), thereafter. — *Sono uyé* (其ヅ上ξ. 且), or after the *Yédo* pronunciation: *Sonó uwí*, moreover, besides, also. — *Sono αtó*, behind that, thereafter, there upon. — *Sono yaéni*, for that cause, so, therefore. — *Sono ta wa* (其ヅ他ヅハ), else, otherwise. — *Sono todsri ni*, thus.

Sono kata, contracted: **sonáta**, his (or its) side, yon side, the familiar word for *Nandzi*, your Honour, you; vulgo *Sonó fóo, Sonó boo* (其ヅ方ξ), plural *Sono fóo dumo*. — *Sono fóo tori-tsúkurí ye*, undertake it! ← *Nandzi kádeé yo!*

Sono moto (其ヅ許ξ) = yon domicile or seat, for „yon, ye." — *Koko moto ni* (於ヲ茲ヅ土ξ), at this place. — *Kami no moto*, seat of gods. — *Fitó ga moto ni*, at the place where someone dwells. — *Tsuku-yumi no mikoto mikoto-nori wo ukéte kudári-mású. Tsui ni aki-motsú no kami no moto ni* (許ξ) *itári-tamgru*, the god of the moon-bow receives the divine charge and descends. At length he comes to the seat of the goddess of the harvest. — *Sono moto motsi-kitu*, you have brought. — *Kuni-guni nite iro-iro no si-fgu ari; ono-ono sono yorósiki ni sitagáru besí*, in every country different ways of acting exist; people ought to keep to the best (*yorósiki*) of each (*ono-ono-sono*). — *Ono-ono-sono bun wo u*, = each gets his share. — *Sono í ni makáse* (任 ξ 其 ζ 意 ʅ), leave it to his pleasure.

Tá no or Tó no, commonly **Dé no** or **Dó no** (何 ʒ, ʅ), or **Donna** (何 ʒ ϝ), the interrogative which? what?

Dóno fitó, which (what) man? who? — *Dóno tokóro ni*, at which place? where? — *Dóno káta*, or contracted *Dónata*, which (what) side? where? — is at the same time used as the „who?", polite interrogative — *Dónata ye yúka zo*, whither, or to whom, are you going? — *Dónata ga anátani kori wo osiye-mdeita ká*, who has taught you this? — *Donna kotozo* (何 ʒ ϝ 事 ξ ϝ), which matter?

Dóno ygu (何 ʒ 樣 ʅ), pron. *dono yóo*, = which way? how? — *Yóru do no ygu na*, how is the night?

In the popular language *Dono ygu* or *Dóygu* resolves into **Doo**, which is written ¿ or ¿ also ʅ. Thence: *Doukí* (乎 ʅ), pron. *dioká*, *Douzó* (何 ʅ 卒 ʋ), how? — *Dóu mó*, however. — *Ano koto wó dou náttaká*, = the matter how is (it) become? what has become of the matter? — *Ano fitó no ná wó don iáká*, = his name how is it called? what is his name? — *Koré wa dou tsukurúi yúkarido ká*, = what concerns this, by what making will it be good, i. e. how will people have to make this?

Dou-si, = how to do? — *Ka-ygu-si* (彼 º 樣 ʋ ϟ), contracted *Kgu-si*, *Kóo-si*, so to do. — *Dóu-sitá* (何 . 何 以 . 爲), = how doing? — *Dou-sité makóto de adí to iwarru zo*, = how could people say, that it is not true? — *Waré dou-sité sómukyu só*, how should I be against it?

Dou-sitá (an abbreviation (apocope) of *Dósitára*), = how done? how? is used adjectively. — *Dósaitá koto gá dru*, what sort of matter is there? — *Dósaitá koto zo*, = what sort of matter? what matter?

e. Substantive pronouns.

By suffixing *re* the adverbs of place become substantive pronouns, which refer to something (whether person or thing, remains undetermined) as being present in a place. The termination *re* is indeed an abbreviation of *are*, which, by a mutation of sound, has arisen from *ari*, to be. The pronouns thus formed are declinable as every other noun, with the genitive termination *no*, are used as attributive adjectives, and, in this form, answer to our pronouns possessive

(„mine, thine"), they are, however, used as substantives also, in which case they, as every other noun, are declinable.

These substantive pronouns are:

1) Wáre, ワレ, the „I," understood as that which is in the midst, in the circle (wa), by which the person thinking or speaking supposes himself surrounded. The characters used for it are ²我, ²吾, ²自, ²僕, ²印, ²身, ²予, ²吾. The Mikado uses for „I" ²朕 *Tsin*, for which formerly *Maro* (麻呂) was used, which word however has at present become an appellative of youth. The Tai-kun generally uses for „I" ²余 or ²予 (not to be confounded with 才). — *Wáre fitó* (我ニ人ト, ²自²佗), the I and another. — *Ware ware wó wasúru* (吾ヲ忘ルヽ我ヲ), I forget the I, — I forget myself. — *Kono kása wa ware no nari* (此笠ハ我ノナリ), this hat is mine ¹).

Plural: *Wáre-ware*, *Wáre-ware-dzúrá*, *Wáre rá* (我ラ等), *Ware domo*, we; *Warerá gá*, ours.

Ware properly belongs to the book-language, nevertheless it is used in the conversational, when the speaker exalts his „I." Then it answers to our WE.

2) Aré, アレ (彼, 佗), something that is somewhere, he, she, it, German *er*; plural *Aré-are*, *Arera*. Being short in matter it, just as he or it, refers to something (person or thing) of which no case is made.

Are ga hon, that one's book, his book. — *Are wa tare?* = something what? i. e. what is it? who there? — *Are wó mi-tái*, I long to see him (or it).

In old-Japanese *Are* occurs, as a variation of *Ware*, I.

Are mé, = that there, also *A-itsu* and *Ko-itsu*, = that there and this here, or *A-itsumé*, *Ko-itsumé* are opprobrious terms.

Oré (意ナ鳴), variation of *Are*, in the mouth of a plebeian of Yédo *ôra*, refers with derogation to another person, whereas from humility, the speaker, with it, also designates himself.

„*Oré wa fitó wo iyáshimete iru kotoba nari; kon-ari midzukára wo iu.*" Oré is a word, with which one mentions another disrespectfully; in later times persons have applied it to themselves. — *Ferd-taitō no kusi.*

3) Karé, カレ (夫, 伊, 架), something that is there, he, she, it, that.

4) Koré, コレ, something that is here, this. (²此, ²是, ²兹, ²之).

---

¹) Here a contraction takes place, as the word *Kasa*, which belongs to *Ware no* also, is represented but once. Comp. pag. 66, line 4 from the bottom.

Kore wa amari tiisai (是ヲ余リ小キイ), this is too small[1]. — *Kore wo moto wo siru tó iu*, this is called knowing the foundation. — *Are kore*, that and this, those and these. — *Kore kara inuru*, to go from here. — *Kore ni yotte* (依ヲ之ニ), therefore. — *Konite yoi*, so far well, good so!

Plural: *Kore-kore, Korera*. — The isolated *Kore wa* is often superseded by *Ko wa* (此ノ者ハ), and the attributive *Kore no* continually, by *Kono*. — *Ko wa ao-fuό-kao no fazîmé no oya nari*, this is the progenitor of the human race. — *Kono nedan wa ikura si-másaká*, the price (*nedan*) of this (article), how much is it?[1]

5) **Soré,** ソレ (夫. 爾. 其), something that is so, such. Plural *soré-sore*, so or such. — *Sore kore* (其ソ斯ソ), = such ones. — *Soré wa deki-másika*, can such happen? — *Soré wa náni dé gozáru*, what is such? — *Ware soré wo wdya mono ni sitá*, I have made such (or that) my property. — *Soré no toki no fan yóri tsugi no toki ni itáru made*, = from the half of such an hour till it comes to the next hour (till the next hour). — *Sore ni tsuité* (就テ夫ニ), concerning that. — *Sore ni wa oyóbi-maséna*, = it comes not to such, such is unnecessary. — *Sore dé wa yói*, also so it is good, also that is good. — *Sore dé wa, kai-makoo*, so (this being so or then) I will buy it. — *Soré kara ayé*, = from there upwards; in relation to time, earlier than, before. — *Sore yóri mayé*, = proceeding from there forwards, i. e. earlier than.... — *Sore yóri simo*, = proceeding from there downwards, i. e. afterwards, there upon (以後). — *Sore yori kono kata* (爾來), = proceeding from there on this side, i. e. since. — *Soré-sore no monóeú*, things which are so or so. — *Soré-sore ni sitagátte*, = according to the so or such, in proportion as it is so or so.

If *Soré* happens to be at the beginning of a sentence as attributive definition (such) of a noun immediately following, then it reflects on that, which has previously been said of the same subject already; e. g.: Mention has been made of the historical commencement of Japan; after some general remarks the writer continues: *Soré Nippon-goku en Tsiu-kwa ko tai yóri figisi ni atáru yué ni Nitsu too tó iu*, what concerns such country Japan, as it lies towards the east of the Central Blooming country (China), so it is called the *Nitsu too* or country eastward of the sun. Evidently *sore* is here, not as a mere expletive particle, but is of the same value, as the Latin relative *qui* at the beginning of a

---

[1] *Shopping-Dialogues*, pp. 2, 23, 24.   [2] Ibid. p. 34.

CHAPTER II. SUBSTANTIVE PRONOUNS. § 8. II.

sentence such as: *Quae consuetudo non fregit eum sed erexit.* (C. Nep. Themistocl. 1. 3). In cases such as this, we supply the place of the reflective pronoun with the demonstrative, and the Japanese *Soré Nippon goku* is equal to: this country Japan.

Sorógfusí = such a man, formerly used only by princes as a modest indication of their own persons towards higher [1]), latterly it has come into vogue with inferior persons, and is used by them to speak modestly of themselves. It is taken for a amalgamation of *Sorr ga nusí*, Mister such a one, and is placed on a footing with the Chinese 其 or 人, = somebody, *quidam* [2]).

6) *Tore* is not in use.

7) *Tare*, タレ, old language, now usually *Dare*, ダレ (誰, 孰), = who? Lat. *quis?* — *Dore*, ドレ, which of many? By suffixing the interrogative particle ゾ *zo*, is formed *Darézo*, abbreviated *Dozo*, who? — *Darega*, whose? (*cujus?*), is often superseded by *Daga*.

Ka ri (*kare eú*) *dáre* (彼ハ誰ソ), who is there? — *Kawá-daré-túki* (= the who is there?-hour), the hour at which objects are still too faintly lighted, to be recognized well, the morning twilight. — *Kawá-daré-bosi*, the morning-star. — *Sore wa dare no O ko de gozarimásuka*, what boy is that? vulgo: *Are wa dare no ko dakú* (*dakú* = *de áru ka*). — *Sumíre daré ga tamé ni niwóru*, = the violet for whom does it smell? — *Nokó ni doriya dráz ó*, who is there? — *Daré ga yókú sirite óru*, who knows it well? — *Kono fitó wa daré de áří-másukú*, = this man who is he? = vulgo *Ano fitó wa* (or *Arewá*) *daré da ká* (properly; *daré de áru ká*), who is he. — *Nandzí wa daré de dra zú*, who are you? — *Daré tó óndzí koto*, with what identity? — *Daré tó fanási súru*, with whom to talk? — *Daré tó tomoní óru zú*, with whom to dwell together? — *Daré ni yoródzu*, indifferent who. — *Korera no siyo no naka de doriya nandzí ni yúkizó* (此 等 ノ 書 ノ 中 ニ 何 レ ヲ 好 = ス ゾ), which of these books pleases you? — *Doré mo*, whatever, each. — *Doré-fodo* (何 レ 程), how much? — *Koko yori tsugínó matsí madé doré-hodo arimásu*, = from here to the nearest town how many (miles) is it?

Remark 1. The Japanese does not distinguish the interrogative sentence

---

[1]) In the *Nippon wa dai isí run* (39th Mikado, 10th year, 10th month), the Emperor's brother, addressed by him as *Nandzí*, calls himself *Sorogusí*, whereas now every one speaks of *Sorogisí ga kíita fumí*, = the letter written by me.

[2]) *Wa-gun risuri*, under *Sorogusí*.

from the affirmative by an altered order of words; the sentence „who is it?" must, therefore, as „it" is the subject of discourse, be expressed by *Sore wa dare da arimdsuka*, and not, as in the *Ban-go zen* [1]), II, 30 r. is the case, by *Darega sore de arimdsaká*.

Remark 2. The question, if perhaps *Dare*, just as the Latin *quis*, with the signification of *aliquis*, = somebody, is thus used as an indefinite pronoun, has been answered negatively by a literate Japanese [2]).

Idsure, イヅレ (誰. 孰. 何), mostly イヅレ Izure, who?, what?, which? — used rather in poetry and in the epistolary style, is superseded in the ordinary conversational language by *dore, doko, dotsira* or *dou*.

Idzure ga masaru (孰か 愈る), who surpasses? which is the better? — *Imada idzure ka* [3]) *kore* (Fou-rai-san) *nára yi tsumibiraka narazu*, it has not yet been settled, which (of the mountains mentioned) this (the *Pung-lai-san*) is. — *Idzure no tokoro ni ka* [4]) *te wo kudasan* (何處 下手), at which place will one lay hands on? where to begin? = *Doń kara fazimen zo?* [5]). — *Idzure no fito*, which man? — *Idzure no yo*, which age? — *Idzure no tosi*, which year? — *Idzure no kata*, which side? which province? — *Idzure mo, Idzure tomo*, whoever, whichever, = *Dore mo, dotsira mo*. — *Idzure to* (or *Idzure tomo*) *naku*, = without whatever, i. e. without anything whatever, = *Dori to icu koto naku*. — *Idzure mo idzure mo*, plural, whichever, all. — *Idzure nari tomo*, whoever it may be. — *Idzure no utsuwa ni te mo*, in somewhere a vessel.

III. Determinative and reflective pronouns.

Self, determinative pronoun in I myself, he himself, reflective pronoun in myself, himself, herself, is expressed by

A. 1. **Onóre**, = Individual; ónódsukára, apart, by oneself.
2. **Mi**, = body, person; **Midsukara**, personal; **Waga-mi**, = own body.

1. **Onóre**, オノレ (己 (vulgo 巳) 身. 躬), from *ond*, = single, and *ore*, = are (being), thus something that is single, single being, individual, — allied in sense to *fitóri* (= *fitó* + *ori*, being alone, single, alone); plur. *onóredomo, onórera*, also *onóra* (己 等) in old Japanese.

——

[1]) 豊語筌.
[2]) Mr. TSUDA SIN ITSIROO.
[3]) *Ka*, an interrogative suffix, just as *zo*.

As the subject of a proposition *Onóre* answers to he, German *er*, *einer*, and, just as these words, indicates a person, without any compliment. Therefore, when the speaker applies it to himself it betrays modesty, whereas applied as a demonstrative pronoun to any one beyond the speaker it shows a want of respect and, just as the variation *Olóre* (オドレ), is understood as a epithet expressive of contempt. The Princes of the Empire call themselves, *onóre*, to the Emperor, and make this word equal to the Chinese expression 寡人 *kwá-zin*, Japanese *sukunáki fitó*, i. e. an insignificant man [1]).

Onóre, used attributively (genitively), or objectively, refers to the subject as being itself the object of its action, and answers to: his own, himself. Examples:

Onóre fitó no oyi wo uyámaréba, Fitó mata onórryú oyí wo uyámaru.

Onóre gá mi wo tadzentó kósaureba, Múdzu ta-zin wo tadzar-sumé yó.

If an individual honors the parents of others, Then others honor the parents of the individual.

Will you improve yourself, First improve others.

Any one may now substitute for the word „individual," in the first saying „I myself, thou thyself (you yourself), or he himself," and say: „If I honor another's parents, then the other also honors mine." In the second saying, however, *onóre*, in consequence of the Imperative there used, may be referred to the second person (thou, you). — *Onóre gá kokóro-sdaiwo okonáu* (行己之志), to do his own will. — *Onóre wó okonau* (行己), to behave oneself, one's own conduct. — *Onóre wó sutete, fitó no tamé ni su* (舍己為人), to set oneself aside and to act for the advantage of others, = *Waga koto wo bú sumúité, fitó no koto ni wá sewayaku*, to give up one's own business and serve the interests of others. — *Onóre wó taddsuí suté, fitó ni motómédzuréba, sunaráki aráuú nási*, when one rules himself (his individual) and seeks nothing of others, then one experiences no hatred. — *Onóre ni katsú*, self-victory. — *Onóre-yúri* (自己ヨリ), = from oneself.

リオノレ 寡キ人ニ 辭シ 倹シ 自シ 利シ.

CHAPTER II. DETERMINATIVE AND REFLECTIVE PRONOUNS. § 8. III.   91

Remark. If we have derived *onóre* from *onó* and attributed to this the signification of one, the word *ono-ono* pleads for this conception, for *ono-ono*, as a repetition of *ono*, has the signification of „one and one," i. e. each one, answers to the Chinese 各 *ko*, and is equal to *fitó-bito*, = man and man, i. e. each man, everyone. As derivatives from this *ono*, which, singly, is no longer in use, comes under notice: **Onasitu** (同一事), not individual, i. e. identical.

Onóre is frequently superseded by **Ore** (己 *t*) ¹), which some Japanese philologers consider an abbreviation of *onóre*.

2. **Mi** (身 ²), body, person, understood as the concrete self, whereas the idea of self, when it is taken in opposition to all that does not belong to self, is indicated by *ware* or *onóre*. — *Mi wo tatsuru mono*, = one (*mono*) who makes his body stand, is one who makes the most of his person; *ware wo tátsuru mono*, on the contrary, is one who places his I, his will, his interests on the foreground, and by which is, in general, understood a self-willed person. — *Sono mi wo usinavázu mono*, is one who does not throw himself away, does not lose sight of his personal dignity; on the contrary *Ware ware wo wasurénu*, I do not forget my I, do not lose sight of my own interest. — *Kare onóre wo wasurénu*, he does not forget himself (his individual in opposition to others). — *Onóre wó homeru*, = to praise oneself as an individual; *mi wo homeru*, to praise one's own person.

Examples: *Mi ten-ka no ken-mei wó usinavádzu* (身を不失天下之顯名ぢ), he himself (by his personal conduct) does not lose his brilliant name in the Empire ³). — *Kun-si sono mi wó fudzukésimezú*, the noble man brings no disgrace upon himself. — *Mi wo osimáru yuén wo sirebá*, *sunavátsi fitó wó dsakuuru yuén wo sira*, if one knows the way to rule oneself, then one knows the way to rule others. — *Mi wó m'má ni makásité nigé-sórinu*, yielding himself to the horse, he escapes.

Wága-mi wo uru, to sell his own body (himself); said of girls who prostitute themselves for hire. — *Wága-mi wo yásumére*, to let one's own body rest, to allow oneself rest. — *Wága de ni wága-mi wo wárusu súru mono*, one who deforms himself with his own hand.

Women use *Waga-mi* and *Mi*, plural *midomo*, for I. — *Midomo ga saditta toki*, when we have come — at the time of our coming ¹).

Mi-mi (御 ª 身 ª), = Highness' self, in old Japanese the self of illustrious persons, e. g. *Kono futa fasirano kami mo ... mi-mi wo kikusi-tamariki*, also both these gods kept their sublime persons (themselves) concealed.

Midsu-kara, ミヅカラ, componnded of *mi* (body), *dsu* (piece, i. e. something that, as a part of a whole, exists apart for itself, so that *mi-dsu*, means a separate something that is body) and *kara* (from), answers to our *of itself*, *from itself*. It is expressed by the Chinese characters 自. 自然. 身自. 躬. 親. 化来.

Remark. As the Japanese etymologists do not satisfactorily explain this word, as they leave the *dsu* unnoticed, we must explain the derivation given here. We acknowledge now, and that for the first time, *dsu*, — to be distinguished from the genitive termination *tsu*, — to be the same suffix, that, added to the radical numbers (*fito*, *futa*, = one, two), forms of them proportional numerals, (thus: *fito-dsu*, *futa-dsu*, = single, double, simplex, duplex), and which, by means of repetition, used in the form of *dsu-dsu*, gives to these numbers the character of distributives: *fito-dsu-dsu*, *futa-dsu-dsu*, = singuli, bini, one at a time, in couples. Whereas now in *mi-kara* (= from a body) the idea of body is taken quite generally, and only opposed to something else, *midsu-kara*, refers to a separate body, to a separate person (opposed to all other persons).

By means of the same derivative elements (ヅカラ), from *Te* (テ), hand, and *Kokóro* (ココロ), heart, will, are formed the words **Te-dsu-kara** (手自. 手親), = from a separate hand, i. e. with one's own hand, and **Kokóro-dsu-kara** (心ヅカラ), from a separate heart, i. e. spontaneous (from one's own free movement).

According to its form *Midsukara* is originally an adverbial definition (= of itself), and as such not susceptible of declension; e. g. *Midzukárá toriwdre fitó tó nári*, he becomes a prisoner of himself, he surrenders himself a prisoner. — *Tedsukára kuwá wo tóru*, to pluck feeding leaves of mulberry trees with one's own hands.

---

¹) The words given in ADDENDULE *Elémens*, pp. 11 and 60 ought, for the correction of typical errors, to be reduced to the forms:
    Sei = *Mi no*,   *Waga-mi no*,' *Ware-tomo no*
    Sibi = *Mi ni*, ... *mi*, ... *ni*
    Zo = *Mi wo*, ... *wo*, ... *wo*.

Midzukara also occurs there with the inflectional terminations *no*, *ni* and *wo*, although in original texts it is always undeclined.

CHAPTER II. DETERMINATIVE AND REFLECTIVE PRONOUNS. § 8. III.   93

However it is also used (in the quality of subject or of object), for I myself or he himself, and for they themselves.

Midzkara is used as subject, whenever another object is mentioned before the verb of the predicate; e. g.: *Midzukara omóedkua fakâri-kato wo yetdri*, he has himself, as he thinks, attained what he intended. — *Midzukara* is also characterized as the subject in the proverb:

即 ○ 見 他 人 之 愁
自 共 可 患

Tu-nin no uréi wo miba ed sunavátsi waidzakara tomoni urúra bési, If one sees another's grief, then one must oneself be grieved with him.

As object (= himself), on the contrary, *Midzukara* is used, whenever it is immediately followed by a transitive verb; e. g. *Mina midzukara akirakani miru ndri* (皆自明也)[1], all (these sayings) mean: to enlighten oneself. — *Midzukara azdmuku* (自欺)[1], to deceive oneself, self-deception. — *M. osimuru* (自修)[1], to cultivate oneself, self-culture. — *M. óru*, to stand on oneself (to rely on oneself). — *M. kokúromi*, to take the proof of oneself. — *M. yomin-suru mono* (自好者), one who is fond of himself. — *M. itdmi*, self-torture.

Onódzukára (オノヅカラ, 自, 自然, 已アカシ, 化來), = from the individual, from oneself, of self, Lat. *sponte*. What has been said of *Midzukara*, is, with regard to its adverbial character, applicable to *Onodzukara* also.

Onodzukárd kuru-kuru to masúru mono, things turning themselves, having their own revolution. — *O. maukíru fitó*, one who, of his own accord, immigrates. — *O. náru kotowdri wo miyo!* behold reasons, which are self-evident!

II. As Chinese expressions of the determinative and reflective pronoun self are in use:

1. 身ヒ, *sin*, body, self, opposed to 人ヒ, *zin*, others.

2. 自身ヒ, *zi-sin*, often pronounced as *dzi-sin*, own body or person. — *Zi-sin wo aisúru fitó*, one who loves his own body, i. e. who is fond of ease, the same as *Sono mi wo aisúru fitó*. — *Watdkusi zi-sin ni itdrinódita*, I have done it in my own person (myself). — *Andta Go-dzi-sin ni* (御自身ヒ=) *itdrinásda*, = You have done it in your Honor's own person.

---

[1] *Dai Gaku*, 1, 4 [2] *Ibid.* VI 1. [3] *Ibid.* III, 4.

3. 自ゞ分ゞ, **zi-bun**, = own part, his part. — *Zi-bun wo mi-outéru mono*, one, who loses sight of himself, his interest. — *Zi-bun ni suwétte óru*, *midzukara óru*, to be substantive. — *Zi-bun no sai-ku wo suru*, to do one's own work. — *Zi-bun no mono to naru*, to become property.

4. 自ゞ然ゞ, **zi-zen** (by some pronounced as *dzi-zen*), also *zi-nen*, = being of self, original, natural, unworked. — *Zi-zen ni*, or *zi-zen to*, = Lat. *sponte*. — *Sore fitó no tri-druied zi-zen nari*, that this human understanding is there, is something natural. — *Yama nó uyé ni zi-zen no fo óri*, on the mountain there is a natural fire. — *Yumé ni zi-zen ni miru*, to see something in a dream, of oneself (involuntarily). — 自ゞ然ゞ生ゞ, to exist of itself (spontaneous existence).

Besides these, there occur many more expressions compounded with 自ゞ, *zi* (self), in which *zi*, at one time, has the meaning of „own," then of „self." In the former case it stands adjectively before a substantive, in the latter objectively before a transitive verb.

自ゞ, *zi*, enters adjectively into compounds, as:

自ゞ国ゞ, own country.	自ゞ業ゞ, own trade.
自ゞ家゜, own house.	自ゞ作ゞ, own fabric.
自ゞ身ゞ, own body, self.	自ゞ筆ゞ, own pencil.
自ゞ巳゛, own person.	自ゞ画ゞ, own drawing.
自ゞ巳゛流ゞ, own clan.	自ゞ問ゞ, own question.
自ゞ体ゞ, own person.	自ゞ答ゞ, own answer.
自ゞ力ゞ, own strength.	自ゞ慢ゞ, own neglect.
自ゞ性ゞ, own disposition.	自ゞ炊ゞ, own boiling.
自ゞ儘ゞ, own whim.	自ゞ得ゞ, own interest.

Zi is objective to the verb in standard compounds as:

自ゞ愛ゞ, self-love.	自ゞ棄ゞ, self-prostitution.
自ゞ賛ゞ, self-praise.	自ゞ害ゞ, self-injury.
自ゞ在ゞ, self-existence.	自ゞ買ゞ, self-sale.
自ゞ頁ゞ, self-confidence.	自ゞ殺ゞ, self-murder.
自ゞ縛ゞ, self-bondage.	自ゞ盗ゞ, self-destruction.
自ゞ称ゞ, self-nomination.	自ゞ滅ゞ, self-annihilation.

These compounds by suffixing the verb *si*, *su*, *suru* (to do), can be changed to verbs, as *si-jitu-suru*, to write with one's own hand; *si-san-suru*, to praise oneself.

IV. Expressions of reciprocity.

The reciprocity of an action is expressed in Japanese not by pronouns, but by the adverbial (modal) definition **Tagávi ni** (タガヒニ, pronounced *ta-ngái ni*, 互に. 迭. 遞), or **Ai-tagái ni** (アヒタガヒニ), = reciprocal, or also by the verb *Aví* (アヒ), vulgo *Aí* (アイ). The last means „meet each other" and signifies, whenever it is prefixed to another verb, that the action takes place reciprocally or mutually. The meaning of *Tagai*, is generally explained by *Kare kore*, this and that; *Ati kasi*, here and there; *Ware hto*, self and another.

Remark. Japanese etymologists[1]) ascribe to *Tagávi* the meaning of 手ヲ換へ, *Ta-kuei*, changing of hands, by which nevertheless the change of the *k* to the troubled *g* (ng) is not explained. To be able to give a reason for this, we think we must consider *Tagari* as a fusion of *ta + mukiri*, = meeting of (or with) the hands, as this takes place in weaving when the shuttle is thrown with one hand and caught up with the other. We, thus, see in *g* (ng) a fusion of the *m* with the *k*; a phenomenon that frequently takes place. In *Fugái* (pron. *fi-ngái*), = East, likewise the troubled *g* in *gdai* is called into existence by a fusion of *mukiini* to *ngini*. *Fi-mukdai*, originally *Fi-mukiiní kdta*, means: the side (*kata*), whence the sun (*fi*) has come to meet (*mukiini*).

Examples: 互に 爲し賓と主と, *Tagái ni fin-ziyu tó nẛru*[2]), by turns he becomes guest and host. — *Tagári ni nikomu*, hate each other. — *Tagávi ni miru*, see each other, meet. — *Kwan-nin idí-mukári*, *Pekkin yori no okuri-fitó tó tágdźíni ai-sótsu tanuhiki*, Mandarins came out of (the town) to meet, and exchanged welcome-greetings with the people sent from Pekking.

Ari-nitaru mono (相に似たる物ミ), things resembling one another. — *Ari-dási*, strike each other, come to blows. — *Ari-siru*, know one another. — *Ari kataru*, converse (speak together). — *Ari-tagaini* (相ニ互ニ), reciprocal.

V. Pronouns Indefinite.

In Japanese, if the subject of a proposition is indefinite, it remains unex-

---

[1]) *Wa-gun awari*. [2]) MENCIUS (LEGGE, *Chinese classics*, Book V. Pt II (Ch. III. § 5.)

pressed; there, propositions without subjects are something very common. Our idioms do not permit this, and having to represent the subject of a proposition by a pronoun indefinite, in such sentences we make use of our „one" (people) or „it."

Besides, for our „one," in a more definite sense are also found Fitó, man, and Arû-fitó, some person, e. g. Fitó ga áru ya (有人麼), is there anybody? — Fitó ga nandzi wo tôru, someone asks for you. — Fitó ga dríte (or attu) O me ni kakári tási, there is somebody, who wishes to appear before you.

„Something" or „anything" is expressed by Mono, which „thing," means, however it is also applied to living beings. — Kore wo káku mono (書之者) is „a this-writing-individual," some one who writes this, distinguished from Kaki-mono, = a written something, a writing (文牘), and from Mono-kaki, a something writing, a writer, - fumi-bitó (史). In Kaki-mono, mono, has the signification of thing or something and is defined by the verbal root Kaki ns, something written; in Mono-kaki, mono is the objective definition to the same verbal root.

Nani, = what? is also used as our „somewhat," with the signification of „something."

If by „nothing" is intended something without contents or substance, it is expressed by the noun-substantive Nai, = something of no value; e. g. Fitó wo nai ga sirani su, to consider anyone as worth nothing.

Our „nobody," when no particular accent falls upon it, is superseded by „somebody" with the negative form of the verb connected with it, the negative („not") being thus taken from the noun or pronoun and incorporated in the termination of the verb. — Fitó ga ari-másu, there is somebody. — Fitó ga dri-masénu, in the written language Fitó nasi (無人), somebody is-there-not, = there is nobody.

If, however, it is wished to bring out „nobody" and „nothing" with emphasis, the expressions which signify „whoever, whatever," are used in connection with a negative verb.

Dare kore wo siránu means: who does not know this? (sirónu, verb negative = not know). — Dare mó kore wo siránu, whoever (who it may be) knows not this, nobody knows it. — Kare nani wo sénu, - what does he not? — Kare naní mo sénu, = he does not whatever it may be, i. e. he does nothing. — Doko ni mo arázu, wherever not to be, = to be no where.

Consequently the instance, cited in the *Elements of Japanese Grammar*, Shang-hai 1861, page 23, *Dare mo kokoni kimasinanda*, will mean: „whoever has not come here," and not „nobody here came (honorific) has not." We are not at liberty to assign to *Dare mo* the meaning of *Nobody*, and to overlook, that in Japanese the negation of a negation is equal to a confirmed assertion.

VI. Relative pronouns are wanting, because the Japanese, having no relative clauses, substitute for them adjective clauses, which precede the word, to which they refer. Instead of „the man, who is present," an expression is used, answering to „the present man" (*Iru fitó*); instead of „the town, which the enemy has sacked," — „of the enemy-to have-sacked-town."

In such cases, moreover, the substantive Tokóro (所), place, is also used to intimate the passive something.

Tsukúru koto is the fabricating, the fabrication;
Tsukúru mono, a fabricating being;
Tsukúru fitó, a fabricating man, one who fabricates;
Tsukúru tokóro, the place of fabrication;
Fitó no tsukúru tokóro no mono is something (mono) of a man's (*fitó no*) fabricating- (*tsukúru-*) place (*tokíro no*), i. e. something that somebody fabricates. — *Inisige yóri motiyúru tokóro no nen-ggu* is a year-name (*nen-ggu*) of a place, where (not which) one from ancient times has used, i. e. a year-name used from ancient times.

Thus we, although the Japanese philologers do not do so, give to *Tokóro*, in that position also, in which it seems to do the work of a pronoun relative, its proper signification, namely that of „place."

In the Syntax this construction will be treated again.

VII. Interrogative pronouns.

In the previous pages, treating of the formation of the pronouns, those, of which the interrogative elements Ta or To, vulgo Da or Do, and Itsu, vulgo Idsu are the foundation, have already been explained. To embrace them in one glance, they are:

CHAPTER II. INTERROGATIVE PRONOUNS. § 8. VII.

Ddno, which? p. 85.	Doko, where? p. 80.	Idzuku, where?	p. 81.
Dare, who? 88.	Dotsi, „ 82.	Idzukunk'd, „	„
Dare ga, whose? „	Dotsira, „ „	Idzukuuzd, on what ground? how? „
Daga, „ „	Doisatsi, „ „	Idzure, who, which?	82.
Daro, who? „	Ddno, which? 85.	Idzurcno, whose?	„
Darenoka, whose? „	Donna, „ „		
Dareno zo, „ „	Dinata, who? „		
	Donoyou, how? „		
	Doyou, dou, „ „		
	Dousite, „ „		
	Dore, which? 87.		

Besides there are still **Nani**, what? and **Ika**, how?, which from the important part they play, deserve an acquaintance more than superficial [1]), whereas **Iku**, how much?, as being related to the numerals, will be treated of with them.

1. **Nani**, ナニ (何), abbreviated **Nan**, ナン, obsolete **Nam**, ナム, plural **Nanra** (何等), what? which? Lat. *quid? quod?* It is used both substantively, and adjectively, and very often strengthened by an interrogative suffix, ka or zo.

Substantively, with the meaning of „what?", *Nani* occurs in expressions as: *Nani wo yerabi mdsi ki?*, what do you choose? — *Nani wo toru ki?*, after what do you ask? — *Nani wo nandzi ga motomuru ya?*, what do you seek? — *Nani wo O kai mudru ki?*, what do you buy? [2]). — *Nani wo motte?*, wherewith? whereby? — 何ヲ以テ利ヲ吾之國ゾ [3]), *Nani wo matte waga kuni wo risen*, wherewith shall I advantage my empire? — *Naniyd dri-mdruki?*, what is there at hand? [4]). — *Kore wa nani ni moteii-marutu?*, what is the use of this? — *Sore ca nani ni yoi ka?*, for what is such good?

---

[1]) The greatest stumbling-blocks in oral intercourse with the Japanese, are the interrogatives (we understand by the term every word, by which inquiry after anything is made), and the ways of using them. Uncertainty in that respect brings about misunderstanding on both sides; one swerves to what the other has not asked; and the speakers, weary of the continual deviating answers, probably end by thinking each other reserved, if not by suspecting each other of a want of understanding. With a view to this, the interrogative pronouns, and the combinations formed with them are here treated of with the differences required.

[2]) *Shopping-Dialogues*, p. 2.   [3]) MENCIUS (LEGGE, *Chinese Classics*, II. Book I. Pt. I. Ch. I. § 4).
[4])   „   „   p. 2.

CHAPTER II. INTERROGATIVE PRONOUNS. § 8. VII.

Nani to, = to what, whereto, as appositive definition¹). — Anata no O na wa nani to ii-masuka?, = your name what (how) is it called?, what is your name?²).

Nani to fu (何と云フ), in the popular language contracted to ナンデフ, pronounced Na-ndeo, for which 何ン條フ is written, = what to call? how? called. — Nani to iru koto, = a what calling matter? i. e. what sort of or which matter? — Nani to mousi-masuka?, what do you say? — Nani to naku, without anything (無大小).

Nani to so (何ト卒ヤ), what says it?, supersedes, like doo zo, our „if you please."

Nani to te, also ナドテ Na-ndote, from Nani to site, = to what? tending, whereto? wherefore? — Nani to te kore wo itasimasita ka, to what end have you done this?

Nani yori (於テ何ニ), Nani kara (自ラ何ニ), = of what?, whereof?

Nani ni yotte (何ニ由リ, 縁テ底ニ), = on what ground?, whence? — 何ニ由リ 知テ 許ソ 可ンヤ也 ³), Nani ni yotte waga kuidru-koto wo siran? on what grounds, (how) do you know that I am able for that?

Naze ni, from nan-se-ni, = for what? to do, why? — Naze ni sore wo sezu ni oraka?, why does not one such? — Naze ni O ugori nasaronu ka? = why does not your rise happen?, i. e. why do you refuse? ⁴).

Nani-si ni, Nani-si ni ku, variation of Naze ni, why? — Nan sore so, properly Nan sure zo, how doing, on account of which, why? 何左.

Wgu mani kore wo yosi to subu, sunaouisi nansure zo okonaro-
寡之王 zaru ⁴), if the king considers this as good, why does not
不則如 he carry it out?
行何爲

Nani so (ナニソ, 何), abbreviated Nan so (ナンソ), also Na-nso (ナン), how? in what way, for what reason? — occurs also as a mere characteristic of a direct question. — 王何曰利 ⁵), Wgu nanso ri wo iwan, = the king, why does he mention the word advantage? — 何 可感也 ⁶), Nanso faien beken, how can one abolish (such)? — 牛羊 何擇焉 ⁶), Uia yga nanso eraban, why to choose between ox and

¹) See page 70, V.   ⁵) Shopping-Dialogues, p. 19.
²) MENCIUS (LEGGE, Chinese Classics, vol. I, p. 15).   „   „   p. 21.
³)   „   Ch. V. § 4.   ⁴) MENCIUS (LEGGE, Vol. II. Book I. Pt. I. Ch. I. § 9).
⁴)   „   Ch. VII. § 4   ⁷) Ibid. Ch. VII. § 7.

100

goat? *Nanzo O ki ni iri-mőru mono ga gozári-másın*, is there anything that pleases you? — 盍反其本矣 ¹), *Nanzo sono moto ni kaverazáru*, why not return to the foundation?

Nanzo ya, ナンゾヤ, obsolete ナゾヤ・何也, 何如, how is this, how does it happen? as predicate closing the sentence, and preceded by a subjective clause.

多民何也不加

Tami ohokikoto wo kuraverarn ra nanzo ya ²), that the people does not increase its number, how is this?

Naso-naso, how? how?, riddles.

Nani naru ³), what? being. — *Nani naru mono*, or *koto*, what thing, or what matter?

Nani no, **Nanno**, adjectively what? in the expressions: *Nani no ji* (何日), what day? vulgo *itsu*. — *Nani no koku* (何剋), what hour? — 是真何心乎機 ⁴), *Kore makoto ni nanno kokoro zo ya*, what was really (my) opinion concerning that?

Nani and *Nan* occur adjectively in the expressions *Nani-goto* (何事), what matter?, what? — *Kimi komima tokoro nani-goto zo*, that which you willingly have, what (is it)? — *Nani-goto de?*, wherefore, why? — *Nani-bun* (何分), what part? — *Nani-yju* or *Nani-zama* (何樣), what manner? *Nani-ren* (何扁), what volume? — *Nani-fodo* (何程), what quantity? the quantity. *Nani-mono* (何者), what being, what? — *Nani-gokiro* (何心), which heart, which sense? — *Nani gokiro naki* (無何心), without any purpose. — *Nani-yué* (何故), what cause? — *Nani-yué ni sore zo?*, why that? — *Nani-kore*, obsolete *Nani-kure* (何是), what one?

Nani-gusi (何其), after Jap. etymologists from *Nani ga nusi*, = whereof? master, what somebody, now in use only with the signification of the indefinite pronoun „any-(some-)one" (其) and applied by the speaker to himself. Compare *Sore gusi*, pag. 88.

Combinations with *Nan* (ナン) are: *Nan-nen* (何年), which year? — *Nan-gwats* (何月), which month? — *Nan-doki* (何時), which (what)

---

¹) Mencius (ibid. Ch. VII. § 28).   ³) Ibid. (Ch. II. § 1).
²) Sal *Nasiru*.   ⁴) Ch. VII. § 7.

time? what hour? — *Nan-doki-goroni* (何ニ時ノ頃ゾ), against what time? [1]. — *Nan-dan* (何ニ段ゾ), which pieces? — *Kono iro ga nan-dan drimásíka?* [1], what (how many) pieces are there of that color? — *Nan-gin!* [1] (何ニ斤ゾ), how many pounds?

Nani, Nanzo occur also with the signification of the indefinite pronoun *any-(some)-thing.* — *Nandzi ra sono koto ni tsuité nanzo kikite óru ka*, have you heard anything about that matter?

2. **Ika, イカ** (如何, 云何), how?

Current combinations with *iki* are:

Ika-mono (何ら者ゾ), what thing.

Ika-sama, vulgo **Ika-yŋu, Ika-yoo** (何ら樣ゾ, 何方), which way. — *Ika-yŋu ni*, in what way, how. — *Ika-yŋu ni mo*, however. — *Ika-yŋu ni naru tomo*, however it may be. — *Ika-yŋu naru mono*, what sort of thing. — *Ika-yŋu naru mono nite uo*, what sort of being or thing it may be, who or whatever. — *Ika-yŋu na koto de mo súru*, do whatever thing it may be, do every thing.

Ika-fodo (何ら程ゾ), quantity. — *Ika-fodo ka*, how much? — *Ika-fodo no taikóra*, how much power. — *Ika-fodo no wida*, how much interspace, how long? — *Sore wo iki-fodo ni uru ya*, for how much is such sold? — *Ika-fodo ookú tomo*, however much? how much soever?

Ika-bakári, how yet (still). — *Sono koto wo iku-bakari kurúshi*, how will people yet (still) be sorry for that.

Ika-náru, how being, of what sort. — *Ika-naru kotozo*, what sort of thing? — *Soko ni iku-naru fíto zo*, what sort of man is there? — *Ika-naru sei-mei zo*, what (is your) name?

The modal terminations of *Iki* are: **Ikani**, イカニ, — *Ikani ka*, イカニカ, — *Ikani zo*, イカニゾ, abbreviated **Ikan**, イカン, — *Ikan zo*, イカンゾ, or even **Ikade**, イカデ (pronounce *Iku-nde*), イカヅデ, *Ikade ka*, *Iku-nde ka*, how? Lat. *quomodo*.

Sore va ikan? : such — how? how is such? According to the rule of the Japanese arrangement of words *ikan*, as predicate, follows *sore va* as subject [4]. The subject may also be a subjective clause, e. g. ...*aru rá ikani*, how does it happen, that there...is? — *Ikade* (vulgo *donde*) *iraserare misashí*, how goes it? — *Ikade arazaran*, how should there not be, why not?

---

[1] *Shopping-Dialogues*, p. 17.   [3] Ibid. p. 35
[2] Ibid. p. 11.   [4] See Introduction, p. 64, 15, A.

Ikága, イカゞ, pronounce *ikâ-nga* (如何, 云何), how?, probably a fusion of *iká ika*. — *Ikága On watári worooya*, = how is your passage?, how do you do? — *Sokó-moto ikága O kurási zo?*, = how do you let (the time) go round? how do you do? — *Ikága sen*, how will one do (anything)? — *Ikága suru* (or *Ikága na*) *koto*, what matter? — *Ikága nó obósímésizo*, what opinion? what do you think?

Interrogative pronouns with the suffix *mo*.

Connected with the suffix *mo*, 毛 (= also, Latin *que*, *cunque*), the interrogative pronouns embrace all that is comprehended in the interrogative as individuals together. *Dare mó*, the same as *quicunque*, whoever, everyone that may be reckoned under *Dare* or *qui*.

If the interrogative is joined to a substantive, *mo* is placed after it, and if it is declined, after the inflectional termination. — *Idzure no ya mo kara tó iu tou*, every arrow may be called *tarn* (shaft). — *Doko ni mo* or *Doko dé mo*, wherever, everywhere.

Instead of *mo*, *te mo* (テ モ) is often used; e. g. *Dare té mó sono zi wo hómétári*, whoever it may be (everyone) has praised this poem. — *Idzure no tosi ni te mo*, in whatever year it may be; *te mo* having, by aphæresis, arisen from *sité mo* (= also is), whereas *to te mo* in expressions as *Nani to te mo*, = whatever people (may think or say), is the same as an ellipsis, being the verb that means think or say, and that governs the apposition [1]) characterized by *to* (*nanito*), not expressed itself, but only indicated by the termination *te*. *Nani to te mo*, thus stands elliptically for *Nani to iyu te mo* [2]), = whatever it may be called or be. An abbreviation of which is *Nanito mo*, *Nán tó mó*. — *Nán to omoeuka*, what do people think of it? *Nán to mo omoweinn*, people think nothing of it, people do not trouble themselves about it.

VIII. Arrangement of the personal pronouns in the conversational language.

The choice of the words, which are used in the oral intercourse as pronouns, is not indifferent, but it is prescribed by etiquette. From our own experience, if after an intercourse of more than two years with Japanese we may speak of it, and from the information given by a learned Japanese gentleman [3])

---

[1]) Compare p. 70, V.   [2]) *Waiyau iiwori*.   [3]) Mr. ︎︎︎︎ ︎︎︎ ︎︎︎︎︎.

the following expressions, used as pronouns, enter into the conversational language.

1. For I.

1) The humblest expression is Te-máe, plural Te-máe-tátai, in the popular tongue of *Yédo* which frequently changes *a* to *e*, Temée, = at hand, i. e. that which is at hand or present to the person opposite.

2) Watákúsi, plural Watákúsi-domo, a modest, and, in confidential intercourse, most usual expression. Every respectable man speaks of himself thus; and the man of the people at *Yédo* says for it Waki (*waachi*).

3) Oré, plural Orára, in the *Yédo*-dialect Oíra, after the mention on page 86 supported by a quotation from the Dictionary of the old-Japanese language, a self-humiliating expression, is now considered as one of pride at *Yédo*.

4) Wáre, plural Warera, the „I" and „We" in the mouth of a prince, when he speaks to his people.

2. For the person spoken to, THOU, YOU, YE.

1) Wáre, plural Wárera, the most humiliating expression, which is applied only to low people. Probably confounded with *Are?*

2) Te-máe, the same as given above for „I," is fit for subordinate persons and servants, and answers to the well known German „*Er*" and „*Sie*."

3) Temáe-sáma, plural Temáe-sáma-gata, is equal to You, Sir, You, gentlemen, used by a person of quality towards those somewhat below him.

4) O-máé, in the *Yédo*-dialect Omée, plural O-máé-gata, in use among the middle class.

5) O-máé-sáma, = Your Honor, more periphrastical and consequently more solemn than *O-mée*.

6) Anáta, plural Anáta-gáta, used, with preference, by polite people towards their equals ¹).

7) Anáta-sáma, plural Anáta-sáma-gáta, is expressive of the greatest respect towards the person addressed.

3. For the person spoken to, HE.

1) Are, plural Arera, is put down for disrespectful.

---

¹) The members of the first Japanese embassy, which came to Europe in 1862, and to which the author was appointed as one of a committee by his Government, generally used *Anáta* mutually.

2) **Ano mono,** = that person there, characterizes the person spoken of as a mere object (*mono*), deserving of no respect.
3) **Ano fitó,** plural **Ano fitó-gata,** polite indication of one's equals. On officer or functionary speaking of another intimates him by *Ano fitó*.
4) **Ano O fitó,** plural **Ano O fitó-gata,** somewhat more stately, is used when the person spoken of is related to the person spoken to.
5) **Ano kata,** plural **Ano kata-gata,** the side there, and **Kono kata,** the side here, looking from the person, and only indicating the direction, in which he is, both belong as our Your Honor, to the very respectful expressions.
6) **Ano O kata,** plural **Ano O kata-gata,** is indicative of the highest respect.

The above arrangement of the pronouns of the conversational language agreeing, in general, with that adopted by R. ALCOCK in his *Elements of Japanese Grammar*, page 21, contains, however, a few deviations which, the reader will please to observe, rest upon the authority of Mr. TSUDA SIN ITSIROO.

CHAPTER III.

THE ADJECTIVE.

§ 9. The adjectives attributing to the idea, expressed by a noun substantive, one or another quality, have, in proportion as they represent an attribute or a predicate, different forms which, though strongly prominent in the written or book language, are, on the contrary, more or less obsolescent in the conversational. The forms of the written, will, therefore, be treated before those of the spoken language.

I. THE ADJECTIVE IN THE WRITTEN LANGUAGE.

A. Construction of the adjective in its radical form with a noun. — If the quality expressed by the adjective is represented as present in the object from the very beginning, then the adjective is, as a subordinate attributive definition in its radical form, joined to the substantive in a compound word: *Taka-co*, Highland, German *Hochland*. Thus also:

Nagu-siki, Long-cape.	*Kuro-tsutsi*, black-earth.
Akā-tsutsi, red earth, ruddle.	*Ami-sake*, sweet-beer.
Siro-gine, white ore (silver).	*Furu-tōsi*, the old-year.

B. Adjectives in ki.

1. *a*. Ki. termination of the adjective used as attributive. — If the quality is first to be attributed to the object expressly, the adjective, to be used as attributive, acquires a conjunctive, or properly a derivative termination, which

for a particular class of adjectives, is ki; Takaki no, = a high land, land that is high, distinguished from Takano, = highland. Thus also:

Nagaki saki, a long cape.   Kuroki tsutsi, black earth.
Akaki tsutsi, red earth (ruddle). Amaki saké, sweet beer.
Siroki gane, white ore.   Furuki ato, old traces, ruins.

The adjectives belonging to this class generally express a quality, to which activity is not allied.

Remark. The termination *ki*, whose vocal *i* is the root, from which the contlemative verb *ari* = to be, is derived, means „being so" that is to say, as the essential part of the word implies. The relation of the essential part to the verbal element can be no other, than that of an adverb to the verb, whereas the mutual relation of *Takaki* and *Yama* is that of a compound word. — Compare what has been said on page 96 line 15 et seqq. concerning *Kati-momo*.

The vulgar language of *Nagasaki* substitute, *ka* for the adjective termination *ki*, thus *siroka* for *siroki*, white [1]).

b. The adjectives with the termination *ki* may be used substantively, as nouns concrete, and then as such are declinable. — *Yama takaki* or *Yama no takaki* is the high of mountains, i. e. eminently high, or the highest of mountains, *yama* now being a subordinate definition to *takaki*.

2. **Ku,** adverbial form. — If an adjective of this class is used as an adverb, then its radical form assumes the termination *ku*. *Takaku tobu*, to fly high. The adverb in *ku* under all circumstances remains an adverb, yet represents in the coördinate sentence, whose predicate verb must be in the unconjugated radical form [2]), the undefined radical form of the adjective verb terminating in *si*.

Isolated by the suffix *ro* (§ 6) the adverb acquires a position separated from the verb, which brings out its idea with more emphasis. — *Ooku ro ro*, = manifold, often (frequently).

3. *a.* **Si,** form of the adjective as praedicate. — When an adjective of this

---

[1] The question, formerly mooted in the Proeve voor Japansche Spraakkunst by j. curtius, 1857, p. 84, if the termination *ka* is really peculiar to the dialect of *Nagasaki*, has since been answered affirmatively, as well by Japanese orally, as in writing by the late s. j. de saint aulaire, who was stationed, as Dutch interpreter for the Japanese language, at *Nagasaki*. „The adjective termination in *a*," wrote the latter to me, „is really used generally in *Nagasaki* and the lower class of the people understand nothing else; those however who have had a little education, know very well, that it is not right."

[2] See Introduction, p. 15, Coördination.

class is used as a predicate, its radical form acquires the termination si, = to be, is. *Yama takasi*, = the mountain high to be, i. e. the mountain is high [1]). The relation in which *taka* stands to *si*, is, in the spirit of the Japanese language, again no other than that of an adverb to its verb.

This *si*, placed by Japanese grammarians among the auxiliary verbs (*Ziyogo*) [2]) and designated *Gen-sai no si* [3]) or the *si* of the present tense, undergoes no verbal change.

b. If now a verbal change to indicate tense and mood is required, then instead of *si*, the continuative verb *ari*, *aru* [4]) (= exist), is used, which added to the adverbial form *ku*, fuses with this into *kari*; from *Takaku ari*, = continually high to be, comes **Takakari**, a derivative verb, which is now to be conjugated in accordance after the general plan of conjugation [5]). Instead of *ari*, *ori* is also used, as synonyme.

4. By the change of *si* into *sa* these adjective verbs are made nouns abstract: **Takasa**, = the height.

> *Remark.* *Si* is a construction of the *si* predicate, and the isolating *sa*. *Takasa*, therefore includes the *Takisi* predicate = „is high," whereas *sa* raises this idea to a noun substantive „the height." The Chinese follows the same way, when it expresses the abstract idea of „height" by 高也者.

5. LIST OF THE PRINCIPAL ADJECTIVE ROOTS IN KI.

1. *Taka-ki* 高き, high.		2. *Fiki-ki*, *Fika-ki* 低き, low.
3. *Fuka-ki* 深き, deep.		4. *Asa-ki* 淺き, shallow.
5. *Naga-ki* 長き, long.		6. *Midzika-ki* 短き, short.
7. *Firo-ki* 廣き, wide, broad.		8. *Seba-(Sema-)ki* 狹き, narrow.
9. *Futo-ki* 太き, thick, coarse.		10. *Foso-ki* 細き, fine.
*) [*Ooi-naru* 大なる, large.]		11. *Tsiisa-ki* 小き, small.

---

[1]) In s. brown's *Colloquial Japanese*, p. XXXIX, line 26 et seqq. *si* is cited as the termination of the adjective predicate, and *si* is wholly overlooked; a capital mistake that we may not leave unnoticed.

[2]) 助語.

[3]) 現在之止. — *Wa-gun siwori* under Si. Compare endeavour, pag. 65.

[4]) Not *ara*, nor *uru*, as it is printed in alcock *Elem.*, p. 27, line 9.

[5]) See § 10.

*) The adjectives placed between brackets [ ] do not belong to this category, and are inserted only for the antithesis.

12. Fíru-ki	平ら, level, even.	13. Kewai-ki[1]	險い, steep.
14. Naka-daku-ki	凸き, gibbous, convex.	15. Kubo-ki	凹き.窪, hollow, concave.
16. Firata-ki	扁き, flat.	17. Máro-ki (Maru-ki)	丸き.圓.圓, round.
18. Atsu-ki	厚き, thick.	19. Usu-ki	薄き, thin.
20. Nuo-ki	直き, right.	[Mugaru	曲き, crooked.]
21. Tói-ki	遠き, far, distant.	22. Tsiká-ki	近き, near.
23. Imane-ki	普き.遍.徧, everywhere.	24. Saka-ná-ki	寡き, seldom.
25. Oó-ki	多き, much, many.	26. Sukúsi-ki	少き, little, few.
27. Sigé-ki	茂き.繁.敷, dense.	28. Muná-si-ki	空き, without contents, void.
29. Matta-ki	全き, entire, whole.	30. Ná-ki	無き, without, ...less.
31. Kosi-ki	剛き, hard.	32. Moro-ki	脆き.脆, brittle.
33. Tsuyo-ki	強き, strong.	34. Yowá-ki	弱き.柔, weak.
35. Ara-ki	暴き.麁.荒.戚, harsh, rude, waste.	[Yawaraganáru	軟らき, soft, weak.]
36. Omó-ki	重き, heavy.	37. Karú-ki	輕き, light.
38. Káta-ki	難き, difficult.	39. Yásu-ki	易き, facile, easy.
40. To-ki	銳.疾, pointed, sharp; quick.	41. Nibu-ki,	鈍き, blunt.
42. Hayá-ki	早き.急.速.疾, early; quick.	43. Osó-ki	遲き, late; slow.
44. Waka-ki	少き.若, young.	[Oitaru,	老い, old.]
[Arata-náru	新き, new.]	45. Furú-ki	古き.舊, ancient, antique.
46. Yo-(oldj Ye-) ki	善き.能, good, well.	47. Wáru-ki	惡き, bad, base.
48. Sámu-(Sábu-) ki	寒き, cold.	[Ataka-naru	暖かき, warm.]

---

[1] Kewasi, and the adjectives cited under Nos. 28, 30, 66 and 73 have sdi (N°. 71) for their derivative form.

CHAPTER III. THE ADJECTIVE. § 9.   109

49. *Suzu-ki*   涼 ろ, cool.   50. *Nuru-ki*   温る遅, lukewarm; lazy.
51. *Ko-ki, Kwo-ki* 濃゜ゝ, strong (of taste or color). 52. *Ara-ki, Awa-ki* 淡ゝら, faint (of taste or color).
53. *Ao-ki*   青ら, pale blue, pale green.   54. *Aka-ki*   赤ら紅, red.
55. *Siro-ki*   白ら, white.   56. *Kuro-ki*   黒ら, black.
   [*Akiroki-nara* 明らか, light, clear.] 57. *Kura-ki*   暗ら, dark, dusky.
58. *Ama-ki*   甘ら, sweet.   59. *Su-ki*   酸ら, acid.
60. *Uma- (Mu-ma-) ki* 旨らか美, sweet, nice, beautiful. 61. *Niku-ki*   醜ら, ugly.
62. *Kayu-ki*   痒ら, itching.   63. *Niga-ki*   苦ら, bitter.
64. *Sibu-ki*   渋ら, raw, acerb.   65. *Yegu-ki*   蘞ら, tart.
66. *Kawhasi-ki, Kawrasi-ki,* 芳らしら, fragrant. 67. *Kusa-ki*   臭ら, stinking.
68. *Sira-ki*   惜らから, covetous, scant. 69. *Ta-ki*   欲゜度, desirous, willing.
70. *Goto-ki*   如ら, 比, like.   [*Kotonaru*   異らか, different.]
71. *Si-ki*   如し, 敷, being such as (substantive suffix ...ish, ...like). 72. *Sika-ki*   然ら, being so, or such.
73. *Be-ki*   可～, allowable.

THE SAME ROOTS ARRANGED ALPHABETICALLY.

Aka .. 54.	Fika .. 8.	Kawhasi 66.	Maita .. 29.	Omo .. 30.	Su .. 59.	Uma .. 60.
Ama .. 58.	Firo .. 12.	Kayu .. 62.	Midzika 6.	Oo .. 25.	Sukosi 86.	Um .. 19.
Amane 23.	Hisasi 16.	Ke .. 51.	Moro .. 32.	Osa .. 43.	Safama 24.	
Ao .. 53.	Firo .. 7.	Kerasi 13.	Mane .. 20.		Sare .. 49.	Wata .. 44.
Ara .. 52.	Fusa .. 10.	Ko .. 51.	Manasi 22.	Sora .. 45.		Waru .. 47.
Asa .. 4.	Fuka .. 5.	Koro .. 31.		Sida .. 5.	To .. 69.	
Atra .. 18.	Furu .. 48.	Kuku .. 15.	Na .. 20.	Sizu .. 5.	Taka .. 1.	Yasa .. 39.
Aro .. 52.	Futo .. 9.	Kuru .. 57.	Naga .. 5.	S .. 71.	Tuim .. 4.	Yega .. 65.
		Kuru .. 56.	Nao .. 20.	Siro .. 72.	Taka .. 29.	Yo .. 46.
Be .. 73.	Goto .. 70.	Kusa .. 67.	Niku .. 41.	Siro .. 64.	To .. 40.	Yasu .. 34.
			Niga .. 63.	Sigo .. 27.	Tu .. 21.	
Faya .. 48.	Kata .. 33.	Maro .. 17.	Niku .. 61.	Siro .. 33.	Tsuyo 23.	
Fiki .. 2	Karo .. 37.	Maru .. 17.	Naru .. 50.	Siro .. 56.		

Remark. The termination ki, as the distinguishing characteristic of this class of adjectives, ought to be placed on the foreground, deviating from the method in the Japanese dictionaries, which give these adjectives as adjective verbs with the termination *si* and, so doing, do not distinguish them from those, which terminate in *siki* (= ish). So, to give an instance, their expression 久**ζ**.**し** is defective, since *fisási* (= is of long duration) as a syncope of *fisasisi*, is in all respects the form of the adjective verb, has but *fisasiki*, not *fisiki*, for adjective form, whereas the adjective form of *nagasi* is not *nagasiki*, but *nagaki*.

6. Examples of the use of the forms cited.

[XI.] *Sibu-kaki no tane wo ukte, amaki kaki wa fayezdru*, if people sow seed of the sour fig, then do not grow figs, that are sweet. — *Tanba-kani yori karoki hitsuzi wo sasdyzi*, from the country of Tanba people offer a fox which is black. — *Tsikira-naki yumi*, a powerless bow. — *Tsikira-naki koto*, powerlessness. — *Nezumi no sirúki wo siro-nezumi to iu*, the white of mice (= mice that are white) are called white mice. — *Furúki wo sutete atarasiki ni tsuku*, forsaking the old, to apply oneself to the new. If objects are previously mentioned, from which a choice is made, then the expression is good: *Furúki no wó sutete, atarasiki no wó toru*, to reject the old (objects) and take the new ones [1].

不ｘ 山ｓ
貴ｒ 高ｓ
故ｓ

Yáma' takáki ga yáeni tattobarizu, a mountain is not considerable, because it is high; *Kídru wo muitte tattoni tó su*, because he carries wood, people consider him to be respectable.

下ｓ 下ｓ 顚ｓ
ヨ ニ ハ
リ オ サ
高ｓ モ 商ｓ
ニ ム ヨ
ノ ク リ
ム ．

Musasali va takáki yori fikiki ni ómomuku. Fikiki yori takáki ni noboru-koto atawadzu [2]. The bat turns itself with its head from above towards below. To climb from below towards above it may not.

[Xn.] *Kono fa akáki térite firagawaru*, the tree-leaf shining red flies around. — *Iy̓e wo takáku tsukúru*, to build a house high. — *Kari va takáku tonde tooku yori kítári*, the wild goose flying high, comes from afar.

---

[1] With regard to this construction compare, page 88, line 10, in connection with note 1.
[2] *Kenzo-gaki his-mon das-i.* XII. 11. verso.

CHAPTER III. THE ADJECTIVE. § 9.   111

Kuma-taka ré taka no oói-naru mono nari. Tsubasa tsu-yóku, ku-tsiu takúku tobi-meyuru ¹), the eagle is the biggest among the birds of prey; strong in the wings, he soars round high in the space of the air.

Tsubasa tsuyóku stands to the next sentence in the relation of coördination, in consequence of which its grammatical relation is left undefined and the adverbial form *tsuyóku* is used instead of the predicate *tsuyósi*. (See above, page 100 b. 2.). The same is the case with *ydsuku* in the proverb: *Aku-dgu ni iri-yásuku, zen-dgu ni iri-gátasi*, = to turn into the way of evil — (is) easy, to tread the way of virtue is difficult. — *Kore wé sore yóri yásuku ari-masu*, this is, from that out, cheaper, = this is cheaper than that ²). — *Nomi-tóku ori*, desirous of drink, to be thirsty. — *O kle háyaku ari-masu*, or merely *O háyaku ari-masu*, your rise is speedy, a greeting at setting out on a journey, and on the way. — *Yóku O kle nasáre-masita*, = well, your arrival has happened, i. e. be welcome. — *Wáruku nari*, to become bad. — *Wáruku natta*, has become bad. — *Yo foito takúku nari-masu* ³), it is too high (too dear).

Remark. Do the adverbs in *ku* in the three last expressions, which we have taken expressly from s. brown's *Colloquial Japanese*, p. XL, retain their adverbial character, or are they predicate adjectives? this question is answered in the place quoted in that work, „that whenever the form (the adverb in *ari* precedes a substantive verb, it is an adjective or a predicate adjective," a conception with which we cannot agree. As the Japanese has no properly called nominative termination, an adjective, to stand as predicate, cannot agree with the subject; these adjectives are governed as subordinate definitions, by verbs which, as regards their signification, answer to our „be" and „become," but their complement, when it is a noun, to the question where? how? or whereto? is in the case of *ni* or *de*, and, if it is an adjective, have *to* before them, in the equivalent adverbial form. *Ten-ki yóku ori* (*yahari*) or *Ten-ki yóku nari*, the weather is good, or the weather becomes good, is in a language nearer perfection in all respects expressed by *Tempestas bona est*, or *bona fit*, but the Japanese expression is, as far as form is concerned, equal to *Tempestas bene est*, or *bene fit*.

[§ L] *Kono misáki wa kunahada nagási*, this cape is very long. — *Ne no adzi amási*, the taste of the root is sweet. — *Kari ga tobu-kota takasi*, the flight of the geese is high. — *Yama toosi*, the mountain is far. — *Kono sodo nite*

---

¹) *Kasira-gaki hiu-mro dzu-i*. XIII. 6. recto.   ²) *Slopping-Dialogues*, p. 85.
³) Ibid. p. 87.

112   CHAPTER III. THE ADJECTIVE. § 9.

aiso faydai, in this strait the stream is swift. — *Siya ni udziudru mono ei akai* (変朱者丹), whoever goes about with red is red. — *Hi no atdru tobiro, taki-fi no kin-ziyo re dku kato daisi. Sahite daki nirori uo imu bʼsi*, in a place where the sun comes, (and) in the neighborhood of fire (the eggs of the silkworm) to lay is not good. In general people ought to avoid the nasty smell. — *Kono sima fito nasi*, this island is without inhabitants. — *Yosi to omóru*, to think that it is good. — *Ne no adri asisi yotte*, because the taste of the root is nasty.

[8a.] *Kono misaki nagusa san ri takari nari*, the length of this cape is only three ri (miles).

II. THE ADJECTIVE ACCORDING TO THE SPOKEN LANGUAGE.

The spoken language suppressing the k and the s of ki, si and ku, thus retains only the i and the u, which now immediately follow a vowel. Thereby they acquire

for *aki* and *asi* the form *ai* and for *aku* the form *au*, pronounced as *gu, go, ōo*.

„ *eki* „ *esi* „   „ *ei* „   „ *eku*   „   „ *eu*,   „   „ *eo*.
„ *iki* „ *isi* „   „ *ii* „   „ *iku*   „   „ *iu*.
„ *oki* „ *osi* „   „ *oi* „   „ *oku*   „   „ *ou*,   „   „ *ōo*.
„ *uki* „ *usi* „   „ *ui* „   „ *uku*   „   „ *uu*.

The easy written style, which follows the spoken language, has for *au, eu* and *ou*, no fixed written form; it supersedes the form of writing to be used by choice

タカウ (high)   also by タカ／, タコウ and ダコイ
ナガウ (long)   „   „ ナガン, ナゴウ „ ナゴイ
タウ (desirous)   „   „ タン, トウ   „ トイ
イウ (without)   „   „ ナン, ノウ   „ ノイ
レグウ (close)   „   „ レグン
トヲウ (far)   „   „   トヲイ.

Examples of the use of the forms.

[i for ki]. *Nagai matsu yori otauru yuki*, snow falling out of the long (high) pine-trees. — *Karoi kemuri noboru*, light smoke ascends. — *Hāna mimo no susuui uo osiru*, the flower fears the cold of the rime.

[i for si]. *Kure no jign akai*, the evening-sun is red. — *Kari ga tobu-koto takai*, the flight of the geese is high. — *Kore wa amari tiisai* [1]), this is too small. —

---

[1]) *Shopping-Dialogues*, p. 2.

CHAPTER III. THE ADJECTIVE. § 9, 10.   113

..*nagai* ¹), is long. — ..*takai* ²), is high. — *Futoga nai* ³), there is no one. — *Kore wa dziyai ga usui* ⁴), this is thin of texture. — ..*atsui* ⁵), is thick. — *Kore wa iroya koi* ⁶), this is dark of color. — ..*iroya usui* ⁷), this is light of color. — ..*iroga warui* ⁸), this is bad of color. — *Osoi kara* ⁹), as it is late. — *Yasui nara, tori-maioo* ¹⁰), as it is cheap, I shall take it.

[u for ku]. *Ari-gitau* or *Ari-gitoo*, difficult to be, abbreviated for *Ari-gitaku ori-masu*, it is difficult to be, - I am obliged to you. — *Yoo moosu*, for *Yoku mousu*, to speak well. — *Kasikoo suru*, for *Kasikiku suru*, to do wisely. — *Fukoo madzurdo*, for *Fukuku midzurden*, to be deeply involved in difficulty.

In Japanese vocabularies the expressions of the conversational are mostly distinguished from those of the book language by an antecedent △ or ○; thus

可 ¦ △ ソレデモコイ. — 否 ¦ ○ ソウレタ 事 ワナイ. カウアワナイ.

that is: the word *Kenari* of the book language is equivalent to *Soredemo yoi* of the conversational. — *Inaya* (= should not ...) of the book language is the same as *Soonito koto wa nai* (= such sort of thing there is not) or as *Kouto wa nai* (= so is there not) of the conversational.

DERIVATIVE ADJECTIVES.

§ 10. Adjectives in karū and garū.

By a fusion of the adverbial form *kū* with *arū* (being), the form *karū* is obtained (so being as the previous adverb indicates). *Nomi-tika-aru*, passes into *Nomi-takūru* (ノ ミ タ ク ル), desirous of drink or being thirsty.

Derivatives of this stamp take the same inflections as *ari*, — *aru* being the attributive, *ari* the predicate form; and as the adjectives in *ki* themselves, express a quality, to which the idea of activity is not allied, the derivative form *k + ari* expresses merely the continual presence of the not-active quality.

Waka-ki, young. — *Waka-ki toki ni*, in youthful time. — *Wakakūru toki ni*, while or as long as one is young. — *Wakakūri si toki yiri*, since the time when one was young.

Naki, not at hand, being without. — *Nakari*, continually not to be at hand.
Siró ki, white. — *Sirokūru*, continually white.
Yasuki, easy. — *Yasukūri*, continually to be easy.

¹) *Shopping-Dialogues*, page 8. ²) page 12. ³) page 6. ⁴) page 23. ⁵) page 24.
⁶) „ page 23. ⁷) page 33. ⁸) page 34. ⁹) page 41. ¹⁰) page 87.

Remark. This illustration of the derivative form *ari* explains the obscure §§ 65 and 67 of acominous *Kibō*. The *poru* there mentioned on page 65, lines 8 to 12, is a fusion of the genitive-termination, *ga* and *aru* peculiar to the conversational language exclusively. Joined to the Chinese word *Yet-ki* ¹), gladness, with it, it forms *Yekkigiru*, being full of gladness, synonymous with *Yekkinaru*, *Yokkiua*, being glad. See § 19.

§ 11. Adjectives in aru.

Ari, aru (有 ル), verb continuative, to be at hand, to be there, to exist, antithetical to *Naki* (無), not at hand, ... less. *Ari* is the radical (to be) and at the same time, but by exception, the predicate form (= there is); *aru* the substantive form (the being), which is at the same time used attributively (being), to derive adjectives from substantives. — *Iro ari*, = there is color or colors are there. — *Kumo ra iro ari*, = what concerns the cloud, there is color, i. e. the cloud has color. If the definition: „there is color" is to become attributive, then *ari* acquires the attributive form *aru*; the subject *iro* now becomes an attributive proposition of *aru*, and assumes the attributive form, thus the genitive termination *no*, in the spoken language, *ga*. *Iro no* or *iro ga aru kumo* means, literally: colors present being clouds, i. e. colored clouds or clouds which have colors.

The genitive termination *no* is often omitted in similar expressions, particularly when the attributive definition joined to *aru* is a verb, which is in its radical form: e. g. *Aski niroi aru ki*, wood (*ki*) of a bad smell. — *Niroi*, to smell, smell.

Examples. *Tsumi ari*, there is guilt. — *Tsumi aru mono*, a guilty person, criminal. — *Futá-kokóro no aru fito*, a man who has two hearts, a double-hearted man. — *Omoi fúdátsu aru kotoba*, a word (*kotoba*), that a couple (*fútátsu*) of meanings (*omoi*) has, an equivocal word. — *Kokóro-ada aru mono*, one who has a will, a firm character. — *Aya-aru ori-mono*, flowers having texture, flowered silk-stuff. — *Sai-rai-aru*, happy. — *Yamari-aru*, sickly. — *Koto-aru*, having business, busy. — *Fima-aru* or *sukima ga aru*, having free time. — 有ル功 人 *Kou-aru fito*, a man who has merit. — 有ル益 *Yeki-aru*, profitable.

§ 12. Adjectives in naru, na and tárá.

By means of the substantive suffix *narō*, which is, in my opinion, a fusion of the local *ni* and of *ari*, *áru*, and thus means „being lasting in...," from

¹) 悦ビ 喜ビ.

substantives and adverbs adjectives are formed, which indicate a possession of that which the root expresses.

The familiar conversational, and the epistolary style abbreviates naru to na. — Ki, yellow. Ki-uri, the yellow pumkin [1]. Ki-nāru or Ki-na nri, a pumkin that is yellow. — △ Fimóna tokóro, a place of rest. — △ Kirei-na nisi, a beautiful rainbow.

With the inflectional termination ni the radical forms of this class are used as adverbs. — Oŏi ni, greatly. — Tsuné ni, commonly. — Sugu ni, directly, straightly.

As words, which have naru for their derivative form are to be noticed:

1) Ooi [1] 大, great.   Ué 上, above.
    Tsuné 常, common.   Sitá 下, below.
    Mare 希, rare, seldom.   Maé 前, before.
    Sugu 直, right.   iya 不欲, unwelcome.

Examples of the use of the forms.

Fitó sono naye no ōi nāru wo sirū koto nāsi [3], = it is not the fact (koto nasi) that a man knows that his rice-crop is so large (ample). — 音ム呼ブハ大ヂ小ヂアリ。オヽイナレバハトノ大サアリ, In to ra doi wo ari; doi nāru ra fato no dotai ni, of parrots people have big and little ones: those which are big have the bigness of a dove. — Sono kou doi nari, his merit is great. — Kuri-ko no kataʷara naru taka-tokōro, a high place at the side of the silkworms. — Sukini nevuri si kaēiko ra doi (or sū) naru kawa wo nugi idzuru, = the silkworms that have previously slept, throw off the skin being (which is) upon them.

2) By means of naru, or na, Chinese words are made Japanese adjectives.

仁 ジャル, Zin-nāru, humane.
忠 チャル, Tsiu-nāru, sincere.
不忠 チャル, Fu-tsiu-nāru, insincere.
勇 チャル, Yuu-nāru, brave.

---

[1] Cucurbita Pepo ovifera LINN.
[2] Ooi, great, after the old writing 大, and the forms oohi, ooi, in the conversational language ooi, derived from oo, much, are frequently interchanged; the same writer frequently uses by turns ooisa (オヽイサ) and ooa (オヽア) for „great," and ooi-nari and ooki nari for „is great."
[3] Dai Gaku, VIII, 2.

眞シ實ジャル, Sin-zits-ndru, solid, real, sincere.
丁寧ジャル, Tei-nei-ndru, courteous.
綺麗ジャル, Ki-rei-ndru, beautiful, fair.
不綺麗ジャル, Bu-ki-rei-ndru, not beautiful.
樣ナ, Yau-na, ...ly, being as... — Yamino yau na, archwise.
悦喜ナ, Yekki-na [1]), glad, joyful.
笑止, Sio-si [1]), = cease laughing, feel pain. — Sio-si nari, it is not to be laughed at, it is sorrowful.

Tarú (タル), = te aru, is also used to form Japanese adjectives from Chinese words. — 現然タル, Gen-zen-tarú, apparent, public.

If more adjectives thus formed follow, linked to one another, then only the last has the attributive form tarú, whereas those preceding have the indefinite form tari.

君有側惡 Sü-tari, kan-tari, fi-tóru kun-si ari [1]), there is a prince,
子斐分分 stately, worthy, perfect.

§ 13. Derivative adjectives in ka.

The termination ka, in my opinion, allied to the adjective radical forms ke and ko (page 109 n°. 51), just as these, indicates, that the quality expressed by the radical word is present in a large degree or is strongly prominent. As evidence of the mutual affinity of ka, ke and ko may be adduced that the forms kanaru, kanari and kani, the first being attributive, the second predicate, the third adverbial, are frequently superseded by kiki, kisi and kiku. — For kanaru and kanari the conversational language uses only kána.

Adjectives of this class are:

Akiráká 明ラカ, bright, clear, light; allied to Ake, light.
Atatáká 温ラカ, warm; allied to Atatameru, to warm.
Furúki 遠ки, far. — Sono áto furuki wari or farukiri, his trace is far.
Kósiki 幽ки, remote, solitary. — Umi no kaze wa karaká nári, the sea-wind is no solitary. — Mitsi ga kósikami farukuna, the way solitary and far.

_____
[1]) Both expressions are taken up here, to illustrate the forms occurring in aoristorm Kiwras, p. 15, line 9 and 10 aloisa, „avois de regret" end pethias, „se rejouir"
[2]) Dai Gaku, III, 4.

Kiráraká 烏ラカ, brilliant; from *Kira-kira*, glitter; *Kirari*, glimmer, *mika*.

Komakí 細コカ. 細暫, fine; allied to *Komaméru*, to make fine, to make small. — *Komakana sand*, fine sand. — *Komakani*, adverb, to the most minute particulars; minutely, exactly.

Naderaká 椅ラカ, smooth, ironed out; from *Nadero*, to iron, to stroke.

Nameraká 滑ラカ, smooth, slippery; allied to *Nameru*, suck, and to *Namésu*, to make smooth.

Nodoká 悠然, set fair (of the weather); from *Nodo*, calm.

Ogosoka 荘ソカ, severe, strict. — *Oroka* 愚カ, 癡, stupid, obsolete *oróki*.

Orósoka 疎ソカ, negligent, lazy. — *Orósokanisu*, to neglect; allied to *órósu*, to lay down, put off.

Sadaka 異ク, 定, certain, sure, definitive. — *Sadaka ndri* or *Sadakrai*, it is certain; allied to *Sadámeru*, to define, fix.

Sidzuká 靜ク. 寂然, calm, still. — *Asa-ji ga sidzuka nari*, or *sidzukéna*, or *sidzukési*, the morning is so calm. — *Sidzukdai*, old-Japanese also *sidzukuni yuku*, to go softly, slink, sneak. The old form *Sidzukuni* pleads for the influence of the vocal harmony. (Compare page 62, line 2). The radical word *Sidzu* is preserved in *Sidzu-kokóro*, a calm mind.

Taviraká 平ラカ, or *Tairaki*, even, plane, flat; from *ta*, hand and *jira*, flat, thus hand-flat-ish.

Tsumá-biraká 詳ラカ, clear and plain, decided, settled; after the *Siwori* from *Tsumári*, concise and *hiraku*, to open. — *Tsumuibirakámi*, or old-Japanese *Tsumabirakéki*, adverb, plainly.

Wadzaki 僅ク, 僅, scarce; *Wadzakáni*, scarcely, hardly.

§ 14. Derivative adjectives in yaka.

Attributive *yakénaru*, predicate *yakúndri* (in the conversational language *yakánu*), adverbially *yakani*.

The derivative form *yaka* means as much as having the appearance of that which the root points out [1].

To the words of this class, which have passed from the old language to the new, belong:

---

[1] This notice of the meaning of *yaka* agrees with that which a Japanese etymologist gives of it: ヤカ、凡ソ物ノ形チ貌シノ詞ニシ. *Wa-gun-siwori*, under *yaka*.

Ashyaká 鮮ヤカ, 鮮明, fresh and bright as the morning (*asa*). Also *Azayaka*, *Azayagu*, *Asayuga*, *Azarakeki*. — *Asayakú náru iro*, a bright color. — *Kurenai no iro hana-huda asdyakú nari* 紅藍花ハ色ぞ甚ダヤ鮮ト明ラシ, the safflower is very bright of color.

Fiyiyaká 冷ヤカ, bleak, cold. — *Aki-kaze va fiyayaka nari*, the autumn wind is bleak. From *fiyu*, cold.

Ke-zayaka 氣ヶ晃ヤ, bright (of the weather).

Kirdriyaká 晶ラヤカ, glittering; also *kirabiyaka*, from *kirámi*, to glitter.

Komiyaká 積ミヤカ, 1) tight, close, dense; from *komi*, *komu*, to fill. — *Kusá ki komayukuno*, grass and wood close growing. — *Komayaka naru saké* 濃酒, strong beer. — 2) narrow, precise.

Maméyaka 眞メ成ヤ, sincere, unfeigned, true; from *Mamé*, reality.

Miyabiyaka 艶ビヤカ, 媛, splendid, beautiful; allied to *miyaburi*, courtly.

Nagóyakú 奶ゴ妖ヤカ, maidenly, graceful; from *Nayo*, maid.

Nigiyaka 賑ヤカ, busy, bustling. — *Nigiwari*, bustle.

Nikoyaka 婉ヤカ, fine, tender, soft, mild; from *Niko*, pleasing; fine.

Nobiyaka 舒ビヤカ, elastic; from *Nobi*, *u*, to stretch.

Odiyaká 隱ヤカ, calm, still; from *odáti*, *u*, to become calm.

Sawáyaká 爽ニ快シ, bright; gay; brave.

Sayaká 清ニ明ナ, ook *Sayakeki*, clear (of light and sound).

Sindiyaká 娜ドヤカ, 煖, supple, pliant; soft, flexible; also *Sindbiyaka*, from *Sinámi*, to bend (oneself).

Sindbiyaka 忍ビヤカ, secretly; from *Sinobi*, *u*, to hide; to suffer.

Sukúyaká 健ヤカ, 勇健, strong, full of power; also *Sakúyaká*, *Sakúyoká*, *Sukiyaká* and *Sukiyaká*; allied to *Saké*, support. (?)

Sumiyaká 速ヤカ, quick, swift; allied to *Susúmi*, pronounce *sumi*, to advance. — *Kawa-oso va midzu-naka wo fasiru-koto sumiyaká nari*, the motion of the river otter under water is quick.

Taweyaká 嫋ヤカ, also *Tawoyaka*, pliable, supple, soft; after Japanese etymologists from *Ta*, hand, and *Yowa*, weak, being the weaker sex, opposed to the man, called *Tawoya-me*; — allied to *Tawame*, *eru*, to bend. — *Nami kaze no tawóyakáni naru*, waves and wind become softer.

Wakayaká 天ヤカ, juvenile. — *Waka-ki*, young. — *Wakayaka náru samurai*, a youthful warrior. — *Yuruyaka* 徐ヤカ, limp; slow; allied to *Yurusi*, to loose.

§ 15. Derivative adjectives in **kóki** or **kóki**.

Kéki or **Kóki**, radical form **Ke** or **Ko** (濃), strong (of taste or color), already mentioned among the adjectives in *ki*, whenever it is joined to the root of another word, signifies that the object richly possesses that, which is mentioned by this word. Words of this stamp are chiefly characterized as old-Japanese, although not totally excluded from the modern language. The conversational language supersedes the attributive *keki* or *koki* and the predicate *kei* or *koi* with *kei* or *koi*, and the adverbial *keku* or *koku* by *keu* (*keo*) or *kou* (*koo*). The forms *keki* and *koki* frequently mutate with the derivative form *ku* (§ 13).

To this class belong:

Azara-keki 鮮ヶキ, quite fresh.	Ne-koki 睡濃キ, lying in a deep sleep.
Fúra-kvki¹) 亮ヶキ, very clear.	
Kiyo-keki 健ヶキ, 尤, very strong.	Nure-koki 濡濃キ, thoroughly damp.
Sámu-keki 寒ヶキ, very cold.	
Sidzu-keki 悄ヶキ, very calm.	Siton-koki 湿シ(濕)濃キ, wet-through.
Tsuyu-keki 露多キ, full of dew.	

§ 16. Derivative adjectives in **siki**, = ..like.

Adjective **siki** (レキ), adverbial **siku** (レク), predicate **sisi** (レシ), often, but not generally, **si** (レ); in the conversational language by the elision of *k* and *s*, mostly **sii** (レイ) and **sin** (レン), the last mentioned frequently pronounced as **hu** (ヒュ); substantive **sisa** (レサ); continuative verb **sikari, u,** = so to be. Root **si** (如レ), = so, Lat. *sic*°).

Siki means, just as ..like (German ..*lich*, Dutch ..*lijk*, ..*aardig*), equality with that, which is expressed by the root, to which it is joined. Being of a similar sound to the transitive verb *Siki*, *Siku*, = to spread, Chinese 敷, 發 or 布, it is indicated in writing also by these Chinese characters, thus by a rebus, which places the word indicated in a false light.

As in old-Japanese many of the adjectives in *ki* (§ 9. B.) occur with the termination *siki* or *ziki*, the Japanese philologers consider the *ki* as an abbreviation of *siki*.

---

¹) Distinguished from *Fáru ke-siki*, spring-weather.
°) 如シ。似シモノト云フ事シ。

CHAPTER III. THE ADJECTIVE. § 16.

Siki forms adjectives from nouns, from adverbs and interjections, and from verbs.

1) Denominative and Adverbial i. e. derived from nouns and adverbs are, e. g.

A-siki 悪シイ, 邪, bad. — *Kokoro no asiki mono*, any one bad in disposition, a person of bad character. — *Asiki tsuwa*, bad tools. — *Asiku manabu*, to learn badly. — *Fino teri-kōmu ca kanchada asisi*, ·· the entrance of sunshine (in an apartment where silkworms are bred) is very injurious. — *Yosi asi wo wakimaiesu*, – not once to distinguish the „it is good and it is bad," not to distinguish good from bad. — *Asikaru*, continuative verb, from *asiku* and *aru*.

Ara-siki 淡シイ, frothy; faint of taste; also *Ara-ara-siki*.

Aya-siki 奇シイ, 怪, wonderful; singular; from *aya!*, exclamation of surprise. *Ayasiki ame*, a wonderful rain, e. g. a stone-rain.

Bibi-siki 美シイ 敷, handsome. — *Faye-siki* 烈シイ, heavy; eager.

Fana fusiu- or *Hana kada-siki* 甚シイ, very, uncommonly; from *kanakada*, very.

Fisi-siki 久シイ, long ago, antithetic to *Sibiruku*, shortly, lately. — *Fiku-sii Hon-tsiyyu ni toworu koto fisisi*, it is long, that *Fiku-sii* has intercourse with our empire. — *Fisisa*, length of time. — *Iku fisisa ni mari-nubeki*, = what lapse of time is it?, how long is it ago. In *Fisa* is placed the meaning of 日去, i. e. the sun or the day goes hence, or has gone hence, which refers to *Fi nisisi*.

Fitó-siki 均シイ, 等, = of one sort; agreeing.

Fuso-siki 太シイ, thickish, stout.

Ikignsiki 如何シイ, interrogative, inquisitive.

Iya-siki 賤シイ, despicable, mean; from *Iya*, no!

Kana-siki 哀シイ, painful, pitiful; from *Kana!* alas! *Kanasiki kana!* how pitiful!

Kibi-siki 厳シイ, originally *Kimi-siki*, · masterly, authoritative, strict, severe.

Kudu-kudu-siki 瑣々シイ 敷, piecemeal.

Kuru-siki 苦シイ, *Kuru-kuru-siki* 苦々敷, tiresome, disagreeable, grievous. *Mi-kuru-siki*, disagreeable to be seen, ugly, misformed. Root *Kuri*, u, to reel (reel off cocoons).

Kuwsi-siki 妙シイ, 美, 委, fair, neat. — *Kuwsi-siki ma*, a fair horse. — *Kuwsi-siku*, neat, precise.

Madzu-siki 貧シイ, poor, shabby.

Mám-siki 正シ , real; from *Mám*, truth.

Munái-siki 空シ , without contents, empty; in vain; from *mi*, kernel, fruit and *na*, without; thus fruitless. — *Munái-siku niru*, to become empty; to give up the ghost.

Onó-ziki 同ジ , identical.

Sibi-siki 寂シ , 閑寂. 淋. 孤, rusty; alone (solitary).

Suzu-siki 冷シ , cool. — *Suzu-sikéru*, continually cool.

Tadái-siki 但シ , 眞 , proper, real.

Tuye-daye-siki 斷エ々シ 敷ヶ , often interrupted, by pausing.

Uré-siki 喜シ , glad, merry, joyful, pleasant. — *Watókuni mo uresiku gozáriimásu*, also I am joyful. — *Urísisa*, gladness. — *Urésisa kagiri nakéri*, the gladness was boundless. — *Urésikiru* or *Uresigáru*, = *urésiku-aru*, continuative verb, to rejoice. — *Fi-kdzu no ooi wo uresigáru*, to be glad at the greatness (*ooi wo*) of the number of days (at a long life). — *Urésusu*, transitive to make glad. — *Uré*, Yakutic *Yór*, joy. — The *Wa-gun Siwori* gives 得 (*e, uru*, to get, acquire) as root.

Utsukú-siki 美シ , lovely; agreeable; handsome; old-Japanese *Itsuka-siki*; allied to *Itsuku-simu*, or also *Utsuku-simu*, to love.

Yasá-siki 温和 , meek; honest, graceful.

Yoró-siki 宜ロシ , 雅 , apt, fit; well.

2) Verbal, derived by means of *siki*.

The transitive or intransitive meaning of the verb, from which adjectives are derived by means of *siki*, passes over to the adjective too, because *siki* is, by nature, neuter. On the manner, in which the derivation in one case or another is brought about, the Japanese etymologists, at least those, whose works are within our reach, preserve silence; they talk about it, indeed, but leave the matter itself in the dark. To be able to treat thoroughly and satisfactorily, this class of words, which, from an etymological point of view, belong to the most intricate, we ought also to be able to compare the forms, in which they occur in the different dialects of the popular language. As these are still unknown to us, we think we must confine ourselves to a mere indication of the most conspicuous phenomena.

Adjectives with a causative meaning derived by means of *siki* from causative or factive verbs, from verbs, by which, as it is known, to cause an action to take place or be carried out is indicated, and which in Japanese, as it will be seen, hereafter, are formed by changing the verbal termination *i* into *asi* (or for vocal-harmony sometimes into *osi*). From *Konómi*, = to like, to be fond of, is formed the causative *Konomási*, = to cause fondness for, to make one to be fond of, and from this the adjective *Konomdsiki*, = lovely. The adjectives, so formed, thus show, that in the nature of the object lies the action, expressed by the causative verb, to exercise or to bring to light.

To this kind of adjectives, among others, belong:

Ibukásiki 訝シ數ヤ, strange, wonderful: polite expression for: doubtful, unexpected: from *Ibukási*, и, to excite surprise, and this from *Ibuki*, и, to be surprised at something.

Isogásiki 閙シ數ヤ, 奈, 忙, busy; from *Isogási*, и, to make busy; and this from *Isogi*, и, to make haste. — *Isogásiki tokóro*, a busy place. — *Watákusi* wa *kon-nitsi* wa *isogásii* (私ワ今日ワ多シ忙シイ) [1], I have much business to day. As a variation of *Isogá-siki*, we have *Isogarasiki*, derived from the causative form *Isogarasi*, = to make busy, which proceeds from *Isogási*, и, = to be busy.

Itamdsiki or *Itasásiki* 傷シ數ヤ, 痛數, smarting, painful; from *Itamási*, и, to torture, and this from *Itámi*, и, to feel pain, to suffer.

Kónomásiki, lovely, agreeable, from *Konomási*, и, cause to like, to excite one's love, to attract a person; and this from *Konómi*, и, to be fond of. 好.

Medzurdsiki 珍シ數ヤ, 奇, exciting interest, interesting; from *Medzurási*, и, to excite interest, and this from *Mede*, *Medzuru*, also *Medzuri*, to take interest in..., to have gladly (愛). Distinguished from *Medzuráki*, important; costly. Every thing that is strange and rare, and however insignificant, an object of taste, is called *Medzurási*. If from *Me-tsuki* or *Mi-tsuki*, = to fix the eye upon a thing, an adjective with the signification of „attractive to the eye," must be formed by means of *siki*, we should obtain *Metsukdsiki*, as derivative from the causative form *Metsukási* (= cause one to look), but not *Medzurasiki* [2]).

Mutsukásiki, tiresome, grievous, vexing, 難, or also, by means of rebus, ex-

---

[1]) *Shopping-Dialogues*. p. 16.

[2]) This is an answer to the question, proposed in a. brown's *Colloquial Japanese*, XLI.

pressed by 六ヲ借ケ and 六ヲケ° 數ケ; from *Mutsukusi*, u, to vex, to grieve, make sad, and this from *Mutsuki*, u, whence the continuative *Matsukiri*, u, » to be grieved (or sad), is more in use.

Natsukdsiki 娚 綏, vulgo 慊ケ 數ケ, attractive, engaging. — *Fánanó miedri matsukdsi*, the scent of flowers is attractive. — From *Natsukisi*, u, make disposed, excite inclination or love; and this from *Natsuki*, u, to be inclined, have inclination to.

Omómakósiki 傑 歴ケ, also by contraction *Omogúsiki*, pronounced as *Omomydsuki*, attractive, engaging; from *Omó-mukdsi*, u, to attract, and this from *Omó-muki*, u, to turn oneself with the face (*ómó*) towards a thing. 趣. 趣一向. From *muki*, = to go to meet, arises a continuative verb *mukdsi*, u, to be turned towards; whence *mukurusi*, u, the causative form; from this is derived *omómakurdsiki*, to be continually attractive.

Omoósiki, causing to think of one, keeping another's thoughts engaged, and that in a good sense, thus engaging, dear, kind; from *Omordsi*, u, also *Omósisi*, u, to cause to think, and this from *ómóri*, u, to think (思).

Osorósiki 恐ラレヤ, frightful; from *Osorósi*, u, to make fear, and this from *Osóri*, uru, to fear.

Sawagúsiki 樂ラ 數ケ. 騷, full of rustling and noise, stormy, turbulent; from *Sawagúsi*, u, to make rustle, to disturb, to confound, and this from *Suwogi*, u, rustle, make a noise, be uneasy (慊ケ. 不安也). — *Siro sawoyusi*, the sea is stormy. — *Kokóro wo suwagdsu*, make the mind uneasy. — *Siru ca ari sawagusiku site mono wo kui-su* [1], = the monkey makes much noise and injures every thing. — The old-Japanese has as variation of *Suwogi* also *Sawugari*, rage, tear; *Sawayasdsi*, u, courage, and *Sawagúsiki*, full of noise.

Tanomósiki 可賴, trusty, a thing upon which one can rely; from *Tanomosi*, u, make trust, and this from *Tandmi*, u, to trust to, to rely upon.

Urámdsiki, exciting disgust; from *Urámasi*, u, make have disgust, to prejudice against oneself, and this from *srdmi*, u, to be disgusted with. 怨 . 恨.

Urdyamdsiki (vulgo, and by way of rebus 浦ヲ山ニ 數ケ), worthy of envy; from *ardyamdsi*, u, to make one envy, excite envy, and this from *ardyami*, u, to envy. 羨. 歆.

---
[1] *Kawa-yohi ha-ugo dsu-i*. XII. II. recto.

Uruwsiuki, uruwsiúsiki 悦ゞシィ. 美, charming; from *Uruwisi*, и, enliven, and this from *uriri*, *uróri*, to be enlivened, or charmed.

Udgawsiuki 訝ゞシィ. 不審, doubtful; from *udgawisu*, make doubt, and this from *utagari*, и (疑. 嫌. 忽), to doubt.

Utomsiuki, despicable, from *Utomulsu*, to despise, properly to estrange, and this from *utómi*, и, to be strange, to be despised. 陳.

Wadzuruwsiuki 煩ゞ敷ィ. 煩, tiresome, teasing, plaguing, from *Wadzuruasi*, и, to tease, and this from *Wadzaróri*, и, to be plagued.

Yddorisiki, hospitable; from *Yddorisi*, и, to lodge, take anyone in, and this from *Yadóri*, и (宿ィ), to lodge somewhere.

Yuwsiuki 和ゞレィ, calming, from *Yusdsi*, и, to make rest, to reduce to calmness, and this from *Yusi*, и, or *Yumi*, и, to come to rest.

Yorikobiniki, joyful, rejoicing, from *Yorikobisi*, и, to please anyone, and this from *Yorikobi*, и, to rejoice, to be glad. 歓. 喜.

Yakdsiki 悒ゞシィ, urging on, impatient; from *Yakúri*, и, to make go; to drive; and this from *Yuki*, и, to go.

§ 17. Derivative adjectives in KA-SIKI.

To the adjectives in *siki* unite the derivatives in ka-siki, ka-siku, ka-si; terminations, which are considered by Japanese etymologists as contractions of kamasiki, kamasiku, kamasi (for which *kawasiki* etc. also occur), and which are indicated in writing by 通ゞ敷ィ. The sign 通 means to go through or to make go through for...., in Japanese *Kayori* or *Kayowasi*. Is this character to be remarked as a rebus here, or is its signification allied to that of the Japanese termination? This question remains unanswered by the Japanese philologers. The writer of the present, leaves the rebus for what it is, and sees in the *kasiki* in question nothing more, than the frequently occurring abbreviation of sika-siki, of which the radical form *sika* (然ィ) is quoted among the adjectives in *ki* (page 109 n°. 72) with the meaning of „being so, such." Kasi is met with, and that as a substantive predicate verb with the signification of „is as much as," in simple expressions such as „Heer (Mister) *to ca kimi zo kasi*" [1]), – the word Heer is as much as *kimi*; whereas the continuative verbal

---

[1]) I borrow this satisfactory example from a metrical list of Japanese and Dutch words, by a Japanese dilettante.

form *Karu* (for *sikáru*) in *Karu ga yuéni* (= for reason (*yuéni*) of the (*ga*) being no (*káru*), that is therefore, on that account), is generally in use, and that to exclusion of *sikáru*. The derivative forms *kúsiki*, *kúsiku*, *kúsisi* or *kasi* thus answer to …ish, …some; whereas *kamásiki* is equivalent to a fusion of *siká-andsi-siki* (*masi*, = to be).

To this class of derivative adjectives, among others, belong:

Fódzi- (vulgo *Fúdzu-*) *ka-siki* 愧ヅ通ク敷ク 耻敷, timid; also *Fadzi-* (vulgo *Fadzu-*) *ka-andsuki*, or *-karésiki*; from *Fadzi*, blush; *Fadzu*, *Fadzuru*, to blush.

Fáru-ká-siki 晴ニ通ク, clear (of the weather); also *Fáru-karésiki*; root *Fare*, clear.

Kara-kari ga misiki, droll, jocose; from *Kura-gari*, to laugh, and this from *Kara kara*, = ha! ha!

Ne-ka-siki 寐ヅ通ク敷ク, sleepy, also *Ne-kamu-* (or *kara*) *siki*; from *Ne*, sleep.

Ya-kamdsiki 喧シク, noisy; from *ya!* an exclamation like Heh! holla! ho! [1]). — *Koko de yakamsiki wo sakeru*, here people prevent what is noisy. *Sidzuka ni site yakamasi nai* (寂不喧), it is quiet and without noise.

Yumé-ka-siki 夢ヅ通ク敷ク, also *Yumé-kama-* (or *kara-*) *siki*, as in a dream; from *Yume*, a dream.

§ 18. **Derivative adjectives in rá-siki**, = having a resemblance to....

They are generally denominative. **Ra** is instead of **ara**, which has arisen by the strengthening the final vowel of *ari* into *a*; *ará-siki*, by apheresis **ra-siki**, thus means: „such (*siki*) as were there…," or „so as if there were." **Makoto**, = truth; **Makoto-naru**, = being truth, true; **Makoto-ra-siki**, such as if it were truth, i. e. probable. *Makoto-rá-siki koto*, or *Makoto-rá-sisa*, probability.

Ra-siki therefore answers to the derivative termination ..ish, so far as it means having a resemblance to that, which is indicated by the root, as bluish [2]), whereas the Japanese termination given at the same time, to the adjective formed with it, a diminishing, frequently also a contemptible signification in addition.

The old way of writing the predicate form *Arasi* is 有ノ見ノ志ヅ. The presence of 有, which is here ideographically, with 'the signification of „to be

---

[1]) *Ya*, *yobi-kakeru koye ni iveri*, = *Ya* is said of a calling voice. — *Wa-gun siwori*, under *Ya*.
[2]) BRILL, *Nederl. Spraakleer*, 1854, § 49. 1. 1).

on hand, = Jap. *ari*," pleads for the correctness of the assimilation of *ra-si* to *ara-si*, and therefore against the supposition, that the *ra* used here might be the characteristic of the plural (§ 5. III. 1. page 50).

The dialect of *Nagasaki* has *rsaka* for *rasiki*.

Examples of derivative adjectives in *ra-siki*:

Otóko, man; *Otóko-rdsiki únna*, a manly woman.

Onnágo, woman; *Onnágo-rdsiki otóko*, a womanish (effeminate) man, = *onnáno yōu ni akondi-mōru otóko* [1]), i. e. a man conducting himself like a woman.

Warabe, *Warambe*, boy; *Warambe-rdsiki*, boyish.

Ko-domo, child; *Kodomo-rdsiki*, childish. *Kodomo-rdsiki hansi*, childish-talk. *Kodomo no yōu ndrá*, childlike.

Kimi, gentleman; *Kimi-rdsiki*, playing the gentleman.

Dai-miyou, = great name, imperial prince; *Dai-miyou-rósiki kélamoto*, a vassal, who plays the prince.

Baka, fool, madman; *Baka-rósiki*, stupid, foolish; *Baka-rdsiki koto*, stupidity, folly.

Uso, gossip, untruth; *Uso-rdsiki*, trifling.

The derivative *Fito-rdsiki*, from *Fito*, man, answers formally indeed to „human," must however, with a view to the examples quoted, have a signification, by which it is only applicable to a not human being, that acts humanly [2]).

Also words of Chinese origin are compounded with *rdsiki*, e. g.

Kou 功 ゞ, merit; *Kou-aru waza*, = a merit being deed, a deed, that really is meritorious. — *Kou-rdsiki waza*, an apparently meritorious deed.

Ri-kou 利 ” 口 ゞ, whetted mouth or tongue, eloquence. — *Rikou-ndrá fito*, an eloquent, witty (but not blunt) man. — *Rikow-rdsiki fitó*, a man, who plays the witty person or the orator.

Ai 愛 ゞ, kind; *Ai-rdsiki*, amiable.

Ka-wai, proper 可 ” 愛 ゞ *Ka-ai*, kind, agreeable. *Kawai-rdsiki*, amiable, lovely.

Kawai-rasiku naki koto, ungraciousness.

Bin-bou 貧 ゞ 乏 ゞ, poverty; *Bin-bou-rdsiki*, poorly.

---

[1]) Thus Mr. Oaas Y., when requested to describe the meaning of *Onnagarasiki otoko*, defined it.
[2]) We know this word alone from a Vocabulary, in which it was translated „menschlifierweise."

CHAPTER III. THE ADJECTIVE. § 19, 20.   127

§ 19. Derivative adjectives in beki.

Placed after the attributive form of a verb baki (可 き) signifies, that what the verb expresses may, can, must and shall happen. The predicate form is besi, the adverbial beku. — *Onna komo tsukasa wo sa-béki*, women may, can or will do this work — *Kore wa onna no sa-beki tsuwam nári*, this is a work to be done by women. — *Sa-beki*, = being allowed or able to do, is here conceived in an active sense, whereas the genitive *onna no* precedes as definition. Compare page 97 § 8. VI. — *Fitó-bitó kono tama wo tattomü*, every one values this jewel highly. — *Kore wa fitó-bitó no tattoma-beki tama nari*, this is a jewel, which every one may, can and shall value highly.

In the chapter on the verbs we shall refer again to *Beki*.

§ 20. Derivative adjectives in naki, = without, ...less, indicating the want of that, which is mentioned in the radical word.

Na-ki 無 き, in the conversational language Nai, from the radical word Na, = not, used substantively means „the good for nothing" or „something good for nothing," = nothing, e. g.: *Fito wo nai ga siro ni su*, to consider a person as good for nothing (of no value). *Nai ga* is genitive.

Used attributively it means „not existing;" *Naki-fitó* is a not existing man, one deceased; *Nai-mono*, a good for nothing, a not existing thing, a nothing. — *Fitó no naki-koto wo kiku*, to hear of a person's not existing (his death).

When *Naki* is preceded by an attributive definition of what does not exist, it answers to the suffix ...less. — *Tsikára-naki* or *Tsikara no naki yumi*, a powerless bow.

The predicative form Nasi, in the conversational language Nai, means the not being at hand of anything, be it thing or circumstance. — *Kono yumi wa tsikára nasi*, this bow is powerless. — *Iwou-ga-sima fitó nasi*, the sulphur island is without inhabitants. — *Ari nasi wo tow* 聞 き 有 き 無 き, to inquire about the existence or non-existence of a thing.

Adverbially Nakū (無 き), in the conversational language Ngu, Noo (ナ ゥ. ナッ. ノ ウ. ノ ッ). — Thence the continuative verb *Nakari* (= *Náku + ari*), not to exist. — *Náku nari*, to go to nothing, to die. — *Naku ni, su*, to be without..., to want.

Na and the forms derived from it will be found treated more diffusely in the chapter on the verbs.

§ 21. Adjectives with the negative prefix **Na**, or the Chinese 不 **Fu**.

Na, with negative power comes before adjectives as well as substantives, and causes them to express the contrary. This use of *Na* peculiar to the old language has been preserved in expressions as: *Na-yami*, = no rest (不安); *Na-yi* (ナキ), = no seat, for „earthquake" (地震); *Na-iri zo*, = not speak, = be silent!

The Chinese 不 *fu*, = not, as a pure negative prefix to Japanese words expressive of quality has also got into use. To the few compounds of that nature belong:

Fu-deki 不ﾃ出ﾃ来ﾙ, mis-chance, bad-growth. *De-ki*, to proceed, to be produced.

Fu-nari 不ﾃ實ﾘ, bad growth. — *Fu-nari no toxi*, a bad year.

Fu-nari-naru 不ﾃ形ﾉナル, misshapen; *Nari*, shape.

Fu-katte-naru 不ﾃ勝手ﾅル, uncomfortable, disadvantageous; uneasy; *Katte*, the winning hand.

Fu-mi-motai-naru 不ﾃ身ﾆ持ﾅル, behaving badly; *Fu-mi-motai*, bad behavior, Fr. *inconduite*; *Mi-motai*, behaving as it should be.

Fu-rachi no 不ﾃ埒ﾉ, extravagant; absurd; improper, irrational; from the Chinese *láei* (埒, vulgo 拶), after the Japanese pronunciation, *Ratxi*, limit, fence. — *Fu-rachi no koto*, what goes beyond limits. — *Ratxi no naki zon-zi yori* 埒ﾉナキ存ﾁ寄ﾘ, an irrational opinion.

Fu-sai-wai-naru 不ﾃ幸ﾋﾅル, unprosperous; *Sai-wai*, prosperity, luck, blessing; from *saki*, development, and *sawi*, growth.

Fu-shi-awase-naru 不ﾃ仕ﾚ合ｾﾅル, not lucky; from *Shi-awase*, chance.

Fu-sugure te inasu 不ﾃ勝ﾚﾃｲﾏｽ, not excellent, not being particularly well.

Fu-tsu-ggu-naru 不ﾃ都ﾃ合ｸﾅル, unfit, inconvenient, incongruous; from the Chinese 都ﾃ合ｸ, = altogether, the sum; thence *Toki no tsu-ggu ni yori*, according to the time.

More numerous are the compounds with 不ﾃ, which, adopted from the Chinese, and sanctioned by use as classical expressions, have penetrated even to the language of daily life.

As attributive definitions prefixed to Japanese words, they occur with the suffixes *no* or *naru*; e. g.:

不和ナル, discordant.	不作法ナル, unfashionable.
不幸ナル, disastrous.	不断ノ噺, unceasing gossip.
不孝ナル, unchildlike.	不朽ノ親シミ, imperishable friendship.
不足ナル, insufficient, not enough.	
不快ナル, indisposed.	不意ノ難, unforeseen difficulty.
不図ナル, indisposed, not well.	不圖ト, unexpectedly, by chance.

If the pure negative 不, of similar expressions is superseded by 無 (bu, = without), the meaning of the word undergoes a considerable modification, which is still frequently lost sight of. 不風ナル Fu-rei-naru, is uncourtly, and equal to coarse, clownish. 無禮ナル, = „without ceremony," and may also be rude behavior, which does not wound. 非禮, is a behavior, antagonist to the nature of politeness, thus misbehavior. 不時 fu-zi is untimely, i. e. not at the time fixed; 無時ニ, without fixed time, i. e. always; 非時ニ, wrong-time, the improper time, the time at which something may not happen.

§ 22. **Adjectives with a previous definition.**

Nouns, prefixed to an adjective as definitive, form with it a compound word, provided they are not characterized as an attributive addition by the termination *no.* — *Te*, hand; *Naga*, long; *Te-naga zaru*, long-armed ape. — *Kutsi*, mouth; *Omoki*, heavy; *Kutsi no omóki fitó*, a man heavy of mouth or tongue.

Examples.

Inisihé imá no na-taiáki fitó, High named (celebrated) persons of old and new times.
Te-bayu, asi-faya, = of hand quick, of foot quick; quick-handed, quick-footed.
Kotoba-fayasi, he is ready of speech. — *Kotoba-ooi*, he is woordy. — *Kutsi-jiróki*, broad-mouthed. — *Me-akáki*, red-eyed.
Mimi-tóki fitó, a man, sharp of ears, a quick-hearing man.
Fara-bútó, thick of belly, a paunch-belly, name of a fish.
Faráka akó (for *fara-aka akó*), a fish red of belly, the red-belly.
Omó-siróki, white or clear of countenance, friendly.
Mono-koye no naki yo, a night without sound, a dead night.
Kokóro-ne no firóki kotoba, a word ample of meaning.
Kokóro-ne wo warui fito, a man bad of disposition.
Ke-no ara-mono, ke-no niko-mono, rough haired beings, soft haired beings.

§ 23. The definition, that the quality in any object in full or relatively full measure is met with, is expressed by adverbs or definitions equal to them, which precede the adjective; as such are worthy of notice:

1. **Ma,** 眞ヾ, 真, in conversational language generally **Man,** = effectively, really; genuine unadulterated, indicates the full measure of the quality. **Ma-naka,** or **Man-naka,** 眞ヾ中ム, the just middle. — *Yumi no ma-naka wo tóru*, just the middle of the bow to seize, to seize the bow just in the middle. — *Man-naka no iye*, the middle house, standing between two others. -

Mán-firáki 眞ヽ平ヶヲ, quite level, even.
Mán-máraki 眞ヽ圓ヽヲ, quite round.
Má-yásaki 眞ヾ安ヶヲ, quite easy.
Mi-siroki 眞ヽ白ヶヲ, quite white, snow-white.
Má-kuroki 眞ヽ黒ヲヲ, quite black, jet-black.

Ma, = effectively, really, variation of *Mi* (實), in the same radical word, that occurs in *Ma-koto* (眞事, 眞言), = reality, truth. *Ma-gokóro*, an upright heart; *Mawe*, truth; *Mama-siki*, really.

2. **Itai-dan,** — 一段ヾ, a whole piece, adverbially: wholly. *Itai-dan utsukúsiki onna*, a woman in all respects beautiful. — *Itai-dan kek-kyu nóru*, in all respects excellent.

3. **Ikani mo,** = however, in all respects. *Ikani mo tsiisaki*, as small as possible. — *Ikani mo tayásiki*, as easy as possible.

4. **Zui-bun,** 随ヽ分ヲ, comparatively, so much as possible. — *Zui-bun fayáku*, pretty early; is also used with the signification of „very early."

§ 24. Absolute comparative.

Adverbs which, expressing a higher degree of the quality, come before the words of quality, are:

1) **Mo,** 最ヘ, vulgo 猛, yet, yet more; to be distinguished from *Mo,* = real, with which it frequently mutates.

Mo-yásaki 最ヘ安ヶヲ, easier.   *Mo-fayí* 最ヘ早ヶ, still quicker or
Mo-gami 最ヘ上ヘ, higher up.   earlier; already.
Mo-sotto 最ヘ些ヶヲ, yet less.   *Mo-sukini* 最ヘ少ヶヲ, yet a little.

Mo-sukasi saki ni, still rather earlier; just now. — *Koro wa onóri tsiisai*. *Mo-*

sukósi ookii no wo () mise ¹), this (case) is too small. Let me see one rather larger.

2) **Ookini**, 大キニ, greatly, very. — *Ookini furúki*, very antique. — *Ooki ni arái*, very rough.

3) **Sukósi**, 少シ, little, in slight degree. — *Sukosi takai tokóro*, a place high only in a slight degree.

4) **Nao** 猶ㇳ, old-Jap. **Navo** 猶ㇳ, once more so..., still more. — *Sore de nao yoks nari*, thereby it becomes so much the better. — *Sore dake nao yoróxi*, it is so much the better.

5) **Iyá** or **Iyó**, also **yá** or **yó**, 彌ｲ, ㇳ, 弥, = once more so..., farther, more; to be distinguished from *iya*, no. — *Iyá taka yáma*, the mountain once as high. — *Iyá medzurásiki*, still more interesting.

6) **Iyá-Iyá** or **Iyó-Iyó**, 彌ｲ ヤｸ, 彌ｲ ヤｸ, more and more; in the conversational language *Iyá ga iyá ni* also. — *Iyó-Iyó fukáki*, still much deeper.

7) **Masu-masu**, 益ス, more and more. — *Riyyu-kóku no mudzirari mdsu-mdsu átsuki nári*, the intercourse of both the empires extends more and more.

§ 25. The relative or real comparative.

1. If a quality be attributed to one object in the same measure as to another, the likeness, if it is quantitative, is expressed by **Fodo**, if it is qualitative by **Yguni**. Fodo (程) means quantity, Yguni, or Yooni (様ｽ), in the manner.

Nami va yáma-fodo takasi, the waves are as high as mountains. — *Nami va yuki no yguni siróxi*, the waves are white as snow. — *Yama-fodo*, = size of mountains, and *Yuki no yguni*, = in the manner of snow, are here adverbial definitions, which, as such, precede the words of quality *takási* and *siróxi*. The particle *va*, vulgo *wa*, is here necessary to separate the subject *nami* from the following substantive (*yama*, or *yuki*), which, as subordinate definition, belongs to the predicate word of quality.

San ri fodo tóoxi, it is so far as three miles. — *Iniyyu ni katakí*, = stony hard, i. e. so hard as stone. — *Zen fodo tai-setsu nárā mono ra nasi*, 無シ 善ｽ 程ｽ 大ｸ 切ｽ + ㇵ 者ｽ ハ, there is nothing so important as virtue; in the conversational language: *Zen fodo tai-setsu na* (or also *tai-zi ta*, 大ｸ 事ｼﾞ ﾀ) *mono wa nai*.

---

¹) *Shopping-Dialogues*, p. 2.

2. If a quality is ascribed to one object in a higher degree, than to another, with which the comparison is made, the latter is considered as the point of departure in the ascription and, as such, characterized by the termination yori (out), immediately precedes the word of quality, which does not assume a comparative form; thus *Nami va iye yori takasi*, = the waves are from houses out high, i. e. the waves are higher than houses. In this form of speech also the isolating particle va or wa is indispensible.

The Mongolian and Mandju, in respect of the comparative, follow the same way [1]). To the expression: „The horse is higher than the sheep," is equivalent in Japanese the expression: *Mumá va fitsúzi yori ooi nari* (馬ハ 大キ 於 羊 也 ナリ), = the horse — from the sheep out high is; in Mongolian *Morin anu chonin etse jeke*.

Examples.

Mei va koo-mooyori karosi (命ハ 鯉 於 鴻 毛 ナリ), the life is lighter than down. — *Ookami vo yama-Inu yori takesi*, the wolf is bolder than the wild dog. — *Olanda-funé ró Too-sen yori saki ni tsuyiku-yan ru*, the Dutch ship lands earlier than the Chinese. — *Kukuretáru yóri arúarúru va naxi*, = something more manifest than the hidden, is there not, there is nothing more manifest, than the hidden. — *Ri vo kiramete, Ten-ka vó osámuru-koto va — siyu yori ooi-náru va nasi*, what concerns the forming of the understanding, and the government of the state, there is nothing greater than the doctrine of CONFUCIUS. ... *yori sukúsiku naru*, less becoming than ...

Remark. No comparison is contained in the sentence: *Kono saka yori tsutai fikisi*, = the land (tsutsi) is of this steepness off low; as the words „of this steepness off (*kono saka yori*)" are an attributive definition of „land (*tsutsi*)," and not of the word of quality „low (*fiki*)."

The relative comparative may also be defined by means of one of the adverbs (§ 24), which indicate a higher degree of the quality; e. g.: *Wasi va kuma-taka yori mata-mata ooi nari*, the eagle is twice as big as the bear-falcon (the horned falcon). — *Kuma-taka va me-o mo dai-niyyu nina taka ni onáziku, taka yori ooi-nuru koto san bai veri*, with the bear-falcon (Spizaitos orientalis) the size of the female and the

---

[1]) Compare L. J. SCHMIDT, *Grammatik der Mongolischen Sprache*. St. Petersburg, 1831. S. 39. — CANON DE LA GABELENTZ, *Élém. de la Grammaire Mandchoue*, 1832, page 86. — *Characteristik der hauptsächlichsten Typen des Sprachbaues*, von Dr. H. STEINTHAL, Berlin, 1860 page 201

male generally is as with the hawk; his size (*ooinaru koto*) with relation to (*yori*) the hawk amounts to threefold (*san bai*); i. e. it is thrice as big as the hawk.

The object, with which the comparison is made, is also isolated by *va*, when the word expressive of quality does not immediately follow it, but is separated from it by a subordinate adverbial definition; e. g.: *Kono iyé yori va mata takasi*, is as high again as this house. — *Kono iyé yori va nao takasi*, is yet higher than this house.

If the object, with which the comparison is made is something which either has remained without notice, or is not expected, then it is characterized by the suffix *mó* (. also, even). *Kore yori mó oosi*, more than this also, or more than even this. — *Fuyêbusa to iru tori va taka yori mó fuyási*, the bird, called *Fayêbusa*, or the quick flier (it is the noble falcon) is fleeter than even the hawk. — *Kono fitó va are yori mo nao gakusiya de ari*[1]), this man is more learned than even he. — 草木ノ花ノ形ハ牡丹ヨリ大ナル物ハナレ *Sqŭ-moku no kwa-kiyŭ va Botan yori ooinaru mono vá nasi*, among the flowers of the vegetable kingdom there is none bigger than the piony.

Verbs also, which express a more or a less, such as **Mási**, **Masári**, **Masárari** (飯シ、ス、勝、優), « to be more, to excel (*praestare*); **Otórari** (劣ニ), « to be less, are used in the forming of comparisons; e. g.: *Idzure ga nandzi ni masáru* (孰飯於汝), who is more than you? — *Kono kuni ni masárite takara no iru kuni* (飯ラ茲ノ國而有ル寶ノ國), a country better than this country and rich in treasures. — *Ware ni masireri*, he has excelled me. — *Siro-mayu-kariko ni masáreru mono va nasi*, there is nothing, that surpasses the silkworm of white cocoons. — *Fitó ni otóru*, to be less than others.

Remark. When in the saying: „It is better not to go, than to go," deviating from the usual order of words, according to which one would be obliged to say „*Yukinu va* (the not going) *yuku yori* (than the going) *masi* (is better)," is expressed by *Yuku yori va yukónu ga mási*, a rhetorical inversion takes place, to make it appear, that the predicate „it is better (= Lat. *praestat*)" is of the most importance. Therefore the subject *yukinu*, as a subordinate definition precedes the predicate, but is emphatically characterized by *ga*, whereas the *yuku yori*, contributed to the comparison,

---

[1]) Compare RODRIGUEZ *Élémens*, p. 61.

isolated by va, is placed in front. Compare what is said on this subject, on page 64.

The poet supersedes yori ra by kara koso or gura koso; e. g.:

Uve miyo! Fana no sodatanu sato rd ndsi.
Kokóro gúra kiad mi ra igasikere ¹).

Plant and look! There is no village where flowers do not come up.
My outside is worse than my heart.

§ 26. The absolute superlative.

The absolute superlative is expressed by one of the adverbs, which imply the highest degree of the quality and precede the word expressive of quality. The adverbs are:

1) **Fana-fada, or hana-háda**, 甚 ハナハダ, very; old-Japanese Fata-fata, from futa, yet again. — Fana-fáda tukaki, very high. — F. sebáki, very narrow. — F. tôkasan ndru, very plentiful. — Tsubame tobi-kakeru koto fana-fada fayá-si, the flight of the swallow is very quick. — F. tai-atsu ni omóru, to consider of the most importance.

2) **Mottomo**, 最 モットモ. 甚. 尤, originally Mótomó, almost, quite. — Akabane no nari mottó mo yorúsiku, bitte mare nari, as to the standard of copper (the coin) is quite good, it is however extremely rare.

3) **Ito, Ito-Ito**, 最 イト. 太. 彌. 甚. 痛, very. — Ito yásaki, very easy. — Ito ósiki fime, a very lovely girl.

4) **Itatte**, 至 イタッテ, the gerund of itári, = arrive at the place to which one will come; as adverb complete, entire; utmost, highest. — Itatte yorósi, it is quite good. — Itatte fayáku, very early. — Sasakira katatsi itatte taiisóku sité koyé ooi nari, the wren is in form very small, yet in voice strong. — ...to kokóro-yaru ed mukoto ni Itatte oróka nari, mean that..., is indeed utterly stupid. Instead of it place the inversion: makutoni oróka nó Itári nari, is indeed the highest point of stupidity, if the logical accent is to be placed on itari. — En-in ainori ki no-doku no itari ni soro, 延を引し和す成ち気ろ毒ルノ至を=ソロ, delay is the summit of vexation.

The Chinese 至 si, = itátte, also is used to express the superlative, and that in composition with Chinese words: e. g.:

---

¹) A leaf in an album, written by FF AU-RAVA, 1862.

至ニ極ヲ, *si-góku*, top-point, utmost.

至ニ善ξ, *si-zen*, highest good, perfectly good.

至ニ妙ナ, *si-beo*, excellent.

至ニ要ξ, *si-yoo*, needful in the highest degree.

5) **Meppo** (メツポウ), which is said to be in use with the signification of „most," but only at Yédo, is known to us only under the form of *Meppou-ndru*, as synonym of *Mono-oudre nasi*, = caring for no danger, fearless, bold.

6) **Itai no**, —イノ, first; **Dai-itai no**, 第ダイ—イ, = the first. — *Tsuruga kita-kuni itsi no yoki mindto nari*, Tsuruga is the first good (the best) harbour in the northern provinces. — *Nippon itsi no takeki mono*, the bravest man in Japan. — On the other hand *Itsi* stands for *utsi*, = blow, in *Itsi fayáku*, = quick as the lightning. — *Tēn-ka dai-itsi no gáku-siya*, the first scholar in the empire.

7) **Itsi-ban**, —イ番ン, = first rank (see § 31. 1)). — *Itsi-ban yorósiki*, the very best.

8) **Sugurete**, 勝レ, excelling, surpassing. — *Sugurete medzuránki*, most interesting.

9) **Kitsúku, kitsuu** (酷ク), heavy, very. — *Kitsuu sui mono*, something very sour.

Very common also, are the following Chinese compounds with 最ξ, **Sai**, = very, utmost, which express a superlative:

最ξ上ジャウ, uppermost, best. 最ξ頂チャウ, the highest.

最ξ中チウ, middlemost. 最ξ前ゼン, first; with relation to time.

最ξ下ゲ, lowest, least. = just now, presently, a few mo-

最ξ初シヨ, very first, first begin- ments ago.

ning. 最ξ勤キン, most diligent.

§ 27. The relative superlative.

The relative superlative is characterised in that, that the objects surpassed are expressly named, and this naming, whether in the genitive, or in the local, is placed before the word expressive of quality, by way of a definition, and thus subordinate to it. The brighter of (or among) the stars is, after the Japanese manner of speaking, the brightest of (or among) the stars, *Fosi no* (or *Fosi no naka ni*) *akiraku ndru va*.

Examples. *Karasi fazikami va na no tattoki nari*, mustard and ginger are the principal of vegetables; or: *Na no tattoki va karasi fazikami nari*, the principal among the vegetables are mustard and ginger. — 薬之ノ中ニ之ノ勝ル [劣ル]者ヲ, *Kusuri no naka no masareru [otoreru] mono*, the best [the least] among the medicines.

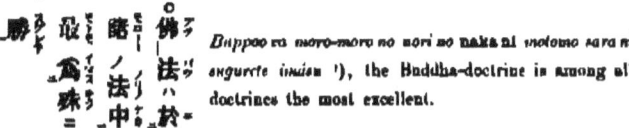
Buppoo wa moro-moro no nori no naka ni motomo sara ni sugurete imasu [1]), the Buddha-doctrine is among all doctrines the most excellent.

§ 28. The excess in a quality is expressed by:

Amári, 餘リ, 余, = excess, adv. excessively, too..., *Tsikara no amari*, excess of strength. — *Amári gin*, excessive money. — *Kore wa amari tsiisai*, 是ワ余リ小サイ [1]), this is too small. — *Kore wa amari nagai* [1]), this is too long. — *Kore wa amari iro ga koi* [1]), this is too dark of color. — *Kore wa amari dzi yai ga dzusi* [1]), this is too thick of stuff.

Yo-fodo, 余ス程ド, = excess, excessive, too..., = *Amári*. — *Sore de wa yo-fodo takáku nari-masu*, 夫レデワ余ス程ド高ク直グナリマス* [1]), then it becomes too high (too dear). — *Yo-fodo osói* [1]), it is too late.

---

[1]) *Nippon-ki*, Vol. 19, page 25 verso.
[2]) *Shopping-Dialogues*, page 2.   [3]) page 5.   [4]) page 23.
[5]) „ page 24.   [6]) page 37.   [7]) page 41.

CHAPTER IV.

NUMERALS.

The Japanese language has its own numerals; but with the introduction of the Chinese system of measures, weights and reckoning of time, the Chinese numerals and the Chinese marks of number came early and generally into use. Thefore one has to do with two sorts of numerals, with the Japanese and with the Chinese. The Japanese are connected with Japanese words, and the Chinese with Chinese.

§ 29. The ancient Japanese cardinal numbers are:

ヒト,	Fitó (F'tó, H'tó) . . . one.		コヽノ,	Kôkónó . . . . nine.
フタ,	Futá (F'tá) . . . . two.		トヲ,	Tóo, : once ten.
ミ,	Mí . . . . three.		ソ,	So, ten, termination of tens.
ヨ,	Yo . . . . four.		モヽ,	Momo . . . . hundred.
イツ,	Itsú . . . . five.		ホ,	..fo, ..vo, as termination of hundreds.
ム,	Mû, Muyu . . . . six.			
ナヽ,	Naná . . . . seven.		チ,	Tsi . . . . thousand.
ヤ,	Yá . . . . eight.		ヨロヅ,	Yórúdsú . . . . ten thousand.

The vulgar may say for *Fitó* (1) and *Fútsemo* (9), by way of abbreviation, *Hi* and *Kokó* also. Oral enumeration by *mono* t.

These radical forms are used in the forming of compound words in which, according to the principle fixed in § 0. I. A., the idea of number is supposed to be already combined with the object, e. g.:

Fitó-ei no fána, = one day's flower. — *Fitó-go no sake*, = one night's rice-beer, i. e. *sake*, that is only one night old. — *Fitó-fina*, one-flowered.

Fatá-go, a twin. — *Fitá-gokóro*, a double heart. — *Fitá-mari*, an hermaphrodite. — *Fitá-oyá*, the parents. — *Fitá-tabi*, twice. — *Fitá-na no sima*, a two-named island.

Mi-ka, the day (*ka*), which has the number three as characteristic, the third day; also the period of three days (*triduum*). — *Mi-ka-tuki*, = the third-day-moon, the moon of the third day. — *Mi-tose*, the year three, also the period of three years (*triennium*). — *Mi-kusá no kayu*, = three-herbed pap.

Yo-mo, the square. — *Mu-tose*, the year six, also the period of six years. — *Mu-tose no*, six yeared. — *Nana-yáma*, the Seven mountains.

Used as substantive numerals, the cardinal numbers from 1 to 9 take the suffix ツ *tsu*, which just as the Chinese numeral-substantive 個 (*ko*), with which in the most ancient writings [1]) it is assimilated, means, originally, a piece of bamboo and, in a general sense, in the counting of articles, is taken for „piece, number" [2]). Consequently we have the following compound nouns:

Fitó-tsu (*F"tóts'*, *H'tóts'*) . . one.	*Mu-tsú* . . . . six.
Futá-tsu (*F"tóts'*) . . . . two.	*Nána-tsu* . . . . seven.
Mi-tsu . . . . three.	*Yá-tsu* . . . . eight.
Yo-tsú . . . . four.	*K'okáno-tsu* . . . . nine.
Itu-tsú (*Its'ts'*) . . . . five.	

These numerals answer to the question: *Iku-tsu* (幾ツ), how many pieces?

Fitó-tsu-fa, a single leaf [3]). — *Mu-tsú-hána*, or *Mu-tsú no hána*, flowers to the number of six, being *Mutsú* characterized by the genitive termination *no* as a noun used attributively.

---

[1]) *Nippon-li*.

[2]) When, in 1857, I published the *Proeve eener Japansche Spraakkunst* von DONKER CURTIUS, I considered this *tsu* as the old genitive termination.

[3]) The name of *Avratsdam Longue*.

By combination with *ari* or *ori* (= to be), Fitó, Futó, Mi and Yo form the words **Fitári** (獨 リ), **Futari** (二 ツ 人 リ), **Mittari** (三 ニ 人 リ), and **Yottari**, individual, alone; — pair, both; — triad, three together; — four; — nouns, which are only applicable to persons, and thus are used as substantives, as well as attributively. — *Kwa-si ra wno fitóri no tsutsdhimu*, the philosopher attends to his own person, himself alone. — *Ika-tari*, how many persons?

The tens: 10, 20 to 90, consist of the cardinal numbers followed by ソ, so, which means ten (just as ..ty in twenty). *Mi-so*, three ten, " thirty. If they are used as substantive numerals, they take as suffix, (instead of ソ, *tsu*) チ, tsi, which is only a modification of *tsu*, and for the sake of euphony also changes to チ", dsi. *Mi-so-dzi*, = thirty-number. *Mi-so-dzi no hána*, flowers to the number of thirty. Let this チ be distinguished from ヒ *zi*, for *Misozi* means the age of 30 years (三 ニ 十 ソ 歳 ヒ).

The tens are:

Radical form.	Compounds with *tsi*
トソ, *Toó*, also *To*, contracted from F'tóso, = once ten.	トソチ, *Toí-tsi*, one ten.
(ソタソ, twenty, not in use.)	ソタチ, *Futá-tsi*, / ハタチ, *Fatá-tsi*, } two tens.
ミソ, *Mi-so*, thirty.	ミソヂ, *Mi-so-dzi*, number of thirty.
ヨソ, *Yo-so*, forty.	ヨソヂ, *Yo-so-dsi*, number of forty.
イツソ, *Itsu-so* (Iso-so), commonly:	イソヂ, *i-so-dzi* (iso-si-dzi), number of
イソ, *I-so*, fifty.	fifty.
ムソ, *Mu-so*, sixty.	ムソヂ, *Mu-so-dzi*, number of sixty.
ナソ, *Naná-so*, seventy.	ナソヂ, *Naná-so-dzi*, „ seventy.
ヤソ, *Yá-so*, eighty.	ヤソヂ, *Yá-so-dzi*, number of eighty.
ヨノソ, *Kókono-so*, ninety.	ヨノソヂ, *Kókono-so-dzi*, „ ninety.

モ ヽ, *Momo*, a hundred; in combinations ṇ,, -jó. -ro, -λo; thence Yo-ro, 400, — I-ro, 500, — Ya-ro, 800); others we have not met with.

チ, *Tsi*, thousand; チ ヽ, *Tsi-tsi*, thousands.
ソタヽ, *Futa-tsi-tsi*, two thousand. — ナヽチ. *Nanú-tsi*, nine thousand.
ヨロヅ, *Yóró-dzu*, ten thousand. — モヽチ, *Mamo-tsi*, a hundred thousand.
モヽヨロヅ, *Momo-yórúdzu*, a hundred times ten thousand, or a million.
ヤモヨロヅ, *Yaso-yórúdzu*, eight hundred times ten thousand, or eight millions.

140 CHAPTER IV. NUMERALS. § 29.

The Japanese numbers *Momo*, *Tsi* and *Yórodzu* are generally used in a general sense for many and all; *Momo-kusa*, all plants; *Tsi-tose*, many years; *Yórodzu no mono*, all things; *Momo-tsi-dori*, all birds ¹).

If a numeral precedes another numeral in its radical form, then it is the attributive definition of such: *Mi-yotsu* is thrice four; *Miso-yotsu*, thirty times four.

Two and thirty, on the other hand, is expressed by *Misodzi amári* (or simply *mári*) *fitátsu*, i. e. a number of thirty plus a number of two. One counts thus:

        Eleven . . . . *Tod-tsi mári fitótsu.*
        Twelve . . . . . .   „ „ *futdtsu* etc.
        One and twenty, *Fatátsi mári fitótsu* etc.

Mu-si-tsi mári mitsi no kuni (六十余り六之國), the six sixty and countries, — *Ya-so yorodzu no kuni*, eight hundred times ten thousand gods.

The saying: „It is more than 1792470 years, since the heavenly parents descended from heaven," we find in the ancient chronicle *Nippon-ki* III. 2 verso, expressed by:

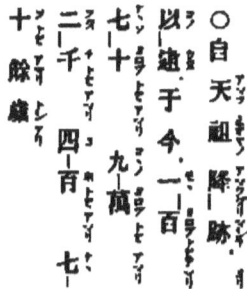

Amatsu mi-oyá no ama-kudári-másite yóri konokata.

Momo yórodzu tose (100 × 10000 years) *amári nanáso yórodzu tose* (70 × 10000 years) *amári kokonó yórodzu tose* (9 × 10000 years) *amári jutátsi tose* (2000 years) *amári yo-so tose* (400 years) *amári nanáso* ²) *tose* (70 years) *amári tosi ári.*

The numerals in *tsu* and *tsi* serve as nouns substantive and are also used, with or without the genitive termination no, as attributives. *Kono sima en ni fitátsu ni site, omó yotsu ari,* this island (the island of the four countries, *Si-kóku*) is of body a unit, and has of faces four in number.

---

¹) *Momo-tsi-dori* is also the name of the thrush, that imitates the voice of all birds.
²) The original, printed with some worn out forms, has *nono* instead of *nanaso*.

§ 30. The Chinese cardinal numbers, after the Japanese pronunciation. The first column contains the number in full.

壹 . 一チ, ヅ, Itai, Itsŭ (*its'*) .... one.
貳 . 二ニ, Ni .... two.
參 . 三ミ, San .... three.
肆 . 四シ, Si ¹) .... four.
伍 . 五ヅ, Go (*no, ngo*) .... five.
陸 . 六ヅ, ヅ, Rokŭ, Riku .... six.
柒 . 七チ, Sitsi (*s'tsi,* at Yedo *h'tsi*) .... seven.
捌 . 八ヅ, Fŭtsi (*hitsi*) .... eight.
玖 . 九ヅ, ヅ, Kiu, Ku .... nine.
拾 . 十ヅ, ヅ ¹), Siyu (at Yedo *dziu, dśiu, dźi,* Eng. *ji*), ten.
百ヅ, Fiyak' (*hyak'*) .... a hundred.
千ヅ, Sen .... a thousand.
萬 . 万ン, ン, Man (*bun*) .... ten thousand.

The number of the tens, hundreds, thousands and tens of thousands is more definitely determined by the units preceding them, thus:

イヅヅユ, *In-siyŭ*, ten.	ヅ ビヤク, *Go-fiyak'*, five hundred.
ニ ヅユ, *Ni-ziyu*, twenty.	ロクビヤク, *Rop-piyak'*, six hundred.
サンヅユ, *San-ziyu*, thirty.	レチビヤク, *Sitsi-fiyak'*, seven hundred.
レ ヅユ, *Si-ziyu*, forty.	ハチビヤク, *Fap-piyak'*, eight hundred.
ヅ ヅユ, *Go-ziyu*, fifty.	ク ビヤク, *Ku-fiyak'*, nine hundred.
ロクヅユ, *Rok'-ziyu*, sixty.	イヅセン, *In-sen*, one thousand.
レチヅユ, *Sitsi-* (*h'tsi*) *ziyu*, seventy.	ニ セン, *Ni-sen* etc., two thousand.
ハチヅユ, *Fatsi-ziyu*, eighty.	イチマン, *Itsi-man*, once ten thousand.
ク ヅユ, *Ku-ziyu*, ninety.	ニ マン, *Ni-man*, twice ten thousand.
イヅビヤク, *Ip-piyak'*, one hundred.	ヅユマン, *Ziyu-man*, 10 × 10000.
ニ ビヤク, *Ni-fiyak'*, two hundred.	ニヅユマン, *Ni-ziyu-man*, 20 × 10000.
サンビヤク, *San-biyak'*, three hundred.	ビヤクマン, *Fiyak-man*, a million.
レ ビヤク, *Si-fiyak'*, four hundred.	ニビヤクマン, *Ni-fiyak-man*, two mill.

---

¹) The numeral *Si* (4) is mostly avoided in composition with nouns, and superseded by the Japanese numeral *Yo* because *Si* also means „to die."

²) The written form *チウ* would, in all respects, answer rather to the Yedo pronunciation, is however, in

142   CHAPTER IV. NUMERALS. § 30, 31.

By the suffixing additional numbers all possible numbers are expressed; thus: *Ziyu man itsi*, 10000. — *Is-sen sap-piyak' roku ziyu roku nen*, the year 1866. The number is intended here as an attributive definition belonging to this year. If however the meaning is 1866 years, then the number is preceded by the adverbial definition *Oyóso*, 凡ソ (pron. *óyóso*), = in sum, together, and the number itself followed by a numeral substantive (see § 37). 凡ソ六ヶ年ノ間ニ, *Oyóso roku ka nen no aida*, = within six years. The necessity of taking up *oyóso* in the translation, naturally disappears in every language, that has a plural.

To a Japanese word, the Chinese numerals are connected by the genitive termination *no*. — *Ziyu ni no iro*, twelve sorts.

§ 31. **Ordinal numerals**, the first, the second. As the most in use are:

1) The Chinese numbers *Itsi*, *Ni*, *San* etc., followed by 番ン *ban*, that means watch, and number. To the question 幾ノ番ン, *Iku-ban*, what number?, answer

一ノ番ン, *Itsi-ban*, number one, i. e. the first.
二ノ番ン, *Ni-ban*, number two, i. e. the second.
三ノ番ン, *Sam-ban*, number three.
四ノ番ン, *Yo-ban*, number four, exceptionally for *Si-ban*.

2) The Chinese numbers, preceded by 第ノ *Dai*, = series; thus: 第一ノ, *Dai-itsi*, = one according to order, i. e. the first. — *Nippon-ki ken dai ni ziyu sitsi*, = Japanese chronicle, volume 27, literally: 27 according to the order of the volumes. 第ノ三ノ子ン, *Dai-san si*, the third son.

3) The compounds *Itsi-ban*, *Ni-ban*, *Sam-ban*, etc., preceded by 第ノ *Dai*; thus *Dai-itsi-ban*, *Dai-ni-ban*, *Dai-sam-ban*, first, second, third. — *Dai-yo-ban*, fourth, exceptionally for *Dai-si-ban*; so also *Dai-ziyu-yo-ban* (14th), *Dai-ni-ziyu-yo-ban* (24th).

With the genitive termination *no*, these three sorts of compounds become attributive.

If only two objects are to be counted, the difference is made by 前ン *Sen* and 後ン *Go*, before and after. If the arrangement is limited to three classes,

---

Japan itself, not yet adopted. — By a mutation of the French letters *j* and *y*, in the Supplement to *no wa*. Or. from page 15 *you* is generally found improperly for *jou* (伊).

they are distinguished as the topmost, middle and lowest, by 上 *Zyoo*, 中 *Tsiu* and 下 *Ge* ¹), or as foremost, next and last, by *Saki*, *Tsugi* and *Ato* or *usiro*. — 上, 種, 中, 種, 下, 種 is the seed of the first, second, third quality.

The first, with reference to the time, is expressed by ハヅ *fatsu*, or ハジメノ *fazime no*, = first; *Fatsu-mono*, the firstlings, the first fruits; *Farime no tosi*, the first year (of a period).

§ 32. The iterative numerals, once, twice etc., are:

Japanese, to the question:	Chinese, to the question:
Iku-tabi, 幾 度, how often?	*Nan-do*, 何 度, how often? ²)
Fitó-tabi, once.	一 度, *Itsi-do*, once.
Fiitó-tabi, twice.	二 度, *Ni-do*, twice.
Mi-tabi, thrice.	三 度, *San-do*, thrice.
Yo-tabi, four times.	四 度, *Yo-do*, four times.
Itsú-tabi, five times.	*Si-do*, 4°.
Mu-tabi, six times.	五 度, *Go-do*, five times.
Nand-tabi, seven times.	六 度, *Rok'do*, six times.
Ya-tabi, eight times.	七 度, *Sitsi-do*, seven times.
Kokóno-tabi, nine times.	八 度, *Fatsi-do*, eight times.
To-tabi, ten times.	九 度, *Ku-do*, nine times.
In numbers higher than 10 the Chinese numbers also are compounded with *tabi*; thus	十 度, *Ziyu-do*, ten times.
Ziyu-itsi-tabi, eleven times.	十 一 度, *Ziyu-itsi-do*, eleven times.
etc.	etc.

Momo-tabi, 百 度, a hundred times; many times. — *Tsi-tabi*, 千 度, a thousand times; many times. — *Tsi-tabi momo-tabi*, 千 度 百 度, a thousand times and a hundred times; often. — *Tabi-tabi*, 度 々, as often.

Tabi, with which the Japanese cardinal numbers form a compound word, means journey; *Tabi-bitó*, a traveller.

---

¹) The *pron*.: *Kami*, *Naka*, *Simo*, is in the case in question, according to the oral communication of a native of Yedo, there at least, not in use.

²) Also how many degrees: *Itsi-do*, 1°, *Ni-do*, 2°, etc.

三ゝ 四ゝ 度 ル, *San yo do*, three to four times; *San si do*, 3° to 4°.

By suffixing **Me** (目 ル), which means eye and, figuratively, mark, these iterative numerals become ordinal numbers, which with the genitive inflection *no* are also attributive. — *Iku-tabi-me*, 幾ゝ度ゞ目 ル, what number of times? — *Fitó-tabi-me*, or Chinese 一ゞ度 ル 目 ル, *Itsi-do-me*, the first time. — *To-tabi-me no hanasi*, a story for the tenth time.

§ 33. The doubling or multiplying numerals, single, twofold etc., consist of the Jap. noun へ, ye or he, vulgo 工, ye or e, = fold (German *fach*), preceded by the Japanese cardinals. To the question *Iku-ye* (幾ゝ重 ル), = how manifold? answer:

Fitó-ye, single.   *Itsu-ye*, five-fold.   *Yá-ye*, eight-fold.
Fitá-ye, two-fold.   *Mú-ye*,   } six-fold. *Kokúno-ye*, nine-fold.
Mi-ye, three-fold.   *Mu-ed* (obsol.),}   *To-ye*, ten-fold.
Yo-ye, four-fold.   *Naná-ye*, seven-fold.   *Fatá-ye* (obsol.), twenty-f.

Fitó-ye no fana, a single flower (*flos simplex*). *Yo-ye no fana*, an eight-fold, i. e. a full flower (*flos plenus*).

The counting by pairs is expressed by the Chinese 倍 ア (also 陪), *bai*, double, pair, in connection with Chinese numerals, thus:

一ゞ 倍 ア, *Itsi bai*, one (or a) pair.   四 ス 倍 ア, *Yo bai*, four pair.
二 ア 倍 ア, *Ni bai*, two pair.   十 ジ 倍 ア, *Ziyu bai*, ten pair.
三ゝ 倍 ア, *San bai*, three pair.   百 ヒ 倍 ア, *Fiyakw-bai*, a hundred pair.

Instead of *bai*, 雙 ジ *soo*, pair is also used. — 一ゞ 雙 ジ *Is-soo*, one pair.

§ 34. For sort numbers, as one sort, two sorts etc., serve the Chinese numbers compounded with the Chinese 種 ジ *siyu* (pron. su), which means sort, kind. They are, after the Yédo pronunciation:

イ シ レユ, *Is-su* . . . . one sort.   ロク レユ, *Rok'-su* . . . . . six sorts.
ニ レユ, *Ni-su* . . . . two sorts.   シチ レユ, *Sitsi-su* . . . . . seven sorts.
サン レユ, *San-su* . . . . . three sorts.   ハチ レユ, *Hitsi-su* . . . . eight sorts.
シ レユ, *Yó-* (not *Si-*) *su*. . four sorts.   ク レユ, *Kú-su* . . . . . . nine sorts.
ゴ レユ, *Go-su* . . . . . . five sorts.   ト レユ, *Tó-si*, etc. . . . ten sorts.

Ren-ziyak' ni, wo no nagaki to mizikaki to no ni-siyu ari, of the bird *Ren-ziyak* (*Bombyciphora*) there a two sorts: as well a long- as a short-tailed.

CHAPTER IV. NUMERALS. § 34, 35.   145

With the termination *no* these substantives are used attributively: *San-siyu no sin-too*, the spirit-service of three kinds.

§ 35. To express the distributive numbers, *one at a time, two at a time*, etc. are used:

1) the Jap. adverb ヅツ, *dsú-tsú*, pron. *dzts*, = at a time, preceded by the Jap. numerals *Fitó-tsu, Fatd-tsu* (= one piece, two pieces), or also by the Chinese numerals in connection with the object counted. *Dzutsu*[1]) is expressed by 宛ラ. To the question *ikú-tsu dzutsu*, 幾ィ宛ラ, how many pieces at a time? answer:

    Fitó-tsu dzutsu, 一トッ宛ラ, one piece at a time.
    Fatd-tsu dzutsu, 二タッ宛ラ, two pieces at a time.

Nara wó fatd-sudzi dzutsu fúru, ropes are spun (*fúru*), two pieces at a time. As it appears, here the accusative *nara wo* (rope) is the objective direct to *faru*, whereas *fatd-sudzi dzutsu*, by way of adverbial definition, is placed between the object and verb. — 一ś日ニ二ニ三シ度ドアツ, *Itsi-näsi ni san do dzutsu*, twice or thrice a day each time. — In accordance with this is the saying: *Ano otóko no kodomo ni Too hiyáku* (壹百) *wo itsi-mai dzutsu O yari nasdre*[2]), = give to these boys a *Too hiyáku*, one piece at a time. — 一ś色ś十ゼ二ニ反ゼ宛ラ 有ラマス, *Fitóiro ziyu-ni tan dzutsu ari-másu*, of one and the same color, twelve pieces at a time are at hand. — 二ニ丈ジ八タ尺シ宛ラ、二ś切ニ, *Ni ziyoo fassak dzutsu no fatd-kire*[3]), two pieces of 2 ziyoo 8 šak at a time (= 28 Jap. feet).

One, two, three or four at a time, when persons are spoken of, is expressed by *Fitóri dzutsu, Futdri dzutsu, Mitóri dzutsu, Yottóri dzutsu*. — *Ikutóri dzutsu*, = how many persons at a time? (see § 20.) — *Ko fúudni fitóri dzutsu noritaru fundkató roku-ziyu fodo kogi-kitdri*, sailor to the number of sixty, seated one at a time in a small boat, came rowing.

---

[1]) The common written form 宛ラ is incorrect, as it, according to the rule given on page 11, answers to *dzudzu*. Misled by indistinct examples in badly printed Japanese books we have in our *Spraakleer* of 1857, page 64 improperly adopted *Fito-dzudzu* instead of *Fito-tsu dzutsu*.

[2]) z. BROWN, *Colloquial Japanese*, N°. 171. — *Tsu hyak*, i. e. „a hundred (cash) worth," inscription on the new Jap. bronze coin of the period *Ten-boo* (vulgo *Tempo*).

[3]) *Shopping-Dialogues*, p. 33.

10

CHAPTER IV. NUMERALS. § 37.   151

To show that a quantity counted is spoken of, the word **Oyóso** (凡そ), pronounced ŏyŏso, = in sum, together, is generally placed before the number. — 凡そ十ヶ月, *Oyŏso siyu-ka getsu*, ten months. — 凡そ一ヶ年, 間, *Oyŏso ik-ka nen no aida*, the interval of one year (in counting), i. e. a year long.

3. 匹 ヒキ. 疋 シ., **Piki**, **Hiki** (一匹), objects, which are paired or given in pairs, as horses, horned cattle, some sorts of fish, such as perch (*Tai*), woven stuffs etc. The counting at Yédo is:

Ip-piki ....1.	Go-hiki .....5.	Ku-hiki (s'ki). 9.	Hiap-pi-ki . 100.
Ni-hiki .....2.	Rŏp-piki....6.	Zib-biki.... 10.	Sen biki... 1000.
Sam-biki.....3.	S'tsi-hiki....7.	Ziu ip-piki.. 11.	
Si-hiki......4.	Hatsi-hiki ...8.	Ziu-ni hiki .. 12.	

M'má ip-piki, one horse. — *Sam-biki usi*, three oxen. — *Kinu Ip-piki*, one piece of silk, of the length of 58 Jap. feet, or two pieces of 29 feet each.

4. 把 ハ, **Fa**, vulgo **Wa** (一把), handful, bunch. *Budoo*, *Dai-kon*, *Kari-kusa*, *Wara itsi-wa*, a bunch of grapes, radishes, hay, straw. At Yédo they count:

Itsi-wa ......1.	Si-wa ......4.	Hitsi-wa....7.	Zip-pa.....10.
Ni-wa......2.	Go-wa ......5.	Hatsi-wa....8.	Ziu itsi-wa (ip-
Sam-ba .....3.	Roku-wa ....6.	Ku-wa .....9.	pa?).....11.

This enumerative noun is applied to birds also (except birds of prey), and then expressed by 羽 ハ, *Fa*, vulgo *Wa*, feather. — *Oo-sagi itsi-wa*, a heron (not to be confounded with *usagi*, = hare). — *Ni-wa sira-sagi*, two white herons. *Sam-ba fibari*, three larks.

5. 尾 ヒ, **Bi** (一尾), tail, for fish. *Koi*, *Fasu*, *Funa itsi-bi*, *ni-bi*, carp, white fish, stone carp one piece, two pieces.

6. 口 ?, **Ko** (一口), mouth, for pots and pans.

7. 杯?, vulgo 盃, **Pai**, **Hai** (一杯?), a saucer as a measure of what is drunk; also a numeral-substantive for muscles. People count:

Ip-pai......1.	Rop-pai....6.	Ziu ip-pai..11.	Ni-Hu ip-pai 21.
Ni-hai......2.	H'tsi-hai....7.	Ziu ni-hai..12.	San-hp-pai.. 30.
San-bai.....3.	Hatsi-hai...8.	Ziu san-bai..13.	Si hp-pai..40.
Si-hai......4.	Ku-hai.....9.	Ziu si-hai...14.	Rok hp-pai. 50.
Go-hai......5.	Zip-pai....10.	Ni-hp-pai..20.	Hiap-pai...100.

152   CHAPTER IV. NUMERALS. § 37.

Midzu ip-pai, a saucer or a glass of water. — *Tcha ni hai*, two cups of tea.

8. 枚ﾏｲ, **Mai** (一ｲﾁ枚ﾏｲ), handle, anything single, leaf, for things thin and flat, as boards, paper, prints, coined silver, some sorts of fish etc.

9. 本ﾎﾝ, **Fon, Hon** (一ｲﾁ本ﾎﾝ), stem, stalk, handle, for trees, plants, in general things long and slender, which have the property of length, as a pencil (*Fude*), fan (*Oogi*), spoon (*Tsiya-siydzu*), whip (*Mutsi*), needles (*Fari*), salmon (*Sake*), etc. At Yedo, they count:

Ip'-pon .... 1.	H'tki-hon ... 7.	Žiu sam-bon . 13.	Ni-žiu-ni hon 22.
Ni-hon ..... 2.	Hatki-hon ... 8.	Žiu si-hon .. 14.	San-žip-pon . 30.
Sam-bon .... 3.	Ku-hon ..... 9.	Žiu go-hon .. 15.	Si-žip-pon .. 40.
Si-hon ..... 4.	Žip-pon .... 10.	Žiu rop-hon . 16.	Si-žiu ip-pon. 41.
Go-hon ..... 5.	Žiu ip-pon .. 11.	Ni-žip-pon .. 20.	Hiap-pon ... 100.
Rop-pon .... 6.	Žiu ni hon .. 12.	Ni-žiu ip-pon 21.	Hiak ip-pon. 101.

10. 端ﾀﾝ, **Tan** (一ｲﾁ端ﾀﾝ), a folded piece, for silk and cotton goods. Vulgo 反ﾀﾝ, sometimes 段ﾀﾝ also. In answer to the question *Nan Jan* (幾ｲｸ反ﾀﾝ), how many pieces? the manner of counting is:

It-tan ...... 1.	Go-tan ..... 5.	Žit-tan .... 10.	Si-ht-tan... 40.
Ni-tan ...... 2.	Rok-tan .... 6.	Žiu-it-tan .. 11.	Si-žiu it-tan. 41.
San-dan ..... 3.	H'tsi-tan.... 7.	Ni-žit-tan... 20.	Hiak-tan... 100.
Si-tan ...... 4.	Hatsi-tan.... 8.	Ni-žiu it-tan. 21.	Sen-tan ... 1000.

絹ｷﾇ 一ｲﾁ端ﾀﾝ, *Kinu it-tan*, one piece of silk. — 布ﾇﾉ 二ﾆ 反ﾀﾝ, *Nuno ni tan*, two pieces of hempen cloth. — 段ﾀﾝ 匹ﾋｷ 三ﾐ 反ﾀﾝ, piece-wares three pieces.

11. 挺ﾁｮｳ, **Thoo** (一ｲﾁ挺ﾁｮｳ), handle, for tools with handles. *Nomi it-thoo*, a chisel. So also *Kiri*, borer; *Yasuri*, file; *Teppoo*, gun; *Naginata*, pike; *Sumi*, East-Ind. ink; *Roo*, wax; *Sokw*, flat candlestick.

12. 柄ﾍｲ, **Fei, Hei** (一ｲﾁ柄ﾍｲ), stem, handle, for pikes and articles with handles.

13. 腰ﾖｳ, **Yoo** (一ｲﾁ腰ﾖｳ), the middle, the waist, for swords, which are stuck in the girdle. *Tatsi, Katana, Waki-sasi itsi-yoo*, one sword with belt, one large, one small sabre. *Utsiwo, Yebira itsi-yoo*, one quiver.

14. 蓋ｶｲ, **Kai** (一ｲﾁ蓋ｶｲ), cover, for hats (*kasa*), umbrellas and parasols (*kara-kasa*). They count as with *Ik-ka*: *Ik-kai*, 1. *Ni-kai*, 2. *Žit-kai*, 10. *Ni-žit-kai*, 20. *Sen-gai*, 1000.

15. 脚𦮀, **Kiyaku**, **Kiak** (一𦮀 脚𦮀), foot, for articles of furniture having feet. *Tsukuye*, or *Kew-sok ik-kiak*, one desk. *Siyoo-gi san-kiak*, three conches.

16. 棹𦮀, **Tho** (一𦮀 棹𦮀), swing, for trunks and traveling-articles, which are carried hanging on a stick. *Norimono it-tio*, a litter or sedan chair. *Naga-bitsu* or *Nuya-motsi ni-tho*, two traveling trunks.

17. 艘𦮀, **Soo** (一𦮀 艘𦮀), vessel, for ships. Counting is done:

Is-soo	1.	Go-soo	5.	Kū-soo	9.	Ni-šiu-soo	20.
Ni-soo	2.	Rok-soo	6.	Zis-soo	10.	San-žo-soo	30.
San-soo	3.	H'tsi-soo	7.	Žiu is-soo	11.	Si-žis-soo	40.
Si-soo	4.	Has-soo	8.	Žiu-ni-soo	12.	Hiaks-soo	100.

Is-soo-fune, one ship. *Is-soo gun-kan*, one war-ship. *Ko-büné is-soo*, one boat.

18. 輛𦮀, **Riyoo** (一𦮀 輛𦮀), a pair of wheels, for carriages. *Kurumu itsi-riyoo*, one wagon.

19. 巻𦮀, **Kwan** (一𦮀 巻𦮀), roll, for writings and stuff, which are rolled up. *Siyo(ro)-motsi ik-kwan*, a roll of writing.

20. 幅𦮀, **Fuku** (一𦮀 幅𦮀), breadth, for piece-goods, pictures etc.

21. 軸𦮀, **Ziku** (一𦮀 軸𦮀), axle, for pictures, which are hung on rollers. *Kake-mono itsi-ziku*, a hanging piece.

22. 面𦮀, **Men** (一𦮀 面𦮀), face, for mirrors, flags, fiddles, drums. *Ka-gami itsi-men*, a looking glass.

23. 册𦮀, **Sats'** (一𦮀 册𦮀), volume, for books. *Is-sats' no ho-mots*, one volume. *Hon ni-sats'*, two volumes.

24. 通𦮀, **Tsuu** (一𦮀 通𦮀), for open letters, written declarations, proofs of receipt etc. They count:

It-tsuu	1.	Si-tsuu	4.	Žiu-it-tsuu	11.	San-žit-tsuu	30.
Ni-tsuu	2.	Rok' tsuu	6.	Ni-žit-tsuu	20.	Si-žit-tsuu	40.
San tsuu	3.	Žit-tsuu	10.	Ni-žiu it-tsuu	21.	Hiak'-tsuu	100.

一𦮀 通𦮀, 書𦮀 状𦮀, *It-tsuu no ko sivo*, or 書𦮀 簡𦮀, *So-kan*, or *Te-gami*, one letter. — 二𦮀 通𦮀, 請𦮀 取𦮀 書𦮀 or 請𦮀 状𦮀, two receipts.

25. 封𦮀, **Puu** (一𦮀 封𦮀), seal, for sealed letters. They count:

Ip-puu	1.	Go-puu	5.	Ku-puu	9.	Ni-žiu-ip-puu	21.
Ni-fuu	2.	Rok-puu	6.	Žip-puu	10.	San-žip-puu	30.
San-puu	3.	H'tsi-fuu	7.	Žiu-ip-puu	11.	Hiak-fuu	100.
Si-fuu	4.	Hatsi-fuu	8.	Ni-žip-puu	20.		

§ 42. Enumeration of months.

Months are reckoned in answer to the question *Iku-tsuki* (幾ら月ぞ), or *Nan-getsu*, how many months?

Japanese.	Chinese.			
Fitó-tsuki.	一ら月ぞ¹), *Itsi-gets* or	一ら个ぅ月ぞ *Ik-ka-gets*, one month.
Futá-tsuki.	二ニ月ぞ *Ni-gets*	"	二ニ个ぅ月ぞ *Ni-ka-gets*, 2 months.
Mi-tsuki.	三ぞ月ぞ *San-gets*	"	三ぞ个ぅ月ぞ *San-ka-gets*, 3 "
Yo-tsuki.	四レ月ぞ *Si-gets*	"	四レ个ぅ月ぞ *Si-ka-gets*, 4 "
Itsi-tsuki.	五ヲ月ぞ *Go-gets*	"	五ヲ个ぅ月ぞ *Go-ka-gets*, 5 "
Mú-tsuki.	六ゟ月ぞ *Rok-gets*	"	六ゟ个ぅ月ぞ *Rok-ka-gets*, 6 "
Nand-tsuki.	七ネ月ぞ *Sitsi-gets*	"	七ネ个ぅ月ぞ *Sitsi-ka-gets*, 7 "
Ya-tsuki.	八ァ月ぞ *Fatsi-gets*	"	八ァ个ぅ月ぞ *Hak-ka-gets*, 8 "
Kokúno-tsuki.	九ヲ月ぞ *Ku-gets*	"	九ヲ个ぅ月ぞ *Ku-ka-gets*, 9 "
To-tsuki.	十ぞ月ぞ *Zin-gets*	"	十ぞ个ぅ月ぞ *Zik-ka-gets*, 10 "
	十ぞ一ら月ぞ *Zin-itsi-gets* "	十ぞ一ら个ぅ月ぞ *Zin-ik-ka-g.*, 11 "
	十ぞ二ニ月ぞ *Zin-ni-gets* "	十ぞ二ニ个ぅ月ぞ *Zin-ni-ka-g.*, 12 "

To the question *Nan-gwats* (何ら月ぞ), at Yédo *Nan ngats*, which month? (of the year) the names following answer:

正ぞ月ぞ, *Styoo-gwats*, first month.	七ネ月ぞ, *Sitsi-gwats*, seventh month.
(at Yédo *Soo ngatsu*).	八ァ月, *Fatsi-gwats*, eighth "
二ニ月, *Ni-gwats*, second "	九ヲ月, *Ku-gwats*, ninth "
三ぞ月, *San-gwats*, third "	十ぞ月, *Zin-(Dzin-)gwats*, tenth "
四レ月, *Si-gwats*, fourth "	十ぞ一ら月, *Zin-itsi-gwats*, eleventh
五ヲ月, *Go-gwats*, fifth "	month.
六ゟ月, *Roku-gwats*, sixth "	十ぞ二ニ月, *Zin-ni-gwats*, twelfth "

These names are good for the intercourse of every day life; in chronological writings and in almanacs the months are also named after the sexagenary cycle.

The intercalary month. As the civil year of the Japanese is a lunar year connected with the solar year, the months continually begin with the new moon

---

¹) *Itsi-gets*, = a whole month.

CHAPTER IV. NOTATION OF TIME § 41   182

1. According to one method, the original Chinese astronomical, exhibited on the inside of the dial, ju. as is seen, the civil day divided into twelve equal portions of time (時, Toki, times), which are named after the zodiac, as 子 時, Nê no doki, Mouse-time, 丑 時, Usi no doki, Bull-time, etc. At Yédo they say Kok instead of Toki. The Toki is divided into two halves; the first is called 初, Siyo, = first beginning, the second, 正, Sei, = the true or proper. Each half, being equivalent to an hour according to our reckoning, has four subordinate divisions, called 刻, Kok or notches, each of 15 分, Bun (= 15 minutes), and the Bun has 60 秒, Meo (60 seconds). This cycle begins with the 子 時, Nê no doki or Nê no koku, the middle of which (正) falls at midnight; thus its beginning falls 60 min. before, its end 60 min. after midnight.

子 時 Nê no doki, Mouse-time.   午 時 M'ma no doki, Horse-time.
  初 siyo, = 11 o'clock in the evening.   初 siyo, = 11 o'clock in the morning.
  正 sei, = 12 o'clock midnight.   正 sei, = 12 o'clock noon.

丑 時 Usi no doki, Bull-time.   未 時 Fitodsi no doki, Goat-time.
  初 siyo, = 1 o'clock in the morning.   初 siyo, = 1 o'clock in the afternoon.
  正 sei, = 2 o'clock   „   正 sei, = 2 o'clock   „

寅 時 Torá no doki, Tiger-time.   申 時 Sáru no doki, Ape-time.
  初 siyo, = 3 o'clock in the morning.   初 siyo, = 3 o'clock in the afternoon.
  正 sei, = 4 o'clock   „   正 sei, = 4 o'clock   „

卯 時 U no doki, Hare-time.   酉 時 Tori no doki, Cock-time.
  初 siyo, = 5 o'clock in the morning.   初 siyo, = 5 o'clock in the afternoon.
  正 sei, = 6 o'clock   „   正 sei, = 6 o'clock   „

辰 時 Tatsu no doki, Dragon-time.   戌 時 Inu no doki, Dog-time.
  初 siyo, = 7 o'clock in the morning.   初 siyo, = 7 o'clock in the evening.
  正 sei, = 8 o'clock   „   正 sei, = 8 o'clock   „

巳 時 Mi no doki, Serpent-time.   亥 時 I no doki, Swine-time.
  初 siyo, = 9 o'clock in the morning.   初 siyo, = 9 o'clock in the evening.
  正 sei, = 10 o'clock   „   正 sei, = 10 o'clock   „

One 11 hours 48 min. 2 sec. before midnight is expressed by 子 初

三ツ刻ミ三ツ分ニ二ツ秒ニ, *Ne no tiyo san-koku san-bun ni-meo*, i. e. 3 × 15 + 3 min. + 2 sec. from the beginning of the Mouse-time. Our 12 o'clock midnight is 子ノ正ヒ, *Ne no sei*; our 12 o'clock 15 min. after midnight 子ノ正ヒ初ツ刻ミ, *Ne no sei tiyo koku*.

2. The second method, the Japanese proper, supersedes the names of the zodiac with numbers, by which the hour is made known by strokes on the bell or drum. The civil day retains the division into 12, or properly 2 × 6 times (時, *Toki*); the *Toki* however is subject to the decimal division into 10 刻, *Koku* (notches), which are also called 分 *Bun* (tenths), the *Bun* into 10 厘, *Rin*. The *Koku* or *Bun* is now = 12 min. The numbers which have been added to the successive twice six *Tokis*, are from midnight till noon 9, 8, 7, 6, 5, 4, and the same from noon till midnight; these numbers are obtained, when the number, which should properly belong to a *Toki*, is subtracted from the number 10; thus 1 – 10 = 9. The numbers 1, 2 and 3 are not included in the hour-numbers, as 1, 2 and 3 strokes on the drum or clock belong to the signals of the military and convent service, and a confusion of the two signals has to be prevented.

The newest information respecting this notation of hours does not quite agree with the notices of it formerly obtained, and people in Japan itself, it seems, do not reckon more consistently. Therefore we confine ourselves to the clocks at Yédo. There, at 12 o'clock at noon, the clock strikes 9¹), and the Japanese calls this time *Firu kokonotsu doki*, = noon, time of the nine number, or in short, *Kokonotsu-doki*, or *Kokon-tsu*, or even *Hiru no koku*. From 12 to 2 o'clock according to our reckoning of time he counts 10 *Bun* and calls our 1 o'clock in the afternoon *Firugo kokonotsu han doki*, = afternoon 9½ time, or, in short, *Firu kokonotsu han*; our 2 o'clock *Firugo yatsu-doki*, or *Firugo yatsu* (or also *Hitsi no koku*; our 3 o'clock *Firugo yyn han*, etc., till after the end of the fourth *Toki*, at midnight the clock strikes nine again, and beginning with *Yoru kokonotsu doki*, the other six *Tokis* continue till noon. In consequence of this, for the Japanese *Tokis* the following definitions of time are obtained.

¹) First a stroke is heard, about a minute afterwards a second and immediately after that a third, being the warning. A minute later the strokes of the hour follow, each stroke with a pause of 10 or 12 seconds, except the last two, which follow quickly on each other and show that the clock has finished striking.

CHAPTER IV. NOTATION OF TIME. § 44.

夜ニ, *YORU* or *YO*, at night.	昼ニ, *FIRU*, at noon.
九ツ時ト, *Kokonōtsu-doki*, 9th time, = 12 o'clock midnight.	九ツ時ト, *Kokonōtsu-doki*, 9th time, = 12 o'clock at noon.
九半ニ, *Kokonōtsu-han*, 9½, = 1 o'clock after midnight.	九半ニ, *Kokonōtsu-han*, 9½, = 1 o'clock in the afternoon.
	昼ニ後ニ, *FIRU-GO*, in the afternoon.
八ツ時ト, *Yatsu-doki*, 8th time, = 2 o'clock after midnight.	八ツ時ト, *Yatsu-doki*, 8th time, = 2 o'clock in the afternoon.
八半ニ, *Ygu-han*, 8½, = 3 o'clock after midnight.	八半ニ, *Ygu-han*, 8½, = 3 o'clock in the afternoon.
明ト, *AKE*, in the morning	夕ラ, *YUU*, in the evening
七ツ時ト, *Nanātsu-doki*, 7th time, = 4 o'clock in the morning.	七ツ時ト, *Nanātsu-doki*, 7th time, = 4 o'clock in the afternoon.
七半ニ, *Nanātsu-han*, 7½, = 5 o'clock in the morning.	七半ニ, *Nanātsu-han*, 7½, = 5 o'clock in the afternoon.
明ト, *AKE*, in the morning	暮ニ, *KURE*, in the evening.
六ツ時ト, *Mutsu-doki*, 6th time, = 6 o'clock in the morning.	六ツ時ト, *Mutsu-doki*, 6th time, = 6 o'clock in the evening.
六半ニ, *Mutsu-han*, 6½, = 7 o'clock in the morning.	六半ニ, *Mutsu-han*, 6½, = 7 o'clock in the evening.
朝ト, *ASA*, in the morning	夜ニ, *YORU*, or *YO*, at night
五ツ時ト, *Itsutsu-doki*, 5th time, = 8 o'clock in the morning.	五ツ時ト, *Itsutsu-doki*, 5th time, = 8 o'clock in the evening.
五半ニ, *Itsutsu-han*, 5½, = 9 o'clock in the morning.	五半ニ, *Itsutsu-han*, 5½, = 9 o'clock in the evening.
昼ニ前ニ, *FIRU MAYE*, in the fore noon.	
四ツ時ト, *Yotsu-doki*, 4th time, = 10 o'clock in the morning.	四ツ時ト, *Yotsu-doki*, 4th time, = 10 o'clock in the evening.
四半ニ, *Yotsu-han*, 4½, = 11 o'clock in the morning.	四半ニ, *Yotsu-han*, 4½, = 11 o'clock in the evening.

In agreement with the preceding definitions are the notices of time, occurring in the *Shopping-Dialogues* page 17, after the Nagasaki original, page 42, where is to be read: 九ツ半ニ時トヨウ七ツ時ト近ヂ内ニ=. *Kokonōtsu han*

166   CHAPTER IV. NOTATION OF TIME. § 44. 45.

doki yori nanatsu made ai ni, „between one and four o'clock." — 八 ツ 半 に
時 ？ 頃 ニ =, *Yqu-han doki goro ni*, „about three o'clock."

On the contrary, not in agreement with it are the notices, occurring in s. BROWN's *Colloquial Japanese Grammar*, page XLVIII, where *Nenu kokonotsu doki* is made equivalent to 10 o'clock in the afternoon till 12 o'clock midnight, and also the other *Tokis* begin 60 minutes earlier, than according to our notice.

The measurement of the *Tokis* fixed according to our hours, is, nevertheless, alone of value for an equinoctial day, and change (they become longer or shorter) in proportion as day and night in the different seasons are of unequal length. Thus each of the six *Tokis* from the longest day, if this day including the morning and evening twilight be reckoned at 17 hrs. 58 min. (notices are found which differ from it) has 2 hrs. 58 min. The Japanese almanacs contain, every 15 days, the definition of the changeable length of day and night, and the time-pieces are regulated accordingly, therefore they are so adapted, that the hour-ciphers are on loose plates, which are shifted, whilst the division of the hour-circle into *Koku* or *Bun*, as also the cyclical division of the zodiac is fixed. The changing of the hours is called *Toki wo utsusu*.

MEASURES, WEIGHTS AND COINS.

The Japanese measures and weights, as well as the coinage are for a great deal reckoned after the Chinese decimal system, with which, as a rule, the Chinese names are used, preceded by the Chinese numerals, both modified by the Japanese pronunciation.

In consequence of the modifications, which since 1850 the Government at Yédo has introduced in the measures and money, the definitions here given differ from those given by us formerly and will, probably, sooner or later undergo modifications again, when people, in Japan itself, have agreed about the principle of the measures, viz. about the Japanese foot and its proportion to the French mètre or Netherlands ell.

§ 45. Measures of length, *Sasinome*.

尺 ？ *Saka*, foot (一 ツ 尺 ？ *Issiku*, one foot), the iron foot (*Kane-asi*, vulgo *Kane-isiku*), used by work-people, generally bent to a square and therefore called the bent foot (曲 ツ 尺 ？ *Kiyak-isiku*), the unit of the Japanese measures, formerly (1831) was found by nice comparison with a standard-

CHAPTER IV. MEASURES, WEIGHTS AND COINS, § 45.   167

mètre to be = 0,908 mètre or 0',11",11"' of an English foot, since 1850 fixed by the Government at Yédo at 0,30175 mètre or 30,175 centimètre, the mètre being reckoned at 3,28889 Japanese feet. At the observatory at Yédo the Netherlands ell or French mètre is reckoned at 3,308 Japanese feet (*Kaneśiku*) [1], whereas the Japanese Department of Marine has adopted 3,290248 Japanese feet for it [1], and a manual published at Nagasaki [2] gives 3,31 Japanese feet as the measure of the Netherlands ell. When, in 1861, the manufacture of some comparative measures was ordered of A. VAN EMDEN, by the „Nederlandsche Handelmaatschappij," the Japanese foot was fixed at 0,3835 Netherlands ell.

For piece-goods, except woolen stuffs, a whalebone foot (鯨尺, *Kusira śiku*) is used, being = 1,25 *imo* feet.

Divisions of the *Siku*:

	Jap. foot.	Mètres
尺, *Siku* (一𣶒尺),	1	0,30175
寸, *Sun* (一𣶒寸),	0,1	0,030175
分, *Bun* (一𣶒分),	0,01	0,0030175
釐, *Rin* (一𣶒釐),	0,001	0,00030175
毛, *Goo* (一𣶒毛),	0,0001	0,000030175
糸, *Si* (一𣶒糸),	0,00001	0,0000030175
忽, *Kot* (一𣶒忽),	0,000001	0,00000030175

Multiples of the *Siku*.

間, 間, *Ken* (一𣶒間, *Ik-ken*), as measure of distance = 6 *Siku* (1,8105 mètres); as measure for piece-goods 0,5 *Siku*.

丈, *Zoo* (一𣶒丈, *Itsi-zoo*), 10 尺 *Siku* (3,0175 mètres).

町, *Tjoo*, *Tsoo*, street (一𣶒町, *It-tsoo*), 60 間 *Ken* (108,63 mètres).

里, *Ri*, Japanese mile; 一𣶒里, *Itsi-ri*, one mile, 36 町 *Tsoo*

[1] From a communication by OHNO YASABUROO, instrument-maker to the observatory at Yédo.
[2] Introduction to the Japanese translation, published at Yédo in 1854, of F. B. CALVER, *Leiddraad by het onderrigt in de Zee-artillerie*. Delft, 1852. The title of the work is: 海上砲術全書 *Kai zoo hô-zyuts zen syo*, or „the book on Marine artillery."

[3] 諳語小引 „Japanese Translation of the English and Dutch with pronunciation. Numbers. First part, N°. 2. Nagasaki, October, 1860." Page 120, 121

CHAPTER IV. MEASURES, WEIGHTS AND COINS. § 45, 46, 47.

or streets, = 3910,69 mètres, if the Japanese foot is reckoned at 0,30175 mètres.

According to the Treaty between Japan and America, concluded in 1858, Art. 7, the Japanese *Ri* is 4275 yards (the yard at 0,91438 Neth. ell), thus = 3908.9745 N. ells, whereas it is said to amount to 33 町 48 間 1 尺 5 分.

In the Japanese-Russian Treaty of 19 Aug. 1858, Art. 8, on the contrary the Japanese *Ri* is made equivalent to 3 wersts 332 saschen, which gives to one *Ri* 3908,08192 Neth. ells.

§ 46. Superficial measures.

步, Pu (一步) or Tsübo (一坪, *Fitó tsubó*), = 一間四方, i. e. a square *Ken*, or 方六尺, i. e. 6 square feet (3,27791025 square mètres).

畝, 畝, 畝, So (一畝, *Fitó se*), a rectangle of 6 步 *Pu* length and 5 *Pu* breadth, = 30 square *Pu*.

段, Tan (一段, *It-tan*), a plane of 20 *Pu* length and 15 *Pu* breadth, = 300 square *Pu*. *It-tan* is the regular plane of a rice-field.

町, Tʃṣo, Tʃoo (一町 四方, *It-tʃoo yomo*), a plane of 60 *Pu* length and 50 *Pu* breadth, = 3000 square *Pu*.

§ 47. Measures of capacity (*Masamé*) for dry and liquid wares.

升, Soo, Sʲo (一升, *Is-ʃoo*), unity of the measures of capacity, formerly distinguished by Europeans with the Malay name *Gantang*, is 0,49 Jap. feet long and broad and 0.27 Jap. feet deep, containing 0,064827 Jap. cubic feet, = 1,8833657110629 cubic decimètres, or 1 litre, 8 decilitres, 9 centilitres etc.

Subdivisions of the *Soo*.

伍合, Go-goo, pron. *go-ngoo*, a measure of 5 合 Goo, = 1 升 Soo full 9 decilitres.

合, Goo. pron. *ngoo* (一合, *Itsi goo*), = 1/10 升 Soo.

勺, formerly 偏, Siyaku, pron. Sjka (一勺, *Is-sjka*), = 1/100 升 Soo.

伍勺, Go sjaku, a measure of 1/100 升 Soo, or 1/2 合.

才, formerly 抄 and 撮, Sai (一才, *Is-sai*), = 1/1000 升 Soo.

Multiples of the *Soo*.

伍升, Go koo, a measure of 5 升 Soo, = 9,40682585145 cubic decimètres.

俵, Pioo, or Tawara (一俵, *Ip-pioo* or *Fitó-tawara*), a sack or bale (rice), at present contains 米 三斗 五升 or 3 *To* 5 *Soo* rice.

斗, To, formerly 迻 (一斗, *It-to*), as vessel Tomimi, = 10 升 Soo.

石ゴ, **Góku** (pron. *ngóku*), formerly 斛ゴ (一ノ 石ゴ, *Iti góku*). = 100 升ゼ Sоо, or 180,3365719029 litres.

Remark. The fixed salaries of Government functionaries are based on the quantity of rice, which is allowed them per year or per day, and which is paid in money according to the market-price. The money value of a *góku* (石) was in 1865 ƒ 12.50 Netherlands currency, or according the Japanese exchange 金ゼ 二° 兩ゼ 二ニ 步ゴ, i. e. 2 × ƒ 5 + 2 × ƒ 1,25 = 百ゴ 石ゴ 高ゼ *Fáku gáku tákdau* is an income of 100 Kok or ƒ 1250 Netherl. currency. The pay of a common man (一ノ 人ゼ 扶ノ 持リ) is 伍ゼ 合ゼ, or 6 cent a day.

§ 48. Weights, *Hakarime*. (*Riō*)

1. 才ゼ, **Sai** (一ノ 才ゼ, *I-sai*). − ⅒ 夕ゼ **Sak'**.
   夕ゼ, vulgo 炒ゼ, **Sak'** (一ノ 夕ゼ, *Is-sak'*). − ⅒ 合ゼ **Goo**.
   合ゼ, **Goo** (一ノ 合ゼ, *Itsi goo*). − ⅒ 斤ゼ **Kin**.
   斤ゼ, **Kin** (一ノ 斤ゼ, *Ik-kin*), the Japanese pound, called by Europeans *Catty* (ct.), weighs according to former notices *) 0,6 kilo, according to the later definition *), 0,597 kilo. They reckon, at Yedo:

Ik-kin	. . .	1 ct.	*Rok-kin*	. . 6 ct.	*Ziu ik-kin*	. . 11 ct.	*Hiak'-kin*,	100 ct.
Ni-kin	. . .	2 „	*Sti-kin*	. . 7 „	*Ziu go-kin*	. . 15 „	*Sen-gin*,	1000 „
San-gin	. . .	3 „	*Hátsi-kin*	. . 8 „	*Ni zik-kin*	. . 20 „	*Mon-gin*,	10000 „
Si-kin	. . .	4 „	*Ku-kin*	. . 9 „	*Ni ziu ik-kin*,	21 „		
Go-kin	. . .	5 „	*Zik-kin*	. . 10 „	*Go zik-kin*	. 50 „		

五° 十ニ 斤ゼ, **Go zíu kin**, = 50 catties (ct. 50), or half a picol (pl. 0,5).
百ゴ 斤ゼ, **Hiak'-kin**, = 100 catties or a picol.

2. Silverweight.

Unity: **Mon-me**, pron. *Momme*, from 文ゼ **Mon**, − farthing, and 目ᴬ **Me**, = eye, meaning characteristic, i. e. weight of a farthing. The signs used for *Mon-me* are 匁ゼ, 奴ゼ, 朱ゼ, 朿ゼ, 凡ゼ, abbreviated forms of the Chinese 錢ゼ *) *Sen*, = farthing. In stead of *Mon-me*, in connection with some numbers, only 目ᴬ, *Me* is used. The Europeans have therefore adopted the name **Mace**, Dutch

---
*) Fr. Ph. VON SIEBOLD, *Nippon-Archief*, Division IV.
*) *Ben-yo ryō sū*, see page 167, note 2.

170   CHAPTER IV. MEASURES, WEIGHTS AND COINS. § 48.

Mace. One Mace (一 分 匁², *Itsi mon-me*, or 壹 分 目ᴬ, *Itsi-me*, or 銀
壹 分 錢², *Gin i-sen*), weighs 3,74799 grammes and has, as ₁⁄₁₀ Tael, if the
Taël is counted to be equal to ƒ 1,60 Neth. cour., a value in silver of ƒ 0,16 N. c.
The *Mon-me* is divided into

          10 分², *Fun*, vulgo condrijn, conderein, cent,
          100 厘², *Rin*, vulgo cassie, cash, mokje.
         1000 毛², *Moo*.
        10000 弗², *Hoto*, vulgo wassie.

Itsi mon-me ni fun, = 1,2 *Mon-me*, or 1 *Mon-me* 2 condrijn. — *Ni mon-me
san-bun*, 2,3 *Mon-me*. *San-mon-me si-fun go-rin roku moo*, = 3,456 *Mon-me*, or
3 mace, 4 condrijn, 5 cent (or cash) 6.

    五ᵍ 匁², *Go-mon-me*, 5 mace or half a taël.
    十ᵍ 匁², *Zin-mon-me*, = 10 *Mon-me* or 10 mace, the weight, which, in
silver, makes the imaginary coin Taël, Dutch Tall, = 37,4799 grammes, value
in silver ƒ 1,60 Neth. cour. being according to the Japanese text of Art. 12,
alinea d of the Additional Articles to the Netherlands-Japanese Treaty of 30 Ja-
nuary 1856, 6,25 匁² = ƒ 1,00 Neth. cour. ¹).

With *Mon-me* they count further: *Ziu-itsi mon-me*, *Ziu-ni mon-me*, *Ziu-ku
mon-me* (19 *mon-me*), and in the tens (20, 30 etc.), and in the hundreds, thousands, tens of thousands etc. supersede *Mon-me* by 目ᴬ *Me*: thus 二゛十ᵍ
目ᴬ, *Ni-ziyu me*, 20 *Mon-me*. 三゛四゛十ᵍ 目ᴬ, *San-si-ziyu me*, 30 to
40 *Mon-me*. 九゛十ᵍ一分 匁², *Ku-ziyu itsi mon-me*, 91 *Mon-me*.

    百ᵍ 目ᴬ, *Hiakú me*, 100 *Me* or *Mon-me*, = 10 taels or 374,799 grammes,
or ƒ 16 Neth. cour.

    貫² 目ᴬ, *Kwan-me* (at Yedo *Kdn-me*), —分 〆² 目ᴬ, *Ik-kwan-me* or
one riet (1000) *me* = 100 taels.

    三゛貫². 五゛百ᵍ 目ᴬ, San-gwan go hiakú mé, 3500 *me* or 350 taels.
    拾゛貫². 目ᴬ, Zik kám-me, 10 riets or 10000 *me*, ... = 1000 „
    百ᵍ 貫². 目ᴬ, Hiak kám-me, 100 riets or 100000 *me*, = 10000 „
    千゛貫². 目ᴬ, Sen ngam-me, 1000 riets or 1000000 *me*, = 100000 „
    萬゛貫². 目ᴬ, Mán ngam-me, 10000 riets, ... = 1000000 „

---

¹) In the official Dutch translation instead of it we find: „De zilveren Spaansche mat of pilaar-mat wordt
gerekend tegen de waarde van ƒ 2,50. De Mexicaansche dollar tegen ƒ 2,56 Ned. cour."

CHAPTER V.

ADVERBS.

§ 52. The adverbs in Japanese which, as such, always precede the word (verb, adjective, or adverb) that they qualify, are, so far as their origin is concerned, to be distinguished as:

I. Adverbs proper.

1. Primitive adverbs, such as: *Mu*, truly, perfectly; *Ito*, very.

2. Adverbs ending in kū (in the spoken language simply u), formed from adjectives in ki (p. 106), as *Hayáku*, early; *Osóku*, late.

II. Improper adverbs or adverbial expressions.

1. Nouns with or without the modal case ni or de, included among which the adjectives in ki (p. 100, b), ka (p. 116 § 13) and *yaka* (p. 117 § 14), provided they are used as substantives concrete.

2. Verbs in the gerund, i. e. in the modal case, characterized by te, as: *Sadamete*, definitely; *Kessité*, certainly; *Kakite* (*kaite*), in writing.

If, for convenience, we distribute the Japanese adverbs and adverbial expressions in groups according to their signification, we shall get as:

§ 53. Adverbs of quality, to the question: how?

1. Adverbs in ku, derived from adjectives in ki (see p. 106, § 9, B, 2), as:

CHAPTER V. ADVERBS. § 54.   175

Koto-gotoku, 悉ドヲトク, all over, entirely.   25.
Nokorázu, 不ㇾ 殘ラ, without surplus, without exception. (See p. 58.)
Mattaku, 全クヲ, wholly, perfectly.
Ippai ni, 一ッ 盃ニ, full, abundantly. — Ippan ni, 一ッ 盤ニ, full (to the brim). *fair all' ode, all' estremo*
I-sio ni, 一ッ 緒ニ, together successively, altogether.   29.
Kátsute, 勝手ヲ, wholly, entirely. With a subsequent negation, by no means, not at all, e. g.: Kátsute wakaranai, it is by no means intelligible; Kátsute mairu mai, I shall not go at all.   30.
Kátsu-gátsu, 且ヲ 又ニ, wholly.
Kátsu-mata, 且ヲ 亦ヲ, 且ヲ 又ヲ, so much the more.
Yo-kei ni, 餘ア 計ケニ, in a greater degree, more.
Iyásiku mo, 苟クシモ, 愈, so much the more.
Sui-bun, 隨ヒ 分ブ, proportionably, pretty, tolerably.   33.
Ziyu-bun ni, 十ジ 分ブニ, fully, quite.
Itsi-bun ca, 一ッ 分ブハ, partly.
Mubara ni, 疎ラニ, sparsely, in a scattered manner, here and there, partially, thinly.
Oyóso, pron. oyósso, 凡ソ, in sum, together; very nearly, about.
Tákusan ni (at Yédo), 澤ヲ 山ニ, richly, abundantly, in multitude.   40.
Tai-soo, 大ヲ 壯ヲ, excessively. Tai-soo ooku, far above measure.
Tai-gai, 大ヲ 槩ガ,
Tai-tei, 大ヲ 抵テ,   } in general, more or less.
Oo-kata, 大ヲ 方ガ,
Sakiboru, 頗ブルニ, pretty, tolerably, for three fourths of the full measure.
Sakidaru fisási, it is pretty long ago.   45.
Yoffodo, ヨッホド, contracted from Yoi-fodo, pretty.
Téiygu-do, pron. Tiao-do, 調ヂ 度ド, not テキド, proportionately, reasonably, just. Téiygu-do yoi, it is just good.
Fotondo, 殆ドド, almost, nearly; scarcely, hardly. Sore va fotondo tarya, it is hardly enough.
Fodo-fodo, Naka-naka, 中ヲ 又ク, almost.
Sukunaku mo ookunai naku, 少ヲナクモ 多クモナク, neither less nor more.   50.

Taito, Taitto, 徽ト, 些ミト, 少, a little. *Taito mo,* as little as possible, with a subsequent negation, not in the least. 51.

Yuu-yuu- (yoo-yoo-) *siti,* scarcely, hardly; almost. 52.
Bakāri, 許り, merely, only. *Kore bakari,* only this.
Fu-soku ni, 不足ニ, not enough.
Betsu ni, 別ニ, in particular, particularly. 55.

§ 55. Adverbs of circumstance.

Mu-yáku ni, 無益ニ, vainly. — *Mudd ni,* 虚ニ, in vain. 56.
Mundsiku, 虚シク, in vain.
Ayamátte, 誤ッテ, by mistake.
Ukegatte, 諾ッテ, willingly.
Konondr, 好シヤ (contracted from *Konomitr*), gladly, willingly, readily. 60.
Tasímīte (= *Tasimite*), 嗜シヤ, gladly. — *Nengoro ni,* 懇ニ, gladly.
Iqu-nugara mō, against the grain, reluctantly.
Tomo ni, 倶ニ, 共, with, together, alike.
Itsi ni, Fitátsi ni, 一ニ, together. 64.
Ondziku, 同ジク, in the spoken language *onīziu,* together, at the same time.
Tada, 只, 啻, only, alone, but. *Tada san ka nitsi nomi,* or *Tada san ka nitsi bakāri,* only three days. 66.

Saye, さえ さへ ~, originally park, enclosure for cattle; used adverbially it limits the idea exclusively to what has been mentioned immediately before and answers to but, as it is as much as the Lat. *modo* only. — *Sono na saye siru,* to know by name only. — *Ai-den to saye mōsze,* say only: „Sir." — *Sake wo nomi saye suru mono,* some one, who does nothing but drink spirits. — *Sake wo nomi saye sureba, yowu,* if one does nothing but drink spirits, he gets drunken.

In connection with a subsequent negation *Saye* is equivalent to not even, Lat. *nec quidem,* e. g.: *Mma saye nakari,* there are not even horses. — *Sono na saye sirazu,* not even to know by name. — *Zi saye mi-sirānu mono,* anyone who does not even know the letters.

Dani, ダニ, cognate to *Saye,* as an adverb, has the word to which it exclusively limits the idea, before it with or without inflection, e. g.: *Ima dani nanori si-tamaye,* assume but for as yet a name. — *Ima sibāsi dani orase mas,* now it will only last a short time. 69.

Sard, さへ, even, German, *sogar*, indicates that an unexpected predicate is emphatically given to the subject of a sentence, e. g.: *Kisaki suru kaiko wo kuwa tamayu*, even the queen has silkworms fed. — *Kare sara korewo sirisu*, he even does not know this.

Kata-gata, 隻, single, alone. 70.

Suku-naku-tomo, 少 ラ ク ト モ, at least. *Sukunaju sitimo mu ka getsu*, at least three months. — *Sa-naki-tomo*, at least.

Nâru-dake, 成 ル 丈 ケ, if possible.

Ze-hi, 是 ヒ 非 ヒ, so or not so, in any case; necessary. *Ze-hi itasi-masoo*, I shall do it in any case.

Don bo-don, 動 ヒ 不 動 ヒ, either active or not active, = in any case. 74.

To-mo kaku-mo, ト モ カ ク モ, *To-mo kyu-mo*, ト モ ウ モ, however, in any case. Also *To-kaku* (兎 ト 角 カ), if possible, synonym to *Nâru-dake*. — *To-kaku itsi-you ni naru-beki*, if possible it should happen in one and the same way.

Fu-i ni, 不 意 ニ, suddenly, at once. 76.

Tama-tama, 偶 ニ, unexpectedly, by chance.

Sai-siyo ni vi, 最 ニ 初 ニ ヘ ニ, firstly.
Dai-itai ni ed, 第 ナ 一 ニ ヘ ニ,

Dai-ni ni ed, 第 ナ 二 ニ ヘ ニ, secondly.

Itsi ni ed, 一 ニ ヘ ニ, partly, on the one hand. — *Mata*, 又 ニ, also. 81.
Mata itsi ni ed, 復 ニ 一 ニ ヘ ニ, on the other hand. *Itsi ni vi makoto, mata itsuni ed itsardri*, on one hand truth, on the other falsehood. 82.

Nâkabâ ra, 半 ニ ヘ, half. *Nâkabâ va..., nâkabâ va..., partly..., partly...*

Sara ni, 更 ち ニ, again, anew.

Sono foka ni, 其 ノ 外 ニ, further, farther.

Sono aye ni, 其 ノ 上 ニ ニ, = besides; moreover. 86.

§ 56. Our adverbs of place and space, such as of, by, for, in, after, on etc. are generally expressed in Japanese by connectives expressive of relation, which, when they are accompanied with another definition, have the latter before them (see Introduction p. 44, § 15, B. 1.); e. g.: *ye* or *he*, = wards; *Kotaira-ye*, hitherwards; *yori*, = of, out; *Kotaira yori*, from here. Since compounds with adverbs of place, belonging to this group, have been already treated at pages 81, 82, 83, we confine ourselves here to a mere citation.

Doko ni, where? *Doko ye*, whither? *Doko yori*, whence? *Doko ni mo*, wherever. 87.

Idzukuzo, Dotaira, where? — *Arokō ni*, somewhere. — *Atsira*, anywhere. 89.
Kasiko ni, there. — *Koko ni, Kotaira*, here.
Kono tokōro ni, here. — *Sono tokōro ni*, there.
Yoso ni, elsewhere. — *Yoso ye*, to elsewhere. — *Yoso kara*, from elsewhere.
Ta-syo, pron. *Ta-jo*, 他ｦ處ﾆ, elsewhere. 92.

Besides these, for the definition of place and space, come under notice:

Aminikn, 偏ｸﾁｸ, everywhere. *Siyo-siyo*, pron. *io-io*, 盛ｼﾞｸ, everywhere.
Tsikiku, 近ｸｸ, near.
Tooku, 遠ｸｸ, far; *Yen-foo ni*, 遠ｷ方ﾆ, far. 95.
Is-io ni, 一ｼ所ﾆ, at or to one and the same place. — *Is-io ni yuku*, to go with, to accompany.
Naka ni, or *Tšiu*, 中ﾆ, in the midst, amidst, amongst. 97.
Uti ni, Urǎ ni, 内ﾆ, within. — *Foki ni, Soto ni*, 外ﾆ, without.
Mayę ni, Sakini, 前ﾆ, before. — *Uuri ni, Ato ni, Notsi ni*, 後ﾆ, behind.
Uyę ni, 上ﾆ, above. — *Sǎǎ ni*, 下ﾆ, beneath. 100.
Sokini, Katu ni, Katawara ni, 側ﾆ, near, at the side, beside.
Migi ni, 右ﾆ, to the right. — *Fidāri ni*, 左ﾘﾆ, to the left.
Marōri ni, 廻ﾘﾆ, round, around.
Gururu-guru, around. — *Gurari to*, round about.
Mukōi ni, 向ﾋﾆ, against, opposite. — *Ai-tai*, 相ｲ對ｽ, opposite. 105.
Yoko ni, Yoko sama ni, 横ﾆ, across. — *Nanu-me ni*, 斜ﾒﾆ, aslant.
Sudzi-makāri ni, ｽｼﾞﾏｶﾘﾆ, vulgar. *Suzi-kai ni*, almost opposite. 107.

§ 57. Adverbs of time, to the question: when? how long?

Itsu zo, 何ｼ時, when? 108.
Itsu-ka, 何ｼ日ｶ, what day of the month? See p. 161.
Itsu mo, 極ｸ, 恒, whenever, ever. — *Itsu de mo*, whenever, always, ever; with a negative verb, never. 110.
Imá (imā) 今ｼ, now. — *Ima ni*, 于今ｼ, now. — *Imí yori*, 自今ｼ, henceforth. 111.
Ima-made, 今ｼ迄ｼ, hitherto, heretofore.
Ima-made ra, contracted *mida*, in the spoken language usually *Mada*. 猶, hitherto, still. Lat. *adhuc*; in connection with negation included in the subsequent verb, not yet. 未ｼ 113.

Tadá-ima, 只今二, 即今, 向來, just now. 114.
Maye-katu, 前ニ方ヨ, *Maě-katu yori*, beforehand. — *Madzu*, 先ヅ, first, beforehand.
Hayaka, 速ヤカ, 早, *Hayyu, Hayao*, 1. soon, very soon; 2. early.
Mo-háyu, *Mo-hayyu*, contracted *Moo*, already. — *Moo O kairi-ite gozarimásaká*, do you go again already? 117.
Osoku, 晩ソク, late.
Aru toki ni, 一時, once, at a certain time.
Tsiká-goro, 近き日ニ, 近來, lately. — *Tsiki-dzuki-ni*, shortly, speedily.
Mukáśi, 昔カシ, 古, of old, formerly, of yore. *Mukaśi yori*, of yore.
Iniśiḱé, 往ニ昔キ, of old time, formerly.
Tsui ni, 終ニ, at the end, finally, at last; ever; with a negative verb, never.
Siķiri ni, 頻リニ, every moment, without ceasing. 124.
Nte, 追テ洏, afterwards, consequently; late, henceforth, *sono notsi*.
Otta'ké, サツヽケ, 刻下, forthwith, immediately, directly, - *suguni, oi-no nai*,
Sugu ni, 直グニ, directly, straight.
Ziki ni, 直ギニ, directly, forthwith.
Sibaraku, 暫ラク, in short, shortly, quickly.
Yoa-yaku, Yoo-yaku, 漸ヤク, by degrees. 130.
Tatsi-matsi, 立チ待チ, 忽, at once, directly; suddenly.
Yagate, 頓ヶ而ナ, suddenly.
Soko-ri ni, 即ソ時ジニ, directly.
Fisásiku, 久シク, long. *Hisá-bisá*, long ago. *Fisásii áto*, long ago.
Sai-zen, 最ぜ前ゼ, just now. 133.
Kore-kara, hereafter, thereupon.
Ik-kóo, 一ケ向コ, henceforth, in connection with a subsequent negation, no more.
Sadé ni, 既ニ, 已, already.
Kiu ni, 急ニ, quickly, hastily. 139.
Tsiyoto, Tsiótto (チヨツト), vulgo *Tsióito*, 卒ソ度ト, once, for a moment. チヨトキケ, just hear! — *Tsiiito O matsi nasare*, wait a moment!
Sono toki, 其ソ時キ, then, at that time. 141.

CHAPTER V. ADVERBS. § 57.

Sono notsi, 其ノ後ニ, thereafter. 142.
Notsi-hodo, 後ノ程ニ, by and by. — *Notsi-notsi*, later.
Kono i-go, 此ノ以イ後ゴ, after this.
Kono-goro, 間ノ日ゴ, there, then. 145.
Kono hodo, 此ノ程ド, shortly, lately.
Kono aida, 此ノ間ダ, 以ノ前ゼン, shortly.

Saki ni, 昨キ者ニ, '以ゼ前, before, the time, that has immediately preceded the present, just now. *Mo sukisi saki ni*, a short time ago. 148.
Saki-goro, 先キ頃ゴ, lately.
Saki-hodo, 先キ刻ド, just now, presently. 150.

Definite notices of time like to-day, yesterday, to-morrow etc. are expressed by nouns with or without a previous adjective definition, e. g.:

Kon-nitsi. 今ノ日ニ, *Kon-nitsi wa*; 今ヤ日ワ, *Kro, Kioo*, this day, to-day.
Kesa, 今ヤ朝サ, this morning. 152.
Sikuzits, 昨ゾ日ジ, *Kinou*, キノフ (contr. from *Saki no fi*, 前ノ日ヒ), yesterday.
Siku-getsu, 昨ゾ月ゲ, last month.
Siku-nen, 昨ゾ年ネ, last year. 155.
Asi, *Asita* (*Asu*), 明タ日ス, to-morrow. — *Asu-nude*, till to-morrow.
Miyoo-nitsi, 明ミ日ニ, to-morrow. — *Miyoo-nitsi no jiro*, to-morrow noon.
Miyoo (*nitsi no*) *ban*, to-morrow morning. — *Miyoo-ban*, 明ミヤ晩バ, to-morrow evening.
Miyoo-gretsu, 明ミヤ月ゲ, next month.
Miyoo-nen, 明ミ年ネ, next year. 160.
Miyoo-go-nitsi, 明ミ後ゴ日ニ, the day after to-morrow; also *Asatte*, アサツテ.
Ake no tosi, *Akuru tosi*, 明ル, 年ト, next year.
Akuru fi, 明ル日ヒ, to-morrow.
Rai-nen, 來ラ年ネ, the year still to come, the next year.
Rai-getsu, 來ラ月ゲ, next month. 165.
Firu ni, 晝ニ, by day.
Ya-hun ni, 夜ヤ分フ, *Ya-tsiu*, 夜ヤ中チ, at night. 167.

For adverbial definitions, to the question: how often? are used

1. the repeating numbers cited in § 32, p. 143: *Fitś-tabi* or *Itsi-do*, once; *Fitś-tabi* or *Ni-do*, twice; *Fitś-tabi mi-tabi*, twice, thrice, continually, etc.

CHAPTER V. ADVERBS. § 57, 58.   181

2. *Mare ni*, 稀ニ, seldom.   165.
Suku naki toki ua, 少ナノ, 時ナハ, seldom.
Ōki toki ua, 多キノ, 時ナハ, often.   170.
Ori-ori or *yori-yori*, 時々, now and then.
Ori-fusi, 折々節々, 時節, from time to time, now and then.
Fu-tosite, 非常, sometimes.
Sibi-sibi, 数ヾ, often. — *Sera-seră*, 節ヾ, often.
Tabi-tabi, 度ヾ, at every turn.   175.
Tsuné ni, 常ニ, 恒, generally, always. — *Tsuné-dzuné*, continually.
Obitadasiku, 夥シヲッシク, manifold, often.   177.

§ 58. Adverbs of manner, indicating the form of thought or speech, in which the speaker represents the idea expressed in the predicate.

1. Affirmative.

Hei, ヘイ, with its variations: *kiki*, *ki*, vulgo *hai*, *ha*, yes.   178.
Sa-yoo, 左様, contracted *Soo*, so, thus, considered more polite than *Hei*. — *Soo ma'oo*, it will be so.
Sikito, 屹ト, certainly, truly.   180.
Tasikani, 慥ニ, certainly, truly.
Makoto ni, *Zitsu ni*, 実ニ, in truth, truly, forsooth, indeed. — *Masa ni*, 正ニ, indeed.
Geni, or *Geni-geni*, 現ニヾ, evidently, doubtlessly.
Kessité, 決而, surely; with subsequent negation: by no means, not at all.
Aridei ni, 有体ニ, solidly, to the purpose.   185.
Kitto, 急度ト, certainly.
Fit-zen, 必然, certainly. *Fit-dziyoo*, 必定, certainly, definitely.
Itsi-dziyoo, 一定, definitely.
Ka-ndrozu, 必ズ, certainly, doubtlessly, without doubt.
Motsi-ron, *Mu-ron*, *Ron-naku*, *Ron-nasi*, 勿論, = do not reason! = without contradiction; not to be contradicted.   190.
Sippari, サッパリ, in all respects; with subsequent negation: by no means. *Sappari* .... *sezu*, to do by no means.
Tsu-zen, *Tsu-zen*, 齊然, properly.
Isasaka, 聊ニカ, in short.   193.

182   CHAPTER V. ADVERBS. § 58, 59.

2. Negative.

Iiye, イゝエ, vulgo *iya*, no, *Iiya-iiya*, no, no.   194.

Remark. The negative: not, expressed in Japanese by n, as a rule, is included in the inflection of the verbs, by which a peculiar negative conjugation arises.

Fu-sin ni, 不ﾞ審ｼﾞﾆ, uncertainly, doubtfully.   195.

Fu-dd-sitè, 不ﾞ圖ﾆｼﾃ, suddenly, by chance.

3. Optative.

Doozo, 何卒ﾞ, though, than, Pray! *Doozo*, *kikare yo*, hear, if you please, hear though!   197.

Negawakuwa, 願ｸﾜﾝ, though (contracted from *Negai*, wish, and *Iwaku* sd, so as they say), so as one wishes. (See *Shopping-Dialogues* p. 11.)   198.

4. Supposing.

Mukotorashiku, probably. — *Ta-bun*, 多ﾌﾞ分ﾝ, perhaps.   199.

Toki ni yotte ed, *Koto ni yottard*, perhaps, according to circumstances.

Zi-ji ni yori, 時ｼﾞ宜ｷﾞﾆ寄ﾖﾘ, or *Zi-ji ni yotte* or *yottard*, if time be favorable, according to circumstances; under favorable circumstances.   201.

Uhkyerarikuwa, 疑ｷﾞｻﾞﾗｸﾜﾝ, probably.   202.

Zon-bun no si-dai, 存ｿﾞ分ﾌﾞﾉ次ｼ第ﾀﾞｲ, as I think; also *Zon-bun ni sita-gitte*. — *Zon-bun no si-dai siyo-moketa ari-mdsu ka*, are there books also?

§ 59. Adverbs connecting propositions, such as nevertheless, however, since they are conjunctional adverbs, are treated in the Chapter VIII on the Conjunctions.

ALPHABETICAL SYNOPSIS OF THE ADVERBS CITED.

The numbers correspond with those placed after the adverbs treated in § 53—59.

Ai-tai	103.	*Isoko ni*	68.	*Dèm ni*	55.	*Don bo-don*	71.
Ake no tosi	152.	*Isa*	156.	*Dai-itsi ni sd.*	79.	*Dono-kurai ooki*	81.
Akuru fi,	163.	*Imi-made*	156.	*Dai-ni ni sd.*	80.	*Doozo*	197.
Akuru tosi	162.	*Ama*	156.	*Dan-dan ni*	14.	*Dore-dake*	20.
Anodnekd	93.	*Issta*	156.	*Dani*	58.	*Dore-fodo*	20.
Amari	22.	*Ito ni*	99.	*Doko ni*	87.	*Dotsira*	88.
Ari-tei ni	185.	*Atsira*	88.	*Doko ni mo*	87.	*Fidàri ni*	102.
Aru toki ni	119.	*Iyunatte*	58.	*Doko ye*	87.	*Firi ni*	166.
Asatte	161.	*Ikahiri*	58.	*Doko yori*	87.	*Fissisi dto*	184.

CHAPTER V. ADVERBS. § 59.

Fudsiku	134.	Ippai ni	28.	Kono yoro	145.	Moo	117.
Fū-dziyoo	167.	Ippan ni	28.	Kono hodo	146.	Motsi-ron	190.
Fütütes ni	64.	Isasuku	105.	Kono i-go	144.	Mu-dd ni	56.
Fü-zen	187.	Is-so ni	29, 96.	Kononde	60.	Mukdi ni	105.
Fodo-fodo	49.	Itsi-bun va	37.	Kono toköro ni	90.	Mukdsi	122.
Fokǎ ni	96.	Itsi-dziyoo	198.	Kore-kura	136.	Mukūsi yori	122.
Fotonulo	46.	itsu de mo	110.	Koto-gotoku	85.	Mandsikǎ	87.
Fu-dd ate	196.	Itsu-ka	109.	Kotoni yattard	200.	Mu-ron	109.
Fu-i ni	76.	Itsu mo	110.	Kotsira	82.	Musa-musai to	18.
Fu-sin ni	105.	Itsu ni	64.	Kütsd̄siku, -siu	8.	Miudto	15.
Fu-soku ni	34.	Itsu ni vi	81.	Mabara ni	38.	Ma-ydku ni	56.
Fu-tomte	173.	Itsu zo	108.	Mada	113.	Ndku bsi ra	53.
Geni, Geni-geni	163.	Iya-nagara mo	68.	Madzu	113.	Naka-naku	49.
Giura-yuru	104.	Iyinika mó	34.	Mukǒto ni	182.	Naka ni	97.
Gururi to	101.	Ka-narazu	169.	Mikutorisikā	109.	Nana-me ni	100.
Hdi, Ha	178.	Kata-yutu	70.	Mare ni	168.	Nani-foto	19.
Haydku	4, 116.	Katuka	8.	Muxani	182.	Nüra-duke	72.
Hayju	4, 116.	Kata ni	101.	Mdd	81.	Neyusdiknei	198.
Hayuo	4, 116.	Kitigu	6.	Mata itsu ni vu	82.	Neugoro ni	61.
Hei, Ilthi	178.	Kittoo	6.	Ikataka	17.	Nolordzu	26.
Hi	178.	Katawara ni	101.	Maedri ni	103.	Natsi-hodo	143.
Hind-bini	134.	Kduko ni	69.	Maye-kata	115.	Notal ni	99.
Hulaiku	134.	Kdtsū-yitsu	31.	Maye ni	99.	Natsi-notsi	143.
Idzukun zo	88.	Kdtsū-mata	35.	Migi ni	102.	Obitadūsiku	177.
Iiya	194.	Kütsu-te	30.	Minu	83.	Ondziku	66.
Iiya-iiya	194.	Keo	151.	Miyoo-dea	158.	Oo-kalu	44.
Iige	194.	Ken	132.	Miyoo-ban	158.	Ooki taki ra	130.
Ik-koo	137.	Kessite	164.	Miyoo-gdtsu	159.	Ori-füzi	172.
Ikura	19.	Kinou	163.	Miyoo-go-nitsi	161.	Ori-ôri	171.
Imd	111.	Kioo	151.	Miyoo-nen	160.	Osi-nǎbete	84.
Imada	113.	Kittd	186.	„ nitsi	157.	Osikǎ	3, 118.
Imu-mude	112.	Kiu ni	139.	„ „ no dsu	158.	Osiu, Ousio	5.
Imi ni	111.	Koku ni	50.	„ „ no firu	157.	Otte	124.
Imi yori	111.	Kon-nitsi	151.	Mo-hayu	117.	Ottokǐ	126.
Ininhě	121.	Kono aida	147.	Mo-hayyu	117.	Oyoso	30.

CHAPTER V. ADVERBS. § 59.

Rai-gitsu	163.	Soro-soro	16.	To-kaku	75.	Yámka	7.
Rai-nen	161.	Soro-soro to	16.	Toki ni yatte va	200.	Yásua	7.
Ran-naka	190.	So-io	93.	To-mo kóki-mo	75.	Ya-tsia	167.
Ran-nga	190.	Sota ni	93.	Tomo ni	63.	Yga-yaku	130.
Sai-siyo ni vel	78.	Subite	23.	Tonto	23.	Ygu-ygu aid	52.
Sai-zen	135.	Suté ni	135.	Tsaku	93.	Yen-foo ni	93.
Suki-goro	140.	Sudzi-nakivini	107.	Too-zen	192.	Yoffodo	46.
Suki-hodo	130.	Suya ni	127.	Tsiki-dziká ni	130.	Yo-fodo	22.
Suki ni	90, 145.	Sai-bun	35.	Tsuku-goro	120.	Yo-kri ni	33.
Siku-gu'tan	154.	Sakidara	45.	Tsukaka	94.	Yoko ni	106.
Siku-nen	155.	Suka-naki toki		Tsuyoto	140.	Yoko-sama ni	106.
Siku-zita	155.	ni	160.	Tsuitto	140.	Yoku	1.
Sisniku-tomo	71.	Sukunuku sus	50.	Trito	81.	Yio	1.
Sippari	191.	Saka-adka-towo	71.	Tritto	81.	Yoo-yuka	130.
Sirri ni	66.	Suuriyuki ni	11.	Tsiyyu-to	47.	Yoo-you sid	82.
Saye	67.	Sard	69.	Tsin	97.	Yori-yori	171.
Sengio	179.	Suzi-kai ni	107.	Twito	140.	Yoroska	2.
Sitsu-setsu	174.	Ta-bun	199.	Tzo-do	47.	Yordeu	5.
Sibaniku	129.	Tabi-tabi	175.	Tsui ni	183.	Yoso kara	91.
Subá-mbi	174.	Tsuta	66.	Tsumibirukvini	10.	Yoso ni	91.
Sutzuki ni	9.	Tiudó-iwa	114.	Tsund-dsund	176.	Yoso ye	91.
Sikito	160.	Tai-gai	43.	Tsune ni	176.	You	1.
Sikiri ni	154.	Tai-avo	41.	Ukegatte	59.	Ze-ki	73.
Sutd ni	100.	Tai-tei	43.	Uri ni	98.	Zen-zen ni	15.
Siyo-siyo	93.	Tákumin ni	40.	Usiro ni	99.	Zi-gi ni yottara	201.
Sokí ni	101.	Tamasukuni	13.	Utsiggourákutsa	202.	Zi-gi ni yotte	201.
Soka-zi ni	133.	Tuta-tama	77.	Utsi ni	98.	Ziki ni	136.
Sono foki ni	53.	Tsunkdni	12, 181.	Uyé ni	100.	Zitsu ni	182.
Sono motsi	142.	Tasinde	61.	Wáruku	3.	Ziya-bun ni	36.
Sono toki	141.	Tu-siyo	98.	Wárua	3.	Zon-bun nó si-	
Sono tokiro ni	90.	Ta-io	92.	Ya-bun ni	167.	dai	203.
Sono ne wi	66.	Titsi-motsi	131.	Yugate	132.		
Siw	179.	Tyu-zen	192.	Yara-yara	17.		

CHAPTER VI.

WORDS EXPRESSIVE OF RELATION.
(POSTPOSITIONS.)

§ 60. Our prepositions which show the relation, in which the chief idea of a sentence stands to other objects or ideas, are superseded in Japanese by postpositions. We call them words expressive of relation.

Chief among these words are the inflections (see Chapter I, p. 61), viz:

ヘ, ve, he, or ニ, ye, e, = wards, to. Dative and Terminative (see p. 68).
ニ, ni, = with relation to, in, to (see p. 68).
ト, to, = to (see p. 70).
ニ, ni; テ, te,   } Local, Modal and Instrumental (see pp. 68,
ニテ, nite; デ, de (pron. nde),} 70.
ヨリ, yori; カラ, kara, = out of, from. Ablative (see p. 71).

§ 61. All other relations are expressed either by:

1. nouns which, as such, are declinable and have the further attributive definition, as genitive, before them, as *Yama uye* or *Yama no uye*, the topmost of a mountain; *Yama uye ni*, on the top of a mountain: or

2. verbs, which being, either in their radical form, or in the gerund in テ, te, in proportion as they govern the accusative, the modal, or the dative have their object with the inflectional termination ヲ, wo, or ニ, ni, or ヘ, ve, before

them, indifferently, whether this object is a noun-substantive or a verb used substantively.

§ 62. Nouns, used as expressive of relation, are:

1. Uvé, Uyé, 上ニ, ヲ, 1) above, upon (with reference to a place).

Tsuki no uyé ni ki wo uyuru, to plant a tree upon the grave. — *Tsuki no ue no ki*, a tree upon the grave. — *Aru uyé ni mata fitotsu*, above which there is still one. — *Kono uyé wa deki-masènu*, = what is above that, does not happen, = more I can not give for it [1]. — *Sono uye wa nai* (or *ari-masènu*), there is nothing above that [2].

2) upon, after (with reference to time).

Gin-mi (or *Tadōri*) *no uré fatto wo motte basu* (吟味 (or 科) ノ 上之 法ヲ 度リ, 以ヲテ 罰ヌス), upon inquiry punish according to law [3]. — *Un-ziyan nou-nri no uré rd* (運上 納 濟テ, 上ニヘ), upon payment of the duty [4]. — *Sina-mono wo ukè-totta uyéte* (*dai-kin wo*) *agu-maïou*, = after having received the goods I shall pay (the price) [5].

Chinese compounds with 上 *ziygu*, too, upon.

山ニ 上ニ, upon mountains. — 雲ニ 上ニ, upon clouds. — 座ノ 上ニ, upon the throne. — 以ノ 上ニ, upwards, prior to a time, *sorr yori morr*. — *San nen i-ziygu*, prior to three years ago.

2. Sitá, 下ニ, beneath, under, below.

Sitá-ni sitá-ni, down! down! = kneel! — *Sitá yori waki-idsuru midsu*, water springing up from beneath. — *Siki no sitá*, what is under a foot measure, the divisions of a foot [6]. — *Watakusi wa anata yori sitá de gozáru*, = I am beneath you, I am less than you.

Chinese compounds with 下ノ, ヘ, ヲ.

天ノ 下ノ, 宇ノ 下ヲ, *Ten-ka*, *U-ka*, what is under the heavens, under the firmament, the earth. — 地ノ 下ヘ, under (in) the earth. — 山ノ 下ヲ, *San-ka*, the foot of a mountain. — 以ノ 下ヲ, = *Sono ato*, after, since. — *San nen i-ka*, three years since.

---

[1] Shopping-Dialogues, p. 15.   [4] Ibid. p. 29.
[2] Treaty f. 1858. Art. V. al. 2.   [5] Ibid. III. 6.
[3] Shopping-Dialogues, p. 13.   [6] Ibid. p. 29.

3. **Mavo, Mayo**, vulgo **Mai**, 前之, ミ (of *ma*, eye, and *re*, side, direction), before, local or temporary.

Matsu-maye, = before the pine-trees. — *Yri-zi wo mawe no mare ni kukaete nin-you m*, she holds the suckling to the breast and suckles it. — *Itsu-ka nen mawe ni*, a year previous [1]). — *Kaiko idzūru maye ni*, before the silkworm comes out. — *Go nen yori maw*, = from the fifth year forward, i. e. before the fifth year.

Chinese compounds with 前 ヒ, *zen*, before.

面之前 ヒ, before the front of. — 門 ヒ 前 ヒ, before the door. — 以 ヽ 前 ヒ, previous to. — *Kono fi-giri aruiwa sono i-zen nite mo*, at this date or even earlier [1]).

4. **Notsi**, 後 ヒ, (from *no*, back, whence *nōku*, retreat, and *tsi*, place), behind, after, with a definition of time, refers to a time which is behind, with reference to the present, future.

Kaze okiru notsi, after the rising of the wind. — *Kaze ga fukite notsi*, after the wind has blown. — *Sono notsi*, thereafter. — *Ima yori oyōso ziyn futsi ka gōtsa no notsi yori fitsūzu minato wo firaku bōsi*, after the lapse of 18 months from now a harbour shall be opened [2]). — 自ジ 今ミ 以ィ 後ゞ, from now for the future.

5. **Omote**, 面ヰ, 表, the face, the countenance, the fore-side, before.

6. **Ura**, 裏ゞ, 裡, the internal, the inside of a garment; the reverse of a coin; the opposite.

Iyē no urā, the inner side of a house. — *Urōmi won no urā nari*, disgust is the reverse of inclination.

7. **Usiro**, 後ヒ, after.

Yama wo usiro ni si, kawa wo omote ni si, (the village) has mountains for background, a river for fore-ground, it has mountains behind and a river before it. — Also the inside of a garment, as reverse, is called *usiro*.

8 **Saki**, 先ヰ, 前, point, with reference to time, beforehand, past.

Saki no tosi, a former year. — *Saki ni*, earlier, before. — *Go nen bakari saki yori m*, only since the last five years. — 卯ヒ 先ヰ, *O saki!* you before! you first! after you!

9. **Ato**, 趾ヒ, 跡, footstep; behind.

Fito no ato ni tsuite yuku, go behind any one. — *Sono ato*, afterwards.

---

[1]) Treaty Art. X. al. 1. [2]) Ibid. XI. 1. [3]) Ibid. II. 8.

10. Utsi, 内ヲ, 中. within.

Iyé no utsí ni aru, to be within the house. — *Kiyo-rim-dō no utsí ni* (居ヲ 御ヲ 場", 内ヲ＿), within the ground, where one has residence ¹). — *Hiyoo kikú no utsí yori*, from out both empires ²). — *Utsí yori fokú wo ukúgaou*, to spy from within what is without. — *Mado no utsí re fairu*, to go in by the window. — *Teki no utsí re seme-iru*, to press into the enemy. — *Yumé no utsí de aru*, to meet in the dream. — *Fuyu no utsí ni*, as long as it is winter. — *San-nen no utsí ni*, within a space of three years. — *San nitsí utsí de deki-masu*, it may happen within three days' time ³). — *Hiyākú me utsí de wa uré-masénu*, within (under) ten taels will I not sell it ⁴). — *Kono ni zi no utsí idzure naritomo motsíyu bísi*, of the two signs each (whichever it be) may be used. — *Kuru utsí ni*, while one is eating. — *Sina-mono wo uke-toránu utsí wa, dai-kin wa agerare-nusáínu*, = within the not receiving of the goods (as long as I have not received the goods), no payment will be made ⁵). — *Men-kiyo nakúrisí ga utsí nite*, as long as there was no permission.

Much in use also, are Chinese compounds with 内ヲ, ?, dai or nai: *Kai-dai* (海? 内ヲ), what is within the seas, the continent. — *Kikú-dai* (國ヲ 内ヲ), within the borders of a country. — *Kikú-dai no dai-itsi no yóka-siya*, the first scholar of the empire. — *Kono dzu (dso) wa Nippon kikú-dai ni jun-antsúsa bísi*, this article shall be made known throughout the Japanese empire ⁶). — *Bu-nai* (部ヲ 内ヲ), the inmost, interior. — *Nippon no bu-nai wo riyokó-su*, to travel over the interior of Japan ⁷). — *Ka-nai* (家? 内ヲ), what is within the house, the family.

11. Fōkā, Hōkā, 外ヲ, without; except, besides.

Kono fokú hoku-kiku kisí ni dté fúōtsu minato wo firákú bísi, besides on the north coast a harbour shall be opened ⁸). — *Yáku-suyo no fokú re uru bíkardsa*, except to the government may not be sold ⁹). — *Kri-sei no fokú onna*, women except wry castles (prostitutes). — *To wo fokú yori todzuru*, to shut a door from without. — *Dai-ku mono fokú idku-nin wa kane-idku wi motsí-masu*, carpenters and other workmen use the iron-foot. — *Tan-mono to ara-mono wono fokú ari-masú*, there are piece-goods, and raw materials and so forth.

---

¹) Treaty. Art. VIII. al. 1.   ³) Ibid. X, 1.   ⁵) Shopping-Dialogues, p. 9.
²) Ibid p. 4.   ⁴) Ibid. p. 13.   ⁸) Treaty. Art. II. al. 17.
⁵) Ibid. Art. I al. 3, 6.   ⁶) Ibid. II 2.   ⁹) Ibid. II. 18.

Chinese compounds with 外ゲ, gwai, outside, without, out of:

門ニ外ゲ, Mon-gwai, without the gate. — 口ヲ外ゲ, K'oo-gwai, out of the mouth, out of the mouth of a river or harbor.

12. **Soto**, 外ソ, originally the back door, at present generally: **without**.

Sotó-mo for Soto-omo, the back- or winter-side of a mountain. — Suto no soto ni, without the village.

13. **Mukávi, Mukái**, 向ミ・フ, vulgo also **Múkau, Mukoo**, as substantive, 'the opposite quarter, the direction opposite anything.

Karega sumi-ka wa waga-lyé no mukhi ni dru, his dwelling is opposite my house. — Mukfu no kisi ve fitó wo watdsu, to put people over to the opposite side (of a river).

14. **Avída, Aída**, 間ヒ・ダ, the interval, space between things, between; space between two points of time, while.

Aida no fima, pause, leisure, opportunity for anything. — Kono aida, between. — Sono aida, meanwhile. — Yama no aida ni midzü úru wo tani-gawa to iru, the appearance of water between mountains is called a valley-brook. — Oyiso ik-ka nen no aida, for the time of one year ¹). — Tada siyau-bai wo suru aida ni nomi, tou-riu-suru koto wo u-béni, only while they carry on trade, may they hold residence (there) ²).

Chinese compounds with 間ヒ, ゲ, kan, gen:

田ニ間ニ, between rice-fields. — 石ニ間ニニ 生ゲテ, to grow between rocks. — 人ニ間ニ, Nin-gen, among men; mankind.

15. **Naka**, 中ナ, the middle, in the midst of, amidst; among.

Ta no naka no ly', a hut in the middle of the field. — Riyau san no naka no riu-sii (雨ニ山ニ、中ナノ 流ル 水ヲ), streaming water just between two mountains. — Yo-naka, the middle of the night, midnight. — Kusa no naka de náka kera, crickets that chirp in (between, among) the grass.

Chinese compounds with 中ヂ, tin, in the midst:

Sai-tiu ni (水ヲ 中ヂニ) sumi mono, beings which live in fresh water. — 海ニ中ヂ, 物ヲ, Kai-tiu no mono, something that is in the sea, a production of the sea. — Kai-tiu ni irite aráhi wo toru, to dive into the sea and fetch up pearl-mussels. — 地ナ 中ヂニ, Tsi-tiu ni, in the earth. — 土ト 中ニ, Do-tiu.

---

¹) Treaty. Art. IV. al. 8.   ²) Ibid. 11. 13.

in the ground. — 道ノ中ニ, *Dọu-tạiu*, = mid-way, half-way, on the way. — 雲ノ中ニ, *Un-tạiu*, in clouds.

16. **Soba**, 側ニ, 傍 (from *soi*, come near and *ba*, place), the neighborhood, next, at the side of, by.

Fi no soba ni koi, come next (or by) the fire!

17. **Kata**, 方ニ, 遍ニ, side; with reference to time, as much as about, against.

Fiyási-kata, *Nisi-kata*, *Kita-kata*, *Minami-gata*, the east-, west-, north-, south-side. — *Kita-kata no kazí*, wind from the north. — *Yo-ake-kata*, = the side, on which the night goes open, i. e. about the dawn of the day. — *Sono ji no yuu-kata ni*, against the fall of the evening. — *Sore yori kono kata*, = from there to this side, i. e. since that time.

Chinese compounds: 海ノ邊ニ, *Kai-bin*, on sea. — *Kai-bin no nin*, people that live on (at) sea. — 葦ノ水ノ邊ニ生ズル, *Asi ra midzu ni siyọu ru*, the reed grows on the water.

The spoken language often supersedes *Kata* with the Chinese **Fóo** (**Hóo**), 方ニ, 下, side, quarter. — *Doko ni O kie masiruka?* whither are you going? ... *san no hoo ni* (or *hóoye*), to Mr. N's. — *Anata no hoo ni*, at or to your side, by or to you '). — *Sono fio*, his side, you. See p. 84.

18. **Futori**, 遍リ, round, round about.

Ike no futori no tsutsumi, a dike round a fish pond.

19. **Mawari**, 回リ, 廻, 周, circumference, round about, round.

Yasiki-mạruri ni, within the compass of dwellings.

Chinese expression: 周囲, *Siu-i*, round about. — 其ノ住ノ場ノ周囲ニ門モ墻モ設ケズ, round about their dwelling place people place neither gate nor fence ').

20. **To**, 與ト, with, Lat. *cum*, indicates the express coupling of two or more objects; it is a declinable suffix and, so far, a word expressive of relation.

Ikare-to onaziküto (, 與ト誰ノ同ジク), = identicalness — with which? — *Ybisu-to wa-bokü sità*, peace has been made with the barbarians. — *Kimi-to tomoni suru*, to hold with his master, to be attached to him. — *Hana, tori*, flowers, birds. — *Hana-to tori wo yekaku*, = to paint birds with (and) flowers. —

') *Shipping Inteligence*, p. 14.   ') Treaty, Art. II. al. 10.

CHAPTER VI. WORDS EXPRESSIVE OF RELATION. § 62.   191

Hana tori-to wo yekáku, to paint flowers and also birds. — *Sisi*, lion; *Tora*, tiger. — *Sisi-to tora wa*, as for the tiger with the lion; or also: as for the lion and the tiger, provided the principal accent be placed on „tiger." — *Kane-ziyáku-to kuzira-ziyáku wa doo-kawari másíku?* = as for the whalebone and the iron foot, what difference is there? [1]. — *Asi*, there; *Koi*, here; *Asi kotsi-to*, there and also here.

...*to* ...*to*, repeated after two nouns coordinate, answers to our both... and..., as well, as... also.., Lat. *et..et*, *que..que*.. — *Hana-to tori-to*, both flowers and birds. — *Olanda kikú-wyu to Dai Nippon Tai-kun to riyyu-kóku no konsin kátsu siyyu-bai no tsusimi wo siróka-sen kato wo hossite*, the King of Holland and the Tai-kun of Japan wishing to extend the relations of friendship and commerce of both countries etc. [1]. — *Nippon-to San-kan-to no atsukai no koto*, negotiations of (between) Japan and the Three states. — *Hana-to tori-to wo yekáku*, to paint flowers as well as birds. — *Yuku-to kururu-to ni mato wo iru*, in going to and fro to shoot at the mark. — *Faracu ni Nippon to gwai-koku to no kwa-hei wo motsiiru koto samadake nási* [2]), = there is no obstacle to using either Japanese or foreign money in payments. — The characteristic of the coupling is necessary here, as without that it does not attract notice.

Remark. If, as in the expression: a valley with or without water, the presence or absence of one object near the other is intended, then the verbs *dru*, present and *náki* (see p. 108, n°. 30), not present, are used, thus: *Midzu dru tani*, a valley with water; *Midzu náki tani*, a valley without water.

21. Tonari, 隣 (from *to*, door, family, and *narabi*, row), neighborhood; next, close to.

Yákú-siyo no tonari ni, next the government house. — Kin-siyo (*kinjo*), 近所, a place near, neighborhood.

22. Si-dai, 次第, rank, following, in proportion to.

Negai-si-dai, according to wish, in proportion as it is wished [1]).

23. Toóri, 通, passage; along.

Warada no feri toóri ni witará kaiko, silkworms lying along the edge of the straw-tray. — *Fama toóri no murá mina...*, all the villages along the strand. —

---

[1] *Shopping-Dialogues*, p. 31.
[2] *Treaty*, Art. IV. al. 2.
[3] *Treaty*, at the beginning.
[4] Ibid. IV. 3.

道ヲ理リノ, 通ヒニ, *dyu-ri no todri ni*, according to right. — 別ヲ冊ヲノ
通ヒニ, following a separate writing [1]). — *Waga kokóro ye no todri ni*, after (in)
my opinion.

24. Tamé, 爲ぇ, purpose, aim, end, the destination of a thing. *Tamé ni*,
for, for the service of, on behalf of, for the sake of, on account of.

Fitó no tame ni, for, on account of others. — *Waga-tame ni*, for my sake. —
Simo kami no tame ni su, the less is for the service of the greater. — *Tate-mono no
tame ni kari-uru ikka no ba-siyo*, a place hired for building [2]). — *Kono okite wo
kataka-sen tame ni*, for the maintenance of this article [3]). — *Uru tame ni*, for sale.

25. Kavari, 替リ, 代, barter. *Kavari ni*, in exchange for, instead of,
for. — *Kono fitó no kavari ni,* for (instead of) this man.

26. Mado, 迄ヂ, 迫, 迄, the aim towards which a movement is directed;
to, into, till, until, with reference to place or time, opposed to *yori*, from.

Firato yori Nagasaki made san ziyu jatsi ri ari, from Firato to Nagasaki it is
28 *ri*. — *Itsu made watdkusi mataneba naranu ka?* till when (how long) must I
wait? — *Asu made*, till to-morrow. — *Ten-si yori motte siyo-zin ni itdru made*,
= from the emperor himself till one comes (*itdru made*) to the common man [4]). —
I-fúku, ya-gu, tubi no rui made ge-suru, clothes, bedding, even to shoes, are
distributed. — *Kokonitsu han doki yori nandtsu made utsi ni*, = within one till four
o'clock, between one and four o'clock [5]). — *Yok-ka made ni deki-mdsu*, by the fourth
day (of the month) it will be ready [6]).

§ 63. Verbs in the gerund, used as words expressive of relation, are

A. With a previous accusative, ヲ, *wo*:

1. Motte, 以ヲ, using, by means, with, the gerund of *Motsi*, to seize,
hold, use.

The object that is seized, or taken with the hand, is either the object direct of an action later to be mentioned, or the means of carrying it out.

It is object direct in sentences as:

將ヲ詩ヲ莫シ浪ニ傳ヘシムルコトナカレ, *Si wo motte nami ni tsutsuru koto na-
kare*, i. e. literally: Taking the poem let it not be abandoned to the waves!
= let not the poem be abandoned to the waves.

---

[1]) Treaty, Art. III. al. 1.   [2]) Ibid. II. 9.   [3]) Ibid. II. 9.
[4]) Dai Gaku, § 9.   [5]) Shopping-Dialogues, p. 17.   [6]) Ibid. p. 10.

The object of *Motte* is used as the means of carrying out an action in sentences as:

以テ人ヲ治ム人ト, *Fitó wo motte fitó wo osimú*, to treat mankind as mankind. — *Irova wo motte rui wo wakásii*, to divide the classes according to the Irova.

2. **Tovorite, Toórite,** contracted **Toótte,** 通シテ, going through or along..., the gerund of *Toviri*, go through, pass.

Mon wo toótte, going through the gate. — *Fi no naka wo toótte*, through the midst of the fire. — *Mitsi-suzi wo toótte yuku*, go along a way.

3. **Tsutátte,** vulgo **Ts'tatte,** along, the gerund of *Tsutái*, go along.

Kai-gan wo tsutátte itai ri bakári yukúba, if one goes a ri along the coast.

4. **Fete,** 經テ, through, along, during, the gerund of *Fe*, *Fúru*, to go away, to go along.

Sono fa fuyu wo fete sibomazu, the foliage does not fade in the winter.

5. **Nozókitè, Nozóltó,** 除キテ, setting behind, excepted, except, the gerund of *Nozóki)i*, a (contracted from *notai ni oki*, to set behind).

Nippon siyo kwa-fei ra, tou-zen wo nozóku, yuyuts-su kai (日ノ本ノ諸ノ 貨ノ幣ハ銅ヲ錢ヲ除テ輪ニ出スヘシ), all Japanese money, except copper money, may be circulated [1]).

B. Verbs, used as words expressive of relation, with a previous local or dative, 二, *ni*:

1. ...*ni óité*, in, at, strengthened local form, of *ni* (in, at) and *óité*, or *witté*, (於テ于), = establissant, Fr. *en établissant*, the gerund of *oki*, 置テ, to place, establish, erect. When merely *ni* and when *ni óité* is used, will appear from the following examples. The expression: „The Dutchmen staying in Japan, = the Dutchmen in Japan," is rendered by *Nippon ni óru Oranda-zin* [2]); in the expression: „this document shall be exchanged at Nagasaki," on the other hand the local is expressed by *ni óité*, and the translation runs: *Kono fon-siyo wo Nagasaki ni óité tori-kayésu-bési* [3]). In the first case the definition of place where? is governed by the *óru* or *óru*, dwell, immediately following; in the second case the definition of place, where?, because not dependent on the verb, exchange, it is, by the addition of *óité*, made an adverbial phrase. — This remark agrees

---

[1] Treaty v. 1858. Art. IV, al. 1. [2] Ibid. VII. 1.
[3] Ibid., after the Japanese text Art. XI, al. 1; after the Dutch text Art. X, al. 4.

194   CHAPTER VI. WORDS EXPRESSIVE OF RELATION. § 63.

with all the definitions of place, occurring in the Japanese text of the document cited.

The object of *dité* may also be an action, one is engaged in, e. g.: *Fan-sóku wo okdsu ni dite ed* (法ヲ則ヲヽ犯ス。於テハ), by violating the Regulations [1].

The derivative from *oki*, viz *okéru*, = to be fixed or placed, preceded by a local in *ni*, answers to the expression: the position with relation to; e. g:

而物ヲ君ヲ / 弗テ也愛ス / 仁ビレレ之ヲ / 之ビレ於テ *Kun-si no mono ni okéru, kore wo ai-site zin-nezu,* = relation of the philosopher to the creatures: he loves them, is however not humane toward them. *Hia Meng*, Cap. VII, § 61.

2. **Yorite, Yotte,** 依リテ. 寄. 據. 因, = having its point of departure and thus also its point of support in, from, in consequence of, on the ground of, the gerund of *yori, yoru*, to get out from. Compare p. 71, 72.

Korera naro siro ni yorite, teki ni kudáranu, those yet relying on a castle, do not submit to the enemy. — *Kore ni yotte*, in consequence of that, therefore, — *Tsikara ni yotte*, in proportion to his strength. — *Toki ni yotte wá*, in proportion to time. — *Iro ni yotte nedan ga kawari masu*, as the colors are different there is a difference in price [2]. — *Negai ni yotte* [3], on entreaty. — *Iru ni yotte*, because there is.

3. **Tsukite,** vulg. **Tsutte,** 付テ. テ. 就, concerning, the gerund of *Tsuki*, concern, come to.

Fune kisi ni tsuku, the ship touches the coast. — *Kore ni tsuki*, or *tsuite*, or *tsuite ra*, concerning that, what concerns this.

The attributive form is *Tsuite no*, e. g. 宗ヲ旨ニ付テ, 爭ヲ論ズ, *Siu-si ni tsuite no soo-ron*, dispute concerning (about) religion [4].

Remark. To *Toote ra* also, for which the written forms: *Tottewa* and *Tattewa* [5] have crept in, the meaning of: concerning, *quand à*, have been given, without reference to the limitation of its use. As gerund of *Toçi*, u (問フ), to ask, *Toote ra* means: if one ask, to the question; and the expression: *Oose ra mottomo nareidomo, waga-mi ni tuote ra, kanai-gátai*, thus

---

[1] Treaty. Art. V. al. 4.   [2] *Shopping-Dialogues*, p. 71.   [3] Treaty. Art. VIII. al. 1.
[4] Ibid. VII. 4.   [5] COLLADO. p. 57. RODRIGUEZ p. 26.

CHAPTER VI. WORDS EXPRESSIVE OF RELATION. § 63.   195

means: the command is indeed reasonable, but if one ask me, it is not easy to be carried out.

4. **Itárite**, vulg. **Itátte**, 至リテ, 至テ, = coming to, respecting; with definitions of time: against, towards, the gerund of *Itári*.

Taikun ni itáttera, does it come to the Taikun, what concerns the Taikun. — *Fáruni itátteru*, towards the spring.

5. **Tai-sité**, 對シテ, standing opposite, towards, the gerund of *Tai-si*, to be opposite, being the further definition, opposite to which, characterized by *ni* or *we*, sometimes also by *to*. Compare p. 68.

Oranda-zin wa tai-ni fou wo okâseru Nippon-zin ra, Japanese, who have transgressed the law, towards Dutchmen. — *Nippon-zin ni tai-si fou wo okasitaru Oranda-zin ra*, Dutchmen, who have transgressed the law, towards Japanese [1].

6. **Mukávite**, **Mukáite**, also *Mukirate*, *Mukóte*, 向テ, 向テ, against, the gerund of *Mukuri*, to be pointed against something.

Fito ni mukáite (or *mukóote*) *ku-ron-suru*, to contend against some one.

Mukárite, *Mukátte*, 向テ, the gerund of *Mukári*, to be turned against something; e. g. *Kaze ni mukátte hasiru*, to run against the wind.

Mukité, *Muité*, 向テ, against, the gerund of *Muki*, to turn against. — *Ryogu biu ni muité*, towards both sides.

7. **Sitagaute**, **Sitagoote**, 從テ, according to, complying with, the gerund of *Sitagari*, *Sitagai*, to submit, to yield, to follow.

Sitagátte, 從テ, according to, the gerund of *Sitagari*, to be subordinate. — (*Ni motsu no*) *aturi ni sitagatte wa-ziyou wo osamu beni*, according to the value (of the goods) shall customs be paid [2]. — *Ki-i ni sitagutte* (貴意ニ從テ), according to the noble (i. e. your) pleasure.

ALPHABETICAL SYNOPSIS OF THE WORDS EXPRESSIVE OF RELATION TREATED.

Aida = Awida . . . § 62. 14.	De = Nite . . . . . § 60.	Go = Natsi . . . . § 62. 6.
Ato, behind . . . . 62. 9.	Fite, through . . § 63. A. 4.	Girai = Fuka . . . . 62. 11.
Awida, between . 62. 14.	Fokd, without . . § 62. 11.	He = Ve . . . . . 60.
Ben = Kata . . . . 62. 17.	Fotori, round about 62. 16.	Hoka = Fokn . . . 62. 11.
Dai = Utsi . . . . 62. 10.	Ge = Sitá . . . . . 62. 2.	Itárite = Itátte . § 63. B. 4.

[1] Treaty Art. V. el. I. 8.   [2] Ibid. III. 2.

Itáíte, to, concerning, respecting . . § 63. B. 4.	Maité = Mukité. . § 63. B. 6.	Teia = Naka . . . § 62. 13.
	Makité, against. 63. B. 6.	To, to, with . . . 60.
Ka = Sita . . . . . § 62. 2.	Mukoo = Mukya. . § 62. 13.	To, with, together,
Kan = Aida. . . . 62. 14.	Makóoté, against § 63. B. 6.	and . . . . 62. 20.
Kara, out . . . . 60.	Nai = Utai. . . . . § 62. 10.	Tomiri, next . . . 62. 21.
Kuta, next, to; against, about 62. 17.	Naka, in the midst of 62. 13.	Toôtte = Tororite § 63. A. 2.
	Ni, at, in . . . . 60.	Toote ca . . . . . 63. B. 3.
Karari, for, instead of . . . . 62. 23.	Nite, in, with . . 60.	Toiri, along . . . § 62. 23.
	Notai, behind, after 62. 4.	Tororite, through § 63. A. 2.
Kr = Sitá . . . . . 62. 2.	Nozáite Nozôkite § 63. A. 5.	Traite = Toukite 63. B. 3.
Mide, to . . . . . 62. 26.	Nozôkite, except. 63. A. 5.	Toukite, concerning
Mai = Mare . . . . 62. 3.	Oité, in . . . . . . 63. B. 1.	§ 63. B. 3.
Macari, round about . . . . . . 62. 19.	Onote, before . . . § 62. 5.	Toitdite, along . 63. A. 3.
	Saki, before hand 62. 5.	Tétatte = Toutdite 63. A. 3.
Mare, Maye, before 62. 3.	Si-dai, following. 62. 29.	Uró, inwards . . § 62. 6.
Mate, by means of, with . . . § 63. A. 1.	Sita, beneath . . . 62. 2.	Uairo, behind . . 62. 7.
	Sitayóitte, accord. to 63. B. 7.	Utai, within . . . 62. 10.
Makii = Makari . § 62. 13.	Sitayyute, „ 63. B. 7.	Ure Uyé, up . . 62. 1.
Maktlite = Mukirite	Sitagoote. „ 63. B. 7.	Uyé, up . . . . . . 62. 1.
§ 63. D. 6.	Sin-i, round about § 62. 19.	Ve, wards, to . . 60.
Makilei, contrary § 62. 13.	Soba, next . . . . . 62. 16.	Yori, out, from . 60.
Makirite, against § 63. B. 6.	Soto, without . . . 62. 12.	Yorite, on the
Mukirite, against 63. D. 6.	Tai-site, towards § 63. B. 5.	ground of . . § 63. D. 2.
Mukitte = Mukirite 63. D. 6.	Taind, for, on account of . . . . § 62. 21.	Yitte = yorite . . 63. B. 2.
Mukyu Makóri § 62. 13.		Zen = Mare. . . . . § 62. 3.
Mukyrute, against § 63. D. 6.	Te, in, with . . . 60.	Ziyyu = Uyé . . . . 62. 1.

CHAPTER VII.

THE VERB.

> Man begreift nichts, dessen Entstehung man nicht einsieht.
> STEINTHAL

In the treatment of this chapter, the question, which presents itself most prominently, is, what are the conjugational forms of the Japanese verb, and what do they mean. Included in it is the answer to the question, how are the conjugational forms of the Western languages expressed in the Japanese.

§ 64. The voices of the Japanese verb are:
Intransitive.
Transitive, Factive or Causative.
Passive, but in the form of an Active.
Negative, since the verbal terminations contain in themselves a negative element, n.

§ 65. The Moods are: the indefinite Root-form; the Imperative which, at the same time, is the basis of the Optative; the indicative Closing form; the Substantive-form (Infinitive), at once Attributive form (Participle), and a derivative Adverbial form (see § 107). — The Root and the Substantive forms are declinable, and by declension express the mood definitive of time and cause (Subjunctive) and the Conditional etc.

§ 66. The Tenses are root-tenses (Present, Preterit, Future, 現在, Gen-zai; 過去, Kwa-ko; 未來, Mi-rai), and derivative tenses. A root-tense is indefinite (aorist), when the action with reference to the speaker is present, past, or future, and is not, with reference to a given period of time, represented as perfect or imperfect. The Japanese verb pays attention to this distinction, and also expresses the beginning, the continuance and the ending, as well as the repetition of an action by peculiar forms.

§ 67. Person and number are not noticed in the verb, whereas the grammatical distinction of three persons (I, thou, he) as well as that of singular and plural, have remained foreign to the language. (See pp. 73 and 53).

Instead of a grammatical distinction, a qualifying one steps in, noticeable by the choice of the verb, by which the speaker distinguishes his own being or acting from that of another person, but particularly noticeable, because he adds the augmentative prefix On or O, which plays so important a part in the domain of the pronouns (see p. 75), to the verb also, as soon as the action that it expresses, proceeds from a person, to whom he bears respect, or is a condition imputed to that person. The want of a grammatical distinction of three persons is fully made good by the manner in which a courtly speaker qualifies his own being or acting and that of another.

The way in which courtesy expresses itself in the verbs, is further explained in an Appendix to this chapter.

§ 68. The verbal root. Every verbal root (the essential part or the root of a verb) terminates either in e or i (compare the Latin *doce* and *audi*). These terminations are the verbal element proper, which is subject to transformation or declension. Whereas we, by means of the European letters are able to disengage these elements from the verbal root and treat them separately, the Japanese syllabic system of writing represents them as bound to the final consonant of the verbal root.

As the element i undergoing a strengthening, in certain cases becomes a or o, whereas the element e, in the same cases remains unchanged, this leads naturally to a division of the verbs into two conjugations: a nondeflecting one in e, and a deflecting one in i, called by some a regular conjugation in e and an irregular one in i.

There is a group of about forty verbs derived by a nondeflecting element *i*, which in respect of their transformation are ranked under the nondeflecting conjugation in *e*. They are enumerated and explained in § 92.

The verbal root or the root-form answers logically, but not formally, to our Infinitive. *Ak*, to open; *Kaki*, to write; *Yuki*, to go.

A verb is in the indefinite root-form, when it is the first member of a compound verb, as well as in the coördinate connection of propositions which has the peculiarity, that only the last of the propositions linked together expresses the definition of time and manner, whereas in the preceding sentences the verb is left in the indefinite root form (compare p. 40).

The dictionaries of Japanese origin do not point out the root-form. But as a knowledge of it is necessary to being able to conjugate a verb, we, here, as in our Dictionary, place the root-form on the foreground.

The root-form is equivalent to a substantive, and is declinable by means of suffixes (see § 7).

Ak ni, to the opening, to open. Dative and Terminative; Supine.

Ak ni va, = *Akenba*, = *Akeba*, while one opens. Local, Modal.

Ak te, by opening. Instrumental, Modal.

On this principle forms are obtained, which answer to some of our moods.

§ 69. The imperative mood, *Ge-dzi no kotoba*. The Imperative terminates in the accented *e*.

In the nondeflecting verbs the root is at once imperative: *Ak*, open! — In the deflecting the termination *i* changes into *e*: *Kiki*, to write; *Kak*, write! *Kuri*, to eat; *Kure*, *Kuye*, eat!

This form may be strengthened by suffixing the exclamation *yo* (see p. 62), for which in the eastern countries *ro* is in use [1]. *Ak yo* or *Ak ro*, open! *Yuk yo* or *Yuk ro*, go! *Se yo* or *Se ro*, do!

Instead of *yo* the conversational language of Si-kok uses *si* also, thus *Aki* for *Ak yo*, open! *Sri* for *Se yo*, do! *Yöku O ide nasarri*, for *nasare*, = well may your arrival happen, i. e. be welcome! — *Ki*, come, has *Koyo*, *Koi*, in Sikok *Koi* [2], come! — From *Mi*, to see, and *Kiki*, to hear, appear also in the old-Japanese *Mi ro* and *Kiki so* (見ろ 見ヨ, 聞シ 聞ヨ) as imperatives.

[1] *Nippon kotoi*, under *Ro*.   [2] Ibid., under *Ko*.

200   CHAPTER VII. THE VERB. § 69, 70.

The termination ヰ, *wi* (ヰ) changes into ヱ *we*; from *Midsi*, to watch; *Utsi*, to beat, becomes *Matè*, *Mate yo*, watch! *Ute*, *Ute yo*, beat!

The imperative thus obtained is with respect to its form the vocative of the verbal root (see p. 62). The categorical imperative, used only to inferiors, is avoided in polite conversation and superseded by more elegant expressions.

The imperative, followed by *kasi* or *gana*, has the force of our optative. *O ide nasarri kasi*, oh that you came!

§ 70. Closing form of the verb.

If a verb closes the sentence in the quality of verb predicate, i. e. as finite verb, then the termination *e* or *i* of the root form passes over to the mute *u*. From *Ake* in *Aku*, one opens; from *Yuki*, *Yuku*, one goes. Logically this form answers to our indicative present. The historian uses it for the past also, which he, in his relation, represents as an event taking place before his eyes. (Historical present).

In the application of this rule the following phenomena present themselves:
The terminations *ai*, *ei*, *ii*,   *oi*, *ui* pass into
                   au, *eu*, *iu*,   *ou*, *uu*, which in the spoken language resolve into   *go*, *io*, *iu* or *iyu*, *ou*, *uu*. Compare pp. 12, 13.

Ai becomes *au*, it suits; *Ei*, *eu* (エウ or エフ), one gets drunken; *Ii* (イ ヽ), *iyu* (イユ), one says; *Oi*, *oyu* (オユ), one grows old; *Kui* (クイ), *Kuyu* (クユ), one regrets; *I* (エ), to get, *u* (ウ), one gets; *Iyi*, *iyu* (イユ), it heals. The terminations:

ke, ケ, and *ki*, キ, become *ku*, ク.   *ge*, ゲ, and *gi*, ギ, become *gu*, グ.
se, セ, „ *si*, シ, „ *su*, ス.   *ze*, ゼ, „ *zi*, ジ, „ *zu*, ズ.
te, テ, „ *tsi*, チ, „ *tsu*, ツ.   *de*, デ, „ *dsi*, ヂ, „ *dsu*, ヅ.
ne, ネ, „ *ni*, ニ, „ *nu*, ヌ.   *re*, レ, „ *ri*, リ, „ *ru*, ル.

The terminations アヒ, エヒ, イヒ, オヒ, ウヒ (*awi*, *ewi*, *iwi*, *owi*, *uwi*), for which the spoken language uses *ai*, *ei*, *ii*, *oi*, *ui* [1]), pass into アフ, エフ, イフ, オフ, ウフ (*awu*, *ewu*, *iwu*, *owu*, *uwu*), in the spoken language *ou* (*go*), *eu* (*io*), *iu*, *ou*, *uu*. See pp. 12, 13.

ネガフ (*Kirawu*, one shuns) and ネガフ (*Negawu*, one wishes) sound in the

---

[1]) Compare p. 10, line 7.

street language of Yédo *Kira-u*, *Negu-u*, but in the mouth of a polite person *Kirgo* and *Naggo* ¹).

The difference between *gu* and *qu*, for which LÉON PAGÈS uses ò and ó ²), mostly remains unnoticed in the spoken language, and both forms are then expressed by *oo*; for the sake of etymology, however, a distinction of the two is highly desirable.

To the deflecting verbs of this class belong:

Ari, vulg. *Ai*, to like; *Inori*, pray; *Kanari*, to be sufficient; *Kanden*, it is sufficient; *Samaviri*, pron. *Sooriii*, wait on; サムラウ, *Samavieri*, pron. *Sooroo*, vulg. *soro* (候ふ, 侍ふ), one waits on, is at the service of ³).

Evi, vulg. *ei*, to get drunken, ェゥ or ェゥ, one gets drunken.

Iri, vulg. *ii*, say; イウ, *iru* or イム, *iyu*, one says.

Omoiri, vulg. *omoii*, think; *omoiru* or *omoyu*, one thinks.

Yuri, vulg. *yui*, bind; *yuru* or *yuu*, one binds.

bi, ヒ, and *bi*, ビ, become *bu*, ブ.   *mi*, ミ, and *mi*, ミ, become *mu*, ム.
ri, リ,   *ri*, リ,   *ru*, ル.

Ari, *tari* and *nari* (to be) remain, when they close the sentence as verb predicate, unchanged. See § 68.

§ 71. **The substantive and attributive form.**

Used as noun substantive (Infinitive) and attributive (by way of participle), the nondeflecting verbs supersede their termination *e* with *uru* or *uru*, *i* with *iru*, and the deflecting their *i* with *u*.

Ake, to open, becomes *Akuru* or *Akeru*.
Mi, to see,   „   *Miru*.
Yuki, to go,   „   *Yuku*.

The terminations *eru*, *iru*, *oru* have more or less continuative force, *Akeru*, *Akuru* and *Miru* being equivalent to *Ake-te-oru*, *Mite-iru* or *Mite-oru*, see § 78.

The form *uru* of *Akuru* belongs to the written language and in Kiusiu to the spoken language also; *eru*, less in use, is confined to the spoken language ³).

---

¹) From an oral communication by the native of Yédo SITAROO.   ²) See p. 18, note.

²) On account of the important part, which *Soro* plays as auxiliary verb in the epistolary style, it will be treated still more particularly hereafter (§ 103).

³) From an oral communication by TSUDA SIN ITSIROO.

As noun substantive, the verb is, like every substantive declinable, e. g.

Tooki ni yaku ed, going into the distance. — Kun-si no mitsi tatóyi ri tooki ni yuika ga gotósi, the way of a philosopher is, to use an instance, as a going into the distance. — Tera wó mira ni yuku, to go to see a temple. — Ki árn wó motte, on account of the presence of trees, because there are trees. — Aye-musu kara, after presentation. — Sikáru ni yotte, = on account of its being thus; since it is so. — Yuka yori ni yukánu ga numi, it is better not to go than to go. — Si, to do; Suru, the doing; Surani rd, in the doing. — Mi, to see; Miru, the seeing; Miráni ed, as one sees. — San fgo ydri mirani (or miránied) ydmuno sugáta ondzikóto nari, on looking out from three sides, the form of the mountain appears to be the same. Compare § 73, page 200, Remark.

Kawikitáru, the become dry, is substantive in Fa nd kawikitáru wo mdma, = what has become dry of the leaves one rubs; on the other hand in; Kawikitáru fa wo te nite mdma, = one rubs the foliage become dry, it is attributive.

All the relations, which in a noun are expressed by the forms of declension, may, thus, by the same means, be attributed to a proposition, just as it may be desired to characterise it as subjective, objective or adverbial.

The substantive form with ka as suffix is the form of the question direct. Ara ka? or Ari-mdsu ka? is there? Ari or Ari-mdsu, there is!

The verbal substantive becomes attributive by its mere subordination to a noun following. Akuru-koto, the deed of opening, the opening. — Yuku-mono, the going something, that which goes.

§ 72 Gerund.

1. The inflectional termination *te*, te, or *de*, de, which in substantives indicates the local, modal or instrumental relation, added to the verbal root forms a gerund, which characterises the action expressed by this verb as a subordinate local, modal or instrumental definition of another action succeeding it.

Ake te, by, on or at opening, Fr. en ouvrant. — Mite, on seeing. — Yukite, on going. — Oyóbi, to come to. — Kári-gáta ni oyóbite wagiyi ni kahéri ki, = when it came to the evening twilight, or, in short, at evening, one returned home. — Tewo ayétt ftidwo manziki-yóba, raising his hand (he) winks and calls people to himself.

2. Modifications introduced into the original form of the gerund by the spoken language:

a. The polysyllabic verbs ending in the deflecting ki or gi, mostly drop the k and g; kite or gite becomes ite. Thence:

Yaite	for	Yakite,	from	Yaki, 燒了,	to burn, *trans.*
Taite	„	Takite,	„	Taki, 焚了,	to burn, *intrans.*
Kiite	„	Kikite,	„	Kiki, 聞了,	to hear.
Oite	„	Okite,	„	Oki, 置了,	to place.
Suité	„	Sukite,	„	Suki, 好了,	to like.
Tsuité	„	Tsukite,	„	Tsuki, 付了,	to come to.
Kaide	„	Kagide,	„	Kagi, 嗅了,	smell, *trans.*
Soite	„	Sogite,	„	Sogi, 扮了,	split.
Toite	„	Togite,	„	Togi, 磨了,	grind.

The nondeflecting *Dé-kíi*, iru (出了來), to come out of, proceed, happen (see § 69, N°. 3), has *Ikíté*.

b. In verbs in tai and ri, taite (チテ) and rite (リテ) change into tte, that is written ッテ but not pronounced *tsté* or *tde*. Thence:

Tatte,	タッテ,	for	Tatsité,	from Tatsi,	to rise, to stand up.
Matte,	マッテ,	„	Matsité,	„ Matsi,	to watch, to wait.
Motte,	モッテ,	„	Motsité,	„ Motsi,	to hand, to take.
Atte,	アッテ,	„	Arite,	„ Ari,	to exist, to be.
Otte,	オッテ,	„	Orite,	„ Ori,	1. to dwell; 2. to break.
Natte,	ナッテ,	„	Narite,	„ Nari,	1. to be; 2. to sound. *intr.*
Yotte,	ヨッテ,	„	Yorite,	„ Yori,	to go out from.
Kakette,	カヘッテ,	„	Kakérité,	„ Kakéri,	to turn back.
Mazitte,	ムレッテ,	„	Mazirite,	„ Maziri,	to pluck.
Tsunitte,	ツノッテ,	„	Tsunirité,	„ Tsunori,	to be steady, steadfast.

Here, after the suppression of the weak termination *i* an assimilation of ts (originally t) and of r with the t succeeding takes place.

c. In deflecting verbs the forms *bite*, ビテ, and *mité*, ミテ, dropping the weak *i*, in pronunciation change into nde. Thence:

Eránde,	エラント゛,	for Erámi-te,	from Erámi, to select.
Ayúnde,	アユント゛,	„ Ayúmi-te,	„ Ayúmi, to walk.
Yónde,	ヨント゛,	„ Yómi-te,	„ Yómi, to read.
Nonde,	ノント゛,	„ Nomi-te,	„ Nomi, to drink.
Nomikónde,	ノミコント゛,	„ Nomikomi-te,	„ Nomikomi, to conceive, to understand.
Monde,	モント゛,	„ Momi-te,	„ Momi, to rub.
Susúnde,	スヽント゛,	„ Susúmi-te,	„ Susúmi, to advance, to go forwards.
Musúnde,	ムスント゛,	„ Músúbi-te,	„ Musúbi, to tie.
Yonde,	ヨント゛,	„ Yobi-te,	„ Yobi, to call.

The nondeflecting in *mi* and *bi* retain *mite*, *bite*. *Horóbi*, to ruin, v. i., *Horóbite*. See § 99, N°. 84.

As the old manner of writing used ヒ instead of ヒ゛, thus ムヒ instead of ムヒ゛, and ヒ also passed for ヒ゛, for the terminations ande, onde, unde, the forms aude, oude, uude, were obtained; which in the pronunciation pass into *gode* (*oode*), *oode*, *uude*; thence: *Erpode* for *Erande*, *Yoode* for *Yonde*, *Ayunde* for *Ayunde*.

d. In the deflecting verbs in ヤヒ, *ari*, オヒ, *ori* (in the spoken language *ai*, *oi*) the substantive form is really アン, オン, pron. *ga*, *ro*, to which the termination *te* is added.

Ari, pron. *Ai*, to meet, becomes アンテ, *areté*, in the spoken language *gote*, *oote*.

Naróbi, pron. *Nardi*, to learn, becomes ナランテ, *Naróraté*, in the spoken language *Narpote*, *Naroote*.

Simúbi, pron. *Simdi*, to cease, becomes シマンテ, *Simirate*, in the spoken language *Simpote*, *Simiote*.

Wardbi, pron. *Wardi*, to laugh, becomes ワランテ, *Wardeaté*, in the spoken language *Warpote*, *Wardote*.

Farábi (Harábi), to sweep away, remove, becomes ハランテ, *Farpote (Harpote)*, in the street language of Yédo *Hardtte* also ¹).

Omóbi, pron. *Omdi*, to think, becomes オモンテ, *Omóraté*, in the spoken language *omiote*.

Nóri, pron. *Nui*, to sew, becomes ヌンテ, *Nueraté*, in the spoken language *Nuote*, *Nute*.

---

¹) See E. Brown, Colloquial Japanese, X.

But if it be admitted, that after dropping the weak i, the remaining semi-vowel r equivalent to u, with the preceding a or o passes into go or ɡo (ô. ô), then the forms .tate, Nargote, Omɡote, also, are only euphonic modifications of the regular forms .teite, Narieite, Omoteite etc.

Instances of the use of the gerund.

Kusiri wo idasité miru, to stick out the head and look. — Idisu, to produce, the causative form of the disused idi, to appear. — Kudi wo mitté ten wo ikiñɡio (クダヲ モツテ テンヲ ウカ ガウ), to observe the heavens with a tube, i. e. not to have a broad view. — Motté, from Motsi, deflecting verb, to catch hold of with the hand, to use anything. — Opito fitóno ɡo-fooro ikaɡujiru, kuzira wo motté sigu to su, he who pays attention to another's appearance, considers the head as the principal; literally: taking the head, he makes (it) the chief or the principal.

Isolated by va the gerund becomes an adverbial phrase definitive of time, to va being equivalent to ôba. See § 73. Examples:

Hitóno kimi to ndtte vá, zin ni dru¹), if he becomes another's lord, he dwells in (his position is that of) humanity. — Natte: Narite, from Nari, — to be, and, when an appositive definition with to precedes, — to become. See § 100. III. — Fibári takákn tondé améni itari bu-mei-su; ktabiróté vá, tobi-saɡariti kusa-múrd nákd ni iru, the lark, soaring high, goes to the skies, dances and sings; if he is tired, then he descends and goes into his grass dwelling. — Tonde, gerund from Tobi, to soar. — Kitabiréte vá, = by fatigue, the gerund isolated by ve, from Kitabire, to grow tired. Tobi-saɡiri, literally: fly-descend, i. e. fly downwards. — Iri, iru, go in, with the local, where? one goes in.

Instead of the isolated gerund Nátte vá (by the being, or becoming) often occurs the expression Nátte ukiynsité, becoming, so, etc.

§ 73. The verbal root in the Local for the forming of adverbial phrases definitive of time (Conjunctive or Subjunctive form).

The predicate verb of subordinate adverbial sentences, which describe a time really present, or supposed as present, in the past, and which in our languages are connected with the principal proposition by conjunctions such as when, since, as, in the Japanese is placed in the Local in ni, followed by the isolating particle ル va. Thus is obtained ni + ru as termination, which fuses into ／ſ, ba (= aru, nhi). The subordinate precedes the principal proposition.

This termination in the nondeflecting verbs in *e* and *i* is joined to the root form, thus .Ikébd, on opening, as or when he opens; *Nedz*)*i*, *iru*, to twist, *Nedzibd*, as one twists; *Motsii*, to use, *Motsibd*, as one uses; *Sií*, to die, *Sibd*, as one dies.

In the deflecting verbs the verbal element *i* first undergoes a strengthening of sound, and changes into *e*, by which *eba* is obtained in the same manner; *Yuki*, to go, *Yukébd*, on going, as or when one goes, or when one went.

Hiami, 恢 ?, to long for, *Hoserba*.	*Ivi*, to say, *Irébd*.
Tatsi (= *Tati*), to arise, *Tatebu*.	*Yomi*, to read, *Yomebi*.
Mutsi (= *Muti*), watch, *Matebu*.	*Ari*, to be, *Arébd*.
Taddi, serve for example, *Tatórebd*, for instance.	*Nuri*, to be, *Narébd*.
	Ndkeri, not to have been, *Ndkerebi*.

Examples of the use of this form.

Satoo wo mazebd toya-yo adzuuii amúku náru, = by the mixture with sugar the tea becomes sweet of taste. *Mas)e, uru*, mix in. — *Mi wó osdmuru yaga wó sirébd, sunawdtsi fitó wo osimaru yaga wó siru*, if one knows the means to govern oneself, then one knows the means to govern others. *Sir)i, u*, to know. — *Titsi si-suru toki ago-siki wó su-béki taikóru ndkirebá, waga-mi wó urite ago-rei wó itoadmu*, at the time of his father's death not having the means to bury him, he (the son) sold himself and performed the funeral rites.

Remark. In nondeflecting verbs in *e* and *i*, instead of the form *eba*, here explained the substantive form of the verb with the isolated local termination niva, vulgo niwa is also used. — *Motome*, to strive for, to seek; *Motomuru*, the seeking; *Motomuru ni wa*, in the seeking, as one seeks. See § 71.

§ 74. The concessive form.

The concessive adverbial phrase, which we connect with the principal proposition by means of conjunctional adverbs such as though, although, however, but, is characterized in Japanese by the strong accented form-word *mó* or *támó* (= Lat. *quoque*) and precedes the principal proposition.

Opposed to *Ima-yumó aritá vá* (pron. *attewa*), *ameya furu*, = while rain-clouds are present, rain falls, and *Ima-yumo arébá, ameya furu*, = as rain-clouds are present, it rains, is: *Ama-gumo arité-mô (ittemô), furâzu*, - also in the presence of rain-clouds it does not rain, that is: although there are rain-clouds, it does not rain.

Consequently the following forms are opposite to each other.

The verb as substantive.

Akuru va, the act of opening.	*Akuru mo*, or *Akuru tomo*, the act of opening being granted.
Tatsuru va, the act of erecting.	*Tatsuru mo*, or *Tatsuru tomo*, though erecting.
Miru va, the seeing.	*Miru mo*, or *Miru tomo*, also (or even) the seeing.
Yuku va, the going.	*Yuku mo*, or *Yuku tomo*, also (or even) the going.
Akuruni va, on opening.	*Akuruni mo*, even on opening.
Tatsuruni va, on erecting.	*Tatsuruni mo*, even on erecting.
Miruni va, on seeing.	*Miruni mo*, even on seeing.
Yukuni va, on going.	*Yukuni mo*, even in going.

Gerund.

Akité va, on opening, as one opens.	*Akité mo*, though opening, or even if one opens.
Tatte va, by erecting, as one erects.	*Tatte mo*, though erecting.
Mite va, on seeing.	*Mite mo*, even if one sees.
Yukite va (pron. *Yuité sa*), by going.	*Yukite (yuite)-mo*, though going.

Time-defining local.

Akeba, contracted from *Akuni-va*, as one opens.	*Akedomo*, contracted from *Akunitomo*, *Akrudomo*, though one opens.
Tateba, contracted from *Tateni-va*, as one is erecting.	*Tatedomo*, contracted from *Tateni-tomo*, *Tatendomo*, though one is erecting.
Yukéba, contracted from *Yuki-ni-va*, as one is going.	*Yuku domo*, contract. from *Yuku-ni-tomo*, *Yukudomo*, though one goes.
Tatsureba, contract. from *Tatsure-ni-va*, as one is erecting.	*Tatsure domo*, contracted from *Tatsure-ai-tomo*, though one is erecting.

From this analysis it is evident why it is necessary at one time to say and to write *ri* and *tomo*, and at another *bi* and *domo*. Just as the impure *b* in *bu* is a fusion of *n + f*, so the impure *d* in *domo* is a fusion of *n + t*. The Japanese themselves seem not to appreciate this distinction and forget to characterize ツ (*tsu*) and ト (*to*) by adding the *Nigori*-mark [1] as ブ, *bu*, and ド, *do*.

Instead of *domo*, **tódómé** (イヘドモ, イエドモ) is also used. This is the concessive form of conjugation of *Iri* or *Ii* (イヒ, イヒ), to say, to be called, and therefore means: though one says, though it be called. This verb is preceded by the definition, how or what one calls something, as apposition with the suffix *to* [2]; e. g. *Kuni ari, sono na wo Nippon to iu*, there is a kingdom, its name is called Nippon. - *Sore wa nani to iu ka*, how is that called? — If the apposition is a verb, then this stands in the substantive- or in the root-form: *Akuru to iu*, *Yuku to iu*, it is said that one opens, it is said that people go. — *Akuru tó tedómó*, *Yuku tó tedómó* thus means: though it is said that one opens, or that one is going, expressions which answer to: although one opens, or might open, although one is going. — *Iri tó tedómó*, even granting the existence, although there is.

§ 75. The form of the Future (未 來?, *Mi-rai*).

There are different expressions, that signify that an action or state which is still in perspective, is objective to the willing, being able, having permission or being obliged. Here the derivative form, which expresses the effort, the inclination or tendency to realize what the verb points out, comes first under notice. As it at the same time includes the uncertainty, if anything is happening, has happened or will happen, it has been called *Futurum dubium*. For convenience' sake we retain this name, even were that of modus dubitativus better fitted.

With regard to the form we distinguish the simple and the periphrastic future.

I. The simple future of *Yamato*-language has for characteristic the terminations *mo* and *mu*, which in nondeflecting verbs in *e* or *i* are immediately added to the root, in the deflecting in *i*, however, only after this *i* by a strengthening of sound has been changed into *u* (or sometimes for vocal harmony into *o*). The termination *mu*, according to the oldest writing 牟ハ or 牟ハ [3] and pronounced *m*, has been in later times superseded by ン, n, and in the spoken language by ウ, u. In measure this ン (*n*) counts as a syllable.

[1] See p. 9.   [2] See p. 70. X.   [3] As in the chronicle *Nippon-ki* and in the oldest poems.

CHAPTER VII. THE VERB. § 75.

Ake, to open, future *Akemu* (アケム), *Aken* (アケン), in the spoken language *Akeu* (アケウ), passing to *akeō*.

Mi, to see, future *Mimu* (ミム), *Min* (ミン), in the spoken language *Miu*.

Yuki, to go, future *Yukamu* (ユカム), *Yukan*, in the spoken language *Yukau* (ユカウ), passing to *Yukoo*, vulg. *Yukoo* also.

Remark. The Japanese writing of the forms of the spoken language varies: to express the pronunciation of アシウ, ユカウ, some write アシン, ユカン, and others アケヅ, ユカヅ, and even アケユウ, ユコリ; and instead of アラウ (*aroo*, shall be, from *Ari*, to be), アラン, アロウ, アロン, and even 有 is written.

Shi, s, to do; future *Simu*, *Sin*, in the spoken language *Siu*, at Yédo *iou*, expressed by 爲.

Mats)i, s, to be present; future *Masamu*, *Masan*, in the spoken language *Masgo*, *Masoo*, at Yédo *Maioo* (Eng. *Mashoō*).

Matsi, マチ, wait; future *Matamu*, *Matan*, in the spoken language *Matgu*, *Matgo*, *Matoo*.

Ari, pron. *Ai*, to fit; future *Aeamu*, *Aran*, in the spoken language *Argu*, *Aroo*, *Awoo*.

Negari, pron. *Negai*, to wish; future *Negaramu*, *Negaran*, in the spoken language *Negaregu*, *Negargo*, or *Negawoo*.

Sumi, to nestle, sit up; future *Sumamu*, *Sumin*, in the spoken language スマウ, *Sumgo*, for which the written form スマン also appears.

Ni, to be (see § 100, 1); future *Namu*, *Nan*.

Ari, to be (see § 101); future *Aramu*, *Aran*, in the spoken language *Argu*, *Argo*, *Aroo*.

The termination *mu*, as characteristic of the Future, is according to my idea the regular indicative closing form and the substantive form of a verb *mi*, that expresses a **striving to be or to do something**. *Aramu*, *Aran*, the derivative of *Ari*, consequently indicates a striving after existence and what is called the dubious future, is according to its form, a present. The nondeflecting verb *Motom)e*, s, uru (來る), generally considered as equivalent to „to acquire," but which, as the regularly formed derivation from *Mots)i*, s (持ち), to hold, really has the meaning of strive to hold, shows the nature of *Mr*, *mu* in its full power. In the same way: *Akari*, red light, glow; lighten, glow; *Akaram)i*, s, strive to glow, in particular, the gradually becoming red and ripe of fruit.

In my opinion, there is also a connection between the form *ne*, *nu* treated here, and the verbal derivative forms *mi*, *mu*, which from a number of adjective root-words cited on p. 107 forms a deflecting intransitive verb, that expresses the becoming such, as the root word indicates and is equivalent to a Latin inchoative verb in -*sco*, for instance:

Siro, white;	*Sirómi*, albescere, to grow white.
Kuro, black;	*Kurómi*, nigrescere, to grow black.
Kura, dark;	*Kurámi*, to grow dark.
Taka, high;	*Takámi*, to grow high.
Fira, flat;	*Firámi*, to grow flat.
Firo, roomy, broad;	*Firómi*, to grow broad.
Kata, hard;	*Katámi*, to grow hard.
Naka, warm;	*Nukúmi*, to grow warm.
Maro, round;	*Murómi*, to grow round.
Ao, green;	*Aómi*, to grow green.
Kubo, hollow;	*Kubómi*, to grow hollow.
Naga, long;	*Nagámi*, to grow long.
Yasu, easy, quiet;	*Yasumi*, to grow easy or quiet.
Sige, tight;	*Sigémi*, to grow tight.
Arata, new;	*Aratámi*, to grow new.
Ara, wild;	*Arámi*, to grow wild.

If we put in the place of *mi* nondeflecting *me*, *mu*, *muru*, then the intransitive verbs cited here become transitive or properly factive: *Sirom*)*e*, *u*, *uru*, to make grow white, – to whiten; *Kurom*)*e*, *u*, *uru*, to make grow black, to blacken; *Nukum*)*e*, *u*, *uru*, to warm, to incubate; *Yasum*)*e*, *u*, *uru*, to make rest, whence *Yasume-zi* (休 字), = rest-word, an expletive particle, like *mo*, which causes a rest, but does not rest, itself. The difference between *mi* and *me* is frequently overlooked by the Japanese themselves.

We return to the Future. According to Japanese philologers the termination *en* or *un* of the Future signifying uncertainty, appears particularly in connection with a previous interrogative, i. e. in interrogative sentences, whereas the termination *ru* is used, when the sentence has a definite subject, which is frequently strengthened by a successive *Koso* (= this here); a difference I have not found actually confirmed.

Examples of the use of the forms cited.

Yezo ra furuki kotoba ni miyetarazu. Yemisi no ten-go naran, the name of Yezo does not appear in the old language. It may be a corruption of Yemisi.

Tami no rin-koku yori okokaran koto wo nozomu koto nasi¹), there is no prospect, that the population (here) will become more numerous than that of neighboring states.

<small>Okokari, n., contin. form of Okoki or Ooh, much. Nozomi, n., to hope on.... Nasi, there is not.</small>

Sono jiminiu niti tagaran kotowo osóru¹), he feared that it (the doctrine) might degenerate in time.

Iraku: Kyu-rai tsuini sorobinu nirusi ka²), behold, he said, a sign that Corea will at last perish.

<small>Forobi, undeflecting verb, to perish. See § 99. 84.</small>

Ima sarcin to omóiru, △³) Ima sargu to omói-nadsu, now I think of going. 今欲去.

Niva-tori wa suman to su, △ Niva-toriga munqu to suru (鷄 欲 栖), the court-bird (the cock) is about to go to his roost. Sumar)i, n., to roost.

Nisiyé wataran (△ wataraun) to su (將西度), I shall go westwards.

Idzurino tokóro ni ki te wo kudasan (何處 下手), where shall I lay down my hands? = △ Itoko wo tekakirini niyyu-(zo-)zo? = which part shall I take for handle? i. e., where shall I seize it? S)i, u, to do; future ン, &c.

△ ドレゝ ハジメツ ゾ, Dorekara hasimeo zo? where shall I begin? — △ Ita tnataiye nigryou zo? whither shall I flee?

Nani ka aran (何有), what may there be? = △ Nanno ri-nikui kotoga arun zo? what may there be, that you do not gladly do? = △ Nani no nardnu to iru kotaya arou zo? = what should there be, that you blame?

Ani korewo nasanya? what, should I do this?

△ Naniwo O mçsi kake-maioo ka? what shall (or may) I show you? — Sake wo age-maioo ka? shall, or may I offer you something to drink?

<small>¹) Meng-tseu. I Book I. 3.   ²) Tszhung-yung.   ³) Nippon-ki.

⁴) The sign /, indicates that the words and expressions, to which it is attached, belong to the spoken language.</small>

△ *Kitu no hoo ni kuro-gumo ga ats'mette orimas' kara*, *Yedo no hoo wi ima ame ga fitte ori-masoo* ¹), as in the north black clouds are heaped up, it will be raining at Yedo now. — If the definition of time *ima* (now) is superseded by *sikuya* (last night), then the after sentence takes the signification of: it will have rained at Yedo last night. — △ *Niku-ban ittaroo*, he will have gone yesterday evening.

The certain Future of the written language.

The adverb *Masini*, indeed, certainly (正, 將), in connection with a future followed by *to si*, gives the expression the meaning that something will certainly happen or is at hand. (§ 148). — *Masini sarda tō su*, will certainly go.

天ヲ木鐸ト爲サン天下ノ道也久シ矣
Ten-ka no mitsi naki koto jadsi, Ten masdni Fuu-si wo motte boku-taku to sen tō si ¹), it is long that the empire has been deprived of the way *of truth and righteousness*; but Heaven will certainly use the master (CONFUCIUS) for a signal bell (for a herald).

國家將興必有禎祥
Koku-ka masani okorànto surrbd, kanardzu tei-siyou-ari ¹), if a nation or a family is indeed on the way to raise itself, then there are certainly signs that give notice of it.

II. The periphrastic Future.

A. The periphrastic Future of the written language is formed

1. by grafting アラン, *aran* or アラム, *arama* (shall be) on the substantive form of a verb, by which *aran* by aphaeresis becomes *ran*. E. g.:

Mi, *Miru*, to see; *Miru-ran*, = the seeing will be, *videns erit*.

Kikji, *u*, to hear; *Kiku-ran*, = the hearing will be.

Ir)i, *u*, or *Ii*, *Iu*, to say; *Iu-ran*, = the saying will be.

As the Japanese find these words expressed in the old rebus writing by 見ラ覧ゾ, 間ラ覧ゾ or 聞ラ覧ゾ, 云ラ覧ゾ, they consider *ran* as a particle standing alone. RODRIGUEZ also, on p. 66 line 27, cites *ran* and, on line 8, *aran* as particles of the future.

---

¹) s. ARUWS, *Colloq. Jap.* XII.
²) *Lun yu* III. 24. lin. 1. LEGGE, *Chinese classics*, Vol. I. pag. 28.
³) *Tchong-yung*, XXIV.

2. By suffixing *naramu*, *naran*, or *narame* (= will be) to the substantive form of a verb. — *Miru-naran*, *Kiku-naran*, *In-naran*, = will see, hear, say. — *A.. ca B.. nari to ieru narame*, people will (*narame*) have said (*ieru*) that A is equal to B.

3. In negative verbs by suffixing *aranan* — a euphonic modification of *ari* + *nan*, = shall or may be, to the substantive form. — *Kasumi tatazu mo aranan* [1]), = also the not rising of fog will happen. See § 84.

4. By grafting *su*, *suru*, fut. *suran* (= to do) on the form of the Future, by which the *s* passes into the impure *ns = z*. — *Mi-tari*, have seen; *Mi-taran*, I shall have seen. — *Mitarau-zu*, visurus est; *Mitaran-zuran*, visurus erit.

5. By grafting the auxiliary verb *masi*, u (= to dwell, reside, see § 101) on the form of the Future of deflecting verbs, ..*amu*, ..*an*, by which ..*an'* + *masi* or ..*an* + *masi* passes into ..*amasi*, e. g.:

Ni, to be, becomes *Namasi* (也 ナ 猿 ン), contracted from *Nan* + *masi*.
Ari, to exist, becomes *Aramasi*.
Nari, to be, becomes *Naramasi* (ナラマレ 也 ナ 猿 ？ 矣 ン 止 ン).
Kurō-sikiri, to be fair, neat, excellent (page 120), becomes *Kirō-sikiramasi*.
Siri, nosvere, becomes *Siramasi*, scituram esse.
Mōsasi (pron. *Myosi*), to mention, becomes *Marusamasi*.
Iri, u. to say, becomes *Iramasi* (云 ハ 僭 ン).
Tamatri, u, to grant, to bestow or confer on, becomes *Tamaramasi*.
Saki, u, to unclose itself, to open, becomes *Sakamasi*.

Hito mo naki " Yadomo sakurara " miru tosi no " Haru no sakamasi, the plum-tree of the inn, though there was nobody, would nevertheless open in the spring of last year. The definition of time: *adru tosi*, in last year, also transfers *masi* to the preterit.

If we compare the periphrastic Future *Iru-masi* with the periphrastic Present *Iri-masi* (see § 101, 2, a), it will appear, that the difference of the two forms is not in *masi*, but that it is in the verb connected with it, in the one case being the Future, and in the other the root-form. Thus when the native, on old authority, seeks for the force of the Future *Iramasi* in the termination *si*, and characterises it as the *Mi-rai no si* (未 ニ 來？ノ 止 ン), i. e. the *si* of the Future, he errs. His *Mi-rai no si* does not exist [2]).

---

[1]) *Hyaku-nin*, N°. 73.
[2]) This has reference also to the *Mi-rai no si*, adopted in numerous *Etimos* p. 66 Her 5 and line 16 - 26.

In the rebus-writing this *Masi* is expressed by 問 ▽ ㇺ and the derivative form *Masibi*, *u*, by 問 ▽ 數 ぐ: forms to which the Japanese philologist himself attributes the force of 欲 $\frac{s}{t}$, *hossi*, = will, and 可 し, *besi*, = may, and which are to be distinguished from *masi* (問 ▽ し, see § 95. 2. *)).

B. The periphrastic Future of the spoken language.

It is formed 1. by grafting (at) *su* (ス), *suru*, *sureba*, on the form of the Future, proper to the spoken language, *zi*, *zu* etc. being the euphonic modification of *si*, *su*, *suru*, *suriba*, = to do. — ソケウズ, *likeo-zu*, aperiturus est. *Miu-zu*, visurus est. *Yukoo-zu*, iturus est.

2. By *makoo* or *aroo*, the Future of *masi* and *ari*, = to be, the first suffixed to the root, the second to the gerund of a verb. — *Kaki-makoo*, I shall write. *Kakite* (or *Kaite*) *aroo*, I shall write.

Remark. 1. Let us now just review the nine „particles for the Future" quoted by RODRIGUEZ *Elém.* pag. 66 lines 7 and 8.

Be)ki, *si*, = may, is a verb. See § 101.

Nan, the Future of *Ni*, 1. to go away, 2. to be in... See § 83.

Naran, the Future of *Nari*. See § 83.

Tnuran, a variation of *Naran*. See § 84.

Taran, the Future of *Tari*, to be continually. See § 78.

Turan)zu, *zuru*, Future *zuran*, from *Tari*. See § 78.

Ten, = *Tarikra*. See § 82.

Si, the *Mirai no si*, based on a misunderstanding. See § 75. II. 5.

Baya is a fusion of *u* or *n*, the characteristic letter of the Future, and *baya*, an exclamation, which, as an expression of complaint (*Nageki no kotoba*), answering to our „Alas," suffixed to a Future, indicates that what is at hand is execrated (*Haya negari-mitsuru kokoro no tenira uari*). — *Kanasiki mono to nari-baya!* Alas he will become a pitiful man!

Consequently *Motome-baya*, *Se-baya*, *Mi-baya* signify, he will, alas! strive for.., he will, alas! do, or see. The same may be said of *Yomi-baya*, from *Yomi*, to read; *Narawa-baya*, from *Narai*, to learn; *Nara-baya* (not *Naruwa-baya*), from *Nari*, to be or to become.

Remark 2. The Future is used as a softened Imperative. Thus the poet says: *Yakazu tomo kusa va moye-nen* ⁵ *Kasuka-no va* ⁶ *Tada farmuo ji ni* ⁶ *usikureta-rasau*, even if it be not burned off, the grass will grow luxuriantly, therefore only leave the field of Kasuka to the vernal sun. *Makasetari*, he has left it to. *Makasetaranan*, he shall or may have left it to, is used, according to the *Wagun Siwori*, for the Imperative *Makastare yo*. Just so in the colloquial: *O ide nasareü* for *O ide nasarei*, may your arrival happen, please come.

Remark 3. For so far as they point to something future, the verbs which express the permission or liberty, the power or the obligation to do anything, come under notice here. They are *Be)si*, *ki*, *tu*, I may; *Ata)si*, *ru*, I am able, can, and 當ら然とヌリ, *Too-sen tari*, it ought to be, it must be, it shall be.

Further illustration of them is given in § 104.

THE SUPPOSITIVE FORM.

§ 76. The terminations *eba* or *iba* of nondeflecting, and *aba* of deflecting verbs are the characteristics of the suppositive adverbial proposition, which, as a rule, precedes the principal proposition. They are, in my opinion, a fusion of the form of the future *en* or *in* and *an* with the local termination *ni* and the isolating *va*. From *Aken-ni-va* comes *Akeba*, アケバ [1]), pronounced as *Ikeba*, on being about to open or as one will open; from *Min-ni-va*, *Miba*, ミバ, (*Minba*), on being about to see; from *Yukan-ni-va*, *Yukaba*, ユカバ, on being about to go; from *Naran-ni-va*, *Naraba*, ナラバ, in the spoken language even fusing into *Nara*, ナラ, on being about to be, might it be.

In the deflecting verbs, clearly noticeable is the difference between the subjunctive *Yukeba* and suppositive *Yukaba*; not so in the nondeflecting verbs, since *Aken-ni-va* and *Iken-ni-va* both fuse into *Ikeba*. For the definite indication of the suppositive character the help of the adverbial *Mosikaru*, vulgo *Mosi*, = albeit, in case of, is called in, and it is placed at the beginning of the suppositive proposition. — *Mosi to wo akeba*, might one open the door.

In the ordinary style of speaking the form *Nara* is used not only for *Nareba*, but for *Nareba* also, thus with the signification of „if it is," and „as it is," as appears from the examples following:

Δ *Sore sara* (or *Sore de wa*) *kwi masoo*, as it is so (= then) I will buy it [2]). —

---

[1]) The points, which characterise the impure *ka* (がが) are commonly left out by careless writers.

[2]) *Shopping-Dialogues*, p. 4

210   CHAPTER VII. THE VERB. § 76.

Firu-maye ni wo mairi-ye masenu, before noon I cannot come. — *Sare naru, jiru-goni*, then (the answer is), in the afternoon ¹). — *Nokorizu Ukai naadru nara, onézi nedan de aye-maiiou*, if you buy all, I will sell them for the same price ²). — *Yésuni (.Yasuki) nara, tori-maiiou*, as (if) it is cheap, I will take it ³).

The future in the Local and isolated by *ni* (.Ikuru-ni-ro*, on being about to open, if one shall open) mutates with the substantive form in the Local isolated by *ra* (.Ikuru-ni-ra*, on opening), as appears from the passage following, taken from the introduction to a Japanese-Chinese Dictionary:

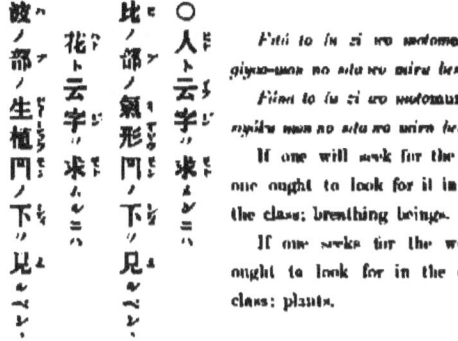

Fitó to fu zi wo motomen ni va, *Fi no bu no ki-giyau-mon no sita wo miru besi.*

Fana to fu zi wo motomuru ni va, *Fa no bu no ari-nyéku mon no sita wo miru besi.*

If one will seek for the word *Fito* (man), then one ought to look for it in the division *Fi*, under the class: breathing beings.

If one seeks for the word *Fana* (flower), one ought to look for in the division *Fa*, under the class: plants.

That the unfused forms *Ikuru-ni-ra* and *Yukan-ni-ra* appear in the written and spoken language as Terminatives as well, equivalent to the Latin *ad aperiendum*, *ad eundum*, cannot surprise us, since the local termination *ni* is also used as characteristic of the Terminative. (See § 7. IV. *b, g*.)

Remark. When in the *Proeve eener Japansche Spraakkunst* of 1857, p. 166, I first explained the origin of the subjunctive and the suppositive form, I raised the question whether or not the Japanese themselves were clearly conscious of it, seeing that they so frequently confound the two forms. Mr. R. BROWN, who has adopted my theory, at p. VII gives the following as answer to it: „Japanese Teachers know nothing of the rational of these formations, and constantly affirm that the conjunctive is the same in sense as the conditional, and that *Yukaba* and *Yukeba* have the same signification; but Mr. HOFFMANN has ably and clearly demonstrated the distinction as above given. Indeed it is remarkable how many obscure points in the structure of Japanese words have been elucidated by

¹) *Shopping-Dialogues*, p. 17.   ²) Ibid. p. 36.
³) Ibid. p. 37.

gan who has derived all his knowledge of Japanese from the study of books." — I admit the last, provided „Japanese books" be understood. Before that time I had not had the opportunity of intercourse with Japanese, which I enjoyed afterwards, in 1862.

THE CONTINUATIVE VERBAL FORM.

§ 77. The deflecting derivative forms ari, iri, ori, uri, as I have shown formerly [1]), are continuative forms of the verbal element i (§ 68), and express the continuance of movement or being in a condition or in an action. The choice of them was originally, and still is under the influence of a vocal harmony, which requires that the vowels of the subordinate syllables be accommodated to that of the principal syllable.

Ari, *Iri* and *Ori* occur as substantive verbs with the signification of 1) to be or exist (有), and 2) dwell, stay (在．居．留), and have i, = to go, and i or ヰ, wi, = seat, as root. These three verbs will subsequently be treated, further in §§ 96, 97, 98.

Examples of the derivation of continuative verbs. Here is to be remarked, that the forms between [ ] have not hitherto occurred to me, yet they must be supposed as basis of the derivative forms.

Iki, light.		*Ikàr)i*, *n*, shine, beam.
Kàki, hook; to hook, *v. i.*	*Kak)e*, *n*, *aru*, fasten, hang, *v. tr.*	*Kakàr)i*, *n*, be hanging.
Sak)i, *n*, unclose itself, to open, *v. i.*		*Sakar)i*, *n*, be in blossom or bloom.
[.ig)i, *u*, rise.]	*Ag)e*, *n*, *aru*, raise.	*.Igar)i*, *n*, be rising, ascending.
[*Sug)i*, *u*, droop, hang down.]	*Sug)e*, *u*, *uru*, cause to droop.	*Sugur)i*, *n*, to be drooping.
Mas)i, *n*, augment, *v. i.*		*Masar)i*, *n*, to be superior.
…zi (= n + si), not to be.		…zar)i, *n*, continually not to be.
Miz)i, *n*, not to see.		*Mizar)i*, *n*, not to be seeing.

[1]) *Proeve eener Jap. Spraakkunst*, 1857. § 57, 61.

218 CHAPTER VII. THE VERB. § 77, 78.

Ara)i, n, not to exist.		Arazar)i, n, not to be existing.
[Sudom)i, n, to be determined.]	Sudom)e, n, uru, to determine.	Sudamar)i, n, being determined.
[Fuzim)i, n, to begin, v.i.]	Fuzim)e, n, uru, begin, v. tr.	Fazimar)i, n, to be begining.
Taidzim)i, n, wrinkle; crimp.	Taidzim)e, n, uru, to crimp, v. tr.	Taidzimar)i, n, to be crimped.
Firom)i, n, to widen, v.i.	Firom)e, n, uru, to widen, tr.	Firomar)i, n. to be widened.
Tsum)i, n, to accumulate, v. intr.	Tsum)e, n, uru, amass, v. tr.	Tsumar)i, n, to be amassed.
Oki)i, n, rise.		okir)i, n, to be rising, the rise.
Ok)i(=Iki), n, breath; flame.		okir)i, n, to be flaming.
Nok)i, n, recede.	Nok)e, n, uru, to put back, to bequeath.	Nokir)i, n, to be remaining.
Nob)i, n, stretch, to become longer or taller.	Nob)e, n, uru, stretch, to make longer or taller.	Nobir)i, n, to be growing higher, to ascend, as smoke. *
Mats)i, n, wait, trans.		Matsar)i, n, to be waiting. **
Ne, sleep. Nem)i, n, to be sleepy.		Nemar)i, n, to be sleeping.

* Thence: Yama ni (not Yama wo) nobiri, to ascend a mountain.

** Kami wo matsuru, attend upon a god, make him a feast. Matsuri (not mataari), the attendance, the feast.

It is obvious that to this category the derivative adjectives in karu and garu also belong. See p. 113 § 10.

§ 78. ..to ari, ..to ori, ..to iri.

1. The continuative verbs Ari, Ori, Iri (= exist, dwell), in connection with a preceding gerund, form a continuative verb. — Akete-ari, Mite-ari, Yukite-ari, (he) is in the act of opening, he is seeing, is going, = aperiens est, videns est, iens est. Matsuteh-ira (pron. Matte-ira, or Matsute-ora, he is in the waiting, Site-ora, he dwells in the doing, he is doing.

In the choice of *Ari*, *Ori* or *Iri*, in the case before us, the vocal harmony, or rather the easy cadence, is noticeable, which had influence on one dialect more than another. In writings which pass for pure Japanese *te-ari* is found exclusively. If the assertion of a Japanese scholar¹) is just, which I may not doubt, the dialect of Yédo uses by preference, *iru*, seldom *óru*, whereas that of Miyako generally uses *óru*²). *Tabĕte-óru*, to eat; *Nomute-* (*Nomde-*, *Nonde-*) *óru*, to drink; *Sirite-óru*, to know. Besides, the dialect of Nagasaki has *óru*. When the same writer at one time uses *te-ari*, then again *te-óru*, he seems to pay attention either to the difference of signification which exists between *ari* and *ori*, or to the ease of the cadence. — *Koto de aru*, the fact is. — *Sobá ni áru fitó*, some one who is near to. On the other hand: *Tono soba-ni óru fitó*, some one who stands near to the door. — *Inisihino kotowo tonónde óru fitó*, some one who is fond of antiquities.

Ari, *Ori* and *Iri* are inflected as defective verbs. See §§ 96, 97, 98.

II. ..tari, ..taru, the contracted form of *te-ari*, is, in connection with a precedent noun, whether Japanese or Chinese, answers to our verb to be, or exist, when, connected with a word expressing a quality, it forms the predicate, e. g. he is glad. Forms of inflection, the same as of *Ari* (§ 96); *tari* is the closing form, *tóru*, the substantive, as well as the attributive; *tarun*, *turan)zu*, *turu*, *zuran*, frequently occur as forms of the future.

Examples:

君と君たらずsin sin
臣と臣たらず*tari*, if the master is a
臣と臣たらずmaster, then is the servant a servant.

王たる*Wgu-sigu tárŭ fitó*, a man
人者who is a ruler.

ソモ佛代 *Dai-kin wo furuwn wta'mo dou-you taru besi*¹), = also at the
モ同金 time of paying the price, it shall be just so (it shall be done
レ像節 in the same way).

220 CHAPTER VII. THE VERB. § 78, 79.

 Tōku wi-zin tari, tattōki koto Ten-si tari, as to virtue he is a saint, as to worthiness he is a son of heaven (emperor).

Kano KI no kuroi wo miréba, rupiku-taiku i-i tari. Hi-tāru kun-si ari¹), if we look at the banks of yon river KI, how luxuriant is the green bamboo! There is an elegant nobleman etc.

FORMS OF THE PAST TENSE
(過去, Kwa-ko).

The form-words of the past tense are auxiliary verbs of time, by means of which derivative verbs are formed.

§ 79. ..tari, ..taru, in the spoken language ta, contracted from te-ari. It, in connection with a verbal root, expresses continuance in the condition or action, which, by the radical form of the precedent verb, is named as something just becoming. „E-tari" and „I have gotten" are both what is called the completed present tense.

The spoken language shortens tari and taru to ta, which ta has also been admitted into the familiar written language. Opposite to Ta yi sono ed furubitāri, field or garden have become old, is, in the spoken language: Ta yi sono gi furuhitā; opposite to Furubitāru ta yi sono, field or garden become old, is, in the spoken language: Furubitā ta yi sono.

Since it is the form of the gerund in te or de on which, after dropping the e, ari (or in the spoken language a) is grafted, the rules given (§ 72) for the gerund are of application to the perfectum praesens also, in other words: the e of the gerund is, in the spoken language, simply superseded by a.

Ikete	becomes	Ikata.	Yonde (= Yomite) becomes Yonda, read.
Mite	„	Mita.	Naroda (Naraute) „ Naratta, learned.
Yuite (= Yukite	„	Yuita.	Atte (= Arite) „ Itta, been there.
Mai'te (= Mairite)	„	Mai'ta, been.	Maite (= Mairite) „ Maitta, has come.

¹) Dai Gaku, III. 4

Whether the perfectum praesens formed by *tari* have an active or a passive, a transitive or an intransitive signification, depends on the precedent root-word.

Fune kisi ni tsuku, the ship comes to the shore, it lands; *tsukitari*, has come to shore. — *Kisi ni tsukitaru fune*, a ship that has come to shore. — *Fune wo kisi ni tsukitari*, one has brought the ship to shore. — *Kisi ni tsukitaru fune*, a ship, that one has brought to shore. — *Sina-mono wo iresi watari*, to import goods. — *Motsi watari taru sina-mono*, goods which one has imported.

Instances of the use of the Perfectum praesens.

Koyju, *uru*, to become thick, fat, corpulent. *M'me ame ni koyu*, the plum becomes thick from the rain. *M'me koyetari*, the plum has become thick. *Ame ni koyuru m'me*, plums, that become thick from the rain. *Koyttaru m'me*, plums, that have become thick. — *Tsuyu kuwa ni tsukitari*, dew has attached itself to the mulberry leaf. *Tsuyu* (or *Tsuyu no*) *tsukitaru kuwa*, leaves to which dew has attached itself. — *Kai-fen wo isi-kake wo tsukite tsigai-do wo tsuraue tari*, along the sea-shore one has built up a wall of stones and placed the houses of the place in a row. — *Mitsi wo satoritaru fito*, some one who has understood the way (the doctrine). — *Anana no kuni yori kildru jito jitsi ni tsuno ari, fune ni norite Yetsi-zen no Finoura ni tsukitari; yueni kono tokiro wo Tsunoki to midzuku*, men come from the country of Anana, have had horns upon the forehead and sailing in a ship reached Finoura in Yetsizen; that is why people call that place: Tsunoka (hornshill). — *Ame no yamitaru asa*, in the spoken language: *yanda asa*, a morning when the rain has ceased. — *Watakusi O tanomi ni mairita*, I have come to beg you. — 承タ忽 レマレタ, *Sootsi si-mavta*, I have understood it, I shall not fail.

Remark. The perfectum praesens in *tari*, formed from transitive verbs, as *Ake*, to open; *Tsugi*, *u*, to pour in; *Ire*, *uru*, to make to go in, remains transitive even though expressions, as *To wa aketari*, *Tsju wo tsugitari*, *Fi wa iretari*, because they are found translated: the door has been opened, the tea has been poured, the fire has been put in [1], seem to plead for the passive signification. Opposite to the subject, isolated by *wa*, door, tea, or fire, stands as predicate: one has opened, poured, put in.

---

[1] Japanese and Dutch Dictionary, by the Prince of Nakats.

§ 80. The form-word *.eri*, *..eru*, *èreba*, deflecting, when in deflecting verbs it takes the place of their verbal element *i*, expresses the continuance in the past, or the praeteritum praesens. — *Mas)i*, *n*, to be; *Maséri*, has been.

Er)i, *a* (to be distinguished from *Er)i*, *n*, that as a substantive verb means to choose] is a variation of *ar)i*, *n* (see § 96), and, just as *ari*, is indicated in old-Japanese by 有. *Eri* is the closing form, *eru* the form of the substantive or attributively used noun; *erame*, *eramu*, *eram*, the form of the Future. Examples: *Fana sikimeri*, the flower fades; *Fana siboameri*, the flower has faded; *Sibonaèru jäna*, a flower which has faded. — *Um)i*, *n*, to bear; *Umeri*, to have born. — *Kisaki no umeru ko*, the son that the Queen has born; *Kimaki no umeran ko*, the son that the Queen shall have born.

Remark. The *eru* used substantively, or attributively is, particularly with the nondeflecting verbs in *e*, superseded by *oal* (§ 81), *otaru* (§ 78) or *erai* (thus *.lkèri*, *.lkètaru* or *.lkerai*), because the form *.lkèru* already exists as a variation of *Akuru*, thus, as participium praesentis.

If it be admitted that, behind *eri* as I suppose, the form *Keri* (§ 82) is hidden, and thus that *Moséri*, by ellipsis has arisen from *Mòsèkeri*, with the meaning of which it is equivalent, then its signification is clearly explained by the origin of the form.

Application of this rule,

..ki becomes ker)i, u.

Kiki, to hear; *Kikèri*, 聞ニ有ル. | *Saki*, to spread; *Sakèri*, 敷ヽ有ル.
Yuki, to go; *Yukèri*, 行ニ有ル. | *Iki*, to live; *Ikèri*, 生ニ有ル.
Saki, to open, *v. int*. *Sakèri*, 咲ニ有ル. | *Kaki*, to write; *Kakèri*, 書ニ有ル.

..si becomes ser)i, u.

Nasi, to make be; *Nasèri*, 成ニ有ル. | *Yudòsi*, to lodge; *Yòdosèri*, 館ニ有ル.
Nokòsi, to make stay behind, to postpone; *Nòkosèri*, 遺ヽ有ル. | *Usùsi*, to remove; *Usunèri*, 遷ヽ有ル.
| *Tèrasi*, to make shine; *Tèrasèri*, 照ヽ有ル.

Remark. The *seri* noticed here is arisen from *si*, the termination of factive verbs, and *eri*; it is to be distinguished from the derivative form *ser)i*, *n* which is a fusion of the *Kwa-kono si* and *eri*.

CHAPTER VII. THE VERB. § 60.   223

..tai (= ti) becomes teri, u.

Tátai, to stand up; Tatéri, 立有. Kátai, to overcome; Katéri, 勝有.
Mótai, to watch; Motéri, 待有. Utai, to strike, beat; Utéri, 打有.
Mótai, to take; Motéri, 持有. Fanátai, to let loose; Fanatéri, 放有.

..vi becomes veri, u.

Ivi, to say, to be called; Ivéri, 云. Nivori, to smell, v. int.; Nivovéri, 匂.
Omóvi, to think; Omovéri, 思. Avi, to meet; Avéri, 逢.
Sitagúvi, to comply, to suit; Tovi, to ask; Tovéri, 問.
Sitagavéri, 從. Navavi, to learn; Navavéri, 習.

..mi becomes meri, u ¹).

Sumi, to reside; Saméri, 住. Susumi, to advance;
Sidzumi, to sink; Sidzuméri, 沈. Susuméri, 進.
Kumi, to bail out; Kuméri, 汲. Sabomi, to fade; Saboméri,
Umi, to bear; Uméri, 產有. Tsubumi, to bud; Tsubuméri, 含有.

..ri becomes reri, u.

Nari, 成, to become; Navéri. Komori, 籠, to stick in, int. Komovéri.
Tsumóri, 積, to accumulate; Tsumovéri. Masiri, 盛, to exceed. Masivéri.
Tsiri, 撤, to scatter, intr.; Tsivéri. Furi, 降, to fall down. Fuvéri.

Examples of the use of the forms ..eri, u.

[Tsudzaki]i, u, to succeed). — Tori-ga akindri-ya fitó sadai ni tate-tsudzaki'ri, Siredó takúro dokúro ni ari-mátai mo ari, the custom-houses and shops (of Simono-seki) succeed one another in one line. Although there are back-streets also.

[Móvi], u, to be; Movéri, has been]. — N... fimé no kami va NN... nusi no kami ya-firo-wani ni narite, miari-maséri, as regards the goddess N., the god NN. having changed into a crocodile eight fathoms long, has paired with her. — Amaterasu kami va fidari no mi mé-wo avari-tamaivi-si tokini mávi mavéva kami nari, the heaven-illuminating god is a god, that came into existence (miri-maséva), when (both the creators) had washed their left eyes. Koru tau-ni miri-maséva (or tau-ni naveriri) kami sari, this is a god that has become a stuff.

---

¹) To be distinguished from the auxiliary verb, Meri, explained in § 108.

[*Sirus*]*i*, *n*, to mention: *Siruséri*, he has mentioned]. *Futa jasirono kami no miradzi koto ni simo ni siruséri*, the pedigree of both the gods — one has noticed it particularly hereafter.

[*Okis*]*i*, *n*, violate.] *Oranda-zin vo tai-si fon wó okineri Nippon-zin ra*, Japanese, who against Dutchmen have violated the law. — *Nippon-zin ni tai-si fon wo okusi-taru Oranda-zin ra*, Dutchmen, who against Japanese have violated the law [1]).

[*Tamar*]*i*, *n*, to condescend, to grant. German *gerahen*, applied to princely persons]. — *Mikoto no fuki-tamaveru hon-ken*, the costly sword that the prince has or had girded on.

[*Sir*]*i*, *n*, to get to know: *Siréri*, he knows]. — *Mitsi wo okonawarezaru wore korewo sireri*, that the way is not practised, this I have gotten to know (this I know).

[*Itar*]*i*, *n*, come to (the point any one will reach); *Itaréru*, the having got at, having reached]. — *Sono itareruni oyinde*, getting at it, having reached it, = reaching the non plus ultra. — *Tsin yon wore itareru kana!* oh that one had reached the middle way!

[*Nokor*]*i*, *n*, to be left]. — *Nokórú mono*, somewhat that is left. — *Nokoreru mono* or *Nokori-si mono*, something that has remained over.

§ 81. The form-words ..ki (キ) or ..si (シ), grafted on the verbal root in *e* or *i*, in the narrative style and in poetry characterise the simple perfect absolute, and, like the Aorist Indic. of the Greek, express the action as completed at a fixed time and without continuance or repetition. *Ki* is the indicative closing-form (= he was); *si*, which passes under the name of *Kwa-ko no si* and is to be distinguished from the *tiwa-zai no si* (page 107), the form in which the verb appears as noun substantive or even as attributive (as participle, = been); *kema*, *kémsi*, *ken*, the future (= shall or may have been).

Ak-ki, *Mi-ki*, *Yuki-ki*, *Ari-ki*, *aperuit*, *vidit*, *iit*, *fuit*, he opened, he saw, he went, he was there.

Ak-si, *Mi-si*, *Yuki-si*, *Ari-si*, to have opened it, to have seen it, having gone etc., or, attributive, the having opened, the having seen, etc.

---

[1]) *The Treaty between the Netherlands and Japan.* 1858. Art. V, al. 1, 2.

Ake-ken, *Mi-ken*, *Yuki-ken*, *Ari-ken*, = *aperuerit*, *viderit*, *iverit*, *fuerit*, he will have opened, have seen, he will have gone, have been.

The action defined by the *Kara-tu no si* is one, perfect or completed, with relation to the period, that is defined by the predicate verb which closes the sentence. With relation to a present, the time indicated by *si* is thus a simple preterit; with relation to a preterit it becomes, logically, our plusquamperfectum, with relation to a future on the other hand our futurum exactum.

Remark. The elements *ki* and *si* are verbs which signify coming and going and with the precedent verbal root, on which they are grafted, form compound verbs. *Ari-ki* and *Ari-si* thus mean the arrival and the departure of existence; forms which express the idea of having been. Compare the expression: *Nous venons de le dire* [1].

In the pure Japanese style the *ki* of the past tense is found explained by 來 (*kii*, - to come), or also by 去, e. g. *Kakeri-ki*, 飯 來, he returned, and it mutates with *nu* and *tsu* (see § 84, 85).

As substantive verb with the meaning of come, *Ki* has the forms of *Ku*, *Kuru*, *Kite* etc., whereas *Si* with the meaning of go away occurs in *Sinji*, *n.*, *new*, *die*, *Sinji*, *iru*, to be dead; whence *Sinime*, dead rice (*Oryza sterilis*); *Me-sici*, dead to the eyes, = blind; *Mimi-sici*, dead to the ears, = deaf. Derived from *Si*, is the continuative form *Sari*; *n.*, to go away.

Ken, old-Japanese *Kemu* (= shall have been), is indicated in writing by 監 (*Kan*), and — by Japanese scholars themselves — explained as a word that „brings the past into doubt" [1].

Examples of the use of 來 as closing form:

此三柱神者　並獨神成坐而　隠御身也

Kono mi fasira no kami wa mina fitori yami nari-masite, mi mi wo kakusi tamori ki, these three Kamis were solitary Kamis, and kept their persons (themselves) concealed.

---

[1] Here, is to be remarked what is mentioned by *The Notitia linguae Sinicae of Premare*, by I. G. Bridgman, page 54, about 來 *lai* and 去 *k'iu*.

リケンハ 過去去ツク 疑ンノ 辞ナリ *Ka-yen Savori*, under *Ken*.

a) Examples of the use of the form in *si* as noun substantive:

Ko-zin no ireri-si mo mmo arinu beri, also what the ancients have said (of it), must have been of this nature. — *Ireri*, continuative past form of *Iri*, *Ii*, to say. — *Simo*, = *Sikuimo*, so, in this manner.

As noun substantive the form in *si* is declinable, thus:

1. *Ari-si ro*, the having been, or what has been. *Ari-si mo*, also what has been (subjective substantive proposition). — *Nokorisi karikono sizyn* (性 ?) *asiku nari si mo kono yué narun*, this may be the reason why the silkworms remaining have become bad of nature.

2. *Ari-si si*, 3. *Ari-si ni ro*, 4. *Ari-site*, while there has been.

5. *Ari-si yori kono kata*, since there has been.

6. *Ari-si-yué*, 7. *Ari-si ni yorite* or *yotte*, while, or as there has been.

8. *Ari-sikaba*, whereas or since there has been. — *Motome-sikaba*, *Yomi-sikaba*, *Narai-sikaba* [1]), as one has sought for, read, learned.

9. *Ari-si nari*, = it has been there.

10. *Ari-si koto ari*, *Ari-si to ari*, = it is a fact (*koto*) that there has been. — *Ari-si to kaya*, it may be that there has been.

b) Examples of the use of the form in *si* as noun adjective:

Nokori-si kuciko, the remaining silkworms. — *Sari-si Fotóke*, the departed Buddha. *Sar)i*, *u*, to go away. — *Kono tane wo motome-si fitó mare nari*, people who have procured this seed, are rare. — *Kan-ki wo sinogi si* (or *sinogi tarn) iri no koto*, the manner in which people have kept off the frost. — *N... ga nori-si funé*, the ship in which N... had sailed. — *Ame furazu " ji-no kasanareba, " take-si ta mo, " maki-si fatake mo " asa gotoni sibomi kare-yuku*, = when there is a repetition of not rainy days, then not only the sprouted field, but also the sown plough-land fades, and dries up every morning — it becomes more faded and drier every day. — *Sikdrani tenno kako ni ya arikan*, he will thus have stood under Heaven's protection.

The *Kwa-kono si* shows itself also in both the words *Figdsi*, pron. *Fingdsi*

---

[1]) By this, is what sonsioure page 66 lier 7 v. o. says explained: „Le conjonctif a encore une forme particulière à la langue écrite, c'est *sikaba*, que l'on ajoute aux radicaux de tous les verbes, comme *motome sikaba*, *yomi sikaba*, *narai sikaba*."

and *Nisi*, East and West. *Finguisi* being a contraction of *Fino-mukai-si kata*, = the side on which the sun has come to meet, and *Nisi* an abbreviation of *Fino ini-si kata*, the side to which the sun has gone away.

§ 62. ..ker)i, n (= ki + eri, = has been), the deflecting continuative form of ki (= was), characterises the perfect present tense. Forms of inflection, the same as those of *eri*, thus:

Keri, *Kesi*, closing-form, = has been.

Kéru, form of the verb, used as substantive and adjective, - the having been, or having been; ...*Keru nari*, has been.

Kereba, as, when, since it has been.

Keredomo or *Kerutomo*, although it has been.

Keran, commonly *Ken*, shall have been. — *Keraba*, if it has been.

Keráku, adverbial form, = as has been, e. g. *Ii-keraku*, as it has been said.

Keras)i, n, negative, = has not been.

Ari, there is; *Ari-ki*, there was; *Ari-keri*, there has been.

Ideographically *keri*, *keru* is expressed by 來了, phonetically by 𠌯, the name of a bird, that cries *géri géri* and therefore is called *Keri* in Japan. 來了則 stands for *Kereba*.

The adjectives in *ki* and *siki* (pp. 105—107 and 109), which form a continuative present in *kári*, instead of *kari* assume *keri* for the form of the praesens perfectum.

Taka)ki, *ku*, high;	*Tika-kér)i*, n, is high;	*Taka-keri*, was high.
Be)ki, *ku* (可 ~), possible;	*Be-kari*, is possible;	*Be-keri*, was possible.
Na)ki, *ku* (無 ᵗ), without, ..less;	*Na-kári*, there is not;	*Na-keri*, there was not.

Distinguish: *Uresisi kagiri nasi*, = the joy is boundless; — *kagiri nakari*, - is continually boundless; — *kagiri nakeri* or *nakesi*, = was boundless; — *kagiri nakari-keri*, = has been continually boundless.

Since this distinction is confirmed by the Japanese spoken and written language, as will be seen by the following examples, we hesitate to agree with the opinion of those [1], who declare *kari* and *keri* to be identical. Nevertheless, we leave the spoken language of Yédo full right to use *keri*, where *kari* is meant.

---

[1] s. brown, *Grammar*, XXIII. § 20.

Examples of the use of these forms.

[*Yasuki*, light, easy]. — *Nippon wi ro tadzuki mka kaeru koto yasukarikeri*, the unmolested return of the Japanese army was easy.

[*Nari* (*Naru*), to become]. — *Sono rei-kon ke nite kariko-to narikeru to kaya*, her soul transforming will have become a silkworm.

[*Siroki*, white]. — *Sei-mei Ten-wau umare nagara ni site mi kami sirokari kereba, Simouno Ten wgu to nadzuke tatematsuru*, as Emperor Seimei's hair was white at his birth, they have called him Emperor White-hair.

[*Tsiisaki*, small]. — *Mayu tiisakereba ito fosokuru*, if the silk-cocoon was too small, the thread is too fine.

[*Asiki*, bad]. — *Kore yori te-ire asikereba, notsi ni iro-iro no yamavi to nari*, as from that point, the treatment (of the silkworm) was bad, afterwards it gets to different diseases (different diseases arise).

[*Yoroshi*, good]. — *Ano kadzukai no tsutome ga yorosikereba, watakusi wo yasiki tsuhke-oitou to imohoniru*, that servant's services having been good, I think I shall keep him.

The adverbial proposition closing with *kereba* may be understood either as causal or as conditional, as in s. BROWN's *Japanese Colloquial* N°. 580, where that expression is translated: „If that servant behaves well (I think I will keep him)."

§ 83. ..tari-ki, ..tari-si, fut. ..tari-ken; ..te-ki, ..te-si, fut. ..ten. By grafting the form-word *ki*, *si*, *keri* on the continuative form *tari* (§ 79) the forms *tari-ki*, = he was being; *tari-ken*, = he shall have been; *tari-keri*, = he has been, are obtained.

The poet supersedes *tari-ki*, *tari-si*, *tari-ken* with *te-ki*, *te-si*, *ten*, also *Omoiri-tesi* and *Tsikiri-tesi* are considered to be equivalent to *Omori-tarisi* (having thought) and *Tsikitaristarisi* (having sworn) [1]).

Wasurururu " mirobu omordzu; " tsikari tesi
Fito wo inotsino " osiku mo aru kana! [2]).

I do not think of myself as being forgotten; oh! the charmingness of the life of the man who has sworn (love) to me, exists still!

---

[1]) *Wagou Siwen*, under *Tesi*.   [2]) *Hyakusin*, N°. 38.

CHAPTER VII. THE VERB. § 84.

§ 84. [..ni], nu, future nan; [nuri], nuru, nureba, future nuran.

Ni, a deflecting auxiliary verb of time, come, by aphaeresis, from ini, inu, = to go away (往, 去), and expressed in the old written language, by 去 (to go or pass away), grafted on the root of a verb, by which its termination e fuses with inu into énu, and the termination i, with inu into inu, implies the passing away of a condition or of an action, i. e. the action coming to an end. Whereas Ake denotes the „opening" as an action first beginning, and Akete-oru „continuance in the opening," Ake-taru „to have opened;" Akinu proper to the old written language, denotes „the ending of the opening." Sitsumi, to sink; Sitsuminu, it sinks away, it goes away into the depth. Fute, disappear; Fi iri futénu, the sun sets (and) disappears. Iri, to go in, appears here as coördinated, in the indefinite root-form (see § 68). The rule on coördination excludes the use of the root-forms ni and nuri; since, however, they form the basis of further derivatives, they must be first brought under notice here.

SYNOPSIS OF INFLECTED FORMS OF THE AUXILIARY VERB NI, Nu, = TO PASS OR GO AWAY.

	Aorist of the Present	Continuative Preterit	Aorist of Preterit	Continuative Preterit
Root-form	[Ni,]	[Nuri,]	Ni-ki, 去來, went away	Ni-keri 去來, has gone away
Closing-form	Nu, 去,		Niki	Ni-keri, Ni-kesi
Noun substantive or attributive		Nuru, 去る, passing away	Ni-si, 既去, gone away	Ni-keru, having gone away
Gerund	Ni-te, 去"而"			
Local		Nureba, on passing away		
Future				
	Namu, ナム, Nan, ナン, 將去, shall go	Nuramu, Nuran, shall be going	Ni-ken, shall have gone away	Ni-keramu, Ni-keran, 去來, shall have gone away
Conditional form	Naba, 也則, if it go	Nuraba, if the passing away shall be	. . . . .	Nikeraba

CHAPTER VII. THE VERB. § 84.

The auxiliary verb *Ni, Nu, Nuru* (to go away) is distinguished from the substantive verb *Ni* (to be) in-as-much as the latter has the appositive definition what something is, before it in the form of a noun. (See § 100, I.)

Remark 1. Attention must be paid to the three forms of the future *nan*, *nurun* and *niken*. From their derivation, as it appears in the synopsis, the logical result is, that they must have the signification there noticed; and this conclusion is confirmed by the definition which the *Wagun Siwori* gives of the three forms.

1. **Nan** *ra mirai wo kakete iru kotoba nari*, i. e. *Nan* is a word used with a view to the future.
2. **Ran** *ra gen-zai wo utagauru no kotoba nari*, i. e. *Ran* (= *Aran*) is a word which brings the present into doubt (should it be?).
3. **Ken** *ra kwa-ko wo utagauru no kotoba nari*, i. e. *Ken* is a word which brings the past into doubt (should it have been?).

Remark 2. Since r + n by assimilation becomes nn, *Owari-nu* (= it ends) passes into *Owannu*, オワンヌ, being the auxiliary verb *nu* (去ル) with a view to this example, called *Owannu no Nu* or the *Nu* of *Owannu*.

Instead of *Ari-nan* (there shall or may be), in the dialect of Yamato *Ira-nan* also occurs for euphony.

Examples of the use of the auxiliary verb *ni, nu*.

[**Nu.**] *Fato ra takani owarete Sjakwon-no fudokoro-ni tobi-iri* nu, the dove, pursued by the falcon, flew into S'akya's lap. — *Sore yori Sado ye tsuki*-nu. *Mata zynn fun urazareba, ni zyu fi-me yo touriu-zu*, thence they came to the island of Sado. As again there was no favorable wind, they stayed there till after the 20th day. — *Uni-nite kaze ni niwaru, kwan-gun ri wo usinarute, Zin-mu no mi iroje san nin* (御 兄 三 人) *tokoro dokoro nite use-tomari* nu, as they were overtaken by wind at sea, and the government's troops lost the advantage, Zin-mu's three elder brothers were lost at different places. — *Kami-agari-si masi*-nu, he (the prince) has gone on high (died). *Agari*, going up; *Si*, do. — *Ko-cin no iccrisi mo saso ari*-nu *besi*, also what the ancients have said, will have been so.

[**Nuru.**] *Ygu-san wo sei-koo* (殺ス 生ス) *no waza kokoroye*-nuru *fito wo arinu besi*, it may be that there were people, who considered the breeding of silkworms a murderous occupation. — *Fisasiku kai-dei ni fanberi*-nuru *aida*, „during my long stay at the bottom of the sea," the beginning of a speech by the sea-god, when he showed himself before the other gods.

[Nan.] *Midzukara sutsurori-sitsyori-namu*, or: *Midzakára sudtsuriri-númu* (自ラ 属ス 突人), one will come under subjection of oneself¹).

[Naba.] *M'awi ro sikarr-naba*, *asiki mitsi ni wo iri-nu besi*, if the horse is led, it may have turned into even a bad road.

[Nureba.] *Fide-yori mo Taiyou-zen sukini yabure-nureba*, *sedamete Ikri-Min yori sukureba-koto wo omoshakidrite*, Fide-yori considering that, when Tschao-sifu should at last have been brought under subjection, help would certainly come from China.....

[Nuran.] *Furuki iwaya iku-yo fe-nuran?* the old stone house, how many ages may it still last? 古窟幾世將經. From the Chinese translation annexed, it appears that by *fe-nuran* the future (may last) is intended, whereas by *fe-niken* the fut. exactum (shall or may have lasted) would be indicated.

The poet, instead of *nu*, *usrs yuku* (行ヲ), = goes, probably to fill up his verse, e. g. *Mákini fatáke mó sihomi karv yuku*, even the corn land, where one has sown, goes to fade (and) to dry up.

§ 85. ..tsū, ..tsūtsū (ツ・ツ・); ..tsuri, n, cba, future an, an auxiliary verb of time proper to the Yamáto dialect and the narrative style, and as such, grafted on the root, as well as on future-form of a verb, it expresses the going away of an action, or of a condition, and characterises the past time absolute. *Tsu, tsuru* passes as a variation of *nu*, *nuru*¹) (§ 84). As predicate closing-form of a proposition *tsu* (or mostly *dzu*, ヅ) is in use by preference, in the dialect of the districts from Owari to Yédo²).

Tsūtsū, as a doubling of *tsu*, implies the repetition (iterative form), *omóe-tsutsu* being made equivalent to *omóuwa-omóuitsu*, = I thought and thought. Tsuri, continuative, has been; *tsuru*, - having been; *tsurdu (tsurdusu)*, - shall have been.

In the old rebus-writing *tsuru* lurks under the character 經, which means *tandzuru*, = to sew to; *Mi-tsuru*, to have seen, is denoted by 見經; *Kiki-tsuru*, to have heard, by 聞經. — Most common are the expressions 云ξヲ,

---

¹) *Nippon-ki*.

²) *Tsuru is also considered as a modification of te-aru. — „Te-aru, te-are" wo tsudzumete „tsuru, tsuru" to iru, i. e contracting Te-aru and te-are, we say tsuru, tsuru. Wagou Simori under Tsuru.*

³) *Ka gos suwori, under Tsu. Vol 10. p. 1. recto.*

Itas, said: 見也, *Mitas*, seen; 聞 タ, *Kikitas*, heard; 思 フ, *omoïtas*, thought; 暗 ヲ, *Kuraïtas*, become dark.

Examples of the use of these forms.

老 御 惡 ○
也 感 給 此
  而 賜 者
  成 之 因

Kono kegare wo nikumi-tamaru mi-tama ni yorite nari mari tas, this (goddess) has arisen, as an emanation from the spirit detesting uncleanness.

Remark. In the same author, instead of *nari-masitas* (= has arisen), *nari-maseri*, *nari-maseru mari*, and *nareru nari* alternately occur. (Compare § 80).

Inuru tosi NN. ni toureresi koro, kuniko no fun-do wo kiki tsu, when, last year inquiry was made of NN., I heard of the manners and customs of that country. — *Kono Kami no sudzi sinomi siridei tas*, or also *siruseri*, = as to the pedigree of this Kami, one has made mention of (it) below [1]. — *Dasu yomai tokoro ni yuite, Ten-wou no sono tsuma wo tsukuwasi tsuru koto wo kikite, tasuki wo motomen to omoiri* [2], when Dasu, going to the place of his destination, heard, that the Emperor had had his wife sent to him, he began to think of seeking help (for her). —

Fotofagisu naiki tasaru kata wo adgamureba,
Tasuki dzuikeud tsuki zo nokoreru [3]),

If I look towards the side, where the cuckoo has called,
Then, there only the moon has remained shining by clear daylight.

Nokoreru fana no kora mo tsiri tsutsu,
Ware mo ukitaru yo wo augumi tsutsu.

The remaining flower, has been strewed to day (leaf for leaf).
Oh I too have passed the floating time of life (step by step).

Fuzi no taki-ne ni yuki zo furi tsutsu.

On the high top of the Fuzi it has snowed (repeatedly).

Remark. In writing, *tsutsu* is frequently expressed by 乍, a sign used for *Nagara*, in the midst of, while (Chapter VIII. III. 2). Probably some identify this *tsutsu*, with the *dzutsu*, = at a time, treated in § 35, p. 145.

---

[1] *tisuzi*, the object of the transitive *sirusi*, to mention, is, by inversion, placed before the verb.
[2] *Nippon-ki*, 14, 18. [3] 百人一首 *Hyoku-nin isso*, N°. 81.

CHAPTER VII. THE VERB. § 86.   253

§ 86. SYNOPSIS OF THE INFLECTED FORMS.

	Nondeflecting conjugation.		Deflecting conjugation.
	ROOT-FORM, declinable.		
	AKE, *open*.	MI, *see*.	YUKI, *go*.
Imperative = Vocative	Ake, *open*.		Yuke, *go!*
	Ake yo, „	Mi yo, *see*.	Yuke yo, „
	Ake i, „		Yuke i, „
	Ake ro, „	Mi ro.	Yuke ro, „
Terminative	Ake ni, *to opening, to open*.	Mi ni, *to seeing, to see*.	Yuki ni, *to going, to go*.
Instrumental, Modal (Gerund).	Akete, *by opening, opening*.	Mite, *by seeing, seeing*.	Yukite (Yuite), *by going, going*.
Isolated	Akete va, } *as one opens*. Akete wa, }	Mite va, } *as one sees*. Mite wa, }	Yukite va, } *as one goes*. Yukite wa, }
Concessive	Akete mó, *though one opens*.	Mite mó, *though one sees*.	Yukite mó, *though one goes*.
With suffixes definitive of time.	Akete kara, } „ yori, } *after the opening*. „ notsi, }	Mite kara, } „ yori, } *after the seeing*. „ notsi, }	Yukite kara, } „ yori, } *after the going*. „ notsi, }
Local, isolated	Ake ba (= Ake + ni + va), *as one opens*.		Yuko ba (= Yuke + ni + va), *as one goes*.
Concessive	Ake domo (= Ake + ni + tomo), *though one opens*.		Yuke domo (Yuke + ni + tomo), *though one goes*.
	INDICATIVE CLOSING-FORM.		
	Aku, *one opens*.	Miru, *one sees*.	Yuku, *one goes*.
	SUBSTANTIVE AND ATTRIBUTIVE FORM.		
	Akeru or Akuru, 1. *the opening*, 2. *opening*.	Miru, 1. *the seeing*, 2. *seeing*.	Yuku, 1. *the going*, 2. *going*.
	Akeru vú,} *the opening*. Akuru vú,} *that o. opens*. „ mó, *though opening*.	Miru vú, *the seeing, that one sees*. Miru mó, *though seeing*.	Yuku vú, *the going, that one goes*. Yuku mó, *though going*.
Terminative	Akuruni, *to the opening, to open*.	Miruni, *to the seeing, to see*.	Yukuni, *to the going, to go*.
Local, isolated	Akuruni va, *on the opening, as one opens*. Akureba, *as one opens*	Miruni va, *on the seeing, as one sees*. Mireba, *as, or if one sees*.	Yukuniva, *on the going, as one goes*.

	Nondeflecting conjugation.		Deflecting conjugation.
Concessive	Akerédomó, though one open. Akuru tó tédomó, though one opens.	Minédomó, though one see. Miru to tédomó, though one sees.	Yuku to tédomó, though one goes.

PRETERIT.

	Akeki, he opened.	Miki, he saw.	Yukiki, he went.
Attribut. and declinable substantive form.	Akeni.	Mini.	Yukini, Yukesi.
Consummative	Akeker)i, u, has opened.	Miker)i, u, has seen.	Yukiker)i, u, has gone. Yuker)i, u, chu.
Future	Akeken, shall have opened.	Miken, shall have seen.	Yuken, shall have gone.
	Aketar)i, u, △ Aketa, has opened.	Mitar)i, u, △ Mita, has seen.	Yukitar)i, u. △ Yukita, Ynita, has gone.

FUTURE.

	Akemn (old Jap.)	Minm.	Yukamu.
	Aken, shall open.	Min, shall see.	Yukan, shall go.
	△ Akeo, shall open.	△ Min, also Miyuo.	△ Yukgo, △ Yukuo.
	Aken to s)i, u, to be about to open.	Min to s)i, u, to be about to see.	Yukan to s)i, u, to be about to go.
	Aken to te, syncope of Aken to ité, being about to open.	Min to te, syncope of Min to site, being about to see.	Yukan to te, syncope of Yukan to site, being about to go.
Conditional	Akeba (= Aken + ni + va), on being about to open, if one open.		Yukaba (= Yukan + ni + va), on being about to go, if one go.

CAUSATIVE OR FACTIVE VERBS IN Si OR So.

§ 87. The causative verbs, which denote a causing to take place or a carrying out of the action, such as our raise (make rise), drench (make drink), are formed by means of the deflecting verb si, su, future san (📖¹), - to do. In nondeflecting verbs in e or i this si is suffixed to the root, by which the derivative forms esi or isi (or sometimes instead of isi, osi and usi) arise, whereas in deflecting verbs their termination i at the same time passes into a (or some-

CHAPTER VII. THE VERB. § 87.   235

times, for vocal harmony, into o, see § 76), by which the derivative forms asu or osu are obtained; e. g. Yuki, to go; Yukasu, make go. Noki, to go back; Nokosu, to make go back. — The verbs, which have ari or uri as continuative form (see § 88), have osu or usu as their causative form. In § 103 Si, to do, is treated as a substantive verb.

Sometimes nondeflecting so, suru, future sou, takes the place of S)i, s. S. passes for a syncope of sim)e, uru, future an, 合ス, have do. See § 88. Iwase, have say, Kikase, have hear, are at least in the Mon yo siu. explained by 合て言ス and 合て聞ス.

The following may serve as examples of the derivation of causative verbs:

1. Káy)e, eru, 歸ル to return, v. i.: Kayesji, u, to make turn back, to return, v. tr. In Yédo: Kairu, Kairu.
2. M)i, iru, 見ル, to see; Mis)e, eru, uru, to make see, to show.
3. N)i, iru, 似ル, to resemble; Nis)e, eru, uru, to make resemble, to imitate.
4. Yuk)i, u, 行ク, to go; Yukas)i, u, to make go.
5. Ugok)i, u, 動ク, to move, v. i.: Ugokas)i, u, to move. v. tr. to make move.
6. Nom)i, u, 飲ム, to drink; Nomas)i, u, to give drink (Fitisi mi-dzuro, water to somebody).
7. Yasum)i, u, 休ム, to rest, v. i.: Yasumas)i, u; also e, uru, to rest, v. tr.; contracted Yasuns)i, u.
8. Si, 去ル, to go away; Sas)i, u, 使ス, 遣ス, to make go away, to send, to dispatch (a messenger).
9. S)i, u, 爲ル, to do; Sas)e, uru, to make do. Ne-sase, to make sleep.
10. Kuds)i, uru, 崩ス, to fall, descend. Kudas)i, u, to make fall, to precipitate, Kudari, 行ク, go from above to v. tr. below; a line of Japanese writing.
11. Ae)i, u, 合フ, to unite, v. i.: Aeas)i, u; e, uru, to unite, v. tr.
12. Tob)i, u, 飛ビ, to soar, fly; Tobas)i, u, to make soar or fly.
13. Asob)i, u, 遊ブ, to play, to ramble. Asobas)i, u, to make ramble, to amuse, to please.
14. Ni, to be; Nar)i, u, to be continually. Nas)i, u, 成ス, to make be, to produce.

15. *Nas)i*, n, to make; *Nusas)i*, n, to make produce.

16. *Nor)i*, n, 鳴, to sound, c. i.; *Naros)i*, n, to make sound.

17. *Ter)i*, n, 照, shine; *Teras)i*, n, to make shine, to illuminate.

18. *Dzi*), 出, — *idz)i*, n, to come out of; *Das)i*, n, or *idas)i*, n, to make go out off. — *Fune wo idasu*, to make a ship start.

19. *Ni*, 荷, burden, load. *Nor)i*, n, to be a burden; to ride, go in a carriage; *Nos)e*, uru, 乘, to make ride, to carry, to convey.

20. *K)i*, uru, 來, to come; *Kos)i*, n, to make come.

21. *Ok)i*, iru, 起, to get up, to rise; *Okos)i*, n, to raise.

22. *Nok)i*, n, 退, to go back, to recede, retreat; *Nokos)i*, n, to make go back; 還, to leave behind.

23. *Ot)i*, iru, uru, 落, to fall; *Otos)i*, n, to make fall, to fell.

24. *Or)i*, uru, 生, to wax, grow; *Oos)i*, n, 生育, to make wax or grow.

25. *Or)i*, n (*Oj)i*, n), 負, to bear (on the back); *Oos)e*, uru, or *Os)e*, uru, 仰, obsol. オツセ, to burden; a charge.

26. *Urur)i*, n, 潤, to get moist; *Ururus)i*, n, to moisten, quicken.

27. *Or)i*, iru, 降, to descend; *Oros)i*, n, 下, to make descend (*ikarios*, to throw out the anchor).

28. *Or)i*, n, 居, to dwell; *Oros)i*, n, 舎居, to make dwell.

29. *Kor)i*, n, 凝, to clot; *Korosi)i*, n, to make clot; to kill, 殺. *Korosi)i*, n, to make kill.
Koros)i, n, to kill;

30. *I*, to go away. *Yor)i*, n, to be going away; *Yos)e*, uru, 寄, to make go away, to send.

31. *Tsuk)i*, iru, uru, 盡, to get exhausted or consumed; *Tsukus)i*, n, 盡, to exhaust, to consume.

Remark. If we do not, as Japanese etymologists [2], reduce *Nusi* (= to cause

---

[1] The sent *i* is preserved in the family name 日之出山, *Hi zi yama*, = sunrise mountain. The change of *i* into *ji* is very common.

[2] *Wagen Siwori*, under *Nasi*.

to be, to give existence to anything) to *Na* (名'), = name, but derive it from *Ni*, = to be, the soundness of such a derivation is pleaded for, not only by the analogy of the Latin factivum *facio*, which comes from *fio*, or the Sanscrit *bhávayámi* derived from *bhû*, to be; but the Japanese causative verbs themselves concur in supporting it. Thus we are of opinion also, that *Asobasi* (= to please) is a causative form, whereas the Japanese philologists ²) see in it a contraction of *Asobi + nusi* (遊ビ 爲シ), = to be pleasing oneself; an opinion with which we could agree, if the passive form *Asobasare*, = be pleased, an ordinary expression of politeness, did not make us suppose a causative *Asobasi* (= to please), as a logical necessity.

The causative verbs derived from intransitive verbs have the object, which is made active, in the accusative before them. *Tsuki ra siro wo terasu*, the moon makes the castle shine, enlightens it.

Examples of the use of the forms.

Titi kore wo nasi, ko kore wo nobu ³), the father originates it, the son continues it. — *Kimi taka wo tobasi*, the prince lets the falcon fly. — *Is-seki wo motte kore wo tsukari nasi-tiri*, one has made this out of one stone. — *Tomi ra iki wo urueosi, toku ra mi wo uruosu* ⁴), riches moisten (quicken) the house, virtue, the person. — *Zin-siya ra mi wo motte mi wo okosi, fu-zin-siya ra mi wo motte mi wo okosi* ⁵), the humane man uses his fortune to exalt himself, the inhumane man his person to push his fortune higher. — *Midare, sidzumarazaru wo yasunzi osien.* he quiets and subdues those, who behave disorderly and unquietly. — *Seki-si wo yasunzaru ga gotosi* ⁶), it is as if one quieted a suckling. — *Kimi ni tsukayuru toki ra sunareteri inotsi wo tsukusu*, when (I my) prince serve, then it is with all my life. — *Kotoba wo tsukusu*, to exhaust his language, i. e. say all that is to be said. —

其ノコトバヲ 盡ス 不レ 得ル *Sono kotoba wo tsukusu koto wo idzu* (pron. *idzu*) ⁷), he does not get (he does not succeed in) exhausting his reasonings.

---

¹) *Wagen Siwori*, under *Asobasu. Yamato Kotoba*, II. 46, r.
²) *Tárkang yang* 13.   ⁵) *Dai Gaku*. VI. 2.
³) *Dai Gaku*. X. 20.   ⁶) *Ibid.* IX. 3.
⁴) *Ibid*. IV. 1.

CAUSATIVE VERBS IN Sime.

(下 知 ス ル 事, tie-dzi-suru kotobu.)

§ 88. The causative verbs in sime denote that an order, or in a less commanding tone, inducement is given to do an action or realize a condition. They are formed according to the same rule as the causative verbs in si, i. e. the causative si or se is superseded by the verb Sime, u, uru, ureba, gerund Simete (contracted site), future Simon, to change. 令 シ, 令 セ.

Ake, to open;   Ake-sime, to make open.
Tairage, uru, to subdue;   Tairage-simé, to order to subdue, to make subdue.
...s)e, uru, do (termination of verbalized   ...se-sime, to change to do, contrive that
  Chinese words);   one does, have done.
Nasasi, u, to have made;   Nasa-sime, to order one to have made.
Ye-sasi, u, to cause to get;   Ye-sasime, to contrive to have gotten.
Ari, there is;   Iró-sime, to order that there be.
Nakuri, there is not;   Nakuré-sime, to order that there be not.
Mátsuri, wait upon, to worship;   Mátsuré-sime, to order to worship.

When Sime unites with the causative verbs in si a syncope takes place: from Karésí + simé comes Karí-sime, to have sent back; from Yukási + simé, Yuki-simé, to order to let (him) go.

Examples of the use of the forms.

Kuni wo tairage-simé, he orders the country to be subdued. — Tsukaí wo kare-sasu, he orders the ambassador to be sent back. — Kawo-kami kore wo mite, utsu-kushi onna nari to omoé, tédzúsaete in-syuku (一宿 爲 セ リ) so-simu, Kawa-kami, seeing him, he thinks that he is a beautiful maiden, leads him by the hand, and charges him to stay the night. — Yase-ki wo nirakáni sei-tera- (成 ラ 長 ス) so-simen to te, koyási wo tsuyoku-su bekarizu, to make lean trees grow quickly, one may not manure too strongly.

Onoregá mi wo susume kosurihú
Mihizá ta-nin wo tasse-sime yé.

Will you advance yourselves.
First let others help themselves forward.

CHAPTER VII. THE VERB. § 88.   29

I'töni yeki (益) *ari-simuru ni sewitsi* (事 —) *tö su*, to manage that there be much advantage for others, I consider the only object. — *Kurauriki wo kiru koto nakarai-sime*, order that the chopping of mulberry-trees do not take place! *Kami wo maturi*, to worship a Kami; *Kami wo maturai-simu*, he gives order to worship the Kami. — *Tor)i*, u, to take; *Tori-sime*, to have it taken. — *Sore takara kari ni motoirite, tori wo tori-simuru tori nari*, the falcon is a bird, that is used for the chace, and (by which) people have birds caught. — *Fukuri*, to consider; *Fukuraî-sime*, to charge to consider. — *Kumoso wo utsu koto wo fukurai-sime* ¹) *tamau*, the Emperor has it taken into consideration to beat the (hostile) Kumâso.

Ni, to be; *Nas)i*, u, to make be; to produce; *Nasisi*, make produce; *Nasi-sime*, charge to have made. He, who orders, charges a second person to have something done by a third. That then is the reason, why *Nasisime* plays so important a part in the courtly style; it is the same as if it were said that a prince gives order, to take measures that something be done. — *Kiku-tei wo nasdameri tö ari*, it is (said) that the Emperor N. has given order, that the wrestling games be held. — *Tsurugi wo sadzakete, Ten-kwau wo korosisimen tö su*, handing him a sword, he will have the Emperor murdered.

Remark 1. The object, which precedes the verb in *sime* in the Accusative, Dative or Local, is, as appears from the examples quoted, the object of the action ordered, not the person who is ordered. If the latter is admitted into the sentence then the old style allows him, as a remote definition, to precede in the Accusative, e. g. *Sukune wo fakira koto wo okonarisima*, (the prince) orders Sukune to hold council. The new style uses the turn of phrase: „by ordering Sukune he has council held," and supersedes *simete* (ordering) by the syncopated form *site*; thus *Sukune wo site* (*simete*) *fakura-koto wo okonarisima*. — *Ten-waja Nunaki Iri-jime wö site N.N. kami wo malturiamu*, the Emperor charges the Lady Nunaki and has the god N.N. solemnly whorshiped.

祭之〇
祀人便
　承天
　　下

Ten-ka no fito wo site . . , matu-ri ni tukuru matsurôsimu ²), the people of the realm are let pay their respects at the feasts.,

---

¹) Not *fakarusime*, as in the original text.   ²) *Tsukung-yang*, XVI.

小人之使　Sеu-zin wo site, koku-ka wo osamé-simurеba, sai-kui suruhi
百官家苗　siru ¹), if one let a man of mean character govern the
皆楽至　country and people, calamity and misfortune rise to the top.

Two zа (長寿) *no moto-wi wo yr-saaiman taru*, to manage that one gets
the foundation of a long life. — *N... wo tsukawaste Idzumo no Oho-yasiro ni osimaru tokoro no kan-takara wo tadasimau*, (the Emperor) sends N... and lets the
Kami-treasure be inspected, which is kept in the Great chapel of Idzumo. —
Tami ni takuwi nyuru koto wo osiyemu, he (the Emperor Shin-nang) lets the
people be taught ploughing and planting.

Remark 2. Site, = *simite*, is also superseded by **mei-site** (命ジシテ) or **rei-
site** (命ゼレテ), giving order to..., with a precedent Dative. — *M.. to iu
Dai-siyau-ni mei-site N.. wo utasimu*, giving order to the general named M.. he
lets N.. be beaten (battle be given him). — 民ヲ民ニ 命ゼレテ カヒコヲ
カハレイ タマフ, (the prince) giving order to the people, lets silkworms be bred.

THE PASSIVE FORM.

§ 89. The Japanese language expresses the idea of „to be rewarded" by an
active form, which answers to „get reward" and by means of the nondeflecting
verb *e* (得ᴇ, = to get, appropriate) forms derivative verbs, which signify the
appropriating of an action coming from without. The Japanese passive verbs,
thus, in nature and form, are derivative active verbs; therefore mention can be
made only of the manner in which they are derived, but, by no means of
passive forms of inflection, for *e* follows the nondeflecting conjugation.

According to their derivation the passive verbs are arranged in three classes:
I. 1. All deflecting transitive verbs in *i* can become passive, when their verbal
element *i* is superseded by **e**, **u**, **eru**, **uru**, e. g.:

Yaki, ヤキ, to burn; *trans.*　　*Yuké*, ヤケ, to be burned, to burn oneself.
Kiki, キヽ, to hear;　　　　　　*Kiké*, キケ, to be heard, to sound.
Saki, サキ, to tear;　　　　　　*Saké*, サケ, to be torn.

¹) *Dai Gaku*. X. 12.

Yomi, ヨミ, to read;		Yome, ヨメ, to be read.	
Umi, ウミ, to bear, bring forth;		Ume, ウメ, to be produced or born.	
Ari, アリ, to exist;		Are, アレ, to become.	
Nari, ナリ, to be;		Nare, ナレ, to become.	
Ori, オリ, to break, e. tr.		Ore, オレ, to break, intr.	
Uri, ウリ, to sell;		Ure, ウレ, to be sold, to be for sale.	
Tsukuri, ツクリ, to make;		Tsukure, ツクレ, to be made.	

2. The nondeflecting transitive verbs in *i*, chiefly monosyllabic, attach *e* to their root-vowel, either with or, according to the dialect of Yédo, without interposition of the *y*. The writing has エ, ユ, エル, ユル; forms, which are frequently confounded with ヘ, ア, ヘル, アル.

Mi, ミ (*Miru*, *Mild*), to see.   *Miye*, ミエ (*Miyu*, ミユ; *Miyuru*, ミユル; *Miyete*, ミエテ; *Miyetari*; or *Mi)e*, u, uru, ete, etari), become visible, appear.

I, キ (*iru*, キル; *ite*, キテ), to shoot.   *Iye*, キエ (*Iyu*, キユ; *Iyuru*, キユル; *Iyete*, キエテ), to get a shot, be shot. Thence *Iyu-sisi*, a shot stag.

Ni, ニ (*Niru*, ニル), to boil; trans. - *Tagu wo niru*, boil tea.   *Niye*, ニエ (*Niyu*, ニユ; *Niyuru*, ニユル; *Niyete*, ニエテ), boil; intr. — *Niye-yu*, boiling water.

Remark. If a nondeflecting verb followed by the verb *e* (= to get) remains in its radical form in *i*, the *e* retains its inherent signification of get; it is equivalent, however, to the expression: get something done, i. e. the being able to realize; thus *Mairi-yenu* (or in the spoken language *Mairi-yemasenu* 行キ得エマセヌ [1]), I cannot come.

II. Some deflecting verbs in *i* have *áye* or *óye* for their passive form, being the verb *e* suffixed to the root in *i*, after the *i*, by strengthening has become *a* or, on account of vocal harmony, has become *o*. This form comes from the old Japanese, and is considered particularly elegant.

---

[1] *Shopping-Dialogues*, page 17.

CHAPTER VII. THE VERB § 89.

Iri, イヒ, to say; to be called; *Irúye*, イハエ, or *Ieú*, to be said or named. 所謂.
Siri, シリ, to know; *Siréye* シラエ, to become or be known. 所知.
Ari, アリ, to exist; *Aráye*, アラエ, to become existing. 所有.
Kiki, キキ, to hear; *Kikóye*, キコエ, to be object of hearing. 所聞.
　　　　　Thence *Kọyé*, the sound, voice.
Omóri, オモヒ (*omoú*), to think; *Omóroyé*, オモエ (*omóoye*), to be thought of or
　　　cogitable. 所想.

Inflection, regular: *Kikoyḗ*, ṅ, *uru*, etc. *ttari* etc., *eba*, future *urun* (= *uru* + *arun*), thus *Kikoyúrun*, to avoid *Kikoyen*, which too much resembles the negative *Kikoyrań*, not to be heard. *Kikoyken* (所聞来矣), it will have become loud.

Remark. The substantive forms *Irúyuru*, *Siriyuru*, *Kikoyuru*, *Omóroyuru* mean that which has been said, called, heard, thought, *Ardyuru*, that which has gotten existence, that which appears, and exists. Used attributively, they are equivalent to our passive participle of the past time. *Siriyuru mono* is, what has been brought to knowledge. — *Kono mi fasira no kami rd iróyaru Sare no kami uḋri*, these three Kamis are the so called Landing-gods. — *Ano tera no kane ga kokomade kikiyu* (in the spoken language *kikiye-mása*), the bell of that temple is to be heard here. — *Aróyuru mono, fitó, Hotóke*, the things, people, Buddhas that exist, = all the things, people etc.

The forms quoted, *Iróyuru*, *Siróyuru*, *Aróyuru* agree perfectly with the Chinese expressions: 所謂 *So iwí*. 所知 *Si tsí*. 所有 *So yeú*.

III. The most usual derivation of passive verbs is effected by means of the undeflecting verb *Ar)e*, *u*, *eru*, *uru*, *ete* etc., = to become, which is suffixed to the substantive form of a transitive verb, by which its weak termination *u* is elided; thus:

Ake, to open; *Akéru*, opening; passive *Akéra + óre = Akerőre*, to be opened.
Mi, to see; *Miru*, seeing; „ *Mira + óre = Mirőre*, to be seen.
Fiki, to draw; *Fiku*, drawing; „ *Fika + óre = Fikőre*, to be drawn.

---

[1] The etymological dictionary *Wayen Siwori*, vol. 37 p. 2 verso splits *áraye* into *ai* and *raye*, declares *raye* as a lengthening of *re*, and *riwoe* as a lengthening of *sire*. What the lengthening means, the author does not say.

CHAPTER VII. THE VERB. § 89.

According to this rule the passive verbs following are formed.

Nondeflecting.

Ag)e, eru, to hoist, raise, lift;   Agerar)e, u, uru etc., to be hoisted.
Wak)e, eru, to share;   Wakerar)e, u, to be shared.
Tat)e, eru, to erect;   Taterar)e, u, to be erected.
At)e, eru, to touch, hit;   Aterar)e, u, to be touched.
Sadam)e, eru, to define;   Sadamerar)e, u, to be defined.
Sim)e, eru, to charge, to let;   Simerar)e, u, to be charged.
Ir)e, eru, to receive;   Irerar)e, u, to be received.
I, Iru, to shoot;   Irar)e, u, to be shot.

Deflecting.

I, u, verbal element, to be;   Ar)e, u, uru, to get existence, to become.
N')i, u, to be;   Nar)e, u, to become.
Nag)i, u, to throw anything forward at its full length. — Kusá wo nagu, to mow grass.   Nagar)e, u, to stream. Kawa, futu nagara, the river, the banner streams.
Nuk)i, u, to draw out;   Nukar)e, u, to be drawn out.
Kog)i, u, to burn, scorch;   Kogar)e, u, to be burnt.
Nas)i, u, to cause to be, to produce;   Nasar)e, u, to be produced.
Idds)i, or Das)i, u, to bring to light, produce;   Idasar)e, u, to be produced.
Kudds)i, u, to drop; trans. to let fall;   Kudasar)e, u, to be dropped, to descend.
Os)i, u, to press;   Osar)e, u, to be pressed.
Koros)i, u, to cause to clot; to kill;   Korosar)e, u, to be killed.
Watds)i, u, to set over; trans.   Watasar)e, u, to be set over.
Fanas)i, u, to loosen; trans.   Fanasar)e, u, to be loosened.
(Itos)i, u, to make fall; to fell;   Itosar)e, u, to be felled.
Fanats)i (tsi = ti), u, to loosen;   Fanatar)e, u, to be loosened; to be banished.

Uts)i, u, to beat;   Utar)e, u, to be beaten.
Mots)i, u, to catch hold of;   Motar)e, u, to be held.
Ir)i, u (Fi, Iu), to say; to be called;   Irar)e, u, to be called.
Or)i, u, to pursue;   Orar)e, u, to be pursued.
Kor)i, u (Kai, Kau), to change, barter;   Korar)e, u, to be or may be changed.

Kw)i, u, to eat; — Kurár)e, u, to be eaten, to be eatable.
Uinar)i, u, to lose; — Uinarér)e, u, to be lost.
Okond'r)i, u, to act, treat, perform, commit; — Okonard'r)e, u, to be treated, performed or committed.
Yob)i, u, to call; — Yobar)e, u, to be called.
Musub)i, u, to knot, to tie; — Musubir)e, u, to be tied, to be knotted together.

Yom)i, u, to read; — Yomdr)e, u, to be read.
Um)i, u, to bear; — Umir)e, u, to be born.
Nom)i, u, to drink; — Nomdr)e, u, to be drunk, to be drinkable.
Ur)i, u, to sell; — Urár)e, u, to be sold, to be for sale.
Kir)i, u, to chop, to cut; — Kirár)e, u, to be cut.
Sir)i, u, to know; — Sirár)e, u, to be known.

Remark 1. Has the Japanese passive verb a potential force? Implicit, yes, but not explicit! Just as our expression: „vegetables that are eaten," includes the idea, that they are eatable, so the Japanese verb, especially its attributive form, may, in the idea of the speaker, have a potential force, and *Kwareru imo*, = a turnip being eaten, may mean that it is an eatable one. Compare the Sanscrit *Amitáb'a*, = *immensa vita*, unmeasured and unmeasurable life.

Thus when the proposition: „Cloths imported from foreign countries, can be sold cheaper than those made in Japan" [1], translated into the Japanese spoken language is: *Nippon de ts'kuremas'ta tam-mono yori, gai-kóku kara watarimas'ta tam-mono wo yasúku úrare-mas'* [2], it declares, that cloths, which have come from foreign countries, are sold cheaper, than cloths which are made in Japan, and the Japanese text has a fact in view, that includes the possibility, whereas the English „can be sold" speaks of the possibility merely. „Not understanding any thing" the Japanese says: *Wakári-masína*, = I don't understand it; not being able to understand it, he says *Wakári dekí-masíná*.

Remark 2. The language of courtesy, which gives to the predicate verb the passive form, although logic requires the active (in treating the forms of courtesy,

---

[1] s. BROWN, *Colloquial Japanese*, p. 8. N°. 60.
[2] Why not rather: *Gai-kokú kara watari-mas'ta tam-mono wa Nippon de ts'kuru mas'ta tam-mono yori yasúku urare-mas'*.

we shall discuss this question further), gives a passive form to intransitive verbs also. Verbs of that character resemble the Greek Middle voice, or even the Latin Deponent Verbs; names, however, with which we shall not embarrass the Japanese.

To the passive verbs derived from intransitive verbs belong, e. g.:

I, iri, iru (居る), to dwell, stay; passive *Irar)e, uru*.
Mair)i, u (参る), to enter;   *Mairar)e*.
Aruk)i, u (歩む 行る), to step;   *Arakar)e*.
Ner)i, u (寝る), to sleep;   *Nerar)e*.
Wak)i, u (分る), to become divided;   *Wakar)e, uru*, to be divided.

Remark 3. Our method of deriving the passive form, first made known in 1857, and afterwards (1868) adopted by Mr. R. BROWN, does not agree with the original Japanese method, according to which for *agen* a verb *Rareru* (i. e. *Rar)e, u, uru*), has been imagined and been inserted in the dictionaries of the country, as equivalent to the Chinese verb 被 *p'i*.

ON THE GOVERNMENT OF THE PASSIVE VERB.

§ 91. 1. The object, which suffers an action, is subject (Nominative), and the verb passive, its predicate, e. g. *Midzu ugokasaru*, the water is brought into motion.

2. The verb passive is considered impersonal and the object undergoing the action, remains as object to the action, in the Accusative, thus *Midzu wo ugokasaru*.

3. The verb passive stands in its substantive form and has its complement, as a genitive, before it: *Midzu no ugokasaruru*, the becoming moved (the movement) of the water, or even that of the water, which is moved, which gets movement.

4. The object, from which the action proceeds, precedes as complement, characterized by the termination *ni*, or by ...*no tame ni*, = in behalf of, for the sake of.....

5. The definition of the material, from which any thing derives its existence or origin, assumes the genitive or even the ablative form in *yori* or *kara*.

Examples of the use of the passive forms.

Midzu ga figasi yi nagaru, the river flows eastwards. — *Sono ye de wi uru-*

masen, for this price it is not sold ¹). *Watakusi kono sina wo sono nedán de wa uri masèna*, I do not sell these goods for that price. — *Káiko umáre-tari*, the silkworm is hatched. — *Umáretaru* or *umarei kaiko*, silkworms hatched. — *Sirasaretaru mono*, things made known. — *Kono mitsi sukèn ni okondearùru to mièydri*, it seems that this way is much practised; *Okona)ri*, vulg. *i*, to practise; exercise; *Mi*, *miru*, to see; *Mie*, to appear, seem. — *Wgu-zi ra idaki torite, manukaretari*, the prince is taken into the arms and saved (from the fire). *Mansik)i*, *u*, to draw out. — *Asàgáwo asa ni umárete yube ni sisu*, = the morning-face (the flower of the winds) is born in the morning and dies in the evening. — *Unáre* from *sini*, to bear. *Fitó wo moto-kuni ye tsukáwasaru*, = the man is sent to his own country. *Miko wo tsukáwasaru besi to sata ari*, it is reported that the prince will be sent. *Ziyau mon* (城 門) *wo seme yaburirùru toki, tou-siya* (刀 車) *nite fusègu nari*, when the gate of a castle is broken by assault, it is shut by means of a scythed chariot. *Yabur)i*, *u*, to break. — *Makíni ra toku wo migi ni sugarrei to nari*, it is a fact, that formerly the falcon trained to sport was made perch on the right hand. *Su)e*, *uru*, to roost; *Suse)i*, *u*, to make roost; *Sugar)e*, *u*, to be set up, placed high. — *Tsumi-nin no kubi wo kiru*, to cut a criminal's throat; *Kubi wo kirarrtaru* (or *kirareta*) *mono*, one whose throat is cut.

Aku-fau ni sarasarete fuku-yau-ni-taru yosi wo tuin-fyo-zu, the report has been spread, that (the ship) has been set adrift by an ill wind and driven on shore. *Funasi*, set free.

Fitó ni tasinamerùru, he is vexed by others, (為 人 所 困). — *Fitó ni nan-gi wo uriru*, = difficulty is caused by others. — *Ten-nyu ni korosùru*, he is killed by the emperor. *Inu ni kamarèdru fitó*, a person bitten by a dog; *Kam)i*, *u*, to bite. — *Kazèni oréru takenu ko*, a young bamboo cane, which is, or can be, broken by the wind. — *Kore ni yotte … fi-you ni idssì. Muta fiyaku-sigyu ni yadowarete, ta-suki, kusá-kari, ine-karite, do-min no mono ni ari omasi*, therefore (the Bonzes of Coren) go out at day-wages. And while they, hired by any one, plough the fields, mow grass, cut rice, they assimilate themselves to the husbandmen. *Yado)ri*, *u* = to hire. — *Fitó ca taku ni orarète Syak'-son no fudokoro*

---

¹) *Shopping-Dialogues*, page 4.

ai tobi-irinu, the dove pursued by the falcon, flew into S'akya's lap. (Or)i, u, to pursue. — *Mimana tsui ni Sinra no tamëni forobosiru*, the state of Mimana is at last demolished on behalf of (= by and for) Sinra. *Forob)i*, u, to perish; *Forobos)i*, u, to demolish. — *Fo no tamë ni yakarete sinu*, burnt by the fire, he dies. 為火所灼死. *Yak)i*, u, trans. to burn. —

鬼所 迷必 ：云 是 人 Kono fïtö kanarazu oni no tamë ni madorasarento iuku, it is said that, that man will certainly be misled by the devil. *Mador)i*, u, to err, to wander; *Madords)i*, u, to make err; *Madorasar)e*, u, to be brought so far, that one errs or wanders. —

Siwo-sawawo kori narëru sima, an island caused by the clotting of sea-foam. — *Koru Fino-kami no ti no nareru nari*, this (spirit) is produced out of the blood of the Fire-god.

THE NEGATIVE FORM OF THE JAPANESE VERB.

§ 91. I. Theory of the Derivation.

In the negative sentence, the Japanese language attaches the negative to the predicate word. It denies that an action or state exists; but it does not deny the existence of the subject or object, while the action or state, in which both are concerned, is existing as positive, as in: "no one comes; he bears nothing." Therefore it unites the negative element, n, with the verbal element i or si (see § 92 and 103) and thereby gets the forms n+i=NI and n+si=SI, 止ジ, pronounced as ndsi or dsi; two root-forms, of which the former is proper to the spoken, the latter to the written language.

These terminations, in nondeflecting affirmative verbs, are immediately added to the root (*Ak=si*, アクシ, *Mi=si*, ミジ), whereas in deflecting ones in *i*, this *i* at once mutates into *a* (*Yuki*, to go, *Yakdzi*, 不ユ往ヰ止ジ, not to go). *Ni* and *si* follow the deflecting conjugation, while the closing form ク *nu* and ズ *su*, at once serve for the substantive and the attributive form. The *Nigori-mark*, so necessary to distinguish スクズ from スクス (to make go), is frequently omitted [1].

248   CHAPTER VII. THE NEGATIVE VERB. § 91.

The root-form *ni*, which we are obliged to adopt as the basis of the negative conjugation, is not in use and, in poetry, appears to be superseded by *ne*.

EXAMPLES OF THE FORMATION OF NEGATIVE VERBS.

Affirmative.	Negative.	
	Written.	Spoken.
Ak)e, uru, *to open*,	Akez)i, u, アケ) ビ, ズ.	(Akéni), Akénu, アケヌ.
M)i, iru, *to see*.	Miz)i, u, ミ) ビ, ズ.	Minu, ミヌ.
Muku)i, yu, yuru (nondef.), *to requite*.	Mukuiz)i, u, ムクイ) ビ, ズ.	Mukuinu, ムクイヌ.
	not to requite.	
Yuk)i, u, *to go*.	Yukáz)i, u, ユカ) ビ, ズ.	Yukánu, ユカヌ.
Sik)i, u, *so to be*.	Sikáz)i, u, シカ) ビ, ズ.	
Nas)i, u, *to cause to be*.	Nasáz)i, u, ナサ) ビ, ズ.	Nasánu, ナサヌ.
Tat)i, u, *to arise*.	Tatáz)i, u, タ) ビ, ズ.	Tatánu, タ、ヌ.
Av)i, u, *to meet*.	Aváz)i, u, アハ) ビ, ズ.	Avánu, アハヌ.
Sorov)i, u, *become equal*.	Sorováz)i, u, ソロハ) ビ, ズ.	Sorovánu, ソロハヌ.
Soorav)i, u, *to serve*.	Sooraváz)i, u, サヲラハビ.	Sooravánu, サヲラハヌ.
△ Sor)ai, o, ,		Soravánu, ソラハヌ.
Nukum)i, u, *to warm*, c. i.	Nukumáz)i, u, ヌクマ) ビ, ズ	Nukumánu, ヌクマヌ.
Nukum)e, uru, *to warm*, c. tr.	Nukumez)i, u, ヌクメ) ビ, ズ	Nukumenu, ヌクメヌ.
Ar)i, u, *to exist, be*.	Aráz)i, u, アラ) ビ, ズ.	Aránu, アラヌ.

In the same manner, every affirmative verb, whether it be active or passive, may assume the negative form; there are, however, a few verbs which depart from the general rule of derivation, to wit:

Ki, Kuru (nondef.), to come;   Kónu, at Yédo Kónu, not to come.
Dek)i, iru (noudef.), to be achieved;   Dekinu, vulg. Dekénu.
Mits)i, uru (nondef.), to be filled;   Miténu (for Mitsinu), not to be filled.
Mds)i, u (not Mes)e, uru), to be;   Mosánu, not to be; — thus also:
Mi-mos)i, u, to be seeing, to see;   Mi-mosánu, not to see.

リ 不ズ 若ヤ

II. INFLECTION OF THE NEGATIVE VERBS.

Synopsis of the negative forms of inflection, compared with the affirmative.
YUKÍ, -u (deflecting), go; YUKAZÍ, -n, not to go.

	Affirmative.	Negative.	
		Written.	Spoken.
	YUK)	YUKA)	YUKA)
Root-form...	-i, go.	-zi, ユカジ, not to go.	-ni, -ne.
Gerund......	-ite, going.	-zite, not going.	-nite, not used.
by elision...	Yuite.	Yukazite, ユカイデ	Yukaide. (*)
Closing-form.	-u, goes.	-zu, ユカズ, goes not.	-nu, ユカヌ.
Subst. and adj.	-u, the going.	-zu.	-nu.
Subst., isolated	-uva, △ -uwa.	-zuva, △ -zuwa.	
„ declined	-uni, -univa, on going, in order to go.	-zuni, -zuniva, -zunba, on not going, for not going.	
Gerund......	-nite, by going.	-zunde, ユカズンデ, ユカイデ, contr. from	-nnde, ユカイデ, -nite, ユカンデ (†).
		-zunite, by not going.	Yukade, ユカデ.
		-zu-site.	-nu ni ötewá, on not going.
Causal- and modal-form.	-eba, as one goes.	-zeba, ユカゼバ, as one goes not.	-neba, ユカネバ.
Concessive...	-u tomó, also the going.	-zu mó, -zu tomo.	
	-é-domó, though one goes.		-né-domó, also Yukádemó.
	-u to iédomo.	-zu to iédomo.	-nu to iédomo.
Suppositive form.	-ábá, contract. from	-zumba.	-nderá, ユカンデバ,
	-au ni va, if one goes.	-zunba, ユカズンバ, contr. from -zuniva, if one goes not.	Yukaderá, ユカデバ, -nu naraba (Yédo).

(*) *Akezite* and *Mizite*, derived from the nondeflecting *Ake* and *Mi*, likewise, in the dialect of Miyako, pass into *Akeide*, アケイデ, not opening, and *Mide*, ミイデ, not seeing.

(†) Just so

Omoranu + te (不思而) passes into オモハデ, *omoráde*, pr. *omoënde*, not thinking.
Aranu + te (勿而) „ „ アラデ, *Arade*, pron. *Arande*, not existing.
Sa (= sika) ranu + te (不然而) „ „ サラデ, *Sarade*, pron. *Sarande*, not being so...

250 CHAPTER VII. THE NEGATIVE VERB. § 91. 92.

Toriñu + te   passes into トラヂ, Toride, pron. Torande, not taking.
Senu + te (不為而) „ „ セヂ, Sede, pron. Se-nde, not doing.
Omoeoyñnu + te „ „ オモヰヌヂ, Omoroyide, pron. omoroyinde, not being thought.

CONTINUATIVE FORMS OF THE NEGATIVE VERB.

§ 92. 1. The written language supersedes the termination ぬ by ザリ, u, which is considered a fusion of ぬ + ari.

Akezi, not to open,   becomes Akezari, アケザリ, not to be opening.
Mizi, not to see,   „   Mizari, ミザリ, not to be seeing.
Yukizi, not to go,   „   Yukazari, ユカザリ, not to be going.
Masazi, not to excel, „   Masazari, マサザリ, not to be the better.
Sikizi, not to be so, so „   Sikazari, シカザリ, continually not to be so.

The forms for the moods and tenses are the same as those of ari; thus: zari, u, uni, eba, eiomo; Future an; Condit. aba; Preterit zari)ki, si, keri, keru, keruni, kerebu, keredomo; Future kerau, ken; Condit. kereba.

2. The written language attaches ar)i, u, to the negative gerund zi-de and opposes to the affirmative form Ake-te-ari, to be opening (§ 78) the negative form Ake-zi-de ari, which, in the spoken language, passes into Akezide ar)i, u, to be in the not opening.

3. The spoken language uses its negative gerund …nu-de in connection with ar)i, u.

    Akinu-de ari,   アカヌヂアリ, commonly pronounced as Akande ar'.
    Minu-de ari,   ミヌヂアリ,   „   „   „ Minde ar'.
    Yukanu-de ari,   ユカヌヂアリ,   „   „   „ Yukande ar'.

From this derivation arise the very common Preterit Minu-de arita, pron. Minde atta, has not been seeing, and the Future Minu-de aran, △ Min-de aroo, will not be seeing.

4. The poet supersedes the negative termination nu with naki, △ nai, naku (= without, see page 108); thence Ave-naku = Aenu, without daring; Omovanaku [1]), = Omoranu, without thinking.

The dialect of Yédo alike, and that by preference, uses nai (= nasi, naki,

---

[1]) Might not these be forms connected with § 107. 3 ?

without) and the thence derived continuative form *Nakuri* and *Nakeri*, as negative auxiliary verb, and supersedes *Ikena*, *Mina*, and *Yukina* with the forms *Ake-nai*, *Ake-nakdr*)*i*, u; — *Mi-nai*, *Mi-nakir*)*i*, u; — *Yuku-nai*, *Yuku-nakir*)*i*, u, = to be without opening, without seeing, without going. Thence ∧ *Yukanaide* for *Yukizu ni*, without going. With the derivative form *nakari* the negative verb follows the affirmative conjugation, as appears from the examples following:

Ake-nakdreba, as one is without opening.	*Mi-nakattdrabd*, if one has not seen.
„ *nakaraba*, if one is without opening.	*Simasa-nakatta kara*, as or after one has not finished; from *Simari* (vulg. *Simai*), to finish.
Deki-nakareba, as it does not issue or proceed.	
„ *nakereba*, as it was without success.	*Tsuké-nakatta*, one has not applied; from *Tsuki*, to apply.
„ *nakaraba*, if it is successless.	
„ *nakereba*, if it was successless.	*De-nakatta*, he did not come out; from *De*, *dera*, to go out.
Mi-nakdtta, he was without seeing.	
„ „ *kara*, as he was without seeing.	*Tobe-nakatta*, did not fly; from *Tobi*, to soar, to fly.

The written language opposes to the forms *Tsuke-nakatta* and *Tobe-nakatta* the forms: *Tsukeru koto nakatta* and *Tobu koto nakatta*, i. e. the beginning and the flying did not happen. Compare *Sore futa-tabi kitaru koto nasi*, it does not happen (*nasi*), that he appears for the second time.

FORM OF THE FORBIDDING IMPERATIVE.

§ 93. 1. The Forbidding Imperative consists of the substantive form of the affirmative verb, followed by the forbidding *na* (Lat. *ne*) or more emphatically *nayo* '). Compare § 60.

Akeru, the opening;	*Akeru na* or *Akeru nayo*, don't open!
Suru, the doing;	*Suru na*, don't do!
Wasdraru, forgetting;	*Wasdraru ni*, don't forget!
Tataku, striking;	*Tataku na*, don't strike!
Nasuru, making;	*Nasuru na*, don't make!
Kiku, hear; *Miru*, see;	*Kiku na*, don't hear; *Miru na*, don't see!
Su, doing, from *Si*;	*Su na* (勿為), do not!

') ナヨ 会ドスル 辭せ ヲスルハナヨ。 *Vegm Suvri*. — Compare § 96.

2. If the idea of continuance is associated with the forbidding, then, instead of na or nagi, Nakaro, ナカル (勿, 毋), the imperative mood of Nakúri, not to be (§ 92, 4), is used. The action which is characterized by nakúre as one that may not be, precedes as subject proposition characterized by koto (thing); thus: Utagau-koto nakóre (勿疑), let the doubting not be!, for: do not doubt!

3. The forbidding proposition begins with Na (= Lat. ne), the predicate verb being in its affirmative root-form, followed by so (compare § 69).

Na iri so, say not. 勿謂. 莫謂. — *Na yurusi so*, grant not! 莫聽. *Na atasi tokoro ni i so*, go not elsewhere. — *Na motome so*, n'acquérez pas¹). — *Nú nakdri si*, pron. *Na nakdsai*, not without! = it must be! — *Nakdr)i*, u, to be without .....

4. The forbidding becomes a wish (optative), when *so* is superseded by *kasi* (= Lat. quaeso). — *Na iri kasi*, may be not say!

Politeness does not allow a person bluntly to use the imperative to his equals or superiors. Instead of *Miru na*, see not, expressions such as *Mi-nasáru ná*, or *Mi-asadre-ndai ná*, = let there not be seen, are used. — *Kuusai na*, = let it not come under notice, is superseded by *O kumui kudasdru na*²); forms, to which we shall return in our illustration of the language of courtesy. Appendix to Chapter VII.

FORMS OF THE NEGATIVE PRETERIT.

§ 94. 1. The negative termination nu becomes nanda, ナンダ.

Akinu, not to open;	*Akananda*, not to have opened.
Dénu, not to go out;	*Denanda*, not to have gone out.
Saménu, not to awake;	*Samenanda*, not to have awoke.
Minu, not to see;	*Minanda*, not to have seen.
Yukinu, not to go;	*Yukananda*, not to have gone.
Masen, not to be;	*Masenanda*, or, in the vulgar language of Yédo, *Mansinanda*, not to have been.
Mi-masén, not to see;	*Mi-masenanda*, not to have seen.

Tsure-datsite modoranandu, they have not come back together (不同歸). *Modori*, to come back. — *Fin wo siruuanda*, he has not learned to know poverty (不知貧). *Siri*, to learn to know.

¹) KOPENUVAL, pag. 66. ²) Shopping-Dialogues, p. 31.

2. The spoken language of Yédo uses the forms *Ake-nakutta, Mi-nakatta, Yuku-nakatta*, = was without opening, without seeing, without going, derived from *Ake-nakviri, Mi-nakviri* and *Yuku-nakviri*. See § 93, 4.

3. The written language employs ..sari)ki, si, kori etc., the preterit of the negative continuative form *zari* (§ 92, 1). — *Onkurazari si inêtoi*¹), the life which was not agreeable. — *Oshi*, agreeable.

FORMS OF THE NEGATIVE FUTURE.

§ 95. 1. The spoken language, which employs the continuative forms *Akenai-de-ari, Minai-de-ari, Yukanai-de-ari*, cited in § 92, 2, makes use of the future of *ari*, thus *argu* (アラウ) or *aroo*, and says: *Akenai-de-argu, Minai-de-argu, Yukanai-de-argu*, he will not be opening, seeing, going.

2. 1) The written language employs ..*zaran*, サラン, the future of the continuative *zari* (§ 92, 1), or, instead of *zaran*, ..*zu to nan*, ..*zu mo aranan* (compare § 75, II, 3), and forms from

Akezari   the future *Akezaran*, or *Akezu to nan*, not to be about to open.
Mizari   „   „ *Mizaran*, or *Mizu to nan*, not to be about to see.
Yukazari „   „ *Yukazaran*, or *Yukazu to nan*, not to be about to go.

2) The written language, moreover, has a negative future in ..*mazi*, マジ, from which by elision of the *z*, the vulgar form *mai*, マイ, has arisen (comp. *Yukuzide* and *Yukuide*, § 91, II).

    Ake-mazi,   vulgo *Ake-mai*, shall not open.
    Mi-mazi,   „   *Mi-mai*,   „ „ see.
    Yuku-mazi, „   *Yuku-mai*, „ „ go.
    Aru-mazi, „   *Aru-mai*, „ „ be.

From these examples it is evident that, in nondeflecting verbs, *mazi* is joined to the root, and in deflecting verbs, to the attributive form.

Since the power to indicate the future, is not to be sought in *zi*, but must lie in *ma*, I consider this the substantive *ma*, which signifies room, space, used also with regard to time, as it appears from the expression: *Ikari wo orosu ma mo adka-site, kaze ni makasete yuku*, = as there is not even (*mo*) time (or opportunity) to cast out the anchor, they abandon themselves to the wind and pass on. — The action now, for which there is no time or opportunity, as it appears

---

¹) *Sigeta-shi*, N°. 50.

from the example, is something that is not yet happening, or has not yet happened (*Mi-rai*), but no real future. — With regard to the negative form *zi* joined to *ma* — it may be considered as an elliptical form of *nazi* (*n + si = nzi, zi, ヅ*), or what is more probable, a fusion of the negative element *n* with the derivative form *siki, siku, sini* or *si* (§ 16) (*n + siki = ziki, ヅ ヰ*) — it only denies, that time or opportunity for something exists, and consequently *mazi* too, is properly a present. The Japanese custom of passing *masi* for *mazi* must therefore be disapproved of.

Inflectional forms of *Mazi*, vulg. *Mai*, are: the adverbial form *mazikuni*, vulg. *maikuro*, and the modal *mazikini*, vulgo *maikini, maini*, no opportunity being; *mai toki*, if, or as, there is no opportunity; *mai tomo*, even if there is no opportunity. Tenses and moods are expressed by the auxiliary verbs *nari*, to be, and *keri*, have been. *Maziki nari* (△ *Mai na*); *Maziki nar)eba; -domo, -do; -aba* (△ *Maziki naru*); *Maziki nar)au*, △ -*go, -oo. Mazi ker)i, n,* (△ *Mai ker)i, n*); *Mazi ker)eba; -domo; Maziken*.

Examples of the use of the negative forms.

When, as it will appear from some of the passages following, not only the subject, but the object also, or even the appositive definition of a negative verb, is isolated by *va*, △ *wa* or *mo*, it is intended to bring out the negation with more emphasis.

[Root-form.] *Ame tsutsi firikesi yori kono kata imi no tóki fodó dai-fei-náru koto arási; nisi va Kikai Yaka no sima yiri figisi Ousyu no Sotogu-fdma muile ggorei no yaki-todókazdru tokóro mó núsi*, since the development of heaven and earth a state of peace so general as at present, has not existed. To the West, from the Yaku-island, which belongs to the region of ghosts, to the farthest shore of the Eastern Osiyu, there is not even one place, to which the authority of the Government does not reach.

Firákesi, preterit of *Firúke*, to open itself, to unfold. — *Arási*, negative root-form, = not exist, used here because, the connection of the sense is coordinative. — *Todókazdru*, attributive negative form of *Todoki, u, = reach to*.

Sonó moto midárití, súé omumóru monó vá árási; sonó atsúšenrú tokóro no mono utaša-šte, sikjušite sono uťsú súrú tokóro no mono dtuski koto imáda koré arásu (Dai Gaku, § 7), = something (*monó ró*), of which the top is regulated, while the root is in disorder, does not exist; neither, is that, which has been made thick, thin, or that which has been made thin, thick. —

CHAPTER VII. THE NEGATIVE VERB. § 85.   235

Yado magura ¹ sigereru yado wo ² sabisiki ni
Fito kozo miyene ³ akiru ki-nikeri ⁴).

In the solitary cell, where the plant *Magura* has sprung up luxuriantly, nobody is to be seen; — Autumn has come.

Miyene, the negative root-form of *Miyu*, to appear. — *Aki*, autumn, light.

[Closing-form.] *Ki-sin no tokoro-tara koto, sore miku mira ki! Kore wo saite setsu; kore wo kiite kikazu; mono ni tai-sité nokosi bekarazu* ⁵), „how abundantly do spiritual beings display the powers that belong to them. We look for them, but do not see them; we listen to, but do not hear them; yet they enter into all things, and there is nothing without them." LEGGE, *Chinese Classics*, Vol. 1, p. 261.

Mite and *Kiite*, gerund of *Mi*, to see, and *Kiki*, to hear, for which in another edition of the text the causative forms *Misedomo* and *Kikedomo*, are used. — *Bekarizu* = may not, from the adjective *Beki* (page 109, N°. 7a).

出ｲ 門ｦ 鬼ノ ○ *Sono kiyo-riu-bu no sai-i ni mon miyou wo mōkesu.*
入ｽﾞ 堵ｦ 周囲ｦ   *Ide-iri zi-zai-ni-sen besi* ⁶), around this abode shall
自 設ｽﾞ 一ﾆ   neither gate nor fence be placed. In going out
在 居ﾆ   and coming in, people shall be free.

勞セﾞ 約ｼ 御ﾆ 山ﾉ *Yama-naka ni kuro-ki no go-miya wo tsukuri, ken-yaku wo*
シ ﾃ 所ｦ 中ﾆ *matsiri, tami wo rō-se-sinezu* ⁷), in the building of a
ﾒｽﾞ 用ｲ 作ﾘ 黒木 palace of barked timber in the mountains (the prince)
民ｦ 偷ﾌ ﾉ considers economy, and does not permit the people to
    drudge.

[Substantive form.]

能ｸ 也ｷ 王ｻ ○ *Wōu no wau tarazaru va se-sura nari, atarazdruni*
也ｷ 非ｽ 不ﾙ 王ｿ *anizu* ⁸), the king's not exercising the imperial sway,
 不ﾙ 為ﾆ 之ﾉ is because he does not do it, not because he is not
   不ﾙ able to do it.

Tarazdru, = the not being, the negative substantive form of *tari*, = *to ari*, § 79, II. — *Atarazuru*, the not being able, from *Atari*.

---

¹) A hermit's farewell, N°. 67 of *Hiyaku-nin issu*. — *Yaho magura lo Gabium ntrigmus* TRUNB.
²) *Tuckung-yung* or the Moon, XVI. 1.   ⁴) *Netherl.-Jap. Treaty of 1858*, Art. II. al. 10.
³) *Nippon o dai ihi ran*, Vol. II. I r. 89th king.   ⁵) *Meng-tse*, Book 1, Pt. 1, § 7.

Mitsi no okonawaresaru, ware kori wo siriri. Tsi-sya ca koni ni sugu; gu-sya va oyobasu [1]), that the path (of the Mean) is not walked in (literally: the not being walked in of the path), this I know. The knowing ones go beyond it, and the stupid do not come up to it.

Okonawaresaru, not being practised, from *Okonaryi*, v. to practise. — *Sugyi*, v., *ore*, *uru*, transflecting v. to overstep, go beyond. — *Oyobisu* or *Oyobisu*, not to reach, from *Oyobyi*, v.

Niru-no to ca uruzi nite aurazu-aita, ji nite mo koyesaru wo ieu mori, concerning the so called pale arrow shafts, people understand by them, such as are not daubed with varnish, nor burnt with fire.

Noryi, v., to daub. — *Koyi*, v., to burn.

Sinzerarezaru wo omonbakarazu (不億不信), what is incredible is not taken into consideration.

Sin-zhe, *uru*, to believe. — *Omonbakaryi*, v., to ponder.

△ *Watukasi kare ga sono koto wo oziwesu ni suru no wo mi-tdi mono de atta*, I should like to see him do that business, undaunted.

Oziru, *uru*, transflecting, to fear.

[Attributive.] *Onori ni sikazaru mono wo tomo tō suru koto nakare*, make not a person, who is not your equal, your mate.

Sikazaru, continuative form of *Sikitzi*, and this from *Sikyi*, v. to equal.

Kono ri wo sirazaru fito, someone who does not know this law.

Mata sirazaru tokóro ari, there is what one does not yet know. — *Mata yoku-sezaru tokóro ari* [2]), there is what one does not yet do well.

Siryi, v. to know. — *Yoku-sye*, *uru*, to do good. — *Sesi*, not to do, thence *Sezaryi*, v.

Yura no to wo " watarn funa-bito " kudzi wo tase!
Yuku ye mo siranu " kori no mitsi kana [3]).

Skipper, sailing over the month by Yura, let loose the helm!
Oh! it is a way of love, that does not know whither it goes!

△ *Me ni miyénu, kutsi ni iwarenu fodo ki-meo* (奇 妙) *na koto*, a matter so uncommon, that it is not to be seen by eyes, nor to be spoken by any mouth.

△ *Fito ni iwarenu yau ni suru*, so to act that it be not remarked by others.

[Gerund.] *Taka ni ye ni sokonawa-sitê, aku ni sokonuru mono nari*, « the hawking-

[1]) *Tsi-sey-yau* IV.   [2]) Ibid. XII.
[3]) *Reu-e-sia*, N°. 46.

falcon is something (*mono*) that suffers no harm by hunger, but is spoiled by surfeiting.

△ *Farawazu-sité tori-age mósu-mai*, without paying I shall not receive (the goods). — △ *Nedan ga kawarazu sité*, while no change in price takes place.

Kun-si yo wo nogarete, sirarezu-sité, kuizu [1], the superior man, retired from the world and unacknowledged, is not grieved at it.

Nogi, *v.*, to push back; *Nogorye*, *era*, being drawn back. — *Sirji*, *v.*, to learn to know; *Sirarye*, *era*, to be known; *Sirarezu*, not to be known. — *Kui*, considering verb, to be grieved at.

[Time-defining Local.] *Kokóro arazareba, mite mizu, kiite kikdzu, kurjute miso adzīrdi wó siedzu* [2], when the mind is not present, we look and do not see; we hear and do not understand; we eat and do not know the taste of what we eat. Compare LEGGE, *Chinese Classics*, Vol. I. p. 292.

Kun-si iru tó sité, zi-tóku-sezdru koto nasi. Zyyu-i ni arite (dtte), simo wo sinoydzu. Ka-i ni arite, kami wo fikdzu. Onorí wó taddsiu-sité, f'tó ni moto-muzareba, simurai nsdmi nasi; Kami Ten wo aramizu, Simo fitó wo toyamezu. Karu ga yuí ni Kun-si ru yasuki ni wite motte mèired mètan [3]. It does not occur that (*koto nasi*) the superior man having once entered on a fixed position, does not continue to be himself. Is he in a high situation, he does not contemn his inferiors. Is he in a low situation, he does not try to pull down his superiors. Rectifying himself and seeking for nothing from others, he has no dissatisfaction. Since he is not averse to Heaven, which is above him, and does not abuse the people, who are below him, so is the superior man always contented and abides his destiny.

Zi-toku, self-preservation. — *Zi-tóku tesdru koto*, = the not remaining what one is, is the subject to *nasi* (is not). — *Sinoguru*, from *Sinogi*, *v.*, to turn off. — *Fikdzu*, not draw or drag, from *Fiki*, *v.* — *Motomuzareba*, the time-defining head of *Matomezari*, not to seek for, and this from *Motoeje*, *era*.

Manabazaru koto ari, kore wo manunde yoku-nezarebe, okdzu. Torazaru koto ari, kore wo toruto sirazarebe, okdzu [4], if it happens that he has not learned something, and when he learns it, does not become master of it, he (the superior man) does not discontinue it. Is it that he has not examined something, and might he not after the examination understand it, he does not give it up.

[1] *Techung-yung*. XI. [2] *Dai Gaku*. VII. 2. [3] *Tchung-yung*. XIV. [4] *Ibid.*, XX. 20.

[Concessive.] *Mi-kari no toki fukaradzu mó taka wo tobasu*, at the time of the princely hawking the falcon is let fly even without design.

Fukaradzu mó = fukaradzu-sité né from *fukai*), n. to consider, to design.

Nippon nite irini zen ni wo arararedomo, mare naradzu, — although (this coin) is not a coin cast in Japan, it is not rare.

Irini, preterit of *Iri*, n. to cast, to found.

心誠求之雖不中不遠未有學養子而后嫁者也 *Kokoro makoto ni kore wo motomebá* (of *motomurebá*), *atarazu tó tatómo, tookarazi: imada ko wo yasinafu koto wo manabude, nikjuaiti notsi tutsugu* (of *ki-sáru*) *mono rá arazu* [1]), if (a mother) aims in uprightness of heart at it (towards the fulfilling of her motherly duty), then even though she do not hit it, she will be not far from it. There never has been (a girl), who first learned to bring up a child, and then married afterwards.

Atarzu, not to hit, not to answer to, from *Atari*. *Tookarzi*, read-form, to be not far off, from *Tooki* (p. 108)

カラズ金銀ノ持行ヘ錢貨幣ト日本銅ハズイハチ持行ニト外國ノ金銀ハヲ日本通用金銀ハ *Nippon tsun-you kin-gin to gwai-koku no kin-gin ra motsi-yuku koto karasukarase to tadomo. Nippon tow-sen to kwa-hei ni kosirogezara kin-gin ra motsi-yuku bekarazu* [2]), Japanese current gold and silver and foreign gold and silver, the export (of it) has no difficulty; but Japanese copper money and uncoined (not made into coin) gold and silver may not be exported.

Siyqu-bai-itási koto karusikardzú tomo (or *to tólomo*), *Nippon kin-si no mua-mono rá niggu-bai-itási bekardzu* [3]), — even if trade has no difficulty, concerning articles which are forbidden in Japan, in them no trade may be driven.

Nandziga sei- (禁ず) siti'mo, si-sesu tomo, kore wo yahari kore wo suru de arzu, if you forbid it or forbid it not he will yet do it.

Mata surudésu, even if it is not so. *Siri*, contracted from *Sikári* (page 103 N°. 71). to be so.

1) *Dai Gaku*, IX, 8.
2) Franco-Japanese Treaty of the 9 Oct. 1859, Art. XIV, al 4
3) Ibid., Art. VIII, al 1.

[Future.] *Koko asikosi tsuru tokira uwo wo āru to nan* ¹), a boy, if he angles at that place, will get no fish.

破レ其ヲ故ニ *Nandzi no kuni waga-kuni no tāme ni yabardren koto ftadsiki ni arū-masi*, it will not last long, before your country will be subdued by mine.

Yuku-sitye kawāru-masi to ni-yon (誓言ジ) *wo tatsuru koto*, the taking of an oath, that in future no change shall take place.

飼ヒ方ノ本ノ口フ *Kavi-kata no ku-den wo okiye, hon-foo wo motte ygu-iku-mbn, naka-naku si-son-zi aru masiki nari* ²), if one observe the oral communication with regard to the feeding (of the silkworm) and rear it according to my prescriptions, it will then probably not happen that one suffers harm.

On-ki-dzukiti-nasdru musika soro, there is (*soro*) no occasion for your care. i. e. don't care about it; don't trouble yourself. — △ *Kāku-bātsu tai-zi-sd koto ni mo nūru-mai*, it will be no matter of extraordinary importance.

大ヲ事ジタフ, *Tai-si-to koto*, a matter of importance. ヲ, an abbreviation of ヲル. If we take ヲ instead of ヲ, we have to do with a fusion of テアル. Compare page 67, line 3.

[Suppositive.] *Ki no uy tomarite orizaru ni va* (or *orizuru kuse araba*), when (the falcon) stays on a tree, and does not come off (or: when he has the bad habit of not coming off).

Foko wo orisunba (of *orizaru ni va*), *ilsu-made mo, ye wo kawdizu-site, kawukihla aydrn běsi*, if (the falcon) does not come off his perch, one must, without baiting, let him suffer terrible hunger.

Iyé wo tsugi, toku wo tsugi, te-waza wo tsugu rui narade va, motairizu, if the expressions are not such as: to propagate a family, to propagate the good, to continue some trade, then (the character 絶, equivalent to *tsugi*) is not used.

Narudzra. トラデハ, the habitual ground of *Narāru*, not to be, used as suppositive form.

Mosi fitō wo osorete midzu wo nomusunba, in case (the falcon) shunning men, does not drink the water.

The negation of a negation involves a strengthened assertion; e. g. *tigu nri* (母を全り) *no yaki-todzikazaru tokiro mi nasi*, there is not one place, to which the authority of the Government does not reach. See page 254.

Sirazunhi aru-bekardzu (不可不知也) for *Sirizu ni ró aru bekardzu*, i. e. in the not knowing — one may not be, — one ought to know.

Fagemi tsutomezumba aru-bekurazu waza nari, it is an occupation in which one may not be without zeal and diligence, i. e. in which zeal and diligence are of the most importance.

Faru aki ca yasezunba aru bekarazu, in spring and in autumn (the hawking-falcon) must be lean. — *Yase*, *nru*, to become lean.

In the oral language the use is very common of the time-defining local ...ne ba, followed by naránü (not to be), to express the „necessity." — *Seyou ni itasneba naránü* (in the Yédo street-dialect: *Siyooni si-nakeri ya mirune*), one must act so. — *Sneba naránü*, it must happen. — *Sneba naránü koto*, the necessity.   *Ide-tatsi sneba naránü de atta*, he was constrained to depart. — *Fitó ru Ten yori ukuru tokiro wo urgami wo uri-gótokoro neba naránü*, man must be thankful for the benefits he receives from Heaven. — *Ari-gatoki*, adj., thankful.

VERBS EXPRESSING THE BEING, THE BECOMING AND THE CAUSING TO BE.

§ 10. *Arü*, n., deflecting continuative verb, derived from I (= empire, go away), signifies being continually in a departing movement, to exist, to be [1]). Its inflectional forms are: *Ari*, the root- and, by exception [2]), the predicate closing-form (= there is); *Aru*, the substantive form, which is also used attributively. Comp. § 11. — *Arute*, *Arutera*, pron. *Atte*, *Attera*, gerund, being, or as one is. — *Aredus*, there or as one is; — *Aredomo*, although there is; — *Arnu*, △ *Aryu*, *Aroo* (アらう. アロウ), future, there will be; *Aran koto kaku no gotosi* (有如此), be it so! (the termination of an oath). — *Aréba* (*Aru* + *ni* + *ra*), conditional, if there is, might there be.

---

[1]) The Japanese themselves seem not to know, that they have continuative verbs, nor that there is a connection between *i* and *ari*. They are, as it appears from the Wa-gun Siwori, in *Aru* a mere modification of 生し, *Naru*, = to become, lat. *feri*.

[2]) By this exception they prevent a confusion of the closing form of *Ari* with that of *Aru* (= to become), which is *Arü* likewise.

Preterit.

Ariki, there was.
Arisi, substantive and attributive form.
Arisi-ya*i*, whilst there was.
Arisikaba, „ „ „

Ariken, there shall or may have been.
Ariker)i, u, contin. (see § 82), have been.

Ariturji, u, △ Attari, Attaru, Atta, has been.

Attaraba, as there has been.
Attaredomo, though there has been.
Attaroo, there will have been.
Attarabu, if there has been.

Negative.

Ardz)i, u, △ Ardnu, not to be, § 91; Arazdr)i, u, contin., not to be.

1. *Ari* has the definition, what exists, as subject, the definition where a thing exists, as Local terminating in *ni*, before it.

   Fitó ari, man is; *Aru fitó*, any one being. — *Itai ni f*itó *ári* (街 有 人), there are people on the market-place; *Fitó úni ni ari* (人 在 街), people are on the market-place. — *Kin-kwa-san kai-tśiu ni dri*, the Kin-kwa-san (gold-flower-mountain) is in the sea. — *Sono kuni ni itsutsu no tanátsu-mono ari*, in that country the five sorts of grain are met with. — *Nin ra kudamono no sane no uŝi ni áru mono nari*, the pith is something being in the middle of the kernel of fruit. — *Suivai ni ari*, being in prosperity, having luck. — *Bin-ka ni ari*, being in poverty and need. — *Dai-Gáku no mitśi ua mŕ-tóku wo akiráku ni aéru ni ári; tami wo arttá ni séru ni dri; ŝi-sen ni todomáru ni ari* [1]), the way of the Great Study consists in illustrating illustrious virtue, it consists in renovating the people (in bringing it back to its primitive state!); it consists in resting in the highest excellence.

2. The definition where a thing is, followed by the subject, that exists, also occurs without the characteristic of the Local.

   終　事　本　物　
   始　有　末　有　

   Mono kon-batsu ari; waza ŝin-śi ari [2]), things have root and top; affairs have end and beginning. Conceived as subject, *Mono* and *Waza* stand for *Mono ua* and *Waza ua*, and the literal translation should be: As to things, there is a root and a top etc. Conceived as local both definitions stand for *Mono ni ua* and *Waza ni ua*.

---

[1] Dai Gaku, § 1.   [2] Ibid. § 8.

3. The spoken language characterises the definition, in what a thing exists, – what it is, by de. — *Sore wó yoki sake de ar'*, this is good wine.

4. If this definition is an action or a state, expressed by a verb, it is put in the Modal characterised by the termination *te* or *de* (see § 72). — *Akete ari*, to be in the opening, to open.

5. If it is a quality, expressed by an adjective in *ki*, as *Takaki*, high (see § 9. B. 1), the spoken language uses the adverbial form in *ku*. — *Tsuki ga takaku aru*, the high-standing (the culminating) of the moon.

6. By fusion of the adverbial form *ku* with *ari karu*, *u* is produced, *Takakar)i, u,* continually to be high. Compare § 10. § 82.

7. If the definition consisting of a subject and *ari* (*Fitó ari*, people are) precedes a substantive as attributive (or relative) quality, the subject of *aru* becomes a genitive definition, and as such generally characterized by *no* or *ga*. *Fitó no aru iti*, a market-place on which are people. — *Iro no* (or *iro ga*) *aru kumi*, colors having (colored) clouds. — *Yoki nioi aru ki*, wood, that has a good smell.

Especially, Chinese substantives are made adjectives by the addition of *no aru* or *ga aru*; *ga + aru* in the spoken language passes into *garu*. — *Sai-tsi* (才智), understanding; *Sai-tsi no aru fitó*, an intelligent man. — *Yekki* (悦ヲ喜ㇵ), mirth: *Yekki ga aru koto* or *Yekkigaru koto*, a merry business. Compare § 10. page 114, Remark.

8. The negative *Ara(zu)i, u,* = not to exist, just as the affirmative *Ari*, has the definition, in which a thing does not exist, i. e. what it is not, in the Local in *ni* before it, mostly, for the sake of emphasis, still isolated by *va*. — *Rei ni arizu* (非 礼), it is not polite; *Rei ni va ardzu*, polite — it is not. — *Sikan va* (*Siku ni va*) *arazu* (不 然), so it is not.

等³ 兄ᴷ 謂³ 神ᴷ 此³
也ᵥ 弟ᵟ 國ᴷ 之⸍ 者^
ᵗ之⸍ 主ᵦ 名ᵟ 非ᴷ
神ᵗ之⸍ ──ᴷ

Yaso Kami. Ko vo fitó faniri no mi-na ni ardzu. (Oho-kuni-nusi no Kami no ani-oto no Kami-tatsi vo igaru nari, Yaso Kami or the eighty superior beings. This is not the illustrious name of one person. Thus people call the row of Kamis of the elder and younger brothers of the Kami named the Great Land-Lord.

9. The Passive *Ar)e, u, aru,* to become, come into existence, is more particularly proper to the written language. — *Ko va togare wó moti usinóru kami*

nari, Mi fana wo arari-tamawu toki ni are-masi-tsu, this (the goddess of the falling stars) is a Kami, who takes and looses dirt. She was (*masi-tsu*) produced (*are*), when (the gods of creation) cleansed their noses. — *Ore* is called *Iru-kane* (= *Are-kane*), as being considered metal in its primitive state (生金).

Remark. **Gozar)i,** a. The courtly epistolary style and the spoken language, instead of simple *Ari*, make use of the more ample **Gozari** or **Gozari-masu,** sounding, in a quick pronunciation, as **Gōzái,** or **Gōzái-más',** in writing expressed by 御ㇲ座ᴵ有り, *Go-za-ari,* which is equivalent to the expression: „to have the honor to be." Courtesy employs this word even where it is = not suited. Like *Ari,* it has the complement of what a thing consists, i. e. what it is, if a substantive, in the Local in *de,* if an adjective in *ki,* in the adverbial form in *ku* (or *u,* page 106) before it. — *Sore wa nani de gozaru?* what is this? — *Nan-doki de gozari-masuka?* what o'clock is it? — *Hiru de gozari-masu,* it is noon. — △ *Anáta de wá gozari-mas'nũ; watákusi zi-sin ni itási-masita,* = it is not you; I did it myself. — *Go ki-gen yorósiu gozari-masu ka?* your disposition is it well? is it well with you? how do you do? — *Ai-kawóra gi mo gozari-masinu,* so as ever, literally: there is no change at all.

§ 97. **Ori,** u, deflecting continuative verb, derived from ⟨ (イ) or wi (ヰ). = *seat,* to sit, means **dwell,** reside, having reference to a living being, that can remove itself. It is preceded by the definition of place, where anything dwells, as also of the condition or of the action, in which anything is, as Local or gerund with the termination *ni* or *de* (sometimes *to*). In definitions of place the spoken language makes use of *ni* or *de* indifferently.

Conjugation, regular: Root, **Ori** (居, 留). Closing-form, subst. and attrib. form *órü,* pron. *ór',* he dwells, the dwelling. — *Or)eba, edomo, oba, ba,* although, if he dwells. — *Ori)ki, si, keri* etc. has dwelled. — Gerund. *Orite* (オ リ テ), pron. *Otte,* which in writing is expressed by オッテ, dwelling; thence the Preterit *Ori)ar)i, u,* △ *Otta.* (オッタ). — *Or)zu,* △ *Ordan,* not to dwell; — *Ori)s)i, u,* 寓居, to make to dwell, to place; — *Ordsim)e, u, eru,* 令居, to order to place. — *Samurái wo siro ni ordsimu,* order is given to place soldiers in the castle. — Passive form, used in speaking, *Ordr)e, u, eru.* — *Sokó ni oras', „hic sedeatur,"* for pray sit down, in speaking to one superior.

Examples of the use of **Ori.**

Utsi ni oru, or *ori-másu,* he is within, is at home. — *Hino moto ni sirú,* he stays at the side of the fire. — *Siwru nisi no kuni ni orisi yori*, since the (people of) Sinru has dwelt in the western parts. - *Kun-si kore ni uru* [1]), the superior man stays there in (in virtue, as in his element). — *Uru ni òtê sono oru tokoro wo siru* [1]), when (a bird some where) nestles, it knows the place where it is at home. — *Hitô no kimi to naite ra, zin ni ori, hitô no sin to naite ri, kêi ni ori, ... kuni-tami to mazirô-ba, sin ni oru* [2]), when he (the noble man) becomes the lord of others, he rests in humanity; when he becomes the minister of others, he rests in reverence (towards the prince); if he has to do with the people of the country, then he dwells in uprightness. — Here we have a succession of three propositions of which only the last has the predicate closing-form *oru*, whereas in both the preceding the indefinite root-form *ori* is used.

Tabe, to eat; *Tabete oru*, to be eating. — *Tabesi)i*, n, make eat, feed; *Tabesate oru*, to be feeding. — *Nomi)*, n, to drink; *Nomite oru*, to be drinking. — *Siri*, to know; *Sirite ori-masu*, to be knowing. — *Hana wo mite zasite oru* (看花坐), he sits beholding flowers. — *Kare ga ima-you ni kimono kite oru*, he is dressed in the fashion. — *Motte wa ore-domo fito ni misinu*, although he has it with him, he does not let others see it.

The causative O*sM*, u (押), pron. *ôsu*, which being derived from the root I (居), has the original signification of to seat, make stay some where, includes the idea of our print, e. g. *Mêki ni in sô ôsu*, to print a mark in wood: *Kami ni katátsi wo ôsu*, to print a figure on or in paper; *Kurâi wo ôsu*, to maintain the throne. Employed as a substantive, it refers to something that presses, and characterises the word *Nézumi-ósi* the mousetrap as something that presses the mouse, and makes it stay.

§ 98, I (伊). Ito, Iru, nondefl. auxiliary verb, = to be in, a variation of OrM, u. *Kunsi wa ydasáki ni ite motte mei wo matsû* [3]), the superior man is quiet and calm, waiting for the appointments of Heaven). — *Dzu-kin wo kaburazu ni iru*, to be without having a covering on the head. — *Tsikara náka narite iru*, or 入 *Tsikara nao naite oru*, to have become powerless.

The root I or wi (居 ï , ﬦ), seat, occurs in compounds as: *Tori-wi* or *Tori-i*, = bird-seat, the name of certain doors, which are at the entrance to Japanese

---

[1]) *Tschung-yung* X   [2]) *Dai Gaku*. III. 1.   [3]) *Ibid.* III. 3   [4]) *Tschung-yung*. XIV.

temples. — *Kurā-i* (位 ?), from *Kurā*, saddle, thus a seat raised as a saddle, a throne. — *Nawi* or *Nai*, the old-Jap. name of earthquake, from *nŭ*, a dis-, and *i*. — *I-sa*, seat-nest, the chair on which one sits with the legs crosswise. *I-toko*, seat. — *I-ziri*, bed. — *Iyĕ* (△ ?), in Eastern Japan *iye*, contracted *yi*, the house. — *I-tsi*, a seat-way, the market-place.

NONDEFLECTING VERBS IN L.

§ 99. As these, with respect to their conjugation, are connected with the verb *I*, *Iru*, to be, they are placed here ¹).

The conjugation of the nondeflecting verbs in i.

	Aorist	Continuative present.	Preterit. pres.	Future.	Continuative Fut.
Root-form....	i.	[iri, ori, yuri.]	itari, △ ita. in, en.	△ iō.	[inzi.]
Imperative...	i-yo, i-sai.				
Closing-form.	u.	iru, uru, yuru.	itari, △ ita.		inzu, △ iōzu.
Subst. and Attr		iru, uru, yuru.	itaru, △ ita.		△ iōzuru.
Gerund	ite.		itarite.		
Local		irebu, urebu, yurebu.	itareba.		△ iōzureba.
as, when.					
Concessive...		ire- ure- yure- domo. domo. domo.	itare-domo.		
although.					
Suppositive...			itaraba.	iu-ra, △ iba, △ iō-naraba.	
if.					

Causative: *isi*, *osi*, *asi*, *usi*.   Negative: *iz)i*, *u*, △ *inu*, *onu*.

Synopsis of nondeflecting verbs in L.

I. Intransitives.

1. Sii), yu, iru or yuru (彌?, ?, ?, ?), to force, compel. — *Site*, by force. ? From *si*, to do, and *i*, iru, to be.

2. Sii, レイ; Siyu, リス; Siiru or Siyuru; gerund *Sŏte*; suppositi. *Sīda*; to be gone; to be dead, from *si* (去レ), to go away (not from 死レ, to die), and #,

---

¹) What Rodriguez in his *Élémens* § 35 says about these verbs, is not of that nature to make a treatment of this subject necessary here.

v. Some also write 了 ヒ, Siri. Causal. Sīsi)i, u, 獻 ず, to dispatch, send out of the world. Compounds with Si are: Me-sii, 盲 る, = to be eye-dead or blind; Mesiitiru, △ Mesiita, has become blind. — Mimi-si)i, 聾 る r, yu, iru, or yuru, ite, to be ear-dead or deaf.

3. KOI, 來 ¹, to come. Imperat. iyo, oyo, oi, in Sikok ei; Gerund ite; Fut. en, old-Jap. óme, on, △ ou, sosu, oszuru; Negat. önu, at Yédo anu.

4. I-KI, 去 ‵ 來 ¹. – go and come; to breathe, live (生). K)iru; Ikite-iru, 在 生, to be living; Fut. △ Ik)iti; Causal. des)i, u, to make live, to enliven.

5. De-ki, 出 ッ 來 ³, – to come out of, to proceed, to be produced, to be achieved; Lat. procedere. Dek)i, iru, ite; Fut. △ iu; Negat. inu, vulg. énu. Caus. Deka)i, u, to produce; thence Dekus' mono, a product. A variation of Deki in déki.

6. Tsuki, 盡 ァ, to come to the end, to consume, v. i., to get exhausted or consumed. Tsuk)i, iru; Negat. inu, not to become exhausted; Causal. Tsukis)i, u, to exhaust, to consume; Pass. Tsukur)e, aru, to be in a state of exhaustion. It is to be distinguished from deflecting Tsuk)i, u, 著 ?, 即, to come to.

7. Oki, 起 ァ, to rise, to get up, se lever. (k)iru, aru, ite, ita; Fut. △ iu; Causal. des)i, u, to make rise, to raise, to establish.

8. Sugi, prou. Su-ngi, 過 ァ, contracted from sué + ni + ki, to go (ki) on the top (of anything), to rise above, to surpass, exceed. Sug)iru, aru, ite. Causal. is)i, u.

9. Fi, 乾 ¹, dry. Firu, to dry, v. n. to ebb. Siro no firu toki, at low water.

10. Ni, 似 ª, to be like, to resemble. N)iru, ite, ite ari = itari; Negat. izu, not to be like; Causal. is)e, u, uru, eru, to make to like; to imitate. Nise-mono, imitation.

11. Ori, 下 ァ, to descend. Or)iru, also uru; ite, itari; Fut. in, △ iu; intosu, to be about to descend; Negat. izu, izar)i, u, not to descend; Causal. Orosi)i, u, to make descend.

12. Otsi, 落 ァ, to fall down. Ots)i, ite, itar)i, u, △ itu; Closing-form (Os)u or i-musu; Attributive iru, also uru, (otsiru ta, a falling stone); Fut. in, △ in; Condit. ñu; Negat. izu. Causal. Otós)i, u, to make fall; to fell.

13. Mitsi, 滿 ?, to be filled. Mits)u, uru, ite. Negat. Mitinu.

14. Kusi, 枯 ?, to rot, v. i. to wither. Kuts)iru, uru, ite.

15. Odsi, 忙 ?, to be afraid. Ods)u, iru, also uru. Causal. Odós)i, u, to make any one afraid.

16. Fudsi, 羞 ッ, 恥, to blush, to be ashamed. Fuds)i, u, uru, ite; Imperat.

CHAPTER VII. NONDEFLECTING VERBS IN I, INT. § 99.   267

iyó; Adverb. *avikaeú*; Adj. *Fudzukàshki*, timid. Causal. *Fudzakàsun)e*, *uru*, to make blush, to shame.

17. **Karab)i**, 枯る, *iru*, *i-aaru*, to dry, *v. i. Karu*, balm; *Kar)e*, *uru*, to dry up.

18. **Kabi**, 黴, mould. *Kabiru*, to grow mouldy; metaphorically: to be grieved.

19. **Sab)i**, *uru*, to rust; metaphorically: to be solitary and still.

20. **Wab)i**, *iru*, also *uru*, *ito* etc. 詫る, intercession, to intercede, to excuse.

21. **Nob)i**, *iru*, *ito*, 延る, 申, to stretch, to be extended. *Nobór)i*, *u*, to be stretching, *v. i.*, to go aloft, to ascend. — *Kemuri no noburu wo miru*, to see the ascending of smoke. — *Fi no nobiri*, the rise of the sun. — *Yama ni nobiri*, to go aloft on a mountain, to ascend a mountain. Fact. *Nobos)e*, *uru*, to make stretch, or ascend. — *Tsukai wo Miyako ye nobosete*, despatching messengers up to Miyako. — *Yaki-mono wo kuruma ni nobosu*, to work up pottery on the potter's wheel. — *Nob)e*, *uru*, *v. tr.*, to stretch, to extend, to raise.

22. **Kobi**, 媚る, to flatter. *Kob)i*, *iru*, *uru*, *ite*; Imperat. *iyo*; Fut. *in*, △ *in*. — *Fúto ni kobiru*, to flatter men.

23. **Korob)i**, *u*, *uru*, corruption, decay, to pass toward destruction. Causal. *ŏs)i*, *u*, to cause to decay.

24. **Fokorob)i**, *u*, *uru*, 綻る, to tear, to burst, *intr.*, to rip as a seam, open as a flower bud.

25. **Forobi**, 亡ぶ, 滅, to become destroyed, to perish. *Forob)i*, *u, i-uru*; Fut. *inu*, *in*, △ *in*. Causal. *ŏs)i*, *u*, to destroy. *Forobosir)e*, *uru*, to be ruined or destroyed.

26. **Fotob)i** (not *Fitobi*), *iru*, *uru*, 滋る, to soften, *v. i.* Causal. *Fotobas)i*, *u*, to make soft.

27. **Furub)i**, *iru*, *uru*, 古る, to get old, to grow old (old, opposed to new).

II. Transitives.

28. **K)i**, *iru*, *ito*, Fut. *in*, △ *in*, 著, to put on (a dress).

29. **Kovi**, 恋る, △ *Koi*, longing for. *Kor)i*, *u*, *iru*, *uru*, to long after, to love. Causal. *Koros)i*, *u*, to cause to love, to attract one's love; *Korinski*, charming, amiable.

30. **Móuši**, 用る, to use, to employ. *Motsi)i*, *u*, *iru*, or *yuru* (よる); *itar)i*, *u* (#ルリ). Fut. *Motsi)in*; Condit. *iba*; Negat. *izu* or *inu* (不て用る), *itar)i*, *u*; Pass. *irure*, to be used, to serve, *v. i.* We consider *Motsi)i*, *iru* the continuative

form of *Motsji*, u (持§), to take hold of, seize, use, of which the Gerund *Métte* (以 ξ) is equivalent to the word expressive of relation, with. Some, although incorrectly, also write モチヒ, モチン etc. The predicate closing-form モチス generally passes for a passive (to be used, to be of use to) perhaps from the analogy of the form with the derivative *iyu* (to get a shot), from *I* (to shoot). See § 89. 2.

On account of the important part, which this verb plays, some instances of its use follow here.

Koré wo mira mono rá toku, koré wo mutsi-aru mono ni sadzukā narábi, sunarútsi sai tsuné ni tira [1], if those which produce them, are quick, and those which use them are slow, riches will ever be sufficient. — *Sono ryōgu-tan wo torite* (△ *totte*), *sono tiu wo tami ni motairu* [2], he takes hold of the two extremes (of good and bad) and employs the Mean of them in his government of the people. — *Gu niste midzukara motairu koto wo konómu* [3], being ignorant he is fond of using his own self (his own judgement). — *Omaé kore wo nani ni motsiiruka?* or, more politely: *Anáta kore wo nani ni O motsii nasáru ka?* for what purpose do you use this?

31. **I**, 射ル, 弋, shooting. *Iru, Ite*, to shoot at, to hit. *Mato wo iru*, to shoot at a mark. *Tori wo iru*, to shoot birds. *Yumi-iru*, to shoot with a bow. Passive *Iye, Iyu*, to be shot. *Iyu nisi* (所射宍), - shot meat, venison.

32. **Mukui**, 報ゐ, 1. reflecting; 2. retaliation, retribution. *Muku)i, yu, yuru*, to retaliate, to retribute; Negat. *izu, izuri*, not to retribute. The recent orthography ムタヒ, ムタン is erroneous. — *Inu ca on wo siri, ata wo mukuu*, 報ヲ知ル 狗ゐ 仇ヲ 恩ヲ, (the dog knows favor and retaliates wrong.

33. **Abi**, *iru* (not *uru*), 浴ξ, - to shoot with bath-water, to splash, to squirt, to cast water up or out. *Yu-abiru*, to sprinkle anything with warm water, to wash it. *Midzu wo abiru*, 浴ξ 水ξ, to squirt cold water. Since, as appears from this expression, *Abiru* has the word water for its object direct, it cannot mean to wash oneself or to bathe.

34. **Mi**, iru, 見ル, to see. Imperat. *iyo*; Gerund *ite*; Pret. *ituri*, △ *itu*; Fut. *in*, △ *iñ*; Negat. *izu*, △ *iun*. Pass. *iye, iyu*, to appear; *iruru*, to become visible. Compounded with *mi*, to see, are:

---

[1] *Dai Gaku* 1. 19   [2] *Tschung-yung* VI.   [3] Ibid. XXVIII.

35. Urŭ-mji, ite, u, uru, 恨ず, to see backwards, to be disgusted with...
Fut. *ima, in,* △ *iii;* Negat. *izn.*

36. Kangámji, tru, 鑒ず, 鑒, 監, to look in the glass; to consider.

37. Kahori-mji, tru, 顧ず, to look back.

THE FOREGOING NONDEFLECTING VERBS IN I, ARRANGED ALPHABETICALLY.

Abi . N°. 33.	Furabi . 25.	Kaki . . 15.	Kobi . . 23.	Mitsi . . 13.	Odsi . . . 7.	Sugi . . . 5.
Dshi . . . 1.	Futebi . 26.	Kangâmi 36.	Korobi . 23.	Motsi . . 30.	Ori . . . 11.	Toshi . . 6.
Yuki . . 16.	Furubi . 27.	Karabi . 17.	Kovi . . 29.	Mukai . 32.	Okō . . . 12.	Urômi . 35.
Ki . . 9.	I . . . . 31.	Kahorimi 37.	Kutsi . . 14.	Ni . . . 10.	Sabi . . . 19.	Wabi . . 20.
Fuborobi 34.	Iki . . . 3.	Ki . . s. 23.	Mi . . . 34.	Nobi . . 21.	Sii . . 1. 2.	

§ 100. I. NI. 爲ル, 爰ル, = to be, is; Gerund *Nite,* Fut. *Nan,* is equivalent to our copula, to be, when in connection with a precedent substantive it implies, that that substantive is a definition, which is ascribed to the subject of the proposition. Derived from the local termination *ni* and from I (= to be, exist, § 94) the verb *Ni* means really an existence or being in...

It is peculiar to the written language, and except the root-form, which is of use in coördination of propositions, only the Gerund *Nite* and the Future *Nan* are to be met with, whereas for the further conjugation the continuative *Nar)i,* u is used (§ 100. II). Examples:

[Root-form.] *Kin to ira fitó eu takumi ni, Nin to ira fitó ei tsuri wo yiku sn* [1]), one Kin is (or was) an architect, one Nin knows (or knew) how to use the angle.

[Gerund.] *Tane wo mi-wake-gataki mono nite, kn-den ooi* [2]), the seed (of silkworms) is a difficult object to judge of, and there are many oral traditions respecting it.

[Future.] The forms ..*ni nan* and ..*to nan,* the first preceded by a substantive, the second, by the substantive form of a verb, have a potential force, *ni nan* being a coupling of *ni,* to be, and *nan,* the Future of *ni, naru* (§ 84), whereas *to nan* stands for *koto nan,* or, as some will, for *tomo nan* also. Compare § 95, 2, 1). — *Kono ori kara mohaya mina mina atari tacamare mote itsudsu koto ni nan* [3]), from this time all (the work) shall be a matter (*koto*) which shall be

---

[1]) *Das Buch vom Tausend Wörtern,* aus dem Schinesischen, mit Berücksichtigung der Koreischen und Japanischen Uebersetzung für Deutsche Shettigere von Dr. J. HOFFMANN 1840 N°. 925 – 928.

[2]) *Tan-zen fi-rok* § 2. [3]) Ibid.

done singing and playing. — *E͡zu to nan*, they will not get. See page 250 line 1. — *Keri no Ihi Miyoo-zin ru kono Ten-wga wo ayame-maitouru* to nan [1]), with regard to the great illustrious spirit of Kevi, this emperor will have been honored (as such). — *Kono sia* (宗⼸) *ni omoi-muki-keru* to nan [2]), he will have been converted to this sect.

Remark. In KLAPROTH' *Élém.* § 64 lines 16, 17 the verb *Ni* here treated is mentioned with the words: „*De, nite, site*, *Etant.* — Ces trois mots s'employent quelquefois au lieu du verbe substantif." — *Site* is the gerund van *Sʼi*, a, *uru*, to do. See § 105.

II. **Nari**, u (也⸺), deflecting continuative verb, derived from *Ni* (= to be, § 100, I). It is immediately preceded by the definition, of what the subject consists, or what it is. Inflectional forms, the same as of *Iri* (§ 90): *Nári* is the root- and, though by exception, the closing-form also: *Naru*, Δ *Na* (§ 12), the substantive form, which is also used as attributive. Gerund *Nárite*, Δ *Nutte*; Causal *Narina*; Fut. *Naran*, Δ *Naroo*; Condit. *Nariba*, in the spoken language generally abbreviated to *Nara* (see § 70).

1. *Nari* is used as closing-form in: *Tóka rā muto núri; Sai rā sué nari* [3]), virtue is the foundation; fortune the top. — *Fi no fúkári ukirúku niri*, the sunlight is clear.

2. *Naru* is substantive in: *Katáti no maduku, aáru wá Ten ni utári, ana no kyta* (or *kuku*) *náru wá Tsi ni nargu*, — that the shape (of the Chinese copper money) is round, answers to the heaven, that its opening is square, is an imitation of the earth. — *Ame náru ru in-yyu no ki núri* (雨⸺ 也之者⸺ 陰! 陽之⸺氣⸺也⸺), that which is rain (= the rain) is an emanation of the tellural and solar principle.

3. *Naru* is attributive in: *Mata ki-naru mayu wo tsukúrú kiiko dri*, there are also silkworms, which make yellow cocoons.

4. The attributive form *Naru*, Δ *Na*, serves to derive adjectives from substantives and adverbs. (See § 12, page 125). *Iyé no katarara naru hayési*, a wood at the side of the house.

5. The Gerund *Narite*, Δ *Nette*, is generally superseded by *Nite* and *Ni-sté* (§ 100, I), probably to prevent a confusion with *Narite*, = giving sound, or

---

[1]) *Nippun wa dai ttairu*. I. 10.   [2]) Ibid. VII. 46 recto.
[3]) *Dai Gaku*. X. 7.

with *Narite*, = *Narete*, = becoming. — *Kokoro-dai makoto nari. Kokoro-dai makoto ni atté, shinja-saté sodai kokoro tadásí* ¹), the will is truth. The will being true, the heart is then rectified.

6. The negative *NaraM*, u (惟 ら 忠 ²), = not to be, is avoided and, as a rule, superseded by the analytical form ni-arasu or ni-aranu. *Waga koto ni arasu*, it is not my business. (See page 162. 8).

7. *Nari*, with its inflectional forms, particularly its closing-form, is in the written language, used periphrastically also, to lengthen or round off a period, and is preceded by the predicate verb proper in its substantive form. The spoken language of Yédo uses *Masi*, s for the same object (see § 101). Examples: *Kono toki ni kuiko tsudre-idzuru nari*, = it is at that time that the silkworm comes out. *Ide, Idzuru*, to come out. — *Kéiko suatad ni tnevsu, si-suru nari*, the silkworm cannot bear frost, it dies. — *Kusa wo kaedsu naraba*, if one gives grass for food. — *Auta no koo ni sobokû gu arimasu nara*, *sore wái kai-másoo* ¹), if you have sapan-wood, I will buy it too. — *Yásei nara, tori-másoo* ²), if it is cheap, I will take it. — *O ni naseru nara*, if you buy.

III. *Nar)e, u, eru, uru* (成る), = to become, Lat. *fieri*, the passive of *Ni*, = to be (§ 100, I). As there is a homonymous *Nar)e, u, eru*, which being formed from another root *Ni*, means to be boiled, become tame, the form *Nare*, when it means to become, is not employed, but now generally represented by the active form *Nar)i, u*, and the immediately precedent, appositive definition, what or how any thing becomes, has to show by its inflectional termination to, ni or the adverbial ku (§ 9, page 111), that *Nari* is not used with the active signification of to be, but supersedes *Nare*, = to become.

Observations concerning the use of *Nari*, as substitute for *Nare*, = to become.

1. The apposition, what any thing becomes, when it is some thing concrete, characterized by the suffix to.

Amé kòrite yuki to naru, the rain, congealing, becomes snow. — *Ten-Tsi no sekiin* ¹) *atutaka-mira toki ra ame to nari, samuki toki ru yuki to naru (or miru nari)* ²), the accumulated tellural matter of the heavens and earth, when it is warm, be-

---
¹) *Dai Gaku* § 6.   ²) *Shopping-Dialogues*, p. 40.   ³) Ibid p. 37.
⁴) 天⁀地⁀積⁀陰⁀.   ⁵) *Kasira-goki kin-mou dsu-i*, I. 7. recto.

comes rain, when it is cold, it becomes snow. — Since they are coördinate, the former of the two propositions closes with the root-form (*ame to*) *nari*, the latter with the closing-form (*yuki to*) *naru*. So, likewise, in: *Kumo ra san-sèn no ki nari, Tsi-ki nobirete* (*nobitte*) *kumo to nari, Ten-ki kudarité ame to naru nari* [1]), clouds are the exhalation of mountains and rivers. The exhalation of the earth rising becomes clouds, the exhalation of the heavens descending becomes rain, or, literally: is becoming rain. — *Motsiiru tokinba, nezumi mo tori to nari; motsiiziru tokinbi, tora mo nezumi to naru*, if one make use of it (if one attach value to it), even the mouse becomes a tiger; if one attach no value to it, then even the tiger becomes a mouse. — *Fitó no kimi to nítte ni, zin ni óra* [1]), if (a noble man) becomes a prince over others, he has humanity for foundation. — *Kawa wakarete futatsu to naru*, the river divides into two branches. — *Kore narawasi to nári-taru nári*, this has become a custom.

2. The apposition, what something becomes, characterized by *ni*; a construction peculiar to the classic language.

Kunitsu kami om'na- (*onna-*) *ni narite* (化 ´ 爲 ² 而 ³) *mitsi ni mukaerri* ⁴), the god of that district became an old woman and came to meet (him) on the way. — *Kora tori ni narerini kami nari* (此者於鳥所成之神也), this is a god changed into a bird. *Narerisi*, the attributive form of the preterit of *Nari* (compare § 80 line 10). — *Kora Fi no kami no mi-kabane ni nari-masèru nari*, this (kami) has become the corpse of the god of fire. If *ni* were superseded by *no* (thus *kabane no*), an existence from the corpse would be meant, for the same writer says of another kami: *Kora Fi no kami no tsi no narerri nari* (血之所化也), this is a production from (has arisen from) the blood of the fire-god. — *Nami kazé mo tawayaka ni narite...*, also waves and wind becoming softer... — *Ken-yo* (賢 ? 愚 ²) *ni naru koto*, becoming sound.

3. If the apposition, what something becomes, is an adjective in *ki* (§ 9. B. page 105), it stands in its adverbial form in *ku*.

Kara-kane furinite narite sono iro akaku naru nari, the Chinese metal (an alloy of copper and silver) growing old, his color becomes red. — *Iritaru mono no nôku naritaru koto*, the annihilation of a thing that has been.

---

[1] *Kenzo-gaki* liu mos dzu-i. t. 6 verso
[1] *Dai Gaku.* III 3
[2] *Nippon-ki.* 14. 13 recto.

4. The materials from which any thing becomes, is put in the Ablative or Genitive, characterized by yori or by no.

Midzu yori naru mono, something that has arisen from water. — *Fino kami no tsi no narëru nari*, it has arisen from the blood of the god of fire, — it is an emanation from the blood....

5. The definition, by what a thing becomes, if it is a verb, is put in its root-form before *Nari*.

Kono sima en siro-nama no kori-narëru nari, this island is a clotting of the sea-foam.

6. *Nari*, employed impersonally (without a subject, as in Germ. *es wird*), and preceded onely by an appositive definition what it is to be, characterized by ni or to.

Ni-gwatz' ni narënu, — when it becomes (comes to) the second month. — *Sidzuka ni naru*, it grows calm. — *Mayu ni* (or *Mayu to*) *narëba*, *ito wo torinusu*, as cocoons become formed, one has the thread taken from them. — *Notsini iro-iro no yamahi to udru*, or *naru-nari*, afterwards arise all sorts of illness.

IV. 1. **Nasi**, u, defleeting causative verb, = to cause to be; to make (生, 成, 爲, 化, 作), from *Ni*, = to be (§ 100. I).

Fu-sa wo nasu [1]), to produce evil. — *Fito no zin-ai wo nasu*, originate cleverness in others, make others grow clever. — *Kore wo nasu beki*, this must be done. — *Kore wo nasu koto nakare*, do this not! (§ 93. 2.). — *Ten no nasëru wasawai*, calamities which heaven has caused.

2. **Nasas**)i, u; **Nasazar**)i, u, negat. not cause to be, not produce. — *Korewa nasazëru besi*, = as to this, one ought not to do it, this may not be done.

3. **Nasas**)i, u, causal., to make produce.

4. **Nasasim**)e, uru, cause that one makes be, give order that one makes, to bring about.

5. **Nasar**)e, u, uru, become produced or done, to happen. Imperative *Nasire*, let there become done, sounding in the popular language of Nagasaki *Nakëri*, *Nahui* and *Nakerri* too [2]).

The use, which courtesy makes of the passive *Nasare*, u, uru, will be illustrated in the Appendix to this Chapter.

---

[1]) *Dai Gaku.* VI. 2.

[2]) Observation by the late Mr. G. G. DE SAINT AULAIRE, interpreter for the Japanese language

CHAPTER VII. THE VERB MASI, TO RESIDE. § 101.

§ 101. Masi, u (坐 ざ), deflecting v., to abide, reside, originally imási, u, from ima, abbreviated ma (間 ´). — space, spot, or with reference to time, while, interval and shi, u, to be active, do. Gerund Masde, by elision Maite also; Pret. Maser)i, u, Masitji, ed, u; Masita, Masi'ta; Fut. Masan. Δ Masoo, pronounced as Maiwo (see page 209, line 12). Negat. Δ Mas'nu, instead of Masdnu (see page 248).

1. In the elevated style Masi supersedes the commoner Ar)i, u, to exist, and Or)i, u, dwell, and just as it, is preceded by the definition of place, where something is, in the Local. E. g. Ko ra Oki tsu miya ni mása kami nari¹), this is a kami dwelling in the chapel of Oki.

2. Masi is used as an auxiliary verb, when an eminent subject is spoken of, and is preceded by the verb with which it is connected in the root-form (a) Present or b) Future), or also c) in the Gerund. Examples:

a) Ama-terasu Kami, the Kami enlightening all around, is also called Ama-terási-masü Kami.

[..ni-masi.] A.. ra B.. Kami no mi faru ni-masi, A.. is the mother of the Kami B..²). (Ni, Nite, to be, see § 100, 1.) — Tamayori-fime no mikoto ra Kamo no mi oya no Kami ni-masi ³), Her Highness Lady Tamayori is the Kami of the ancestors of Kamo.

[..nari-masi.] Kono mi fasira no Kami wa mina fitóri-gami nari-masite, mi-mi wo kákusi-tamáriki ⁴), these three gods were gods standing alone, and kept themselves hidden. — Kono fime no gami ra N.. Kami ni mi-dei-masóri, this goddess has matched herself with the god N.. (See § 80). —

也ナ 所ヲ 爲シ 此ヲ
生ミ 胎ヲ 爲ル 者ハ
坐ル 而テ

Kono sima ra ye to yet umi-masuru nari, this island (the gods) have produced (it) as an after birth. — Maseru, the attributive form of Maseri, the preterit of Masi. (See § 80).

[..masi-másí, = to be being.] Ten nyu N.. no miya ni masi-masi, the emperor is residing in the palace N.. — Butz zin ra fitó no wegari ni yotte ka-go- (加 ° 護 ") si-másí-masedomó, sono mi (其身) kari-kata ni uromáa narába, ikugaru seny ⁵) although Buddha and the spirits assist, complying with the wish of men: if, in the rearing (of the silkworm) one is negligent, what will it avail? — Siyuh-ke

¹) Kami-yom mi-maki.   ³) Ibid.   ⁵) Ibid.
²) Ibid.   ⁴) Tar-som f-rol 11. 11 recto.

CHAPTER VII. THE VERB MASI, TO ABIDE. § 101.   273

(出家), pron. *sukke*) *no mozhasi masi-masi-keredomo, taitsi yurusi tamawāzu*, he wished to quit the paternal house (i. e. to become a monk), but the father did not grant it him.

b) [..*umasi*.] By grafting *masi* on the form of the Future, ..*am*, ..*an*, by which *amasi* is gotten, a periphrastic future is formed. *Sin)i, uru*, to go away; *Inótsi sinawasi*¹), life will perish. See § 75, 5.

c) Masi in connection with a gerund, used as well in the elevated style as in the polite conversational. — *Kono Kami ra Susano wo no mikoto to tsikara wo awasete masi-tamawaren sori*²), this Kami wrestles with the moon-god Susano wo no mikoto, literally: he is (*masi*) measuring his strength etc. — △ *Kore wa yabaurete imasu*³), this is torn. — *Fitó waru ni ikura faitte imasu ka*⁴), in a bale, how much goes in it? *Fa-ir)i, u* (入?), to enter.

There is no verb of which the polite spoken language makes a more frequent use, than *Masi*, and as it, grafted on the root-form of verb, generally has to express the inflectional forms, whereas the verb itself to which it is added remains unchanged, in its root-form, a knowledge of the conjugation of this auxiliary verb will be found without any other. The forms, which are in use in the spoken language, are limited to:

Másu, △ *Mas'*, is, being.	*Masuba*, as it is.
Másuka? is it?	*Masudomo*, although it is.
Másunu? is it not?	*Masiyoo*, △ *Maśoo*, it will be.
Mase, imperat. be!	*Mase-nara*, if it is.
Másite, △ *Maste*, gerund.	*Masinu*, △ *Maseng*, it is not.
Masita, △ *Masta*, has been.	

The forms *masaru, masareba, masaredomo*, quoted by Mr. A. BROWN, *Grammar* XXIV, for *mase, maseba, masedomo*, I have neither found in any original Japanese writing, nor observed in conversation with Japanese. To what dialect do these forms belong?

From the *Shopping-Dialogues*, published by us, which particularly come under notice as a faithful representation of the polite language of Yédo, it is obvious that *Masi* is used as the final word of a proposition indifferently whether the speaker or the person spoken to or something else, is the subject of it. Thus it may,

---

¹) *Nippon Sowari*, under *Sinu*.   ³) *Kami-yono si-rosi*.
²) *Shopping-Dialogues*, p. 24.   ⁴) Ibid. p. 34.

without the speaker's attaching any importance to it, be used only to round off the proposition, and express our „please" just as little as „have the honor."

Examples of the use of *Masi* in the spoken language, borrowed from the *Shopping-Dialogues*.

Kono fito wa dare de ari-masu ka, = this man — who is he? *Watákusi no toukiyui de ari-masu*, he is my bosom-friend. *Anáta no O na wa nani to ii-masu ká?* your name — what is it called? *Watákusino na wa ... to ii-mdsu*, my name is called ... (S.-D. 19).

Sina wo miru-koto wa deki-mdsu ka? The seeing of your goods — can that take place? (*deki-másu na?* cannot it take place?) *Deki-mdsu*, it can take place. (S.-D. 21).

Anáta wa too-ko no fito de ari-masu ka? Are you an inhabitant of this place? *Watákusi wa too-ko no monode ari-masu*, I am someone of this place. (S.-D. 20).

Kono nedan wa ikura si-masu ká? the price of it — to how much does it (amount)? (S.-D. 34).

Soo-tai si-masita, I have understood you. (S.-D. 41.)

Miyoo-niti (io ken-too itási-masoo, to morrow I will give you an answer. (S.-D. 39.)

Watákusi wa kore wo sonzi-masénu, I do not know it. (S.-D. 26).

Firu-maye ni wa mairi-ye-masénu, before noon I cannot come. (S.-D. 17).

Rok-kin ni atari-mdsu na? Is not that about six pounds? (S.-D. 8) [1]).

Watákusa banáklela (io d'sa-ma (御 邪 魔) *de gozari-masén'ká?* Am I not your disturber? Don't I disturb you? the ordinary question of anyone who unasked pays a visit.

§ 102. Samuravjí, u (侍 ｻﾑﾗｲ, 候, 伺候), also Savuravjí, u, △ Sorai, closing-form Soro, 侯ｽ, ｻﾛｽ, = to be, is; in old-Jap. 佐 守 ｽ, Samorari, from *sare*, at the side, by, and *moruri*, guard. As noun *Samurai* (△ *Sirai*) answers to our „guarde" and is the old general name for people on duty at the court of a prince.

Used as an auxiliary verb in the written language, particularly in the epistolary style, it qualifies the being as a serving being and humiliates the speaker. If, therefore, in a proposition, of which the predicate verb is *Soro*, no subject is named, the unnamed, who speaks or acts, is the speaker not the person spoken

---

[1]) Page 89 of the original edition: *A new famil-ar phrases*. Nagasaki 1859.

CHAPTER VII. THE VERB SORAI. § 102.   277

to, and we assign to those propositions the I or We as subject. With regard to the use of *Soro* the following is to be noticed:

1. The definition, what a thing is, when it is a noun, precedes in the Local, characterized by *ni* or *nite*, △ *de* (not *do*)¹).

2. The definition, how a thing is, expressed by an adjective in *ki*, is placed in its adverbial form in *ku*. — *Kaku no gotōku soro* (如斯候), it is so ²). — *Mǫusi ayu-beku* ³) *soro* (可申上候), = it is possible that I mention, — I shall make mention of it. — *Naku soro*, = *Nasi*, there is not. — *Go-za soro* (御座候), = △ *Gozari-masu*, it is (See § 96, p. 263, line 4). — *Sa-yoo nite go-za naku soro*, it is not so.

3. *Soro*, as an auxiliary verb, expressive of humility, grafted on the root-form of a verb, is appropriate to the familiar, as well as the official form of writing. — *Fino soba ni ori-sōrō*, „I am by the fire" ⁴). — *Yorisiku On agiri-soorū*, eat heartily ⁵), literally: may your rice be good! — *Kyoo-go manōra-beki ka deo ai-tate-soro tame*, to appoint the articles to be kept in future. — *Bu-sata idási-soro tokóro ni*, while I make no mention of it. — *Deo-yáku wo tori-kiwame soro*, one draws up a treaty. — *Sasi-yurusi-soro*, I agree to.

4. In negations as *Ayezu-soro*, I do not raise, — *Motomezu-soro*, I do not try to acquire, — *Irazu-soro*, I do not say, in deviation from the rule, *zu* is used instead of *si*, the root-form. If *soro* be grafted on the negative form of the spoken language, the forms *Ageánu + soro*, *Motomenai + soro*, *Iránai + soro*, are obtained, which forms may fuse into アゲゾ z *Ayezoro*, *Motomezoro*, *Irazoro*, and are to be easily distinguished from the affirmative forms *Aye-soro*, *Motome-soro*, *Iri-soro*. Thus if in RODRIGUEZ *Elém.* page 71 line 10, it is said with regard to the negative form: „cependant on dit aussi *motome soro*, *wazou* (sic) *soro*," then *motome-soro*, *irazoro* are meant.

---

¹) Here the example cited in RODRIGUEZ *Elém.* page 71 line 10: „Christian nite soro," christianus sum, comes under notice.
²) See page 109 n°. 70.   ³) *Beki*, see page 109 n°. 73.
⁴) Nieuw verzameld Japansch en Hollandsch woord-nb. door den vorst van Nakatu 1810. V. 55 recto.
⁵) Ibid. II. 40 verso.

278 CHAPTER VII. THE VERB: NORAI. § 102.

SYNOPSIS OF THE CONJUGATIONAL FORMS OF SAMURAI, △ NOORAI,
NORAI, TO BE.

	Present.		Preterit.		
Root-form....	Sórai,	△ Soraí,	Sórai si.	△ Sorai si.	
	サウライ.	ソライ.		Sórai ni.	
Closing-form	Sórō,	„ Soro,	Sórai-ki.	Sórai no.	Sórai tsu.
	サウラウ.	ソロ.			△ Soro tsu, ソロツ.
Subst. and Attr.	Sórō,	„ Soro.	Sórai si.	Sórai zuru.	Sórai tsuru.
	Sórō koto,	„ Soro koto.	Sórai si koto.		△ Soro tsuru.
Gerund	Sóraite,	„ Sorote.			
	ゐり Mú.	ゐり Mú.			
Local, Causal	Sórayeba,	„ Soroyeba.	Sórai-sikaba.		Sórai tsureba.
and Modal form	候ウれ.		Sórai-sini.		△ Soro tsureba.
	Sórō ni,	„ Soro ni woitewa			Sórai tsurumi.
		„ Soro tokoroni,			△ Soro tsurumi.
Concessive. ...	Sórayedomo,	„ Soroyedomo.	Sórai si to iyedomo,		Sórai tsure domo
	Sórō to iyedomo,	„ Soro to yutomo,	Sórai si kadomo.		Soro tsure domo
	Sórō tomo,	„ Soro tomo.			
	Sórayeba tote.				
Imperative...	Sóraye.				
Optative ...	Sóraye kasi,	„ Soroye kasi,	Sórai si monowo.		

	Future.	Periphrastic Future.		Fut. preterit.
Root-form....	Sórawan	[Sorawauzi, Sorowanzi.]		Sórō beku	Soro bekeri
	サウラン			
	△ Nororan			
Closing-form .	Sórawanzu	△ Soraizu		Soro besi
	サウラハンズ			Soro beku-soro
Subst. and Attr.	Sorawan koto	Sorawan zuru	△ Sorawan zuru	Soro beki
			△ Sórō zuru	
		Sorawan suru-koto	△ Sórō zuru-koto	Soro beki-koto
Local, Causal and Modal form	Sórawan zureba	△ Sorawan zureba	Soro beki ni Sórō bekere-ba
			△ Sórō zureba	
Concessive....		Sorawan zurumo	△ Sórō zurumo	Soro bekere-domo.
		Sorawan zuredomo	△ Sorawan zuredomo	
			△ Sórō zuredomo	
Conditional ..	Sórawaba			
	' Sorowaba			

CHAPTER VII. THE VERB SORAI. § 102.

	Future.	Periphrastic Future.	Fut. præterit.
Conditional...	Sóravan ni woitewa △ Sórô ni woitewa		
Optative......	Soravan monowo △ Sorovan monowo		

NEGATIVE CONJUGATION.

	Present.	Future.
Root-form...	[Sóravazi], not to be.	
Closing-form..	Sóravazu¹), △ Sorovazu, it is not.	Sóro maziku soro, will not be. Sórô koto maziku soro.
Substant. and Attributive.	Sóravazu, △ Sorovazu, the not being, not being.	
Substant. isolated.	Sóravazu va, the not being.	
Gerund......	Sóravade, △ Sorovade. Sóravazu site, not being.	
Time defining Local.	Sóravaneba, when it is not.	
Concessive...	Sóravane domo, though it is not.	Sórô mai heredomo, though it might not have been.
Conditional...	Sóravazunba Sóravazuba } if it is not. Maziku sóravaba.	Maziku sóravaba, if it should not be.

§ 103. Si, u, uru (為 レ, ス, スル). to do. As we have already elucidated this verb, so far as it is used in the formation of causative verbs, in § 87, it is here noticed only in its other relations.

I. The root-form si occurs in compound nouns.

1. as chief word, indicating the person, who is employed with something, in which case it is equivalent to our termination er of tiler, potter etc. — Káwará-si, = a brick-maker; Mono-si, = Lat. opifex, maker; I-mono-si, metal founder; Kusu-si,

---

¹) The regular negative form of the deflecting verb Sórari is Sóramazu. But the spoken language does not use it, Sóramazu, and Sorovazu, which are more easily pronounced, on account of the rule, that the vowels of the subordinate syllables adapt themselves to that of the principal syllable.

medicine-maker, physician; *Nu-si* (contracted from *Nuru-si*), japanner, *Si* being generally explained by 師シ, master; or

2. as definitive member before the chief word, as in *Si-goto*, occupation, where it is generally indicated phonetically by 仕シ, and even by 支シ, with the signification of which characters the pure Japanese root, *Si*, has nothing to do. Thus *Si-goto* is met with under the form of 仕シ事ゴ. — *Sore ra idzure ga si-wazu ka?* (夫ソ䟽ガ仕シ業ザ㆑), whose business is this? 仕シ樣ヨウ, *Si-yoo*, manner of doing; 仕シ法ホ, *Si-hoo*, manner of acting, *Si-kata*, 仕シ方ヨ, manner of handling, also 仕シ形ギ, form of doing, gestures; *Te site no si-kata*, gesticulations with the hands. *Note*. 仕シ手テ, — work-hand, the hand, the person that accomplishes a thing.

3. The root-form *Si* further occurs in compound verbs as an adverbial prefix, to imply that the action expressed by the verb, is done, as a definite act, and, in itself, includes all the activity of the subject. Examples:

Fune wo dasji, u, to clear a ship (compare page 236 n°. 18). — *Fune no dosi-ba*, = the place for the clearing of ships. 其ソ船フ子ノ仕シ出ダ場バ〃港ト ノ名ア, *Sono fune no si-dasi-ba no minato no na*, the name of the port at which this ship is, or has been, actually cleared. — *Ire*, *uru*, to take in, to take up; *Si-ire*, 仕入, the taking in, as exercising a calling, the buying in, purchase of merchandise. 仕シ居ヲ, *Si-ori*, u, to be busy; *Mono-si-ori*, u, to keep oneself busy with one thing or another. — *Nippon ni ote yebumi no si-mairi* (仕シ參マ) ra sudeni fai- (廢ハ) seri [1]), in Japan coming up to the image-trampling has been already abolished.

仕シ打ダ, *Si-utsi*, the deed.
仕シ拂ハ, *Si-harahi*, the payment.
仕シ立タ, *Si-tate*, erection, making.
仕シ遂ト, *Si-tóge*, perfect accomplish.
仕シ直ナ, *Si-naosi*, polish.

II. Acting as verb, *S)i*, u is nondeflecting. On account of the important part it plays, it is advisable that the explanation of its use should be preceded by a

---
[1] Franco-Japanese Treaty of the 9 Oct. 1858, Art. IV, al. 2.

CHAPTER VII. THE VERB SI, TO DO. § 103.   281

SYNOPSIS OF THE CONJUGATIONAL FORMS.

	Nondefecting.	Defecting.	
Conjunctive.			
Root-form...	Si. 為り, TO DO.	[Sar)i, u, not in use.]	...ni, form word of causative
Imperative...	Seyo, Siro, Nei, Senai, do.		verbs, as Nasi, to make
Closing-form...	Su.	Sara.	be; ...seyo, imperative;
Subst. and Attr.		Suru, doing.	...su, closing-form.
Terminative...		Suruni, to doing.	
Local........		Suruni, by doing.	
		Saruni va.	
	Seba.	Sure ba.	...seba.
Conditive....		Sure domo, } if one	
		Sura to iedomo, } do.	
Gerund......	Sité.		...sité, doing.
		PRETERIT.	
Closing-form..	Seri, did.	Si-tari. △ Sita. has done.	...s(tar)i, u, △ ..sita, has done.
Substant. and Attributive.	Seru, the having done.	Si-taru. △ Sita.	
	Sesi.		
	Sesi ni, when one did.		
	Sesi nari, has done.		
	Sesi kaba, as he did.		
		FUTURE.	
	Sen, せん, shall do; △ Seô, 為う.	△ Seôz)u, uru, ん ず)ス. ズ々.	
	Sensu.		...su-be)ki, ku, si, (p. 100 n°. 73. § 104).
		NEGATIVE.	
Root-form...	Sezi, せず, not to do.	Sezari, contin.	
Closing, Subst. and Attrib.	Sezu, △ Senu.	Sezaru.	
Gerund......	Sezu site, △ Sede, 不で 為で.		
		CAUSATIVE.	
			...sse)e, 令て 為て, have done. ...ssa)u.

	Nondefecting.	Defecting.
		..sas)ete, etari, △ eta, Fut. eu, △ eô. Contin. urn, areba, uredome. Neg. Sasenu. ..sasim)e, nondeflect., let do, have done.
	Se-sim)e (爲せ), u, uru, charge to do; Ger. Sesimete, contr. Sasite; Fut. Sesimen.	
PASSIVE.		
	Serar)e, u, uru, nondefl. become done.	..sar)e, u, uru, become done. ..maserar)e, u, uru, 令爲, order is given to do.
	Serareru, △ Serarenu, negative, not to be done.	

Compounds with si.

1. s)i, u, uru (to do) is used to derive verbs from Japanese nouns; e. g.:

Kari, hunting; *Kari-s)i*, u, uru, to practise hunting; *Fira no jura ni kari-su*, people hunt on the plain of Firano. — *Tuta ji-kure ni kari suru koto*, hunting alone in the evening. — *Yome-iri*, = the entrance as a (married) woman, marriage. *Onna wa, — imdda yome-iri-sesaru wo dzyo* (女了) *to iri. sadeni yome-iri-si taru wo fu* (婦?) *to iru. Yome-iri-siteamó fu-bo yonde musume to irû* [1]*, = as to the woman, she who has not yet made her entrance as wife, is called *dzyo* (maid), she who has already made her entrance as wife, is called *fu*. Also if she has been married, her parents may, calling her *musume* (daughter). In the same way, by means of *si*, verbs are derived from:

Yome-tori, to take to wife. — *Kami-agari*, the rising as Kami, the decease of a prince. — *Katsi-waddri*, a ford. — *Kawa wo katsi-waddri-suru*, the fording of a river. — △ *Mama no kasira ga figdsi-su*, the horse's head faces the east. — *Ono-ono nisi ya fiyasi-su*, each turns either to the west or to the east, every

---

[1] *Kasira-gosi his-mos dzu-i.* IV. 2. r.

one does this or that. — *Kono kata ni mukitite tane-maki sezu*, = towards that side the sowing is not done. — *Mainai serarezu*, he is not bribed. — *Kono nedan wa ikura ni-muimaku* (or *uri-muimaku*, or *kakiri-muimaku*)? ¹), what is the price of it? — *Go tu me ni-mdea*, it is five taels. — *Sono kata wa doo ni-muimaka?* ¹), its form — how is it?

2. *a.* Chinese words also are verbalized by means of *si*; their number is legion. Examples:

來ス,	*Rai-si*, to come.	旅行ス,	*Riokoo-si*, to travel.
來朝ス,	*Rai-tvo-si*, to come to court.	坐ス,	*Za-si*, to sit.
對ス,	*Tai-si*, to be opposite to.	通ス,	*Tsuu-si*, to go through...
拜ス,	*Fai-si*, to greet, salute.	用意ス,	*Yon-i-si*, to provide...
廢ス,	*Fai-si*, to abolish.	用心ス,	*Yoo-sin-si*, to be attentive.
勞ス,	*Rju-si*, to weary.	敵ス,	*Teki-si*, to be hostile.
令ス,	*Rei-si*, to order.	着ス,	*Tsaku-si*, to arrive.
死ス,	*Si-si*, to die.	着岸ス,	*Tikuqan-si*, to land.
餌ス,	*Zi-si*, to allure with bait (飼ス). ... *Zi-serarje*, n. usu, allured with bait (bribed).	違ス,	*Tiu-si*, to make known.
		微ス,	*Tsu-si*, to penetrate; understand.
		合ス,	*Gio-si*, to fit, agree.
在留ス,	*Zai-riu-si*, to keep abode.	熱ス,	*Ne-si*, to be hot.
居留ス,	*Kiyo-riu-si*, ,, ,,	失ス,	*Sit-si*, to lose.
住ス,	*Dziu-si*, to dwell.	沒ス,	*Bot-si*, to sink.
住在ス,	*Dziu-zai-si*, ,,		

b. Of the thus verbalised Chinese words some, by way of exception, have. *zi*, *u*, *uru* (ジ, ズ, ヅル) instead of *si*, *u*, *uru*. The impure *z* occurs in:

按ズ,	*An-zi*, to remark (to distinguish from 安ス, *An-si*, to bring to rest.)	感ズ,	*Kan-zi*, to affect, stir, excite the feelings.
散ズ,	*San-zi*, to scatter.	獻ズ,	*Ken-zi*, to offer.
御覽ズ,	*Go-ran-zi*, to please to see.	現ズ,	*Gen-zi*, to appear.
		減ズ,	*Gen-zi*, to lessen, to diminish.

¹) *Meppring-Dialogues*, page 3, 34.   ²) Ibid. p. 11.

轉レジ, Ten-si, 1. to make revolve; 2. to transform.

合戰レジ, Kassen-si, to be hand to hand (teki to, with the enemy).

吟レジ, Gin-si, to sing.

損レジ, Son-si, to suffer damage. Sonzasji, u, to injure.

命レジ, Mei-si, to give order.

存レジ, Zon-si, 1. to maintain; 2. vulgo, to think.

論レジ, Ron-si, to discourse.

相論レジ, Soo-ron-si, to converse.

生レジ, Soo-si, to come forth, grow; to produce.

報レジ, Hoo-si, to reward.

應レジ, Oo-si, to answer to.

Examples of the use of Chinese-Japanese verbs in si.

Ken-bun (見 キ 聞 ク) suru koto wo kaki tomeru, to note down what one sees and hears. If suru be superseded by seru, it means to note down what one has seen and heard (remarked). — Hi no tooki tikaki wo ron-zu, = people speak of the far and near (of the distance) of the sun from the earth. — △ 承 ハ 知 リレ レ ス, Soo-ti-si-ma'ta, I have understood! = very well. — △ 左 ノ 樣 ニ シマシマツ, Soo-si-maioo, I shall do it. = I shall satisfy your desire. — Hisaku suye-okite fanasasureba, dai tsukarete yamai wo siyan (生 ズ) zu, if the hunting falcon be kept long perched, and not let fly abroad, his feet get exhausted by weariness, and he grows sick. — Sore taka ra tsune ni nessuru (熱 ス ル) yuyeni mi-midzu wo konomu mono nari, the falcon, because he is continually hot, is very fond of fresh water. — 庶 ノ 民 ニ 令 シ レ テ カ ヒ コ ア カ ヒ レ ム ヌ マ フ, charging all people (the emperor) has silkworms bred. — Furansi-biko no jad Nippon ni kio-riu- (居 ス 留 ス) seva (read seba), sono fito-bito wo Nippon ni ito nengoroni atsukiru besi [1]), if the French remain in Japan, that people will be treated well.

Remark. If the accomplishing of a thing, instead of the being occupied with it, is to be expressed, then Itas)i, u (致 ス), to accomplish, is used instead of si, both in Japanese and Chinese words. Itasi has arisen by syncope from itarasi, which is the causative form of itar)i, u (至 ル), = has gone (whither he would go) and as such signifies the accomplishment of an action. For the rest, the spoken language seems to use itasi also, merely for euphony, as being more harmonious than the simple si.

Examples:

---

[1]) Franco-Japanese Treaty of 1858. Art. I. al. 2. Ibid. IX. 8. XV. 1. 2.

CHAPTER VII. THE VERB SI, TO DO. § 103. 285

○ 日本人佛蘭西人ヨリノ借財ヲ佛ハズレテ出奔イタシ候節ハ日本役人吟味イタシ佛ヒ申スベキ方イタスベシ

Nippon-sin Fransi-sin yori no haku-zai wo jiu-ridasauté ippon itasitaru toki ra, Nippon yakunin gin-mi itasi, farsi-kata itasasu besi [1]), when Japanese, without having paid their debts to Frenchmen, have taken flight, the Japanese authorities shall make inquiry and make them pay.

○ 商ヒ昔シ Soo-bai-itasu koto kurusikardzu [2]), trade is not unwelcome, — it will not be thwarted.

△ Miyoo-niti Go ken-too itdsi-makoo [3]), to-morrow I shall give you an answer. — △ Go soo-dan itasi- (tasi = itdsi) makoo, I shall speak with you about it. — △ Sayoo itdsi makoo, I shall do so. — △ O-itoma itasi-makoo, I shall take leave of you [4]).

III. ON THE GOVERNMENT OF SI, U, URU, TO DO.

When this verb has an object direct, in the accusative, before it, it is transitive, but when not, it is intransitive.

1. [..wo su.] The definition: what a person does, stands, as object direct, in the accusative. Examples:

Karera nani wo sitaru ka? what has he done? — Ware kore wo sesu (吾 之 為 之 矣) [5]), I do not do this, — this is not my business. — Zin wo suru mono (為 仁 者), one who practises humanity. — Tedsukara kuwa wo torite (totte) ko-gai wo si-tamaru, = with her own hands (the princess) plucks the mulberry leaf, and practises the nourishment of children (the breeding of silkworms).

2. [..ni su.] The definition of the state or of the quality, in which one is engaged or is (intransitive), or in which one causes a thing to be, what one makes of a thing (transitive), provided it be a noun, is put in the Local in ni, the form ..ni-si, u, uru, sometimes mutating to ..n-si, whence ..nasi (ど, き, ず) proceeds [6]). From the Gerund ni sité the form nite arises, by syncope.

---

[1]) Franco-Jap. Treaty. Art. XVIII. al. 1.   [2]) Ibid. VIII. 1.
[3]) Shopping-Dialogues, p. 29.   [4]) Ibid. p. 41.   [5]) Terdmay-yung. XI.
[6]) The s in nsi — I have observed it myself, — is so softly pronounced, that one thinks he hears ssi instead of nsi, therefore even RODRIGUES in Elém. § 19 has adopted the written-form si.

Examples:

a. Si, with an intransitive signification. — *I-nakára ni site* (or *nite*) *kóri ten beri* (可坐而致也), one may do it while sitting. — *Fa, roku-mi ni site karu,* the leaf, being in the sixth year, dries up. — *Zai-wi ku-nen nisité* (or *nite*) *Ten-wau fou-zu,* being in the ninth year of his reign, the Emperor dies. — *Nomi yotsu kado nisité, sue toyaru,* the fruit is quadrangular, and pointed at the top. — *Kono sima ra mi fitatu ni sité ono yotsu ari, ono gotoni na ari,* this island (Sikok, or the four countries) is one and has four faces: these have each a name. — *Tatsi-tokóro ni sité saitsi tou bési,* 可立而待也, standing on the point of departure he must wait. — *Saki,* the point. *Sakin'zuru tokin'ra* (= *saki ni suru toki ni ru*) *fitó wo mi-su,* when one is at the point (is the chief), one leads the others (先則制人). — *Fitu fako ni nan gin tri ni si-ma-raka?*[1]), how many pounds shall I put in a chest? *Fyak-kin iri ni nasére,* put a hundred pounds in. — *Roo no kata wa doo si-nawa ka?* the shape of the wax — how is it? — *Atsukuri ni surebu, musi, taiiséka sité, mayu wo taiisuki wo tsu-kuru*[2]), by overfeeding, the (silk)worm will remain small and also make small cocoons. — *Sika ra mima no gotéku ni sté wo* (小豕) *suri,* the stag is much like a horse and is smaller. — *Yama-inu ra iro ki ni sté, fou miroku, wo nayasi*[3]), the wild dog, being yellow of color, has white cheeks and a long tail.

b. Si, with a transitive signification. — *Makoto,* truth. *Sono kokóro bue wo makoto ni su,* he makes his meaning truth. — *Tóku wo akirdka ni su,* he lets virtue shine. — *Moto wo hokí ni sté, sué wo utsi-ni surebá, tami wo arasosisimáte, abéru koto wo kadokim*[4]), if one excludes the root (virtue) and includes the top (fortune), one teaches the people strife, and rapacity. — *Fútokóro,* bosom, heart. *Kore wo futokóro ni si-tsu besi,* one ought to take this to heart. — *Omote,* face, front side. *Nisi ra gawa wo omote ni su,* on the west one has a river in front. — *Tairiku,* level, smooth. *Ten-ka wo tairaka ni suru koto wa kuni wo osimuru ni ári*[5]) (平天下在治其國), the making the whole empire peaceful and happy depends on the government of his state. — *Meate ni suru,* to set for aim. — *Ti-kon ni suru,* set for example. — *Itsi-setsu* (大切) *ni suru,* to consider im-

---

[1]) *Sheppoug-Dialogues,* p. 11.

[2]) The inversion *mayo wo taisuki* instead of *taisaki mayo wo* serves to bring out *taisuki* (small) with emphasis.

[3]) *Kasira-gaki.* XII. 5 r.   [4]) *Dai Gaku.* X 5.   [5]) *Ibid.,* R. 1.

portant. — *Atataka ni suru*, to warm. — *Komaka ni suru*, to make fine. — *Tsumabiraka ni suru*, to make clear. — *Karo*, light (of weight); *Karonzi*, to consider lightly, despise. — *Omo*, heavy, weighty; *Omonzi*, to consider weighty. To be distinguished from *Karoku si*, *Omoku si*, to make light, to make weighty. — *Sora*, empty; *Soranzi*, to learn by heart. — *Ama*, mead, sugar juice; *Ama ni su*, or *amon'zu*, to think sweet. — *Fakowa soye ni sita kudasure* [1]), please to give the chest into the bargain. — *Oki-tokei wo fitotsu soye ni si-masiwo* [2]), I will give a timepiece into the bargain.

3. [..ku su, ..u su.] If the definition of quality is an adjective in *ki* (§ ?), e. g. *Nagaki*, long, its adverbial form in *ku* (or merely *u*) is used to unite with *s)i*, *u*, *uru*, and the so formed compound (*Nagaku-si*), as long as there is no object direct, expresses the mere carrying out of the idea of the adverb, and, as it appears from the examples quoted, is equivalent to the predicative closing-form *Nagasi*, = is long; if however an object direct is involved, then the verb *s)i*, *u* has its transitive signification (the causative form *se-su* = *se-simu* seems to lurk behind it). In the example quoted at page 209: *Tsuri wo yoku-su*, he handles the angle well, *yoku* is a modal definition of the transitively used *s)i*, *u*, to do, handle.

a. With an intransitive signification ..*ku s)i*, *u*, *uru* appear in propositions as:
Wo nagaku site tobu koto atawazu [3]), he (a certain bird) has a long tail and cannot fly far. — *Ituwa ... kubi nagaiku sit'*, asi takasi*, the camel has a long neck and high legs. — *Sono ke no-kega* (温？厚？) *ni sita, kitsune no ke yori mo atataka nari; natsuru suzusi* [4]), his hair is warm and close, and warmer even than the hair of the fox; in summer it is cool. — [*Tsikiki*, near.] *A.. ni B.. te tsikaku site C.. to koto-nari*, A.. comes near B.. and differs from C.. - [*Usuki*, thin, *Karoki*, light.] *Kutsibiru usuru-site, kotoba karuru-su*, if the lips are thin (if the tong is smooth), the word weighs light. — [*Aruki*, rough, wild; *Arakasu*, act wildly, behave wildly.] *Ten-wan undere-tanki aruku-site jito wo korosu kotowo konomu*, the emperor, fierce by nature, was fond of killing men. — [*Gotoki*, like.] *Kaku no gotoku suretu*, when people are acting in this way. — [*Yasuki*, easy.] *Notonizu () koi masuru mori, yasuku-site age-mawoo* [5]), if you buy the whole

---

[1]) *Shopping-Dialogues*, p. 12. [2]) Ibid. p. 20.
[3]) *Kaira-pahi*, XIII. 11. r.   [4]) Ibid. XII. 9 r.
[5]) *Shopping-Dialogues*, p. 86.

stock, I will let you have it cheap. — [*Naki*, not existing. *Naku si* (△ ナクシ, ナシ pron. *ngosu*), 1. to be wanting, to fail, 2. to think paltry (of no value).] 1. *Yaku ni koto nakusite*, *Kami no tasuki ari*, medical treatment failing there is God's help. 2. △ *Fitó wo mandomo ngu su*, he considers others as of no value.

b. With a transitive signification ..*ku s)i*, *u*, *sru* is found in propositions as: [*Takaki*, high.] *Me-ate wo takaku suru*, to exalt one's aim, not to give up one's intention. — [*Fikiki*, low, humble.] *Me wo fikiku site utsubusite miru*, to cast the eyes downwards and look below. — [*Tadisiki*, right, upright.] *Sono mi wo osa-merito hossuru mono wa madzu sono kokóro wo tadásin-su. Sono kokóro wo tadasiu-sento hossuru mono wa madzu sono kokórobase wo makoto ni su* [1]), who ever will govern himself, first makes his heart right. He who will make his heart right, first aims at truth. — [*Mattaki*, whole; *mattaku-* (*mattan*, *mattou*, △ *mattoo*) *su*, to make whole, to perfect.] *Zin wo suru to ro sono kokóro no toku wo mattou suru yuén nari* (為仁者所以全其心之德也), the practice of humanity is the means to perfect the heart. — [*Toki*, quick, ready.] *Kore wo toku su*, he does it quickly. — [*Atsuki*, hot.] *Atsuku or Atsuu suru*, to make hot. — [*Suzu-siki*, cool.] *To wo firaki suzusika su beni*, you may open the door and let in the coolness. — [*Fitósi*, = one-ish, of one sort.] *Kuni ka wo fitósu su*, he makes the country and people conforming to one mode. — [*Ondziki*, identical.] *Tomo ni tsu-kóku wo ondzin sézu*, not having the middle kingdom in common. *Tsiri wo ondziku sezu*, not having the dust in common, not staying at the same place with anyone. — [*Fakáki*, deep; *Katóki*, hard, fast.] *Ne wo fukyu si, faso wo ka-toku suru kusa nari*, = it is a plant, that shoots its roots deep, and makes its stalk hard.

4. [to *su*.] The appositive definition, what a thing is made, whether in fact or in imagination merely, is characterized by the particle *to*, = to, (see page 70. V). If an object direct is mentioned in the proposition, the apposition has reference to the object and *si* has the transitive signification of make (to), take for, consider as; on the other hand if no direct object is mentioned in the proposition, the apposition has reference to the subject, and *si* has the intransitive signification of: to be actually.

α. Appositions referring to the subject we have in sentences, like:

---

[1] *Dai Gaku*, IV, 4.

Fito to site kyu naki rei (or *naki mono ra*) *tsiku-iyu ni kitondrazu*, he who is a human being and is destitute of filial love, does not differ from the brute; or: he who as a human being is devoid of etc. — *Inuḋi no sima ri ena to site umi matsru nari*, the island of Awadsi arose (at the creation of the Japanese archipelago) as an afterbirth. — *Fosi atsuru to ieu ra fosi ni arazu. Fito no me ni fosi to suru nomi*, concerning the assertion, that stars fall, they are not stars. Only for the eyes of men do they appear as stars.

b. Appositions referring to the object we have in sentences as:

Onore ni sikazdru mono wo tomotó suru koto nakare, it may not be that (you) make any one, who is not as your self (who is your inferior), (to) your fellow. — *Kono fau wo dai-itsi to su beki*, this rule must be considered as the first (the principal). — *Fau to su* (為゛法゛ト), make (to) a rule, consider as a rule. — *Te-fon ni su; mote ni su.*

Remark. 1. The object that is taken for anything, is found as object still governed by a separate active verb, which most frequently gives the way in which it is made. — *Ten wau ... fime wo tatete kisagi to si-tamawu*, the emperor appoints Lady ... and makes her (to) consort, = the emperor takes Lady ... for consort.

Remark. 2. Much used is the formula: *A.. wo motte B.. to su*, he makes A.. to B.., considers A.. as B.., has A.. to B. — *Wauki wo motte taitsi to si, Buwau wo motte ko to su*[1]), he has Wangki for father and Wu wang for son. — *Kuni ra ri wo motte ri to sezu; gi wo motte ri to su*[2]), a government does not make advantage pass as advantage; it considers justice as advantage. Or: a government does not find its advantage in advantage; it finds its advantage in justice. — *Hi to suruni gi wo mottesu*[3]), to use justice as being advantageous. —

主ト以テ觀ル   *Yen-sin wo miru ni ra, sono siyu to suru tokoro wo mottesu*[4]),
其ノ所ヲ居ル   to judge of a foreign minister people take as stand him whom he makes his host (him in whose house he stays).

Remark. 3. By the omission of *site*, instead of *..to site*, we meet with *to* alone. — *Yuru yuru*, loitering, hesitating, by degrees. — *Yuru yuru ayumi*, to go step

---

[1]) *Tschung-yung.* XVIII.   [2]) *Dai Gaku.* X. 22.   [3]) Ibid. IV. 5.
[4]) *Meng-tseu,* Lib. II, Cap III. § 45.

for step (slowly). —. *Yuru yuru to suru*, slowly, by degrees to do. — *Yuru yuru to site* (or *Yuru yuru to*) *sappoo* (八方) *ve firogu*, it spreads gradually in all directions.

5. If the appositive definition, what any thing is made (to), and that in imagination, is a verb with or without complement, it is put in the closing-form followed by *to si*, *u*, *uru* etc.

Kakuru koto nasi, there is no want. — 爲ˣ 無ᵇ 缺ᵃ1, *Kakuru koto nasi to su*, people think, that nothing is wanting. — △ *Kore yori afwa nai*, there is nothing that surpasses that. *Kore yori afwa nai to su*, people consider, that nothing surpasses it. — *Itari*, come to.. *Itareri*, is come to.. *Ware itareri to su*, I think to have come to the extreme, to have reached the topmost. — *Faru-aki va kage wo tattomi*, *fuyu va finata wo yosi to su*, in the warm season (spring—autumn) the shadow is prized; in winter the sunshine is thought the best. — *Tada sikure ni kari-suru wo yosi to suru nari*, people think it for the best, to hunt only in the evening.

6. [an-, in-, an-to su.] The definition expressed by a verb with or without complement, to what purpose a person is occupied, is put in the Future followed by *to si*, *u*, *uru*; whence the forms: ..*an to su*, ..*in to su*, ..*an to su* (△ *eó-*, *iu-*, *oo to su*), = he is busy about.., he is about to.., he tries to..; Lat. *in eo est ut*, *id agit ut*. These forms are equivalent to the Lat. verbum meditativum (*moriturio*), and, as it, express an effort towards something.

Kassen ni yukán to su, he is about to go to battle. — *Yebisu domo no mi fi wo fandite mikoto wo yaki-korosan to suru toki*, *mikotono saki-tamaveru fou ken midsukara nukete*, *moye-kitaru kusa wo nagi-faravu*, when the savages setting the field on fire tried to burn the prince, the sword which the prince had girded on, unsheathed itself and mowed the burning grass away.

7. [..*to site*, = ..*to te*.] Instead of the gerund *to site* the syncopated *to te* is often met with. Examples:

Kono aida ni, *Hayatomo seto to* ¹) *te*, *siro haydai*, being between them (between the two banks) the isthmus of Hayatomo, the stream is rapid. — *Kono hoka Kooraitaka*, *Yeso-taka*, *Kiu-kiu-taka to te*, *kuni-guni ni ari*, moreover there are, since

---

¹) In our opinion, to estimate *to*, rightly as it is here used, what has been said at page 70, V, respecting *No to ru*, must be observed.

CHAPTER VII. THE VERB ri, § 103. BEKI, § 104.   291

the falcon of Corea, that of Yezo, that of Liu-kiu are met with, (falcons) in every country. — *Kano seki wo Fotoke ni nitari to te, Buts-zgu-seki to mo iwi*, people call that rock, because they think that it resembles a Buddha, the Buddha-image-rock. — *Iwi wo tsumide* (△ *tsunde*), *siro to site ... tatakaeru*, he heaps up rice-balls to a fort and fights. — *Yase-ki wo niwaka ni oi-siru* (威シ長ズ *we-simru* to te *koyasi wo tsuyoku-su bekarāzu*, to make meagre trunks of trees grow, they may not be too strongly manured. —

人ズヲ 日ヲ 奥ヲ *Go koku no waō wa Nippon wo semen to te su-man no nin*
數ズ 數ズ 國ヲ   *ziyu wo wataśu*, the king of the country U, intending
穐ヲ ノ 王ヲ   to make war on Japan, sends a force of many tens
              of thousands thither.

§ 104. **Beši**, may, can, shall; **Beki**, adjective, *Beku*, adverb possibly, expressed in Chinese by 可．宜．應．須．合．好．謂．

I. Derivation and signification.

Be (ベ), after the old form of writing ムベ, *mabē* (pronounced as mbē), also ウベ, *obē* and ウメ, *ume* (pronounced as mmē), is in Japanese dictionaries, called a word of assent [1] and made equal to the Chinese 宜 *i* [2].

If, although this definition of the idea is practically sufficient, an investigation of the origin of *Be*, is still required, it must be sought in the exclamation *m*, which, as our *hem*, implies that a person understands something, and in *he*, = our *yes*. The original form, *m-hé*, according to the rule of euphony passes, in pronunciation, into *mbē*, expressed in writing by ベ, for which we write *be*, whereas in the mouth of a Yedo gentleman it sounds clearly as *mbe*.

The old form ムベ, *Mabe*, occurs as a substantive with the signification of consent still, in expressions as *Mabē nari* (宜ニナリ), it is granted, = one has the liberty to do, one may do; *Mabē narēzu*, it is not allowed, it may not be; whereas ベ (*be*), occurs as a substantive in the every day expression *Su-be nari*, it is possible, *Su-be masi*, it is impossible.

[1] 古ハ譜ヲフメウバイト ヲケリ, i. e.: Formerly the Chinese word 譜 (= consent) was trans-lated with *Ube* or *Ume*.

[2] 宜 f. suitable, proper, fit, becoming, ought, should." MEDHURST, *Chinese and English Dictionary*

The forms derived from the root *Be*: the predicative *beu*, the attributive adjective, *beki*, and the adverb, *beku*, thus include the idea of may, and of can, i. e., no external cause preventing the doing of a thing. A command to do something is not included in it, and we do injustice to the politeness of the Japanese, if we give to this word the signification of our „one must, you must, you shall." The idea of consent on the one side does not include that of obligation on the other (must), and can, at its strongest, only contain an inducement.

II. Be belongs to the root-words treated in § 9. I. B., of which the so called adjectives in *ki* are derived. In accordance with the rule given there, *Beni* and *Beki* in the old-Japanese and in the popular language are superseded by the syncopated form *Bei* (可 ？) and the adverb *Beku* by Beo (可 ：．ク．可 ｀歴 ？), and that particularly in the countries east of the Hakone-pass, whereas in Sinano *Mei* (可 ？) is said, instead of *Bei* [1]).

With regard to the inflectional forms, they cannot be better elucidated than by a systematic synopsis. The writer confines himself to those forms, which have actually come under his notice, and with regard to such as, according to the rule, may yet exist, he refers the reader to the Synopsis of the Inflectional forms of *Nasi*, § 100.

INFLECTIONAL FORMS OF BESI, MAY, CAN.

	Aorist		Contin. preset.	Preterit.
Root-form	He, can.	Béku-ai, may.	Bekári, arises from Beku + ari, is being able.	Bekéri, arises from Beku + eri, has been able.
Closing form	Besi, ∧ Bei, Mei, Beku-au, it can.		Bekári, Be nari.	Bekési.
Subst. and At-tributive.	Beki, ∧ Bei, Mei, Bekusuru, possible.		Bekáru.	Bekéru.
Subst., isolated	Beki va.		Bekáru vá.	
Gerund		Béku-sité, contr. Bete.		
Lond. as, when, there			Bekáre ba.	Bekére bá, when he could.

[1]) Wa-gun Siowa, under Mei. Vol. 17. p. 1. recto.

CHAPTER VII. THE VERB BESI, MAY. § 104.   253

	Aorist.	Contin. Pres.	Preterit.
Concessive... although		Bekare domo,	Bekére domo.
Adverbial....		Bekaraku.	

FUTURE.

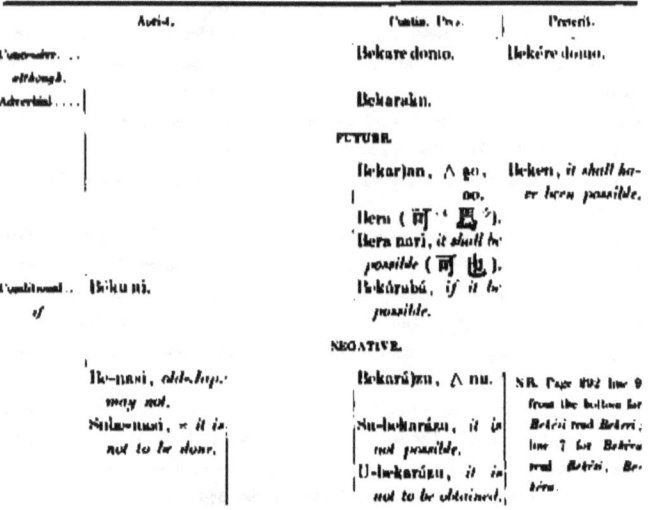

	Beka(ra)ṅ, 可 go, oo.	Beken, *it shall have been possible.*
	Hem (可 し).	
	Bera nari, *it shall be possible* (可也).	
Conditional.. Beku ni, *if*	Bekúrubá, *if it be possible.*	

NEGATIVE.

Be-nasi, *alds. hip.: may not.*	Bekarážzu, 可 nu.	NB. Page 252 line 9 from the bottom for Bekéři read Bekéri; line 7 for Bekíra read Bekéri, Bekéru.
Suba-nasi, = *it is not to be done.*	Su-bekarážzu, *it is not possible.*	
	U-bekarážzu, *it is not to be obtained.*	

III. ON THE GOVERNMENT OF Besi.

The verb, which, preceding *Besi*, expresses what one may, can, shall or will (do) is put, either in its root, or its attributive form. In nondeflecting verbs both forms are used, in deflecting verbs in *i*, only the attributive form in *u* or, instead of it, in the root, in *i* with nu or tsu as termination. Examples with nondeflecting verbs:

Ake-beri, one can, may open. — *Mi-besi*, one can, may see. — *Fiyori yoki wo mite, tané wo age-besi. Soro-wato ni touri, jikage-nite kawakasu-besi*, if you see, that the weather is fair, you may take out the seed (of the silkworms that have been put in water). Suspend it on sticks and dry it in the sun. — Δ *Wakeruru*, to be divided; *Wakeriruru-beki*, divisible. — Δ *Mi-wakeruru*, to be distinguished at night; *Mi-wakeriruru-beri*, it is to be distinguished at night. — Δ *Arururu*, to be visible; *Aruraruru-beki koto*, visibility. — *E, Ite* (or *Ye, Yete*) *U, Uru* (get) becomes *U-beki* instead of *Uribeki*; うべき *Ubeki mono*, something one can get, something obtainable. — *Sesume*, have it done; *Sisum-beki* instead of *Sei-*

mör'beni, one can have done.   Tasuke, help, save; Tasuku-beni instead of Tasukur'beni. — In a legend N'äkyu speaks to the falcon: Nandzi kono fato wo tasukubini, spare this dove. — The falcon answers: Ware kono fato wo tasukêbâ, ware uete ni-nu-beni, if I spare the dove, I shall die of hunger.

Examples with nondeflecting verbs:

Nari, to be. Kono sima busarazu Okino-sima naru-beni, this island will undoubtedly be that of Oki. — Si, to do. Su-beki (可為), feasible. Su-beki koto ari, there is a possibility of doing (this). — Onna kono tewaza wo su-beni, women ought to do such work. — Kore wa onna no su-beki tewaza nari, that is a work which women can or ought to do. Su-beki (being able, or about to do) is here conceived in an active sense, whereas the genitive onna no precedes as attributive definition. — Tomo ni iru-beni (可與言), people may speak with one another. — Nivakini fusegu-beki yau mo nakereba, Kawatsi ye nige-yuku, as in the hurry it was impossible to offer resistance, they fled to Kawatsi. — Kore wa nasazdru b'si, with regard to this, it may remain undone. — Kore wa nasaru bekarazu, with regard to this, one may not do it. The former allows, that something may not happen, the latter forbids that it happen. — Tsumabiraka ni su-bekarâzu (不可為), I cannot make it clear.

The terminations nu and tsu occur in deflecting verbs, e. g. Ari, to be; Ari-nu-b'si, it may or can be.   Iri-nu bisi (可入), one may go in. — Itari-nu-b'si (可至), one may or shall come to. — Iri (Ji), to be called; Iri-tsu-b'si, it may or can be called. — Tana-kokoro ni megurasi-tsu-b'si, one can make it run round on the palm of the hand.

I refer both terminations not to the closing-forms tsu and nu, treated in § 84 and 85, but to 曼 s nu (a variation of no) and 津 y tsu, which, as characteristics of the attributive relation, are derived from the old language. See page 67.

IV. 1. The ability to do any thing is expressed by Yôkasu, u, uru, to do good: 能, 耐, 克, 巧. Negative Yokuséznu, △ Yokusénu. From the expression: U'ru koto wo yôkû su, = I am able to get, it appears that the definition what one is able for, precedes as object in the Accusative.

Also used adverbially Yôku expresses the ability to do anything, e. g. Omonbakâtte sikjusite nôtsi yôku u, by reflection is one able consequently to attain (his object). 慮而后能得. Dai Gaku, l. 2.

能ク惡ム仁人 Tādi zin-zin yóka hitó wo ai-si, yóka hitó wo nikúma koto
能ク愛ス人ヲ wo su¹), the humane man alone is able to love others,
人ヲ 人ヲ to hate others. — Sri-zin to Vdowo, mata yoku-wzuru tokoro ari ²), even if he were a saint, there would still be
something that he could not do.

2. The inability to do a thing is expressed by Atavāzṅ, u (不能ハス), = Lat. non valet, = Uru koto atardzu, = the acquisition is not brought about. Atávi, of which Atardzu is the negative form, is composed of Ate, = equivalent, and av)i, u, = to fit, or, after the Wagun Siwori, from Atakavi (宣ヶ易ヒ), = to take the place of a thing, as an exchange, and means, substantively used, the value (直ヒ) of a thing; thus, as a verb, to be of value, to be worth (Lat. valere). The Japanese language considers the treatment, and not the person treating, as that which is not of value, or cannot be brought about.

吾レ弗ス能ハ已ム矣, Ware yamu koto atardzu¹), = that I (halting half-way) should rest, is not brought about. = I can not rest. — Ken wo mite aguru koto atardzu, agete sukinzaru koto atarazaru ni nai nari, Fu-sen wo mite sirizikuru koto atardzu, sirizikete tsoodigaru koto atarazdra ra ayamatsi nari ¹), to see an excellent man and not be able to raise him; to raise him and not be able to promote him, is fate. To see a good-for-nothing and not be able to remove him, to remove him and not be able to put him away, that is a mistake. — Kore wo motoiite tsukusu koto atarazaru mono aran ⁴), = that this (principle) be

盡ヶ有ル用ス exhausted by the application, will be something impos-
者ニ不レ sible. — 不能無敝ス, Tsuiye naki koto ata-
矣 能ハ之ヲ rdzu, it is not possible, that (a thing) do not perish.

V. To dare, is expressed by Ahete, Aete (敢テ), the gerund of Ake or Ar)e, u, uru, = to answer to... — Ahite atardzu (不敢當ヲ), he dares not attempt it. — Ahite kotowari-iru, he dares judge of it. — Ahite koto-wari-iradnu, he dares not judge of it. — Tarazdru tokoro areba, akete tsutomezunba ardzu ¹), = if there is any thing that does not suffice (if he comes short of), he (the man of character) does not dare not exert himself. — he dares not be negligent.

¹) Dai Gaku. X. 16.   ²) Tschung-yung. XII. 2.   ³) Ibid. XI. 2.
⁴) Dai Gaku. X. 16.   ⁵) Tschung-yung.   ⁶) Ibid. XIII. 4.

Remark. The negative *Idz̆u* or *Idz̆uu* (不致), joined to the root of a precedent verb, means the not accomplishing of an action; it is made equivalent to *Fatasazu* (不て果ず), not to accomplish. — *Omoi-*, *Iri-*, *Tori-*, *Nagare-ahi'zu* or *ah'zu*, mean: not continue meaning, saying, taking, flowing.

VI. That an action or a state is fitting, or is as it should be, is expressed by *Too-zen tari*, u (當ぅ然とzり), « it is as it should be. Joined to it are also the ideas, that one is obliged or even entitled to it. The definition what is fitting, precedes as substantive proposition, and is characterized by *koto* (affair). — *Oidôru wo uyamagu koto too-zen tari*, that age is respected, is as it should be. —

日 府 又 粟 當
本 ノ 役 組 然
政 船 人 ス タ
          ル リ

Nippon mi-fu yori … fune-hunc ni … yaku-nin nori-kumamuru koto toosen taru bexi[1]), it will be proper that on the part of the Japanese government custom-house officers be placed on the ships; or, after the official translation: the Japanese government shall have the right ... to place.

§ 105. The desiderative verbs.

1. Desiderative verbs are formed by grafting on the root of the verb, the word expressive of quality *Ta*, desirous. Belonging to the adjectives in *ki* (see page 100 n°. 69), *Ta* (ideographically expressed) by 欲, phonetically by 度多) has all the inflectional forms common to them, thus *Taki*, the substantive and attributive form, desirous; *Tasi*, predicate, = is desirous; *Taku*, adv. — The spoken language, which according to § 9 II. suppresses the *k* and the *s*, supersedes *Taki* and *Tasi* by *Tai* (タイ, for which タヒ is improperly written), and *Taku* by タウ, *Tou*, *Too*, for which inadepts also write タフ.

Mi-taki (Δ *Mi-tai*), desirous to see; *Mi-tasi* (Δ *Mi-tai*), he desires to see; *Mi-taku* (Δ *Mi-tou*, *Mi-too*), adv. — 欲Σ見ㇼ 見タ度ジ. — *Mi-takuba*, if he whishes to see. — *Mi-taku* (or *Mi-too*) *mo mai*[2]), he will not even see.

From the adverbial form *Taku* or *Too*, by means of the verb *Si*, *s*, *sru*, to do (§ 103), is derived *Takusi* or *Toosi*, to desire; gerund *Takuste* or *Too-site*,

---
[1]) Regulations by which the Dutch trade in Japan shall be carried on. Art. II.
[2]) This is the „*tomo nai*, je ne veut pas," occurring in some. Kōn. pag 55 § 50 line 4.

in the spoken language passing by elision into *Takn-te* or *Too-te*, = desiring; *Takate wa* or *Toote wa*, the gerund isolated by *wa*, = if one desires; *Takate mo* or *Toote mo*, though he wishes.

The adv. *Taku* or *Too* is further used in compositions like *Taku-* or *Too-yozari-musú*, = desiring; *Taku-* or *Too-omou*, or *omoi-nasu*, = is desirous thinking, desires; *Taku-omoote iru*, *Taku-omoote ori-masu*, = roundabout polite form for: I desire; *Tiiku-zonzi-nasu*, = I am desirous; *Mairi-taku-zonzi-nasu*, I will go.

II. Continuative forms.

1) If according to § 10, to the adv. *Taku* or *Too* we join the verb *Ari*, to exist, we obtain the continuative form *Taku* + *ari* or *Too* + *ari*, which in pronunciation, and in writing also, passes over to **Takari**, たかり, = continually to be desirous. Inflection, the same as of *Ari* (§ 86).

Pres.   *Mi-taku ari*, *Mi-too ari*, *Mitakarʲi*, u. is desiring to see.
Gerund *Mi-taku-arite*, *Mi-taku-itte*, *Mi-too-itte*, *Mi-takarte*, ∧ *Mi-takatte*.
Concess. *Mi-taku wa aredomo*, also *Mi-toi-keredomo*, though he desires to see.
Condit. *Mi-taku-ba*, *Mi-takereba*, *Mi-toi-naraba*, if he desires to see.
Future   *Mi-takaroo*, he may desire to see.
Pret.   *Mi-tooatta*, *Mi-takatta*, he was desiring to see,
         Mi-takatta keredomo, though he has desired to see.
Fut. Perf. *Mi-takattaroo*, he may have desired to see.

Derivative verbs of this stamp are:

Kiki-taki, desirous to hear. 聞？度？
Yuki-taki, desirous to go.
Si-taki (支 度？), desirous to do, ready.   *Si-taku-* (*si-tyu*)-*suru*, to be ready.
Itasi-taki (欲？致？), desirous to bring about.
Manabi-taki, desirous to learn.
Nomi-taki, desirous to drink.
Medi-taki, desirous to love, in love.

Ure-taki, desirous to mourn, sympathetic.
Nemu-taki, desirous to sleep, sleepy. — ∧ *Nemu-tai*, I will sleep. — *Nemu-taku nasi* ("*Nemu-tyu nai*), I am not sleepy. *Ware mata nemu-taku mo nai* (vulgo *nemu-tyu mo nai*), also I am not sleepy. — *Nemu-tasa*, sleepiness. *Wa-takusi*, selfish; the I.

§ 106. The leaving off of an action is expressed

1. by the deflecting transitive verb **Maki**, u. From *Ake*, to open, *Mi*, to see, *Yuki*, to go, are derived by means of *Maki*: *Ake-maki*, *Mi-maki*, *Yuku-maki*,

to leave off opening, to leave off seeing, not to go farther. From the examples given it appears, that, just as in the forming of the continuative, factive and passive forms, the weak i of the deflecting verb undergoes a strengthening. *Maki*, u means to roll up; thence the substantive *Maki*, a roll, or *Maki-mono*, a thing that is rolled. A roll of writing, that has been used, is rolled up again. Thence, improperly: *Sita wo maku*, to roll up the tongue, i. e. cease speaking, grow speechless. — *Ito naki koto wo makite zi wo utóru*, he lays the stringless harp aside and sings a verse.

Joined to a verb with the signification of ceasing to do what the verb expresses, *Maki*, u is expressed by 退 to refuse, to retire, thus 見ㇾ退ぐ, *Mi-maki*, to cease seeing. — 知ゞ退ぐ, *Sira-maki*, to have done with a thing. 欲ㇾ聞ゞ退ゞ數ぐ, *Kiku-maka fôski*, desiring not to hear more of. — 懶聽政, *Mätsuri-koto wo kikamaku fôsu*, he wishes to hear no more of business.

II. **Yam**i, u (止ㇾ), intr., to become quiet, to come to rest, Lat. *quiescere*; to leave off … — *Kaiko kuú wo kuvi-yamu*, the silkworm leaves off eating. — *Kura wo furi-yame*, leave off strowing food on the floor (to feed the silkworm). — *Yami*, as we see, with the root of a precedent verb forms a compound verb.

III. **Sima**i, u, △ **Sima**i, u, 了ぐ, phonetically expressed by 仕ン舞ξ, in my opinion, a distortion of *Sümôri*, to retire to rest, perch as bird, thence improperly to have done with a thing, to leave off. It belongs more especially to the spoken language, and generally has the complement of the action one leaves off, in the gerund in *te* or *de*, sometimes also in the verbal root, before it.

Si-goto wo site simai-maúoo, I shall finish my work. — *Watakusi wa sono siyo-(so) matsi wo tsukáyu yomi-simarúta* (△ *simoota*), I have read this book throughout. — *Kare wa kunde simoota*, he has left off eating, = he has eaten. — *Kunde simaute aroo*, he will have eaten. — *Waki-simauta sake*, fermented beer. — *Imada waki-simaudzu ni oru sake*, beer that has not fermented. — *Kunde simai: nonde simai*, leave off eating and drinking. — *Uri-sarpute simau*, to sell out. — *O ya-siyôkù O simai nasare mase*, may your supper be ended! take your supper at my house! the action being represented as finished. [1]).

---

[1]) Compare what A. REMUSAT in *Élém. de la Gramm. Chinoise* § 343 says concerning 了 *leao*.

Simavăsji, u., causal., to make leave off ... — *Watákusi ni madzu ište-simau-sasyo*, let me first have done speaking.

Simavarjo, u., uru, pass., to be finished. — *Kaki-simararetaru iou-kun*, a written (finished) letter.

§ 107. The adverbial form of a verb, as characteristic of modal propositions, like: as one thinks, as one says, is ..á-siku, ..á-sikûvá, = ..á-ku, ..á-kuvá.

Of the verbals derived by means of siki, = ..like, treated at large in § 10, 2), page 121, some by changing siki into siku assume an adverbial character. From *Omoi*, to think, to mean, is obtained *Omorisiku*, = probably, as one thinks or means. This is the axiom. As nevertheless the *si* of *siku*, is suppressed, for shortness. ..*a-siku* passes into ..*á-ku*; from *Omosisiku* is formed *Omoriku* and with addition of the isolating *va*, *Omoriku vá*, = as one means. The same is good of:

Ie)*i*, *u*, to say, to be called; *Si ni iraku* (詩 ニ = 日 ク), = as it is said in the odes, according to the odes.

Nori-tamde)*i*, or *No-tamde*)*i*, *u*, to bid, enjoin, command; *Si no nori-tamaraku* (子 シ ノ 日 ィ エ ハ ク), = according to the master's sentence, as the master says.

Negde)*i*, *u*, to wish; Δ *Negavákubu*, *m-yoo yorosii*, = as I wish, it is good so, = so it should be according to my wish.

Mgus)*i*, *u*, to say; *Mgusáka*, as people say. — *Fös*)*i*, *u*, now *Füss*)*i*, *u*, to desire; *Fosáka* (欲 サク), as people desire, as people will.

Ireri, has said; *Irerdku ra*, as people have said.

Ivikeri, has said; *Ivikvrasi*, it is as if people had said (compare § 18); *Irikeraku* (云 ヒ 來 ラ ク), as people have said. — *Sen-zi* (宣 ビ 旨 ジ) *ni ivikerákuen*, as it has been said in a proclamation by the Mikado.

Onor)*e*, *uru*, old-Jap. also *Oworí*, to fear; *Omoráku* (恐 ラクハ), as it is to be feared, as I fear; a polite way of expressing doubt.

Nari, to be; *Naráka* (= *Nariáku*). = as it is, preceded by a verb in the substantive form, e. g. *Kiku-naráka*, as one learns. — *Miru-naráka*, as people see. — *Ivu-naráka*, as people say. — *Utagavu-naráka*, contracted *Utagavu-ráku*, probably. *Naráka* is declared to be a contraction of *Nari* (to be) and *Kaku* (= *Sikáku*, adv. so, compare § 17) [1]), and, while it is said that *Naráka* must

---

[1]) 也 ラ 斯 ク ノ 畧 ヒ. See 助語審象, Zo-go sin-seo or Explanation of the auxiliary verbs. III. 31 v.

be expressed by 設 or 辻, people write 聞ラ設シ, 見ヱ設シ, 行ラ設シ or 聞ラ辻シ, etc.

Remark. The derivative form *siki*, elucidated in § 16, predicate *siki*, contracted *si*, which in connection with *ari* (to be) passes into *ari-siki* and *ra-siki* (§ 18), is also joined to verbs to express doubt¹). Consequently *Keri* (= has been, § 82) passes into *Kerási*, it is as if it had been; *Ki-ni-keri* (= is come, § 84) into *Ki-ni-kerasi*, it is as it were come. — *Aki ra ki-ni-kerasi* ²), the autumn is come. — *Fáru sugite* " *nitsu ki-ni-kerasi* ³), the spring is passing away and it seems as if the summer were (already) coming.

§ 109. ...*meri*, = it is as if, it seems, an old-Japanese derivative form, which, as it is said, resembles *Nari* (is) but expresses some doubt⁴). It follows the indicative closing-form of a verb.

Yebisu no kami no koto yo mi smazamu ni icu-meri ⁵), with respect to the history of the God Yebis', people speak about it in the world, as it seems, in different ways.

        Tsuyiri okisi " *sacemo ga tsuynuro!* " *inoti nite*
        Arare! kotosi no " *aki no inu-meri* ⁶).

Oh dew of the sprig, that is planted with promises! In my life, Alas! the autumn of this year, as it seems, passes away (without seeing the promise made to me performed). — *Inu*, from *Inji*, *u*, *uru*, to go away (§ 84), not a negative form of *I*, to be.

As belonging to this category are cited: ⁷)

Ak'eu-meri (明去), it seems to become day.

Nagáre-meri (流), *Fátéun-meri* (滅去), it is as if it flows away, as if it perishes.

This form is to be distinguished from *Tsubúm-iri*, *Nasásm-iri*, being the pret. pres. of *Tsubúmi*, to bud, and *Nasásmu*, to order to be made (see § 80), as also from ..*namuri*, or ..*nanmeri*, shall have been, Future Perfect, of *Ni*, to be (see § 100, I.).

---

¹) *Sukái ni yoru kotobu meri*, *Wagan Sirori*, under *Ran*.
²) *Hyaku-nin*, N°. 47.   ³) Ibid. N°. 2.
⁴) ノナリト 例"ラ 少シ 疑ヒノ意ニ アリト イヘリ. *Wagan Sirori*, under *Meri*.
⁵) *Nimote*. II. 16 verso.   ⁶) *Hyaku-nin*, N°. 75.   ⁷) *Wagan Sirori*.

§ 109. **Nasi**, **Naki**, **Naku**, in the ordinary manner of speaking and writing, by the suppression of the *s* and *k* (see § 9, 11, page 112), **Nai**, **Nai**, **Nau** (ナウ, pronounced as **Nɡo**, whence the written form **Noo**, **Nô** and **Nö**), means not to exist (無), not to be present, to be not at hand, in opposition to *Ari*, a (有, § 90), – to exist.

A general sketch in § 20, when treating of the derivative adjectives in *naki*, has already made us acquainted with this word. Here it requires to be elucidated in further particulars, concerning which all the dictionaries generally leave the student in the lurch.

I. The root **Na**, of which the sound *n* is the negative element (compare § 91, I), occurs

1. as prefix, like our *un*, in compounds as: *Na-yami*, = unrest; *Na-kato*, nothingness; *Na-wi* (ナヰ), *Na-i* (ナイ), = un-seat, i. e. earthquake; *Na-mi*, the un-real, the nothing; whence *Iru-jitó wo muni-su*, – *Nai gu siro ni su* (蔑), to esteem any one as nothing.

2. as the forbidding *not*, followed by an imperative, that closes with *so*. — *Na-sutomé so*, seek not! — *Na-si so*, also *Na-si zo* (勿莫), do not! — *Na-iri so*, say not! — *Na-nakare so*, = △ *Na-nakaeru*?), let it not be wanting! = it must be there.

3. In the spoken language *na* suffixed to the substantive form of an affirmative verb is the forbidding *not*, Lat. *ne*.

Ageru na, raise not!	*Iru na*, be not!
Kiku na (聞ク莫?), hear not!	*Suru na*, do not!
Miru na, see not!	*Agerureru na*, let it not be raised!
Iu na (イウ), say not!	*Yomareru na*, let it not be read!

This imperative is strengthened by the subsequent *yo*. — *Miru-na yo*, you shall not see. — *Wasureru-na yo*, you shall not forget.

4. *Na* suffixed to the substantive form of a verb, occurs as characteristic of a negative question. — *Man gin de wa hyaku nóbi bakari nasenu*? for (the delivery) of ten thousand pounds are not a hundred days needful? — *Ri ni mo iro-iro arimasu nai*? there are also different sorts of miles, – is it not so? *Shopping-Dialogues* p. 31.

---

¹) Compare subs. 66, line 13.

CHAPTER VII. THE VERB NASI, NOT TO BE. § 109.

11. **Nasi**, △ **Nai**, predicate: there is not.

1. *Ato nasi*, there is no trace. — *Kizu nasi*, there is no hindrance. — *Urami nasi*, there is no disgust. — *I nasi*, there is no meaning. — *Yeki nasi*, there is no advantage in it. — △ *Zeni ga¹) aru ka? nai ka?* are there cents or are there not? = Is there money, or not? — *En-rio nasi ni handsu koto*, to speak without forethought, not to care about what one says.

2. To bring it out with emphasis, the subject of *Nasi* is isolated, either by wa, △ wa, or by mo, = also, even. — △ *Fu-soku wa nai*, there is no want. — △ *Fitó koto mó nai*, = there is not even a single affair, = there is absolutely nothing on hand.

3. [..koto nasi.] If the subject, the existence of which is denied by *Nasi*, is a substantive proposition, it is characterized by koto, affair. — *Fitóri kore wo adsu-koto nasi* (無獨成之), = that a person does this alone, does not exist, no one accomplishes it alone. — *Taka wa kure ni sorete, miso-tsoo* (明与 朝ら) ta-dzune yobu toki ra, fitd wo mite, osore tonde tsikádzuku koto nasi*, if the falcon has flown away in the evening, and one seeks and calls him the next morning, he becomes shy at the sight of people, flies around, and it does not happen (nasi), that he approaches. *Tsikádzuku koto nasi* may for rounding off the period, stand for *Tsikadzukinu*, not approach. — *Sari todomaru koto nasi* (△ ..koto ga nai), 無去住, he goes not, he stays not. — *Sikureba kaiko wa surusiki ni nasi-* (冷じ) *taru koto wa nai*, = that however the silkworm has grown in cool weather, this does not exist. — △ *N'da no koto mó nai* (無事), there is absolutely nothing at hand. — △ *N'da no ii-bun mó nai*, there is nothing to say.

[..mono nasi.] △ *Kore wo yóku-suru mono wo nai*, a person who can (do) such, there is not. — △ *Tanósimi-suru mono ga nai*, there is no one people may trust. — △ *Me ni aidru mono ga nai*, there is nothing that comes under notice. — *Okoeiku za-sen* (鹿*銭¿) to miyuru mono nasi*, chiefly those (coins) are wanting which (mono) seem to be counters or model coins.

[..tokoro nasi.] *Ki-suru tokoro nasi* (無所歸), there is no support. — △ *Nokóru tokoro wa nai*, there is no more room, = every place is taken. — △ *Fito ni warun yuwaruru (= iwaruru) tokoro wó nai*, there is nothing, about which ill is spoken by others.

---

¹) For *ga*, see page 84.

4. If the definition that this or that is wanting, is predicate to a precedent subject, it is, for the sake of clearness, willingly isolated by va, △ wa, thus separated from the predicate. — *Iwoo yu sima fitó nasi*, the „brimstone island" is without people, has no inhabitants. — *Kono yumú rú tsikára ndsi*, this how is without strength, is powerless.

5. The appositive definition, what a thing is not, is put in the Local, characterized by one of the terminations ni, de, ni wa or de wa. — △ *Iti fui ni wa nai*, it is not sagacity, it is stupid. — △ *Sono yau ni nai*, it is not so. — △ *..no yau ni nai*, it is not so as... — △ *Kore fodo ni nai*, it is not so much. — △ *Waga mama ni wa nai*, it is not capricious. — △ *Na-koto de wa nai*, it is no nothingness, it is even of importance. — △ *Waga koto de nai*, it is not my business; it does not concern me; I have nothing to do with it. — △ *Waga-tomo de nai*, it is not we. — △ *Sorewa sayau de wa nai ka?* is it not so? — △ *Sgu* (or *Sou*) *de wa nai*, it is not so. (不如是, 不然ヒバアラ). — △ *Doko de mó sou de nai to iru koto wa nai*, it is nowhere said, that it is not so, literally: it does not occur anywhere that people say that it is not so. — △ *Kau de wa nai*, it is not so. — △ *Sou sita koto de wa nai*, it is not a business of that nature. — △ *Minu de wa nai* (非不見), one may not overlook; one may indeed look to. — △ *Iwanu de wa nai* (非不言), one must speak about it.

6. [..ku nai.] The definition denied by △ *Nai*, in the easy manner of writing, also precedes as an adverb. — △ *Kono syok-motu' umaku nai*, that meat is not tasty. — *Umaku nai syok-motu*, distasteful meat.

Remark. The predicate *Nasi* is in compound words used as an attributive also, e. g. *Na-nasi-yubi*, the nameless (the fourth) finger, i. e. the finger, whose predicate definition: *na-nasi* is at the same time its adhering attribute.

III. **Naki**, △ **Nai** (ナイ, vulg. ナヒ also), - ..less, the adjective form.

1. Used as a noun substantive, it means: nothing, and answers to *Naki-mono* and *Naki-koto*, i. e. a thing or a matter that does not exist. — *Naki ni suru*, to consider as nothing, to cipher away. — *Fitó wo nai ga* (vulg. ナヒガ) *riro ni suru* (賤人), to consider others of no value. — *Kore wo nasu mo yúye-naki ni arāzu*, = also that people make this, is not a „cause-lessness," i. e. it is not without reason that this is done.

2. The attributive **Naki**, △ **Nai**, - paltry, in the original signification of not existing. — *Naki-fito*, a person not existing, not present, i. e. a de-

funct. *Naki-mono*, vulgo *Nai-mono*, a thing not existing, a nothing. — *Aru fito no naki-koto wo kiku*, to hear of one's not being (his being dead). *Naki-ato* (亡迹), a trace effaced.

3. As attributive adjective (without, Lat. *absque*, *sine*) *Naki*, △ *Nai* has the definition, what there is not, as a genitive before it, either with or without the genitive termination *no* or *ga*.

△ *Teniye-maki koto ataraizu*, continuance is impossible, — an end must come. *Tsikara-naki yumi*, a powerless bow, a bow without strength. — *Tsikara-naki koto*, power-less-ness. — *Ato-naki nari*, it is a thing without trace — it has disappeared, *Ato nasi*, there is no trace of it. — *Kiwamari no naki koto nari*, it is a matter without limitation. — *Kiwamari no aru koto nari*, it is a matter that has limitation. — △ *Mi no oki-dokoro no nai mono*, a person without a place in which he can settle, a wretch. — △ *Tsigai no nai yau ni wa murana*, it is not of that nature that there should be no difference. — △ *Prinsi no kokiro-gake ga nai*, without a life's exertion or care. — △ *Tanomi ni suru mono ga nai*, without anything or anybody in which one has support. — △ *Kokiro ni mono ga nai*, having no evil in the heart, — *Urami naki*, without disfavor.

Remark. To *ga* and of the last three examples, what is said at page 64 respecting *ga* is applicable.

IV. The adverbial form *Naku* (ナク), without, by the dropping of the *k* in the easy manner of writing passes to ナウ *Nau*, for which ナン *Navu* also is written, sounding in pronunciation as *Ngu*, *Ngo*, — for which *noo*, *nô* or *nō* have chiefly been written. See § 9. II. — *Nani-to naku*, *idzu to naku*, without anything whatever, — nothing at all.

1. The form **Naku** is used, as if it were the uninflected verbal root, in coördinate propositions. See § 9. II. 2. — *Kake-wo naku*, *amari-mo nasi*, there is nothing too little, nothing too much. 无欠无餘.

2. Among Poets **Naku** supersedes the termination *nu* of the negative verb. *Are-naku*, *Aenu*, not to dare. — *Maku-naku*, *Makanu*, not to roll up (§ 100). — *Omowo-naku*, *Omowanu*, not to think. See § 92. 4.

3. **Naku va**, △ **Naku wa**, the adverbial form isolated by *va*, △ *wa*, is used as predicate verb in adverbial propositions, with the meaning of as or if there is not, failing of. — *Ikitaru kizi* **naku va**, *sintaru kizi mo tirubesi*, failing of a living pheasant, one may take a dead one (to feed the falcon).

4. **Nakumba, Nakumba**. The Local *Nakuba* contracted from *Naku ni*, and isolated by *va*, means in case of not existing, if there is not. — *Midzu-*

CHAPTER VII. THE VERB NAS (NAKI, NAKU). § 109.   305

nikinité fétauréru koto naku, *tomite ojoru* koto nakumba, *ikan!* if one, being poor, is without flattery, and being rich, is without pride, how then? (what do you think of it?) Compare BOUR. 56.

This Local form may even close a suppositive proposition, but is therefore no modus conditionalis.

ヤ レ ヌ カ シ ズ | 日モ ソ レ ナ ク ン バ | 業ナ シ ナ ク ン バ | 安民節 一 | 衣食ノ道ハ | *I-siyok' no mitsi ra an-min dai' itai no kro sareba, itni nitai mo* nakumba *aru bekarazu,* as clothing and feeding are the principal acts towards the welfare of a people, they may never fail for a day.

5. △ **Naku to wa,** = **Ngo to wa,** contracted from *Nakusité wa.* See below V, 1, *Nakusi.*

6. **Naku to mo,**   **Naku to tédomo** or **Naku to iú to mo,** though it is said that there is not, granted that there is not,   even if there is not.

V. VERBS COMPOUNDED WITH **Naku.**

As such come under notice: *Naku-si, Naku-se, Nakéri, Nakarésime, Nakeri* and *Naka-nari.*

Explanation.

1. **Naku-si,** n. *uru,* not to be, to be wanting, a coupling of *Naku* and *si,* = to do (see § 103, III, 3), antithesis to *Iri, n,* to be present. The spoken language, which makes from *Naku-si*, **Ngu-si** (ナクシ). **Ngo-si,** changes the gerund *Nakusite,* by syncope into **Nguto, Nooto,** and *Nakusite ru* into **Nguto wa, Nooto wa** [1]), = by or through want of, or; as there is not. Examples:

Yo-sin ni Nippon yaku-nin yuri yursui naku-sité, *ai-oruru-bekarizu* [2]), at night, without permission of the Japanese officers, no goods may be unloaded.   *Nippon yaku-nin tatsi-aei nakusité* [3]), without there being Japanese officers present. — *Zin-sin no ri siru-koto arazaru-koto nakusite* (or *ngu-sité*), *sikin-sité Ten-ka no mono ri arazdru koto nasi* [4]), the spiritual part of the human heart is not without knowledge, and so also are the things on earth not without natural laws. — *Kotoba nakusite kakeri-tamaru,* without (saying) a word (the king) goes away

---

[1]) In SOEMOULE *Elém.* p. 55 line 3 below, *Nowatara* should stand instead of *Nitewa,* = our *Nao to wa*

[2]) Art. II al. 3 of the Regulations by which the trade in Japan shall be carried on, belonging to the Treaty of 1859.

[3]) Franco-Japanese Treaty of 1858, Art. VIII, al. 4   [4]) *Dsu Gaku.* V. e

again. — △ *Kane ga nju-site* (or *Kane ga nakute wa*) *kōnawanu*, without money no success. — △ „*Jnohito wō ori-ori kami-ire wo nākuru* (or *nakusare-masu*), he is always losing (read wanting) his pocket-book" ¹).

Naků-s)e, uru, △ **Ngo-se** (ナツセ), contracted from *Ndků-sim)e*, u, uru, = to despise.

△ *Fitō wo nan to mo noomuru* (ナヲノム) *mono*, = a person, who does not respect others for anything, who respects others for nothing.

2. **Nakari**, n, continuative, not present, a fusion of *Naku* and *ari*, follows the inflection of *.iri*. See § 92. 4. — *Ureua kagiri nakari keri*, the joy has been boundless. — *Kono zeni, men-kiyo nakurisi ga atsi nite, saya iritaru mono ima no go ni nawo nokoreri*, of this coin there are now still several copies (*mono*) remaining, which, while there was no permission, were prematurely struck off.

As a form of the forbidding Imperative, *Nakáre* comes particularly under notice. See § 93. 2. — *Tniu-ziyo mitai wo sdra koto tdokardzu. Korewo onoréni hodokûsite negavazunhā, fūd ni hodokûsu koto nakáre* ²), whoever is honorable and kind, never deviates far from the way (from the moral law). If a person does not wish that this or that be applied to him, he may not apply it to others!

施不施不忽
於 願 諸 遊 想
人亦己 遊
勿而

Derived from *Nakāri* is **Nakarsim)e**, n, uru, = to command that there be not, i. e. forbid. See § 88. — *Kuruuoki wo kiru-koto nākardsimu*, = order is given that the chopping of the mulberry-trees do not happen, = it is forbidden to chop the mulberry-trees.

桑毋
拓 伐

3. **Nakeri**, Pret. pres. there has not been, follows the inflection of *..eri, eri* (§ 80. § 92. 4). — *Nirakéni fusagu-beki yau mo nakereba*, „*Kavataiye nige-yuku*, as in the hurry there was no opportunity for defence, they fled towards Kavatai.

Remark. The spoken language of Yédo seems to use *Nukéreba* for *Nakéreba*, thence „*Sirō- (sib-) ke ga nakerebá* (or *nakutered*) *adziwai ga nai*, it is not good without salt" ³).

4. **Naků-narí**, n, △ **Ngo-nari**, **Ngo-nari**, to become nothing, to come to nothing, to be consumed. See § 100. III. (冤, 沒, 死). — *Tukúra naku-naru*,

---

¹) s. BROWN, *Coll. Jap.* Nº. 591.   ²) *Tschung-yung*. XIII. 3   ³) s. BROWN, *Coll. Jap.* Nº. 631.

CHAPTER VII. THE VERB NASI (NAKI, NAKU). § 109. 307

to become powerless. — *Tsikóra náku-naríte iru*, = △ *Tsikára ngo ndíte iru*, to have become powerless. — *Sake va náku-narita*, = △ *Sake wa ngo-natta*, the wine is consumed. — △ *Uvvi no yumé go naku-narita*, the unpleasant dream has disappeared. — *Aritaru mono no náku-naritaru koto*, the perishing of a thing, that has existed.

SYNOPSIS OF THE INFLECTIONAL FORMS AND DERIVATIVES OF NA)SI, KI, KU, NOT TO BE.

	Form of the Predicate verb.	Substantive and Attributive form.	Adverbial form.	Derivative verb.
Root-form....	NA, = not.	Naki, △Nai, ...less.	Naku, △Ngu, (△Noo, Nò) without.	Naku-si, △Ngu-si, to want, fail of.
Closing-form.	Nasi, △Nai *there is not.*			Naku-su, △Ngu-su, *there is wanting.*
Substant. form, declinable.	Nasi, △Nai Nasi vá, △Nai wá *that there is not.* △Nai ka? *is there not?*	Naki, △Nai Naki vá, △Nai wá *what there is not, the ...less.* △Nai koto	△Naku wa	Naku-suru, △Ngu-suru
Local, derivative of time and manner.	Nasi ni, △Nai ni Nasi ni- △Nai ni- óite wá, óite wá, *while there is not.*		Naku ni va, = Nakunba, △Nakumba.	
Gerund......				Naku-site, = △Nakú te △Ngo te △Nò te △Nakú te wá △Nò te wá *by want of...*
Concessive... though.	Nasi to- △Nai to- iyé domo, iyédomo Nasi to- △Nai to- iu tomo, iu tomo △Nai tomo		Naku tomo, *though there is wanting.*	
Conditional... if.		△Nai-naraba △Nai-nará		
Imperative...	Na! Nayo! *be it not!*			

Continuative.

	Present.	Pret. pres.	Preteris.	
Root-form....	Nakari.	Nakaritari, △ Nakarita, Nakatta, ナカツタ. Nakari-keri, there has not been.	Nakari-si, there has not been.	Nakéri, △ Nai-keri, there was not.
Closing-form..	Nakari, there is not.		Nakari-ki, there has not been.	Nakéri, there was not.
Substant. form	Nakáru. Nakaru wa.	Nakaritaru, △ Nakatta to.	Nakari-si.	Nakési.
Attributive...	Nakaru.		Nakari-si,	Nakési, Nakéru.
Legal, declarative of Case.	Nakaru ni. Nakaru ni óttewa.	Nakaritaru ni △ Nakari ta ui, △ Nakatta ni.	Nakari-si ni.	Nakeru ni.
Gerund......	Nakarite, △ Nakátte.			
Causal form..	Nakareba.	△ Nakattareba.		Nakereba, as there was not.
Concessive....	Nakarédomo. Nakarutomo.	△ Nakattaredomo.		Nakeredomo, though it was not. Nakeru to mo.

FUTURE.

Nakaran,
△ Nakargo
(Nakaroo, Nakaró).
Nakarn z)a, uru,
(△ Nakaró z)n, nru.

Conditional... Nakaraba.

IMPERATIVE.

Nakare.
Optative Nakare kasi.
Nakare guna.

NEGATIVE.

Nakarúnn, it must be there.
Nakerana naranu, 不可無, it must have been.
Nakini arazu, Nakinarázn, it is not without ...
Na nakaseso, it may not be wanting.

CHAPTER VII. COMPOUND VERBS. § 110.   309

REMARKS ON THE COMPOUND VERBS.

§ 110. The subordinate definition, which precedes a verb with which it is compounded, may be a substantive or a verb.

I. The substantive may be its object direct, or indirect. See § 3. II. 1 and 2.

It is the object direct in *Ama-gori*, *Tsi-gori*, to long for rain, for milk; it is the object indirect in *Ama-kudari*, descending from the sky.

II. 1. The verb, preceding another verb as subordinate qualifying definition, remains in its root-form. The chief word of the compound governs the accidental object. *Korós)i*, u, to kill; *Fitó wo i-korósi*, *titsi-korósi*, *sasi-korósi*, to shoot a person dead, to strike dead, to stab dead.

To the qualifying definitions belong verbs like *Os)i*, u, 押シ, to press, to do with emphasis; *Osi-yar)i*, u, throw away; *Osi-ir)i*, u, to intrude.

Uts)i, u, 打ツ, to strike, with a blow, or suddenly; *titsi-or)i*, iru, to pounce, as a bird of prey (§ 99. I. nº. 11); *Siro wo titsi-i)de, dzuru*, to make a sally.

Sasi, 差シ, send away; *Ok)i*, u, place; *Sasi-oki*, set aside, put away; *Fitó wo sasi-tsukaras)i*, u, to dispatch any one.

Mes)i, u, 召シ, invite, call up, qualifies the action as one which takes place by higher command; *Mesi-tor)i*, u, to take by order, to arrest a person; *M.. ye fitó wo tsukarasi, N.. wo mesi-kuresi-tamaeu*, (the prince) sends people to M.. and has N.. brought back.

Avi, Ai, 相ヒ, together. Lat. *con*; *Ai-katar)i*, u, speak together; *Ai-gisu*, consult together.

2. The definition of the particular direction of an action incorporated in a compound verb (as in flying upwards or downwards), is not expressed in Japanese, as in other languages, by a prefix or a preposition, but as the principal part of the expression, by a verb, that is preceded by the mention of the action as a subordinate definition. Leaving the indication of such compound verbs to the dictionaries, we here confine ourselves, for the sake of brevity, to a few examples.

Ag)e, uru, 上ジ, *trans.*, expresses the moving upwards, *Sag)e, uru*, 下ジ, *trans.*, the movement downwards. — *Tori-age*, to take up, to raise. — *Sasi-age*, nudge, to present. — *Motsi-age*, to bring up. — *Fiki-age*, to draw up. — *Mgusi-age*, to mention (a thing to a superior). — *Fiki-sage*, or *Fiki-orósi*, to draw down. — *Agari*, *Sagari*, *contin.*, *intr.* — *Tobi-agar)i*, u, to fly upwards. — *Tobi-sagar)i*, u, to fly downwards.

21

Nobór)i, u, to go upwards. Kudár)i, u, to go downwards. — Fasu-nobóri, to run upwards. — Nagare-kudari, to flow downwards.

Ir)i, u, 入 {, to go into. Ide, Idzuru, 出 {, to come out. — Osi-iru, intrude. — Faye-iru, to grow inwards. — Otsi-iru, to fall into... — Faye-idzuru, to sprout out. — Ir)e, uru, trans.; Otdsi-iru, to make a thing fall in.. — Idas)i, u, caust. — Tori-idds)i, u, to take out of.

Kom)i, u, 込 {, intr., to go inwards. Kom)e, uru, tr., to bring in. — Komas)i, u, to make go inwards. — Fi no teri-komu, the shining in of the sun. — Nomi-komu, to swallow. — Kugi wo (Kuabi wo) utsi-komu, to drive in a nail.

Utsus)i, u, 移 {, to remove. — Fakobi-utsusu, to transport. — Kaki-utsusu, to write over again, to copy.

Kaher)i, u, 帰 {, to turn back; Kahes)i, u, to make turn back. — Tobi-kahru, to fly back. — Tori-kayesu, to take back.

Mav)i, u, 舞 {, to move in a circle. — Mi-mavi, to look around.

Mavar)i, u, continually to go round. — Nagare-mavaru, to flow round.

Mavas)i, u, to make go round. — Fiki-mavasu, to draw a thing round-about. — Tori-mavasu, to turn round.

Tsuk)i, u, 着 {, intr., = on, to. — Kisi ni tsuku, to come ashore. — Δ Fune ga oka ni nagare-tsuku, the ship drifts ashore.

Tovor)i, u, Δ Toár)i, u, 通 {, to go through, to pass. — Fi no nakawo, to go through the midst of the fire. — Nagare-toworu, to flow through.

Tovos)i, u, Δ Toós)i, u, to make go through. — Ori-todsu, to drive through. — Ori-todsaretaru, driven through. Mato wo i-tousu, to shoot through a target.

Watar)i, u, 渡 {, to pass, to go from one side to the other. — Kawa wo watári, to cross a river. — Kawa wo katsi-watdri, to wade through a river. — Tobi-watari, to fly over.

Watas)i, u, to make pass over, to carry over. — Yaku-ho ye futo wo fiki-watdsu, to transport people to the office.

Tsir)i, u, 散 {, intr., to spread, scatter; Tsiras)i, u, caus., spread, scatter. — Fou-bou ye nige tsiru, they fled to all sides. — Tobi-tsiru, to spatter abroad. — Ovi-tsirasu, to scatter.

— — —

APPENDIX.

DISTINCTIVE VERBS AND VERBAL FORMS EXPRESSIVE OF COURTESY.

§ 111. Courtesy in language and writing is, in Japan, not confined to the priveleged classes of society; cast ages ago in distinct forms and, we may add, stamped by the law, it has penetrated to the lowest grades of society and spread over social intercourse a gloss of reciprocal respect, which is indeed not to be found among any other people on the globe.

Besides, courtesy in language and writing is not the consequence of recent development: even the oldest Japanese historical book, the *Yamáto-bumi* of the eighth century (see page 37) is characterized by a courteousness of expression which, the not unfrequent insignificance of the contents considered, cannot be acquitted of extravagance.

So long as courtesy governs the oral and written intercourse of a people, the appreciation of its forms belongs to the study of the language, and since we have treated it in the chapter on the Pronouns, we are obliged to fix the attention on the verbs and verbal forms also with which courtesy gives gloss to its language.

The chief features of the Japanese courtesy are:

1. The polite speaker distinguishes the conditions and actions of persons beyond him by the honorary prefix 御す.* *On* or *O*. See page 75.

2. He does not say or require, that another person, whom he places above himself, should do any thing himself, but says or requires only, that the action be done, i. e. he places the passive form as predicate to the subject, that really performs the action.

3. He considers not only persons of higher station, but even his own equals as being in a higher position, and with the actions of others connects the idea of descent, whereas to his own he gives that of ascent.

4. He is scrupulous in the choice of synonimous verbs, in proportion as he wishes to express the same idea in a more or less exalted style. Letter-writers teach him to distinguish the degrees.

§ 112. To satisfy the demand, which represents the person beyond the speaker not as acting himself and thus as not immediately coming in contact with persons of lower station, the active form of the predicate verb is, as it has been said, simply superseded by the passive form, without — and here is the peculiarity of the expression, — introducing any modification in the construction of the original active proposition (compare § 90. 2). Examples:

Karuno Oho-kimi wo dai-si ni sadamerare [1]) (instead of *sadamu*, or *sadame-tamaou*), (the emperor) declares the Great-prince Karuno hereditary prince. — *Zin-mu Ten-wau aru toki takaki oka ni noborite, kono kuni no katatsi akitsumusi ni nitari wo mite, fazimete Akitsusimato mutsukeraru* (instead of *sudzuku*), = Emperor Zin-mu, once climbing a height, seeing that this country (Japan) resembles the light-insect (the dragon-fly), first gave it the name of Light-island. — *L. wa M. ni N. no kwan wo sadzukeraresi* (instead of *sadzukesi*) to *ari*, people say, that L. has given the office of an N. to M. — *Nani wo iwasare-masita ka?* what have you said? *Iwasare* from *Iwasi*, make say, and this from *Ivi*, to say.

Much in use are the honorary passive forms: 1. *Serare*, 2. *Saserare*, 3. *Nasare*, *Nasare-nasa)i*, n. 4. *Nasasareru*, 5. *Arasare*, 6. *Irare*, 7. *Irasare*, 8. *Iraserare*. Explanation:

1. **Serare**, uru, pass. of *S)e*, uru, to do, to effect. — *Yamato-Take sibaraku ton-riu-seraru* [1]) (instead of *ton-riu-su*), Yamato-Take stays there some time. — *Kei-ko Ten-wau Siga nite fou-gyo-* (崩ぎ御ず) *seraru* (instead of *fou-gyo-su* or *fou-gyo-si tomaru*), Emperor Kei-ko dies at Siga. — *N. no Oho-kimi kau-zi-* (薨を) *seraru*, Great-prince N. dies. *M. wo kiri-korosi, N. wo ru-zai-* (流ぐ罪ぎ) *seraru* [1]), (the king) sabres M. down, and banishes N. If, instead of *seraru*, *sasimuriru* were used, it would mean, that the king gives order to kill and to banish.

2. **Saserare**, uru, it is effected that one does; from *Sas)e*, uru, to make do. The action runs, as it were, over three wheels, by which a person of high station causes an inferior to have a thing done. — *Go-bo* (御ご廟ぎ) *ni mays wo ken-zi-suseraru* (or *ken-zi-saxe-tamaeru*), the prince has cocoons offered in the ancestral temple.

3. **Nasare**, uru, 被ぎ成+, to be done, from *Nasi*, make exist, and this from *Ni*, to be (see § 100). *Nani wo nasaru ka?* what does your honor?

---

[1]) *Nippon wo-dai itsi-ran*. II. 6 verso. [2]) Ibid. [3]) Ibid. II. 5 verso.

CHAPTER VII. VERBS OF COURTESY. § 112.   313

In the familiar style of speaking and writing as an auxiliary verb grafted on the root of another verb, it makes known, that the action which is done, proceeds from the person spoken to, or even merely from another person than the speaker. Examples from the spoken language:

Sayoo nara, O tsuki nasare! if it is so, give it me! — *Koshikake ni O kake nasare!* may Your sitting on a chair happen, = take a seat. *O kake nasare,* sit down. — *Kore wo O kasi- (O tsuki) nasare,* lend (give) me this. — *Kore wo Go-ran nasare,* please look at this. — *Yoku O yasumi nrisari!* = may Your good rest happen! = good rest! — *Doko ni O samai nasaru ka?* where do You live? — *O kai nasarete mo, O yame nasarete mo, kono syzwo deki-masenu,* you may buy it or not, there ends the matter. — *Nokorazu O kai ndaaru nara, yasuku-site age-masoo,* if you buy the whole stock, I will sell it cheap. — *Roowo O kai-nasardnu ka?* don't you buy wax?

Nasare-mas)i, u, the same as *Nasare,* only more round-about, vulgo *Nasari-masu* also (see § 101). — △ *Nani wo nasare-masu?* what are you doing? — *Go un-sin nasare-mase,* depend on it. — *W'atakusi no mynsu koto wa O wakari nasare-masska?* do you understand what I say? — *Si-ygu ni nasare-masi ka?* will you do so? — *O kamai nasare-mari na!* take no pains! — *Sikosi mo O kamai nasare-masu na,* don't trouble yourself about; don't care for it. — *Kono mitsi wo O ide nasare-mase,* go this way. — *Idzureye O ide nasare-masu?* whither are you going? — *Idzure yori O ide nasare-musita?* whence do You come? — *Douzo O hairi nasare-mase,* if you please, walk in.

4. **Nasaserar)e,** uru, 被レ為レ成ル, care is taken that a thing is done or made; the passive of *Nasase,* have made, and this the causative form of *Nosi,* to make. The action or the effect here runs over four wheels.

5. **Arasar)e,** uru, pass. of *Arai,* to have be, and this from *Ari,* to be. — △ *Dore ga O suki de arasare-masu ka?* what is there of your desire? what do you like?

Araserar)e, uru, vulgo for *Irasseru.* — △ *O kasama ikaga de araserare-masu,* how is your son? — *Solute okisama wa ikaga de araserare-masu?* and how is your lady?

6. **Irar)e,** uru, to be placed in the condition of dwelling, pass. of *I, Iru* (居ル), to dwell, be somewhere, stay (see § 98). — *Anata iraruru tokoro wo zonzi-masenu,* I do not know your dwelling-place.

7. **Iraser)e,** uru, pass. of *Irasi,* make dwell, thus to be placed in the condition

of making dwell, = to be (somewhere). — *Mo sükoshi irasare-mase* (low language: *irakkai masi*), stay a little longer. — *Yoku irasare-masita*, you are well placed, = you are welcome. — *Sate, hisabisa ikaga de irasare maru*, come on, how have you been this long time. — *Ikaga de irasare-* (vulg. *irakai-*) *masu?* how do you do?

8. Iraserar)e, uru, to be placed in the state of dwelling, = to be. — △ *Go ka-nai sama wa ikaga de iraserare* (vulg. *irakai*) *masu?* how are your family? — △ *Kwa hen-* (火ろ邊に) *ni iraserare-mase*, be near the fire (come near the fire). — *Itsi bat i rai* (一て別テ以て來?) *ikaga de iraserare-musita?* since our last separation, how have you been?

§ 113. I. Tama)vi, vu, △ Tamai, Tam)au, oo, 賜 シ, タ, 給, to bestow, grant, give, when the giver belongs to a higher sphere. Although the Japanese themselves reduce this word to *Tama*, 玉ノ, = jewel, we take it for a compound of the old *Tabi*, = to give, and *Avi*, 合ヒ, to meet. Thence: *Mono wo motte fitō ni tamaru* [1]), literally: to confer something on a person. 祿ヲ 臣シ= タマフ [1]), *Itoku wo ko-sin ni tamavu*, (the king Zin-mu) grants incomes to his servants.

As an auxiliary verb grafted on the root of another verb, it characterizes the action as proceeding from a higher person, whether divine or princely. It is expressed by 給フ and phonetically by リ, ヒ, answers somewhat to the „please" or „have the goodness" used by courtesy, German *geruhen*, is however, at least in tales, rightly left out by the translator.

Examples:

Tedzukara kawd wo torite ko-gavi wo si-tamaru, (the princess) plucks mulberry leaves with her own hand, and feeds silkworms. — *Sono notsi Tau yori taku wo ken-ze sikōba, Mi-kari wo moyowasare, sio-teo wo torёsime-tamaru*, when afterwards falcons had been brought as presents from China, (the Japanese prince) caused hawking to come more into fashion, and had all birds caught. *Mayow)i, u,* to come into fashion. *Tor)i, u,* to take. — *N.. tatsimatsi mandsiku ndru*, N.. dies suddenly. — *Iku-fodo mo ndkū kano fimé mandsiku nar)se-tamavu*, immediately after, that lady (a princess) dies.

---

[1]) *Nippon-ki*   [1]) *Nippon wat-dai sin-run*.

CHAPTER VII. VERBS OF COURTESY. § 113.   315

軍中ニテ 御
身煩ハレクツ
崩御ナル

Kun-tsiu nite mi mi wadzurawasikusite fodo-ndku fou-kiyo si-tamaru [1], (the prince), while he is with the army, is taken unwell and dies shortly after.

Old writers have *Tabѝ*, u., = to give, instead of *Tamavi* also; thence: *Osame-tabisi toki*, = when N.. governed [2]. —

For further examples see page 270 line 11 from the bottom. — p. 230 l. 8 from the top. — p. 274 l. 20. — p. 290 l. 9 from the bottom.

II. **Tamavari**, u., △ **Tamguri**, **Tamóri**, u., the continuative form of *Tamavi*, which however supplies the place of the passive form *Tamaware*, = to be granted, not in use (compare *Nari* as substitute for *Nare*, § 100. III), and, like *Tamavi*, also as an auxiliary, is joined to the root, or to the gerund of a verb.

Kore Ten no tamaedru nari, 是天所致也, this is a present from Heaven. — *Ko-zi-ki ni Izanagi no mikoto yori Amaterasu Okon kami ve mi kubi-tama wo tamavarisi koto wo iveri*, in the book of antiquity it is mentioned, that by (the god) Izanagi a necklace was presented to the goddess of the sun. — *Kore wo mente go i ni deiyo*- (五´位ニ叙シ) *stnare*, ... *no na wo tamavari*, (the king) inviting him, raises him to the fifth rank and confers on him the name of .. — *Nuno san-byăku-tan wo Hăku-sai kok-uqu NN. ni tamavari* (賜), *ya zyu-man kon wo ... ni tamaru*, (the Jap. prince) gives three hundred pieces of silk to NN., king of Petsi, and presents (his minister) a hundred thousand arrows.

Uke-tamavari, u., △ **Uke-tamóri** (承 拳), to have the honor to receive (from a superior), or to hear. — *Triyăku wo uke-tamarari* [1] (承 勅), to receive the king's orders. — △ *Go i-ken* (御´意´見?) *wo uke-tamvatta* or *tamotta*, I have had the honor to receive your advice. — △ *Sakù-ya yuki ga furi-masita to uke-tamavari-masita*, I have had the honor to hear, that it has snowed during the night. — *Go sa-u* (御´左´右?) *uke-tamavari-tăku zonsi-măsu*, I wish to have the honor to hear, how you do. — *Ka-roo* (家ロ老?) *făni wo idasite tamavari-keri*, we (skippers are speaking) enjoy the honor, that the secretary (of the governor) has our ships cleared. — △ *Midzu wo nomasete tamóre*, = have the goodness to let me drink fresh water.

---

[1] *Nippon wau-dai itsi-ran*. I, 10.
[2]   „   „   „   I, 16

[1] *Wa-gun Surori*, under *Tamoru*.

§ 114. By **Mátsuri**, a the speaker expresses the most profound respect for the object, be it a person or a thing, that he speaks of or to. As continuative form of *Matsi* (待ツ), = to wait (compare page 219), *Mátsuri* (祭リ. 奠. 祠) means continual waiting, solemn attendance, to show respectful homage. Thence *Ten wo mutsuri, Tsi wo mátsuri*, 祀ツ先ヅ, *Sen wo mutsuri, Kami wo mutsuri*, „people do homage to heaven, to earth, to ancestors, to Kamis," by celebrating feasts to their honor, *Mátsuri* being the feast itself.

As qualifying auxiliary joined to the root of a verb, *Mátsuri* unites with it the idea of reverential homage. One says: *Fütári no kimi ni tsukaeuru* (△ tsukûru) *koto atarázu*, serving two masters is impracticable. — More respect is shown by the expression: *Kimi ni tsukaru* (△ tsukû) *mátsuru koto* [1]), to serve my prince with

上ジ
帝テ
ニ
respect. — *Zŏ-tei ni tsuko-mátsuru*, to serve the Most High reverentially [2]).

When the excessively polite speaker says to his equals: *O tomo tsukamatsuri-makon*, I will accompany you, or *O itoma tsukamotsuri-mdes*, I take leave of you, we may put down such politeness to his own account. The role requires *Tsukai-* or *Tsukae-mátsuri*, yet this, for ease in pronunciation, passes into *Tsukô-* (ツ ヅ リ) or *Tsakó-mátsuri*.

Tate-mátsuri, 奉, to offer respectfully and solemnly, from *Tate*, set upright.

Kono toki ama-bito faríkano uwo wo Ten-wau ni tate-matsuri ni koto ari [3]), it appears that, then, the divers solemnly presented a redbellied fish to the Emperor. — *Dewa kuni yori kariko wo kaou mono wo tate-matsuru* [4]), from the country of Deva persons, who breed silkworms, are solemnly presented (to the emperor). — *Tsusima yori sirokane wo tate-mátsuru* [5]), from the island of Tsusima silver is presented (to the emperor). — *Hakusai no tate-matsureru to-fŭd*, artificers, whom Hakusai had presented (to the king of Japan).

Tate-mátsuri is joined to the root of a verb, as a qualifying auxiliary, to characterize the action as respectful, solemn.

On na (御名) *wo Yamáto Takè no Mikoto mousi-tatematsuru* (申ツ率ヅマツル) *besi* [6]), your name I must respectfully call Yamáto Takè no Mikoto (compare

---

[1]) *Tsi-tsup-yeng* XIII.   [4]) Ibid. XIX.
[2]) *Yamato wa dai.* I. 21 v.   [5]) Ibid. III. 4 v.
[3]) Ibid. II. 89 r.   [6]) Ibid. I. 28.

CHAPTER VII. VERBS OF COURTESY. § 115.   317

p. 228 line 6). — *Ten-nguwo sendni tasuke-nose-tate-mdtsuri, Kavatsi ve nige-yuku* ¹), they respectfully help the emperor to mount a horse and escape to Kavatsi.

It is in earnest, not in irony, when the historian says: *Makowa no miko ukagavi kitdrite Ten-ngu wo kordsi-tate-mdtsuru* ²), prince Makowa, steals in and respectfully kills the emperor.

Tate-matsurur)e, uru, the honorary passive, honoring, in the eye of the speaker, also him who respectfully offers or presents. If in the preceding example *tate-mdtsardra* were used, instead of *tate-mdtsuru*, the speaker would show his respect towards the murderer.

The states and occupations to the qualification of which courtesy pays particular attention, and the expressions of which, to be properly appreciated, must be understood also, are: 1. Being, existence; 2. Doing; 3. Seeing, Showing; 4. Saying; 5. Giving; 6. Going and Coming. — Explanation:

§ 115. BEING.

1. The spoken language, which leaves the use of *Nari*, to be, to the book-language, instead of it uses 1. *Masi* (§ 101); 2. *Ari* (§ 90), *Ari-masi* (§ 101); 3. *Ori, Ori-masi* (§ 97); 4. *Gozari, Gozari-masi* (p. 263 *Rem.*); 5. *Soro* (§ 102); 6. *Fanberi* and 7. *Maosi.*

6. Fanber)i, u, Famber)i, u, ハンベリ, ハヘリ, of old ハムヘリ, means wait upon (侍, 陪), stay or be somewhere (在), it is expressed in the epistolary style by 候 (wait upon), and declared as equivalent to *Samurari, Soroi* (§ 102). *A. B. sa-u ni fanberite* (左゛右゛= 侍ふリテ) *mdtsuri-koto wo tori-okondru*, (the ministers) A. and B. taking the places right and left (of the sovereign), carry on the affairs of government. — *Yamira Zin-dai yori fanberi*, the bow has existed from the time of the gods. Compare page 220 line 3 from the bottom.

7. M(a)usi, u, △ Moosi, 叚, 浸, 逵, 寔, 1. to show oneself respectful; 2. 申, to mention. The way in which this word is used, requires the distinction of its two significations, although no attention is paid to it, by the Japanese, who use but one Chinese sign (申) for both.

In the former signification, as definitive or as defined part of a compound verb also, it qualifies the action as submissive, respectful: *M(a)usi-uke* is to receive respectfully; *Uke-mausi* on receiving to show oneself submissive. The

---

¹) *Nippon wou-dai itsi-ran.*   ²) Ibid.

root *Mgu* seems to be the same as occurs in *Mgu-k)i*, *uru* (来朝), to come to court in solemn procession, *Mesi-mguko-* (not *ku*) *sumu* (召来), to send for a person to court, and in *Mairi*, to make a solemn entry. Japanese philologers think that this *Mausi*, „placed after the root of a verb, frequently passes into *Masi*" (§ 101) ¹).

Yamáto Takeno Mikoto Ise Dai-zin-Guu yori fou-ken wo mgusi-ukete, *Suruga no kuni made yuki-tamguru* ¹), prince Yamáto Take receives respectfully from the temple of the Great Spirit at Ise the precious sword and departs to the country of Suruga. — Δ *Kaki-tome-mguru beki ya* (書留可申ya), if I shall take a note of it? — *Sa-yyu naraba O wakare moosi-* (= *masi*) *masu*, as it is so, I take respectful leave of you; the ordinary expression for our: Farewell! — *Ori wo motte On tsikadzuki ni nari-mousi-taku-son-zite, tada ima-made yen-in mgusi soro*, wishing for an opportunity humbly to come in contact with you, I have only delayed it till now. — Δ *O kandri-mousi-soro hitó wo mi-mousi soro*, I see the man of whom you speak.

§ 116. DOING is expressed by

1. S)i, u, uru, to do (§ 103), Si-mas)i, u, to be doing (§ 101).
2. Itas)i, u, Itasi-más)i, u, to accomplish (p. 284 *Rem.*), more stately than Si.
3. Asobas)i, u, the causative form ⁴) of *Asob)i, u* (遊), to play, to be amused (*Suru yeda ni asobu*, the ape is playing among the branches), and further the honorary passive *Asobasar)e, uru* (被遊), to take pleasure in any occupation, are used both for the qualification of what persons of rank do. See page 237 line 5.

Δ *Go ki-gen yoku asobasi-soro*, His Honor's disposition (cast of mind) is good. — *Kore wo asobimesi asobasi-soro*, Your Honor means this. — *Kono hoo ye On-ide asobasaru beku soro*, literally: may your outgoing be to this side, for: please come to my house. — *O noki asobasare!* please to go back (or out of the way)!

¹) *MASU ga-bi ni tsúkete iru wo shukte MACSU no rippata nari.* — *Wa-yun Sioreri*, under *Masu*.

²) *Yamato no dai. I. 83 v.*

³) According to the *Wa-yun Siworri*, *Asobaru* is a contraction of 遊ばせる, *Asobi-naru*. — „*Asuihe yori*," so it adds, „*Ki-nin koto wo nasawaru wo kaku iueri*," it is an old custom to designate by this word the doing of noble persons.

CHAPTER VII. VERBS OF COURTESY. § 117.   319

§ 117. SEEING and SHOWING.

1. **Mi, Mite, Miru** (§ 99 n°. 34), to see. — *Sina wo miru koto wa deki-masu ka?* can I see your goods? ¹). — *Watákusi wa kasuka ni fune wo mi-masu*, I see ships in the distance. Do they say for it really in Yédo *Watakusi wa kas'kani fune ga mie-maru* or *mieru?* i. e. I — the ship comes in view.

2. **Mis)e, eru,** to show. — *Bun-ko wo O mise!* ¹), let me see a desk, or in the more round-about language of Miyako: *Bun-ko wo Go ken* (御 ＊ 見 ゼ) *wo kudasare mase.*

3. **Pai- (Hai-) ken,** 拝 ゜ 見 ゼ, to look on with respect, with interest. — *Kore wo hai-ken itdsi-masu*, or *hai-ken tsakamdtsari-soro*, I have the honor to see it.

4. **O me ni kak)e, eru,** 御 ＊ 目 ゜ 掛 ゼ, = to bring a thing under Your Honor's notice, to show a thing.. — *Nani wo O me ni kake-makoo ka?* ¹), what shall I show Your Honor?

5. **O me ni kakar)i, u,** = to appear before His or Your Honor's eyes. — *Miyoo-niti O me ni kakari-makoo* ¹), = to morrow I shall come under your notice, I shall let myself be seen by you, I shall call upon you. — *Tadai ma hazimete O me ni kakari masita* ¹), it is for the first time that I come under your notice, = it is for the first time that I have the honor to see you.

6. **Go-ran** (御 ＊ 覧 ゼ), the glance of a noble person.

Go-ran-s)i, u, uru, to honor with a glance. — *Ten-wqu no on fara wo-tiygu wo ik-ken Go-ran-* (一 ッ 見 ゼ 御 ＊ 覧 ゼ) *zite, kokóro yoku, warasi-tamawu* ¹), the mother of the emperor, at the first glance upon the prior, becomes glad of heart and smiles.

In the familiar style of speaking and writing the speaker applies *Go-ran* to his equals, to show them respect. — *Kore wo Go-ran-serare*, or *Go-ran nasare*, please look at this. — *Nani wo Go-ran nasóru ka?* ¹), what are you looking at, what do you wish to see? the shopkeeper asks his customer. — *Nani de gosari-masu ka? itte Go-ran nasure*, go and see what it is.

§ 118. SAYING. The idea of saying is expressed by

1. **Iv)i, u, I)i, u** (云), **Ii-mas)i, u.** — *Anata no O na wa nanito ii-masu ka?* what is your name? — *Watakusino nawa ... to ii-masu* ⁴), my name is ...

¹) *Shopping-Dialogues*, p. 23.   ²) Ibid. p. 8.   ³) Ibid., p. 1.   ⁴) Ibid. p. 18.
⁵) L. BROWN, Coll. N°. 1048.   ⁶) *Nippon wau-dai itsi-ran*, II. 15 v.
⁷) *Shopping-Dialogues*, p. 1.   ⁸) Ibid. p. 19.

2. Nori-tamav)i, u, to order, when speaking of the master (see § 107, p. 290 l. 15).

3. Osiy)e, u, uru, 教え, 之, pron. ossy)e, s, uru, to teach, to communicate a thing (*jito ni koto wo*) to a person by teaching, places him who makes the communication above him, who receives it. — *Ware ni* (not *wore wo*) *osiye yo* (教え, 我), = teach me or communicate to me, sounds modest; *Anata ni osiye-mdsu*, = I teach you or communicate to you, is considered presumptious. — *Tami ni takahási uyuru koto wo osiyesimu* [1]), (emperor Schin-nung) has the people taught ploughing and sowing.

4. Oós)e, uru, 仰せ, to charge (*jito wo koto ni*, a person with anything), see § 87 n°. 25. Thence the passive (*Oserar)e*, uru, 被仰, to be charged, instructed. To a superior one says: Δ *Anata ro sono toori ni ooserare-mas'ta ka?* have you spoken so? to an inferior: *Omae sono toori ni itta ka?* — *Oose-tsuk)e*, uru (仰付), speak to, to address. Thence the honorary passive (*Oose-tsukerar)e*, uru, 被仰付. — *Nippon ye to kai wo mo oose-tsukeraruru aida*, as or since (a. § 129, n°. 46) We (the sovereign speaks) have given orders to sail to Japan. — Δ *Tonosama kore wo oose-tsukerareta*, the master has said this to us, or charged us with it.

5. Kikas)e, oru, = *Kikasuru*, to make people hear, from *Kiki*, to hear. — *Ano O kata ni O kiki nasari,* learn from him, ask him. — *Kikasime*, old-Jap. *Kikame!* 令聞, let me hear! tell me! speaking to a nobleman. *Watakusi ni O kikase nasare!* let me hear! tell me. — *Watakusi ni O kikase nasaru koto ya dekimas'ta ka?* can you tell it me? *Fito no kokoroye ni naru koto wo i i kikaseru koto*, to tell that which tends to the interest of others.

Kikó-sim)e, uru, 使聞, to let hear.

Kikosimas)i, u, 聞召, to let hear, inform.

6. Maus)i, u, マウシ, Δ Moos)i, u, to speak respectfully to one's superior, to mention, declare; expressed ideographically by 云. 曰. 申. 白. 謁. 啓. 告. 奏. 言. [¹]). It has the definition of what is said as an Accusative, and, if it is a Substantive objective phrase, this with the particle *to* before it, whereas the more distant object, to whom or where one mentions, as Dative or Local

---

¹) *Jap. Encycl.* vol. 103, l. r.

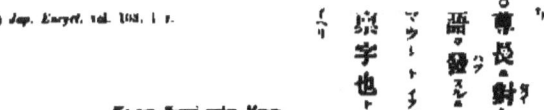

Wa-gun Siwori under *Mawo*.

preceden. — *Tsubusa ni sono koto wo mausi-soro*, I mention this minutely. — *Zooteini mansu*, 告ゲ上ゲ帝?=, to speak to God. — *Buts'ni mausite mausiku* ¹), 白佛言, = as he speaking to Buddha says. — *Mausi-tamaraku ra*, 奏シ許スヲカン ²), a (the prince to the emperor) says. — *Nagaku Nippon no yatsko to narite, midsuki-mono wo sadzuku besi to maosu*, he declares that he will always be the servant of Japan, and pay tribute. — △ *Sore wa Nippon de wa nani to moosi-masu ka?* ³), what is this called in Japan?

It *Mausi* is used as a root, on which another verb is grafted, it is expressed thereby, that the action is confined to the speaking or saying, e. g. *Sadame*, to define; *Mausi-sadume*, to defined with words; *Age*, to raise; *Mausi-ag)e*, *uru*, 申上, = to say towards above, to communicate to a superior; *Moosi-ire*, 申入, proposition to one's equal. — *Nandziye* (or *Nandzi ni*) *ko-kan wo motte moosi-ire-soro*, I have the honor to inform you by letter. — *Yaku-nin ye mausi-tassu-beni*, notice shall be given of it to the officers.

§ 119. GIVING.

1. As from courtesy the speaker places the person addressed above him, even if he is his equal, he qualifies his own giving as an upward movement, and the giving of another as a downward one; he uses *Ag)e*, *uru*, to reach upwards, in opposition to the honorary passive *Kudasar)e*, *uru*, to be let down from on high, to descend (page 241 line 22), and since from this distinction it appears who gives, the speaker or the person spoken to, the express mention of a pronoun in connection with these and similar verbs is superfluous, as the following examples show:

△ *Dai-kin wo age-mōsō kara, uke-tori-gaki wo kadasare* ¹), after I have paid you the price give me a receipt. — *Dai-kin wa agararani* (or *agesare-masdas*) ²), = the price will not be reached upward to you by me, = I will not pay the price. — *Dai-kin wa tadaima kudasaru ka?* ³), will you give me the money for the goods immediately? — *Tadaima kudasaru koto wa deki-masenu ku?* ⁴), cannot you give (it) me immediately? — *Anata-suma yori kudasareta kane itsi-pu mo tsukai wa itasimasenu*, of the money given by Your Honor - it is a Japanese grisette who writes it — I have not yet spent one bu.

¹) *Kousaku*, ur § 107.   ²) *Nippon-bi*. Vol. VII. 14 r.   ³) n. seoux, Coll. N°. 346.
²) *Shopping-Dialogues*, p. 14.   ³) Ibid. p. 13.   ⁴) Ibid. p. 13   ⁷) Ibid. p. 13.

2. **Sasag)e, uru** (from *Sasi*, to show, and *Age*, to raise), 捧. 棒. 擎, holding a thing up, to present to a person in a higher station.

Sinra wo tsukai N.N. kitatte mitsuki wo sasagu [1]), N.N. ambassador of Sinra comes and solemnly offers presents (to the emperor). — *Tanba no kuni yori kuroki kitsune wo sasigu* [2]), a black fox from the country of Tanba is offered (to the emperor).

3. **Kudasare**, joined to the root or to the gerund of a verb, characterizes the action as one proceeding from the person spoken to. It sounds more courtly than *Nasare* (§ 100. IV. 5).

O kai kudasare (vulgo *kudasai*), or *kudasare-mase*, or *O kai nasare!* please to buy. — The chapman: *San-byaku me de kudasare!* 三ミ百ゞ目ᴬ出ʳ 下ゞレ [3]), please to pay 30 taels! The buyer: *Ni-byaka me de agemakoo*, I will give you 20 taels. — *Doozo mioo-nitsi O ide* (御ᵗ 出ヂ) *kudasare!* please to come to-morrow! — *Tsibadzuki ni O nori* (御ᵉ 成ゞ) *kudasare!* [4]), please to approach him, « allow me to present him to you. — *O kamai kudasaru na* [5]), take no pains. — *Mo sukósi nemusite kudasare* [6]), please to set the price somewhat higher. — *Goḱ yasuku-site kudasaru nara, nokordzu kai-makoo* [7]), if you give it as cheap as possible, I will buy all.

Remark. For Kudasari, v see § 87 N°. 10.

4. **Tsuk)é, uru**, 付ヂ, to add to, expresses the idea of giving, without any boast. In ⊿ *O tsuké nasare!* please give it me! *Tsuke* has reference to the speaker and the honorary passive *Nasare* to the person spoken to.

5. **Torasim)e, uru**, also **Toras)e, uru**. That the expression: „to give order to take" places the person ordered beneath the one who orders is self-evident. —

風ゞ百ゞ官ᵗ仁ヒ義ゞ ノノ札ゞ ヲゞ 物ゞヲ 賜ヂヲ

Fyak-kwan ni sin, gi rei, tsi, sin no fuda wo torasimete mono wo tamawa [1]), the emperor orders the assembled officers to take tablets, on which one of the words humanity, justice etc. is written and thereby bestows gifts.

6. **Yar)i, u**, 遣ヂ, to cast, throw, send (*fito ni mono wo*, to send a thing to some one); it humbles the receiver. — *Tsukai wo O yari nasare*, please send me a message. — *Kono mono ni kane itsipu yare!* give that person one *bu!*

---

[1]) *Yamato nen-dai.* III. 8 v.   [4]) Ibid. III. 6 r.   [7]) *Shopping-Dialogues*, p. 88.
[2]) *Shopping-Dialogues*, p. 19.   [5]) Ibid. p. 81.   [8]) Ibid. p. 88.
[3]) Ibid. p. 80.   [6]) *Yamato nen-dai.* III. 6 v.

§ 120. GOING and COMING are expressed by

1. **Mairu**, n, solemn entry, to enter (a palace or temple) in solemn procession. 参, 参, 詣, 入, 参入, 参納. From *Mai*, *Maa*, to walk in procession, to hold a stately procession, and *iri*, u, to enter. The definition: whither one goes or where one enters, precedes, characterized by *ye*, *wo* or *ni*.

Ten-mu unadzuite O-mae ve mairu [1]), prince Ten-mu, yielding, waits upon His Highness (the Mikado). — *Kau-rai mo .. Go tsin* (御￫陣￬) *ni mairite fri-fuku su* (平ケ伏ザ) [1]), also they of Corea come into the imperial camp and submit themselves.

In the familiar style of speaking and writing *Mairi* is used instead of *Kitari*, to come, if one's own coming to the person spoken to is meant, even if one is on an equality with him. If the pronoun of the first person is wanting, by *Mairi* it is indicated that the speaker means his own coming to the person spoken to. — Δ *Watakusi sina wo mi ni* (or *kai-mono ni) maitta* (來ラマ), I have come to you to look at (or to buy) goods. — Δ *Watakusi kono fitó wo tsurete maitta*, I have brought this man with me. (*Shopping-Dial*. 18). — Δ *Firu-maye ni wo mairi ye-* (行ク得ス) *masimu*, I cannot come before noon. (*Sh.-Dial*. 17).

2. **Mairar)e**, uru, if it occurs, is used by the speaker, instead of *Mairi*, by way of an honorary passive, from respect towards the person who comes.

3. **Mairas)e**, uru, cause to enter solemnly, cause a thing to enter solemnly, i. e. to send a thing to a person in a high station, to offer a thing solemnly. 進. 上. 獻. The giver humbles himself, and raises the receiver.

4. **Mairasar)e**, uru (passive of *Mairasi*), to be admitted with solemnity. — An example from NODA. § 105: *S. Joan Baptista Jesu Christoni Baptisma wo sadzuke-mairasareta* or *Sadzuke-tatematsurareta*, S. J. B. was solemnly admitted to the administration of baptism to J. C. — Here by *Mairi* the giver of the baptism is placed beneath the recipient, whereas the passive form *mairasareta* expresses the respect of the speaker towards the giver.

5. **Ide, Idzuru** (出ズ), to come out of, to appear, and

6. **Agar)i**, u (上ル), to come up, rise, are applied only to a person beyond the speaker. The former points to the beginning, the latter to the duration of the action. *Fi no ide* is sun-rise, *O ide* (御￫出ズ), the rising, the appearing of persons beyond the speaker, His or Your coming. — *O ide nasaru* (御出成),

---

[1]) *Nippy i coo-dai sio-ran* II. page 4 r.   [2]) *Yamato san-dai*. I. 66 r

- Your or His rise takes place, i. e. you or he comes. — *Yoku O ide nasare*, or *nasare-mase*, or, abbreviated, *Yoku O ide!* — be welcome! — *O ide nasarei kasi!* oh that he came! — *Dokoni O ide nasaruka?* whither are you going? — △ *Kono mitsi wo O ide nasare-mase*, go this way. — *Idzuku ye* (or *Idzuku yori*) *O ide nasare-masu?* whither are you going (or whence are you coming? — *Watakusi to isho ni* (— 与 所 ㇾ 与) *O ide nasare-mase*, go with me.

O ide also takes the place of the auxiliary verb *Ari, Ori* or *Iri* (§ 96, 97, 98), in connection with a precedent gerund. — *Tasikā ni sirite (tite) O ide nasare-mdsuka?* ¹), do you, or does he know it certainly? — *O ki wo tsukete, mite O ide nasare!* ¹), fix your attention on it and see! — *Atsira ni matte O ide nasare!* ¹), wait there! — *Akari wo motte O ide nasare*, bring a light. — *O agāri* (御 ⁰ 上 ⁴) *nasare*, i. e. may your coming take place, says a merchant for: come in! (*SA.-Dialogues* 1).

Taken in an ample sense, by another's coming the speaker understands a meeting, a concession to the speaker's wish, e. g.: *Sake wo age-maśoo ka?* may I offer you sake? — *Iri gitoo*, no I thank you. — *Nazeni O agari nasaranu ka?* = why do you not rise? for: why don't you concede, — why do you refuse? (*Shopping-Dialogues* 21).

Agarasar)e, u, uru, to be raised, from *Agarasi*, to make rise, and this from *Agari*, to rise. The passive form, for honor's sake used in deference instead of *Agari*; also **Agarasarar)e**, uru.

7. **Makār)i**, u, evidently a continuative verb and as I think derived from *Mak)i*, u, = to leave off (§ 106), means a continual leaving off of work, i. e. to have furlough (Hd. *Urlaub*) or vacation, to be out of service for a time; to go on furlough ⁴). It was formerly used for people in service, who left the capital to go elsewhere for a time, on a visit. It is expressed by 罷. 退. 往. 去. 辞. 向. 至. 就, and must be distinguished from *Makar)e*, eru, to be sent away, the pass. of *Mak)i*, u.

日 俊 辞 *Yamáto fime mikoto ni makari-mousi-tamarite iraku* ⁵), (prince
姫 于 Yamáto take) paying a visit to (the priestess) Yamáto fime
命 (at Ise) says ... — △ *Watakusi wa omae no kata ni makarou*,
or *makari-maśoo*, I shall come and visit you.

¹) s. BROWN, *Coll Jap.* N⁰. 16   ²) Ibid. N⁰. 34.   ³) Ibid. N⁰ 88.
⁴) *MAKARU to wa hito sumite uma ha wo siriseru koto nari.*   ⁵) *Nippon-ki* VII. 16. r.

When the chapman says: *Sono ne de wa makari-masinu*, – for that price I will not come to you, he declares that he is not willing to sell for that price. – *Aru tokoroni uikari-aru*, to be somewhere on leave, to be somewhere; to be there for a time, but not definitely. – *Bu-zi ni makari ari-masu*, ≈ he finds himself for a time at ease, it is well with him. – That *Makari* is, at the same time used for „to die" will, our derivation considered, not appear strange.

Placed before another verb it seems to unite with it the idea „of furlough, on a visit only for a time." – *Mioo-nitsi makari iden besi*, possibly I may just call on you to morrow. – *Makari* therefore indicates discretion, politeness.

8. **Tsiki-dsuki**, u, 近づく, to come into the neighborhood. — *Hiru tomosii ni tsikō-dzuku*, the night moth comes in contact with the lamp-light. Thence *Tsikō-dzaki*, an acquaintance, one known. — *O tsikōdzaki ni nari-masu*, I become your acquaintance, I make acquaintance with you. – *O tsikōdzaki ni nari-masite yoro-kobi-mōsu*, it is agreeable to me to have become acquainted with you.

The going out of the Mikado is called **Mi-yuki-s**)i, u, uru, or 行幸 *Gigo-ggo-s*)i, u, uru, or *ligo-ggo-ari*, to spread happiness in going; on the other hand the going out of the Tai-kun, 御成 *O nari*.

Ten-wau N. kuni ni gigu-ggu-su [1])*, the emperor repairs to the country of N. — *Ten-tsi Ten-wau aru-taki yama-simo ye gigu-ggu arite, kaheri tamaedzu, Ten ni nobori tamacu ni ya?* [1])*, the emperor Ten-tsi once went into the mountains and did not return. Should he have gone to Heaven?

Nippon wa-dai iti-ran II. 10 r.   [1]) Ibid II. 4 r.

CHAPTER VIII.

CONJUNCTIONS.

§ 121. As the relation indicated by conjunctions, in which propositions stand to one another, is either a coördination or a subordination, Grammar distinguishes coördinative and subordinative conjunctions. Consequently we arrange the Japanese conjunctions as follows:

A. COÖRDINATIVE CONJUNCTIONS.

I. Copulative conj.

1. Mo, ..mó, ..mó.
2. Mata, ..mo mata.
3. Katsu, Katsu va.
4. Oyobi.
5. Narabi ni.
6. Kanete.

II. Disjunctive conj.

7. Aruiva.
8. Matava.
9. ..ka, ..ka.
10. ..ya, ..ya.
 ..yara, yaran.

III. Adversative conj.

11. Mottomo.
12. Nagára, ..ga (..nga).
13. Sikasi-nagára, Sikasi.
14. Sari- (San-) nagára.
15. Yavari.

IV. Conclusive conj.

16. Kono-yuý ni. Sore-kara. Kore ni yotte.
17. Sore de, Sore de wa, Soo wa.
18. So site, So goto.
19. Sáte.
20. Sunavatsi.

V. Explanatory conj.

21. Kedási.
22. Tadási.
23. Anzuru ni.

CHAPTER VIII. CONJUNCTIONS. § 121, 122.   327

B. SUBORDINATIVE CONJ., GOVERNING THE ADVERBIAL PROPOSITION THAT PRECEDES.

I. Conjunctions of place and time.

24. Tokóro, Baśo.	27. Setsu.	31. Ma-ma.	35. Noisi.
25. Tokóro ni,	28. Migiri.	32. Aida.	36. Yori.
△ Tokúro de.	29. Utai.	33. Uyé.	37. Kara.
26. Toki.	30. Mo.	34. Mave, Mayé.	38. Made.

II. Conjunctions of quality and manner.

a. *Comparative*,   b. *Proportional conj.*

39. Toóri ni. 40. Yęu ni. 41. Gotó)si, ki, ku.   42. Fodo, Fodoni.

III. Conjunctions of causality,

a. *used in the notice of an actual cause.*

43. Yuf ni.   44. Kara.   45. Ni yotte, Aida, Tsuki, Tsuite.

b. *Conjunctions used in the notice of a possible, i. e. a future and thus an uncertain cause (Conditional conjunctions).*

46. Naraba, Nara, *in connection with* Moukóvá, Mosiva, Mosi.

IV. Conjunctions of the purpose.

47. Tamé ni.   48. Tote.

V. Conjunctions of concession.

49. ...mo.	52. ...hidomó.	55. Sikamo.
50. ...tomo.	53. Sikaredomo, Saredomo.	56. Somo-samo.
51. ...domo.	54. Soredemo.	57. Mamayo.

The relative comparative of propositions. 58. ...yori va musiro.

Explanation.

A. COÖRDINATIVE CONJUNCTIONS.

I. Copulative or coördinative conjunctions.

§ 122. 1. ...mo, 亦 °, adverbial suffix, = too, also, Lat. *que, quoque*, characterizes the word which precedes, either subject or object of the proposition, as added to, or made equivalent to another subject or object already mentioned.

Kore, this;   *Kore mó,* this too; even this.
Kore wo, this, him;   *Kore wo mó,* him too.

328   CHAPTER VIII. CONJUNCTIONS. § 122.

As suffix to an interrogative pronoun it contains all that is included in the interrogative, as individuals together. *Dare*, who? (Lat. *quis?*) — *Dare mó*, whoever (Lat. *quisque*). See page 102.

It characterizes the concessive proposition. See § 131 n°. 50.

..*mó*, ..*mó*, both.. and.., as well.. as also.., not alone or not only, but also.. — *Kaze mó nami mo sidzumarazu*, — both wind and waves do not abate, — neither wind nor waves become still.

扇ヲ 周ノ 武王ツクリタマフトモ (*Aógi* (Δ *Óugi*) wa, Ziyuu tsukuri-tamau tó mó mata Bu-wau tsukuri-tamau tó mó ieri* [1]), — concerning the fan, it is said that (*to*) Seihun has made it, as also that (*to*) Wŭ-wang has made it.

2. Mata, 又ta, 亦ta, twig, something that is double: an adverbial conjunction — too, and, moreover (*mou hitó*), likewise, or also, unites both coordinate names and equivalent propositions, and refers to the word or proposition that follows it. *Anáta no kinu-mono* mata *momen-mono it-tan no nagasa wa ikura ari-másu ka!* [2]), what is the length (and) breadth of one piece of your silk- and cotton goods? *K'e-ori wa kane-zak* mata *ken wo motsii-másu* [3]), for woolen goods the iron foot is used as also the *ken* (an ell of 6 feet).

Mata (亦ta) refers to the predicate in propositions like:

不亦説乎 *Manainde toki ni kore wo narau* mata *yorokobashikarazu ya!* [4]), to learn a thing (and) practise it continually, is this not agreeable too?

..*mó* mata, likewise. If the subject as well as the predicate of a proposition is made equivalent to the subject and predicate of a precedent proposition, the sameness of the subject is expressed by the suffix *mo*, and that of the predicate by the adv. *mata* (亦); thence the formula ..*mo mata*..

Kono futá fasirano kami mó mata.. *mi-mi wo kákusi tamáiki*, also (*mo*) both these gods kept themselves likewise (*mató*) concealed. Compare page 225.

At the beginning of a proposition *Mata* points to the equality of its contents with that expressed in the preceding proposition. — *Mata* (又) *andta no kou ni sa-tou ari-másái nará*, *sore wo kai-makou* [5]), and if you have sugar, I will buy it.

---

[1]) *Kauirogoki*. VIII. 2 r   [2]) *Shopping-Dialogues*, p. 38.   [3]) Ibd p 18
[4]) *Lun-yu*, Cap. I   [5]) *Shopping-Dialogues*, p. 40

CHAPTER VIII. CONJUNCTIONS. § 122.   329

3. **Katsu**, 且多, isolated by *ni* or *wa* also **Katsu wa**, **Katsu wà**, = and also, moreover, Lat. *quoque*, continuative conj., characterizes the proposition or the part of the proposition that follows it, as an addition to the precedent clause.

親多且多商多貿, *Kon-sin katsu šoo-bai* [1], friendship and trade.
有ヲ耻ヲ且多格ヲ, *Fudzi arite kitau itaru* [1], people grow ashamed and come to perfection.

Katsu mata, 且亦, moreover also, then so much the more.
Katsu-katsu, = moreover and moreover, all and all.

4. **Oyobi**, 及ビ, reach to, as conj. to and with, inclusive, unites two objects removed from each other, comprising the series of similar things between them. It is a synonym of „*ni itaru made* or „*yuki-tsukite*, = coming to..., and of *Made mô*. (See § 62, n°. 26).

The stipulation that Japan shall appoint consuls and commercial agents abroad, is expressed in the Treaty of 1858, Art. 1 al. 4, by:

締ヲ取ヲ締ヲ役ヲ人ニ及ビ貿易ヲ勉ムヲ處ニ頂ク役ヲ人ニ任ズ。

5. **Narabi ni**, 並ビニ, besides, also, from *Narabi*, *n.* to place oneself neat, joins substantives and propositions. *Morokosi narabini Bun-yo ni itasu-taru mono*, a person versed in the Chinese as also in foreign languages. — *Nippon no kome narabi ni Nippon no mugi* [1], Japanese rice and Japanese wheat.

At the beginning of a proposition *Narabi ni* is met with e. g. in Art. VII al. 2 of the said Treaty, containing the stipulation: „And these buildings shall not be injured," after the building of churches is conceded in the previous proposition.

6. **Kanete**, 兼ネ而, 兼ヲ, at the same time, gerund of *Kane*, to take with or together, to comprehend, comprise, embrace, characterizes an apposition. — *N.N., Bungo no kami kanete Nagasaki Go-Bu-gioo*, N.N., prince of Bungo and governor of Nagasaki.

II. Disjunctive conjunctions,

between propositions that reciprocally exclude or may supersede each other.

§ 123. 7. **Aruiwa, Aruiwa**, 或ハ、, contr. of *aru iru wa*, = as someone says [1], separates, with the signification of or, or also, substantives and propositions

[1] Netherl.-Jap. Treaty of 1858, in the beginning [2] Lun-yu. II. 3. [3] Treaty. II. 19.
アルイハ 有人ノ略ナルベシ 又一ヒ謝ヒノ義 *Ka-gen Sintori, under Aruiwa*.

which may take the place of each other. — *Kono figiri aruiwa sono i-zen nite mo* ¹), at this date or earlier.

Aruiwa repeated has the power of exclusion. — *Aruiwa kono figiri, aruiwa sono i-zen*, either at this date, or earlier.

8. **Mata va, Mata wa**, the *mata* isolated by *ra*, = or also, then well. The „or" in „consul or consular agent" is expressed in the Treaty Art. I. al. 2 by 又ヲ、 *mata ra*. — 日ヲ本ヱ貫¹官ヲ又ハ委¹任ノ役ヲ人ヲ、 *Nippon ki-kwan mata ra (-nin no' yaku-nin* ²), Japanese officers of rank or also commissioners. — *Andta wa Eyeres mata ra Oran-mo-ziwo O kaki ka?* ³), do you write English or Dutch?

9. **..ka**, 默ヤ、耶、乎, as suffix and pronounced with emphasis, original characteristic of the direct question; e. g.: *Fud kd?* a man? *Ara ka?* is there? *Ari!* there is!

In alternative propositions repeated as a suffix, ..ka, ..ka, takes the place of our disjunctive either.., or.., Germ. *entweder.., oder*... — *Yama ka? Kumo ka? touku-zite siru-koto nasi*, = whether mountain? or cloud? being far off I cannot know it. — *Sore ka ardna ka?* (是耶非耶), is it so, is it not so? — △ *Sore ka, kore ka koi to iye!* tell that or this (one or the other) to come! ⁴).

Remark. In my opinion, *ka* gets its disjunctive power from its original quality of an interrogative particle. *Sore* and *kore* are thus characterized by *ka* as undetermined points of interrogation. Besides the alternative question: is it so or not? is expressed by two coördinate questions, of which one as well as the other closes with the interrogative particle *ka*, thus *Sa-yoo de dri-ındsa ka? Sa-yoo de ari-masina ka?* = is it so? is it not so? The question: Is it silk or woolen stuff? sounds in the spoken language: *Kinu-mono de dri-másu kd? ke-ori de dri-másaka?* ⁵) = is it silk stuff? is it woolen stuff? If this alternative question is put, without any modification, dependent on the subsequent *to omóu* (= to think that), or of *to toru* (= ask if), the expression is obtained: to think that, or ask if it is silk or woolen stuff. Thus, when ..*ka*, ..*ka* answers to our dis-

---

¹) Treaty. XI. 1 ²) Ibid. IX. 6.

³) *Slopping-Dialogues*, p. 16. The original has *O bak i te* for *O baki-mi´mi te*.

⁴) Compare COLLADO, p. 59 lin. 7 from the bottom. „*Pedro ca Ioen ca con to iye*. dic quod vraiat Petrus vel Joannes."

⁵) *Shopping-Dialogues*, p. 16.

junctive either..., or..., it is because the questions themselves are disjunctive or alternative.

Since *Oôkata* means „for the most part, in general" (see page 175 n°. 44), *Oôkata sayoo de gozári-makoo, oôkata sayoo de gozári-másń-mai* of course also means „In general it may be so, in general it may not be so," for which we are used to say: „It may be so, in general, or it may not." Consequently the disjunctive character in those two propositions is not expressed by *Oôkata*, but by the mere antithesis of the propositions themselves ').

10. ..*ya*, や, disjunctive suffix '), = or, Lat. *vel, sive.* — *Ta ya sono va fúrubitári*, garden or field has become old; in the spoken language: *Ta ya sono ga fúrubita.* — *Dzu-kin ya kása wo nuku*, to take off kerchief or hat. — *Siba ya òdòro wo motte seki wo tsakúra*, to make mats of underwood or thorns. — *Hanasí ya warái koye*, noises of talking or laughing.

Also *ya* is, just as *ka*, properly the closing particle of a question, it may be simple or disjunctive, and as that about which a question is put, is uncertain, this particle is also called *ikayuru utagai no ya*, i. e. the so called *ya* of uncertainty." — *Ano fito wá kitáru ya?* is he coming? — *Sikára ya, ina ya?* is it so, or not? — *Mikado kí-an ni másu ya? ina ya?* '), — is the Mikado at his ease or not? = how does the Mikado?

Asa yúru ni ' uyá ni kan-kau (孝を行き) ' suru fito wá
Kami ya Fotoke no ' megumi aru besi.

He who early and late does his duty towards his parents,
Shall have the grace of the gods and of Buddha.

Yara, properly *Yaran*, = *Ya + aran*, if there shall be? — ..*sama ga kuru de arau yara, wotdkwai ra níaggute óra*, I doubt if Mr. N. will come. — *Idzure no koto yara sírarezu*, it is not known what matter it is. — △ *Fitó yara tsiku-boo yara sírazu* '), whether it is a man or a brute — I do not know.

III. Adversative conjunctions.

§ 124. 11. *Mottomo* (improperly expressed by 尤も、尤), though, although, adversative or properly concessive conjunction, originally *Mótte mó*

') Compare a. shown, *Coll. Jap.* Li. line 6 from the bottom.
') 言之、間也. *Wagun Soori*, under *Ya*   ') *Nippon-ki.* XXVI. 9
') Borrowed from COLLADO. pag. 60

332   CHAPTER VIII. CONJUNCTIONS. § 124.

(以をて), = with (this) also, modified for vocal harmony *Motto mo*, is put, in my opinion, elliptically for *Sore wo mότte mό*, = with all this.., though, on the other hand. An example:

引き達し挙し | 尤も外し國人互ノ取リ | 彼ヲ所ヲ外ヲ(向)フ | ○軍用ノ物ハ日本ヲ

Gun-yoo no io-buts wa Nippon yaku-jo no jokέ uri-bakardes. **Mottomo gwai-koku-sin togai no tori-jiki wa sasi-tomai-aru koto nasi** [1]), munitions of war may be sold to the Japanese government exclusively. That foreigners take such from one another will not, however be noticed. — By *Motte* as it appears from this example, the contents of the previous proposition are resumed, whereas the suffix *mo* stamps them as conceded. That the proposition following *Mottomo* contains an antithesis, is the logical consequence of the concessive character of the previous proposition. Compare § 74. The Japanese are accustomed not to distinguish the conjunction *Mottomo* from the adverb *Mottomo*, according to the old manner of writing properly *Mότomό* and ideographically expressed by 似 or 尤, = „utmost, by eminence" (see page 134), and also express the conjunction *Mottomo* by the character 尤, by which it has become a stumbling-block for many a translator. As a proof it is necessary to cite the official Dutch translation of the above mentioned article: „Oorlogsbehoeften zullen alleen aan de Japansche regeering verkocht worden en om dezelve aan vreemde natiën te verkoopen is buiten deze bepaling." — Of another article [2]) also, in which the description of the tedious manner of examining goods is followed by: 尤取調方格別外ニ時日ヲ費サルベシ, i. e. the examination, however, shall take place without any extraordinary waste of time, the Dutch translation drawn up by Japanese interpreters has „EN" (and) instead of however, whence it appears that they, misled by the Chinese character, have misconceived the force of the conjunction *Mottomo*.

Remark. The *Mottomo* occurring in *tio motto mo de ari-masu* (尤モ理デモアリマス), You are right) of the everyday colloquial language, is evidently the adverb used as a substantive, and the phrase, which is elliptical, means:

---

[1]) Treaty II. 16.
[2]) Art. III. al. 5 of the Annals or Tariff belonging to the Treaty of the 18 Aug. 1859.
[3]) *Shopping-Dialogues*, p. 13.

what you have said is incontestable. This expression is, by the by, also connected with a particular shrewd hero of antiquity, one Mr. *Mottomo* (尤), who had applied to himself the name of 道ヲ理¹, *Doo-ri*, i. e. right, reason ¹). We leave this as we find it.

12. **Nagára**, = in the midst of, whilst, properly a word expressive of relation, arisen by syncope from *Naka gara*, which for the sake of euphony has taken the place of *Naka kara* (自ヲ中ヲ), = from the midst, and has a verb in its root-form before it. *Ne-nagára*, in the midst of sleep, not: as long as one sleeps. *I-nagára uru-mono* is a person who sells, sitting: *Motsi-yukite uru mono* on the contrary, a hawker. *Nagára* is to be distinguished from *Nakara* (半ヲ中), = the half. — *Hi no nakara*, noon.

If the subsequent proposition is an antithesis to the antecedent, *Nagára* is

政ヲ 着ヲ 服ヲ 著シ equivalent to: nevertheless, yet, e. g. *So fuku wo ki-nagára matsuri-koto wo kiki-tamaru* ¹), though he wears mourning, yet he attends to affairs of government. — *Kono kuni Dai-Min ni tsudzuki-nagára, kisa aredz*, this country, though it borders on China, has (nevertheless) no elephants.

The antithesis is more emphatically expressed by *Nagára mó*.

The spoken language, which contents itself with putting *Nó* in the place of *Nára-dáke* (if possible), also retains simply *ga* (at Yedo *nga*) of *Nagára*, to which the force of but has been justly attributed ²). It is put, like *Nagára*, at the end of the concessive proposition. *Ano O kata no kokórozasi wa yoroisi gozari-masi'ta ga, matsigai-masi'ta* ¹), though his intention was good, yet he has made a mistake.

13. **Sikási nagára**, since it is so, mostly simple **Sikási**, 併ヲ, 爾, it is so, exhibits the previous proposition as conceded, and is followed by a sentence containing a statement, which must be of value equal to or more than the antecedent proposition. It is equivalent to: although, though, yet, however, nevertheless. — *Sina wo miru-koto wa deki-masu ka?* can I see your goods? — *Deki-másu*. **Sikási** (併ヲ) *koko ni te-hon-gire ga ari-másii kara, koré wo tïo-ran nasáre* ¹), yes; however as I have patterns here, please see them. — *Oke-gai ni wa jikage yori*; **sikási** (併) *amári sanusa ni aisi; mottomo do-mo re dusi-kya-sitsu ra*,

---

¹) *Wagun Siwori, under Mattomo*.   ²) *Nippon wa-dsa itsi-ran* II. 1 v.
²) a. brown, *Coll. Jap.* LV. LXII. f.   ⁴) Ibid. p. 41. N°. 313.
³) *Shopping-Dialogues*, p. 23.

finaie mo yosi '), in the breeding (of silkworms) on tubs, shadow is good, but too much cold injurious, however as soon as (the silkworms) are brought out of doors and fed there, sunshine also is good.

14. **Shri-nagara** or **San-nagara** (然さりする, 雖然, vulgo 仁然), by syncope for *Sikóri-nagóra*, = since it is so, is put at the beginning of a proposition, which contains an antithesis, and therefore is equivalent to: although it is so, notwithstanding, nevertheless. The antithesis is more decidedly expressed by **Sari-nagara mó** or **Sikási-nagara mó**. — *San-nagóra* is phonetically, but not ideographically, indicated by 仁ﾀ. 次. 仁. 佗.

15. **Yavári**, 猶ﾀ. 然. 仍, however, yet, nevertheless, still. — △ *Nan-dzi ga sei-site mo, sei-sizu tomo, kare ra yavari sore wo suru de aru*, whether you forbid him or not, he will do it nevertheless.

IV. Conclusive conjunctions,

preceding the proposition, which expresses a consequence.

§ 125. 16. The adverbial expressions formed with ..yué ni, ..kare and ..ni yotte: *Kono yué ni, Karu ga yué ni. Sore yué ni*, or also simply with *Yué ni*, therefore.

Sore-kara. △ Soreda kara, Sore-ta kara, vulgo *Sosite kara*, thence, then.

Kore ni yótte, Sore ni yótte, therefore. *Sikáru ni yótte*, or *Sira ni yótte*, since it is so, therefore.

Further elucidation follows in § 120, N°. 43, 44, 45.

17. △ **Sore de**, 夫して, **Sore de wà**, so, thus, then, = *ni yótte*. — △ *Watákusi dai-zi na koto wo tásun, sore de O kike!* I communicate an affair of importance, thus listen! — *£ Sore de wá kai-masioo* '), then (as it is so) I will buy it.

△ **Soo wa**, a contraction of *Sikiku ro. Sikyu wa*, so, or in the opinion of Japanese, of 左 様 ﾞの, *Sa-yoo wa*.

左ﾞ程ﾞ! ｎ ..., *Soo wá makóri-masén* '), so I cannot consent to it, so it is not to be done. (For *Makóri* compare page 325, line 1.)

18. **Soo-site**, vulgo **So-site**, 且し, also 卆ｽ 而ｽ, *Sosite* written, contr. from *Sikyu-site*, since it is so, thus, then. See *Shopping-Dial.* page 15. Comp. *£ Soo si-masioo.* I shall do it.

') *Tama-mayo kai-fee hi-dèn*]] ﾞ) *Shopping Dialogues*, p. 10. ﾞ) Ibid., p. 8.

19. **Sáte, Sáte vá**, so, thus, a fusion of *Sikirite, Sikatte*, = (this) being so, according to some, also of 左ㇵ樣ㇼ仕レ而ㇷ *Sçu (Soo) site*, which as far as the meaning goes, comes to the same thing, placed at the beginning of a proposition, expresses a consequence, even if the idea, from which the consequence flows, is not expressed as in: „So then the day approaches, on which" etc. — *Sate* is expressed by 則, sometimes also by 偖.

20. **Sünavatsi**, modified for vocal harmony from *Sunáo-tsi* (正直路), = the right way; adverbially: right, directly (Germ. *geradewegs*); conjunctively: consequently, is placed at the beginning of the subsequent proposition, which expresses the consequence. It is also used with the power of *videlicet*, to wit 則, 即, 乃, 迺, 便, 即便.

則ㇲㇳ○知ㇽ所ㇼ 近ㇱ先ㇳ 迪ㇼ彼ㇲ 矣 *Sen-kon-suru tokoro wo sireba, sûnaotsi mitsi ni tsikdsi*¹), if one knows what precedes and what follows (if one knows the cause and effect), then one is near the path of wisdom. — 安ㇴ政ㇵ 五ㇳ年ㇱ即ㇳ千ㇵ八ㇲ百ㇲ五ㇳ十ㇺ八ㇲ年ㇱ, the Vth year of Ansei, consequently the year 1858 ²).

V. Explanatory conjunctions.

§ 126. 21. **Kedasi**, 蓋ㇾ, = namely, for, though, Lat. *nam*, at the beginning of a sentence, which explains the proposition preceding, mostly giving a reason. — *Yun-dzuka wo nigiri to iru. Kedasi tana-kokoro ni nigiru no tokoro nari*, the hilt of a bow is called *nigiri* (hilt); it is the place at which it is held with the hand though.

The shade of doubt ascribed to *Kedasi* by some philological Japanese is with justice, not admitted by others.

22. **Tadasi**, 但ㇱ, = properly, devoid of other definitions, forsooth, is placed at the beginning of proposition, which explains a preceding assertion by a particular circumstance and generally confines it to that. It is to be distinguished from the adv. *Tada*, = only (see p. 176 n°. 66). — *You-gin ni hiyaku mai, tadasi gulden nari*, European silver two hundred *Mai*, i. e. guilders.

23. **Ansuru ni**, 按ㇲㇲルニ, = in my opinion, Remark. precedes that, which the writer has to remark on the saying of another.

---
¹) *Dai Gaku*, § 8. ²) Neth.-Jap. Treaty Art. XI. al 5.

B. SUBORDINATIVE CONJUNCTIONS, THAT GOVERN ADVERBIAL PROPOSITIONS.

I. Conjunctions of place and time.

§ 127. 24. **Tokóro**, 所ろ, or **Ba-šo**, = place, it answers to our adverbial conjunction of place where (see page 97). — △ „*Andta no sinuru tokóro de watakusi mo mata asoko ni sini-maïoo*, where thou diest, I too will die" [1]. — *Mina mina nige-sariši tokóro ni si* (or *ba-šo ni ed*) *fitóri tatte-oru*, alone to remain standing, where all have fled. — *Kari-tatete omóru tokóro no do-ma* [2], a patch of ground, where people think of breeding (silkworms).

25. **Tokóro ni**, △ **Tokóro de**, characterizes the attributive proposition by which it is preceded, also as an adverbial definition of time, and is equivalent to: whilst, as. — *Mina mina górókóbú tokóro ni, sono yo nieakú ni oo-kaze fúki-kitári-keri*, whilst everyone (on board) was full of gladness, in that night a storm suddenly arose, = every one was glad, as a storm arose etc. — *Sikóra tokóro ni*, as it is so, it being such.

26. **Toki**, 時 じ, time; **Toki vā**, **Toki ni**, **Toki ni vā** = **Tokinvā**, at the time of, when. *Mono-kuu toki ni mono-gatári sězu*, at the time of eating (when one is eating) one does not talk. — *Finó kasá dra toki rā, fiděri; tsuki no kasá dra toki ed, mik niši no uhi ame-furu to iěri*, people say that the weather becomes dry, when there is a sun-hood (a circle round the sun), and that it rains within three days, when there is a moon-hood. - *Sono tate-mono wo ... siyu-fo nado suru koto aran toki ni ra, Nippon ydku-nin kore wo ken-bun suru koto tau-zen taru běsi* [3], when it shall happen that people repair buildings... etc., Japanese officers will have to look after them. — *Sore wo suru na; muyoo ni nirn toki ra seme rarern zo*, do not do that! if it happen so, then you will be blamed, do not do it, otherwise you will be etc. - △ *Yedo e yukimasita toki Rokn-go gawa ni midzu ga masimasita* [4], when I went to Yédo, the water in the river Rokugo was high.

27. **Sótsu**, 節 せ, division of time. (See page 158). - *Tudán idzure no kaze nite mo kiriyoi nari; mottomo no-gái no sètsú ra kuwašikuraza* [5], properly one must avoid every wind; at the time of the breeding (of wild silkworms) in the open fields however, it does not matter.

---

[1] a snown. Coll. Jap. LVII.   [3] *Yama-mayu ś-dēn*. III. 1.   [5] Neth.-Jap. Treaty. II. 7.
[2] a snown. Coll. Jap. LVI.   [4] *Yama-mayu ś-dēn*. I

CHAPTER VIII. CONJUNCTIONS. § 127.

The rest of the words expressive of relation, which define time are used in the same way as *Toki*, i. e. they are preceded by the proposition governed by them in its attributive form. If they occur with a gerund preceding, they then belong, adverbially, to the subsequent principal proposition.

28. **Migiri**, 間?, street-cutting[1]), paving with flag-stones, also the stones of a staircase: fig. step, space of time. Synonym of *Shau* (n°. 27). — *Fune no tsuyāku-kan no migiri ni*, on the arrival of the ship.

29. **Utsi**, 内?, *Utsi wa*, *Utsi ni*, within; while. See page 188. — △ *Yédo ni ori-masita utsi ni*, [*on-sirō no*] *kwa-zi ga ari-masita*[2]), there was a conflagration [in the palace], whilst I was at Yédo.

30. **Ma**, 間 ゞ, 1. space, interval; 2. opportunity. — *Ikari wo orōsu ma mo naku-site, kaze ni makasete yuku*, not even having had time to drop the anchor, they drifted before the wind.

31. **Ma-ma**, 間 ゞ ゞ ゞ, **Ma-ma ni**, 1. at every place, wherever; 2. on every occasion, as often as, every time that. Repetition of *Ma* (see page 54), synonym of *lida-aida*. *Ko-tai mata ca siya-tai wo jorite* (jotte), *na-ma ni ki-seki wo uru koto ari*, at the digging up of old soils, or ground on which temples have stood, rare stones are frequently discovered. — *Kane wo utsi ma-ma ni*, as often as the bell is struck. — *Mono wo tōru ma-ma ni*, as often as any thing is taken.

Tabi-tabi ni, 度ゞゞ ニ ｰ ,
Tabi-goto ni, 毎 度, } as often as. —
Goto ni, 毎 ﾄ ,

Ya wo funditu tabi-goto ni (or *Ya no tobu goto ni*) *koyi wo tatsuru*, to call out at every shot of an arrow (or as often as an arrow flies).

32. **Aida**, 間?, while. See page 189.

33. **Uyè**, 上?, above, upon, on. See page 186.

34. **Mayè, Mayo**, 前 X, vulgo **Mai**, before. See p. 187. — „*Watōkusi no kaeru maeni site sinase*, get it done before I come back"[3]). · · · △ „*Watōkusi wa mairanu maini siyoto wo sité simai-makoo*, I shall finish my business before I return"[3]), — properly: I don't come; I first shall have done my business.

---

[1]) *Mi-giri*, contracted from *Mītsi wo kiri*, way-cutting, or as some say, from *Mizu-kiri*, = water cutting, because the row of flag-stones had at short distances from one another to step on in rainy weather is called *Migiri*. *Wo-gun Suzen*, under *Migiri*.
[2]) a. brown, Coll. Jap LVI.
[3]) Ibid. N°. 164.
[3]) Ibid. LVI.

35. Notsi, 後ニ, after. See page 187.

36. Yori, 自リ, since. — *Ame tsutsi firókuei yori kono kata*, since heaven and earth have developed themselves. — △ *Muiri-masita* (vulgo *masite*) *yori, ano tokōro wo hiraki-masita* [1]), that place has been opened, since they came.

37. Kara, 自ラ, after, see page 72. — *Watakusi-ni wa yomenu kara, tsuu-zi-kata ni tanonde, naosi-te morai-masu*, I cannot read it and thus I shall request the interpreters to translate it. — △ *Age-masu kara uke-tori-gaki wo kudasare*, after delivery by me, please give a receipt. Vulgo also with a gerund preceding. — △ *Tabete* (for *tabeta*) *kara yuki-masita* [2]), he went, after he had eaten.

38. Made, 迄ヲ, to, till. See page 192.

II. Conjunctions of quality and manner.

§ 128. *a*. Comparative conjunctions, equivalent to: like, just as, so as.

39. Toóri ni, 通リ, ニ, in the way, on the passage of... (see page 191), according to, in the way that, properly a word expressive of relation. — 例ヶ之ノ通リ ニ, *Rei no toóri ni*, according to the law. — *Andta no osiyuru toóri ni itdai-masita*, I have acted according to your direction (as you prescribed).

40. Yųu ni, △ Yoo ni, 樣ヲ ニ, in the manner of, in the way that, so that, as if [3]). — *Omóru yųu*, the meaning. — *Fitó no suku yųu ni suru*, to do as others would gladly have it. — *Kariko kard ni fanarenu yųu ni su-besi*, people must go to work so, that the silkworm be not removed from its food. — △ „*Hitti-bitó no osoreru yoo ni okonai-masita*, he behaved so, that people were afraid of him" [4]).

41. Gotó(si), ki, ku, 若シ, キ, ク, 如, to be like... (see page 100 n°. 7), is equivalent to „to be as if," when it, used without a subject, has a proposition before it, as complement. — *Aku wó komí nu mono ró wazdeai wo manúkū; tatore ba jibiki no otó ni oó-suru ga gótdosi*, whoever loves evil, draws upon himself adversity; it is, to use a comparison, as if the echo answered the sound. — *Mosi*

---

[1]) a. snows, Coll. Jap. LVII.   [3]) Ibid LVI.
[2]) Comp. page 25. *Demo pas* etc. and 131   [4]) a. snows, LVII.

sa-yçu ni yomu-beku naraba, in case one must read so. — *Mosi sa-yçu ni yomu-beki ga gotóku naraba*, if one ought to read so (which the speaker doubts).

b. **Proportional conjunctions**, which express a proportion as: in proportion to, how, — so much the.

44. **Fodo** (△ Hodo), **Fodo ni**, 程に, 程に, = in proportion to, for so far as, so much as, so much that. Comp. page 131. — *Tsikara no oyóbu fodo ni*, for so far as my strength reaches. — △ *Watákusi wa kiu-sikü-si-tai fodo ni tsukurete oru*, I am so tired, that I long for rest. — *..ra .. to iu fodo wo kotoba nari, .. is a word that says so much, as ..* — *Fisásiki fodo ooi* (△ *Hisásii hodo ooi*), = much in proportion to the long lasting, i. e. the longer, the better. — △ *(toi hodo yoi* [1]), the more, the better. — *Fisásii-kereba fisásiki fodo ooi*, the longer, the more. — *Hayákerebi haydki fodo yoi*, the sooner, the better. — *Are wa nomeba, nomu fodo kawaki ga tsuyóku ndru*, the more he drinks, the more thirsty he is.

Saru fodo ni, 爾之程ニ, 然程ニ, arisen by syncope from *Sikáru fodo ni*, = for so far as it is so, is placed at the beginning of a sentence. *Sari-fodo ni* is also met with.

III. Conjunctions of causality.

§ 129. *a.* Conjunctions of propositions, which notice an actual, past or present cause.

45. **Yúé**, 故ニ, now commonly written ゆへ, = cause; **Yúé ni**, for reason of, because, as, whereas, while, with an attributive definition preceding, which is sometimes qualified as a genitive by *ga*. — *Sore Nippon-goku wa Tsiu-kwa no tsi yori figdsi ni atáru yué ni Nit-tóu tó iwa*, the country of Japan, as it from the middle kingdom (China) lies towards the east, it bears the name (there) of the (country) to the east of the sun. — *Ten-ka ni keda-mono ooku, den-fata wo sokondeu yué ni fitó ni kari wó osiwe-tamáriki*, as many animals were upon the earth and did damage to the lands, he (a certain prince) taught the people hunting. — *Ten-ka ni midzu ooi yué ni*, as rivers are on the earth in great numbers. — *Mukási wa kinu ni mono wo kakisi yué ni, kami to iru zi ito-fen wo kakern* [2], formerly people wrote on silk; thence the character indicating paper (紙) is combined with that indicating silk (糸). — *Yúma takaki gá yué ni táttokardzu; ki dru wó mótte*

---

[1] a. **BROWN**, LVII [2] *Kosmi-goki*, VIII. 1 r.

táttosí tǒ su, on account of its height, a mountain does not deserve honor; that it bears trees, that makes it deserving of honor. — *Fitó kocchiru ga yuè ni táttokaräzu; tsí árī wā mótte táttosi tǒ su*, a person is not respectable on account of acquired bulk; having understanding, that makes him respectable.

Compounds with *Yuè ni*, placed as illative conjunctions at the beginning of a proposition:

Kono yuè ni, 居之故ニ, = therefore. *Kono yuè ni kun-si wī midzu tóka ni tsutsu sima* [1]), therefore the philosopher applies himself particularly to virtue. — △ *Sore yuè ni*, 夫之故ニ, = for such reasons, therefore.

Káru ga yuè ni, by aphaeresis for *Sikáru ga yuè ni*, = on account of its being so, since it is so, therefore, thence, Lat. *ergo*, is placed at the beginning of a proposition, which contains the consequence of a series of propositions preceding. — *Káru ga yuè ni kuni wó osámuru koto wa chi wo totonouru ni ári* [2]), therefore the management of a country depends upon the management of his own house.

44. **Kara**, 由, 自, = from, Lat. *ex* (see page 71), as an illative conjunction peculiar to the spoken language of Yédo, it characterizes the proposition it governs as the cause, from which the subsequent proposition flows.

It is sometimes also used alone with the signification of after. The verb dependent on *Kara* is used as a substantive. — *Te-hon-gire ga ari-mdsu kara, kore wo Go-ran nasare* [3]), as patterns are at hand, please see them. — △ *Kon-nitsi wa yohodo ósói kara, myau-nitsi kaheri-mansyoo* [4]), as it is too late to day, I shall return to morrow. *Osói* stands for *Osíki* of the written language. — *Hosi wa tsi-soo tóδi kara, tsíadku iniye-mdsu* [5]), the stars seem small, because they are more or less distant. — *Kan-den-si nasuyoo kara, watúkusi no sina wo () kai kudasáre* [6]), = after you shall have thought of it, please buy my goods. — △ *Tabete* (properly *Tabeta*) *kara yuki-masita* [7]), after having eaten, he went.

Compounds with *Kara*, placed as illative conjunctions at the beginning of a proposition:

Sore kara, 自夫, vulgo *Soreda kara*, thence.

△ **Soo site** (properly **Soo-sita**) **kara**, thence, then.

△ **Soo site, So site**, 且, then.

...

[1]) *Da͡i Gaku*, X. 6.
[2]) *Shopping-Dialogues*, p. 23.
[4]) *Shopping-Dialogues*, p. 39.
[3]) Ibid. IX. 5
[4]) Ibid. p. 41.
[7]) s. brown, LVI.
[5]) s. brown, LVII.

45. ...*ni yôtte*, old-Jap. ...*ni yota*, vulgo ...*ni yotte*, 依 因 由 仍, gerund of *yori*, proceeding from... having its foundation on..., because of... It is preceded by the causal proposition, which it governs, in its substantive form with or without the suffix *ni*. *Kumi no budziri ni Awadzi no sima yóri Sado nó sima made ya sima maidzu umi-nasseru kuni mieu ni yorte (to Yasima-kuni tó fu* [1]), the eight isles mentioned in the preceding lines — beginning with Awadsi and ending with Sado are called the „Great land of eight isles," as they constitute the land first produced. *Figiku-kuku wo uyuru koto wo yiku-su yotte mono wo tsukuru mono wo Nou-nin to ieu* [2]), with respect to his ability (*yóksuru*) in cultivating the hundred (all) kinds of grain, the producer is called Nou-nin (husbandman).

Compounds with ...*ni yótte*, as illative conjunctions placed at the beginning of a proposition:

Kore ni yótte, Sore ni yótte, therefore, Lat. *igitur*.

Sikáru ni yótte, or **Sáru ni yótte,** as it is so, for such reasons, therefore, consequently.

Remark. ...*ni yítte* is, in the official style, superseded by the words expressive of relation **Aida**, = between, while (§ 62 n°. 14), and **Tsuki, Tsukite, Tsuite,** respecting (§ 63, B. 3). At least, places have come under our notice, in which both words must have causal force. Compare page 320, line 14.

b. Conjunctions of adverbial propositions, which indicate a future, possible cause (Conditional conjunctions).

We may not pass them over in silence, because they are suggested by others although they do not really exist. We have alone to do with a time-defining local, and thus if, with a view to the spoken language, we confine ourselves to *Nari*, to be, with the form *Naru-toki ni*, when it shall be, for which also simply *Naru-toki ni*, = when it is, is used, or, instead of it, with the suppositive form explained in § 76, thus, to stick to *Nari*, with

46. **Naraba,** △ **Nara,** = if it shall be; it is preceded by a substantive or by a verb in the substantive form. -- △ *Sa-yoo nari*, or *Sore nara*, *kai-maiôo* [3]), if it is so, then I shall buy it. If the speaker intends to say: as it is so, then he takes *Nara* for a contraction of *Nareba*. — *Firu maye ni wá mairi-ye-maséau*. —

---

[1] *Ko-n-ki-dzu.* I. p. 4 r.   [2] *Kawu-gaki.* IV. 4 r.

[3] *Shopping-Dialogues*, p. 4.

„Sore nara, hirugu ni." ¹), I can't come before noon. „In the afternoon then." — △ Nokordzu O kai nasdra nara, ondzi nedan de age-maioo ¹), if you will take all, I will sell them at (··) the same price. — △ Nokordzu frii-kin nedan de O kai-nasare. „Yasui nara, tori-maioo" ¹), Buy all the pieces at one and the same price. — „If it is cheap, I will take it."

If the mere possibility or probability of the statement is insisted on, then, in addition to *Naraba*, use is made of the adverb:

Mósikuwa, or simply **Mosiwa**, **Mosi**, — in case of, if. 荷, 如, 若. = 万ㇲ —{ *Man-itsi*, one against a thousand. Its place is at the beginning, or even after the subject of a subordinate proposition, whereas the predicate verb of that statement, if it is not attributively connected with *toki* (as *Naru-toki*), is put in the suppositive form (*Naraba*) or occurs as the gerund. *Mosi sikára toki ва*, in case it is so; 若シ然ラハ, *Mosi sikáraba*, if it might be so; *Mosi sikárite*, in case it is so.

As *Sikuni* is evidently the adverbial form of *Siki*, — ...ish, ...like, isolated by *ni* (see page 109) n°. 71), only *wo* of *Mo-sikuwi*, remains as the nucleus of this compound. If this *wo* is a variation of the *wa* (前 ¹), — actually, explained at page 130), *Mósikuwi* is equivalent to the Latin *veri-similiter*; if it is an abbreviation of *omoü*, — thought, then *Mósi-kuwi* means probably, likely, peut-être. *Inu ka neko ka?* dog? or cat? *Inu ka? mosikuwa neko ka?* a dog? or perhaps a cat? *Ni-nusi mosi kore wo inamu toki ва* ¹), in case the owner of the goods refuses such. *Mosi ta no kóku-zin so-sei no taku wo gen-zuru toki ва, Oranda-zin mo doü-ggu ni nyo-wraru bei* ¹), if the amount of the import duty be lowered for another nation, the Dutchmen shall be placed on a like footing. *Mosi gi-ron-tchoji gataku toki sei, sono sigiran wo ..., seioju ni uiende nyotai-seritsu bei* ¹), if such may be difficult to determine, this question shall be brought to the knowledge of the government and (by it) be settled. *Niigata minoto, mosi sono minato wo aki-gataki koto araba* (read *araba*). *Nippon nisi no kata nite betsu ni fsitsuwa minato narabini mura wo ..., aku-bei* ¹), the port of Niigata — in case a difficulty might arise about opening this port, a harbor and town shall be opened elsewhere on the West-side of Nippon. *Mosi siygu-zen*

---

¹) *Shopping-Dialogues*, p. 17.   ²) Ibid., p. 84.   ³) Ibid. p. 87.
⁴) Neth.-Jap. Treaty. III. al. 8   ⁵) Ibid III al. 7   ⁶) Ibid. II. al. 9.
⁷) French-Jap. Treaty. III. al. 8

san kin i-ziyyu wo motsi-wataralsi ¹), in case a merchant vessel might import more than three pounds (of opium). *Mosi yao-ji naki ni-ani* **arita**, *kono ki-yen taiu jon-riyo tori-kayesi sunsuzu domo, dru-piku no omómoki ea kono ki-yen yori tori-okonóru-bési* ¹), if there might be some trifling matter, which cannot be avoided, the spirit of the Treaty shall be acted upon, even if the ratification of the document (containing the Treaty) within the fixed term shall not have taken place.

IV. Conjunctions of the purpose.

§ 130. 17. Tamé ni, 爲, of Tamé, purpose, aim, end, for, on behalf of, is properly a word expressive of relation (see page 292 n°. 24), and has, when it is used as a conjunction, the verb in its substantive form with or without **ga**, as suffix of the genitive, before it. *Ki-miku wo siyun-siu-sesimaru ga tamé ni ... siyo-rikisun besi* ¹), in order to have the rules followed, aid will be given. — *Uru tamé ni*, for sale. *Tsutsi suna yu ni fukasunu tané, kazé wo kirynu bési*, take care to shelter the place from wind, to the end that earth and sand be not blown on the food (of the silkworms).

The verb dependent on *Tamé ni* is put in the future with or without the genitive termination *ga*, when the attainment of the object is considered as still belonging to the future. — *Kono okite wo katákusen tamé ni*, in order to carry out this clause, there shall etc. — *Kayami ra sugata no yosi-asi wo miru ma, kokóro no kyaka-tsyoku wo tadási arataram ga tamé nari*, = with regard to the mirror, its object is not alone to see if the countenance is beautiful or ugly, but also to rectify and reform the wrong and the right (i. e. the moral nature) of the heart.

48. **Tote**, the syncopated *to site*, of *to*, to, and *sité*, the gerund of *si*, *n*, *sru*, to do.

Preceded by a verb in the future, .. *tó su* means to be active to carry out the object, which still belongs to the future, (Compare § 103. 6. 7. page 290). *Motomen to su* is thus - *acquisiturus est*, he is about to get; *Motomen to site* or *Motomen to te*, = being about to get, i. e. for the purpose of getting. *Sin-fu to ien mono ju-zi no yasuri wo motomen to te Nippon ve wohiriki*, a certain Sin-fu came to Japan to search for a remedy against death.

---

¹) Neth. Jap. Treaty, III. al. 6   ²) Ibid. XI al. 2   ³) Ibid. XIII al. 2

The spoken language supersedes *Motomen* by *Motomeó* (see page 209), thence the expressions: *Motomeó to suru tokoroni*, on the point of acquiring; *Motomeó to suru mono*, some one who is on the point of acquiring; *Motomeó to te*, that he may acquire.

V. Concessive conjunctions.

§ 131. 49. Mo, 亦 も, also, properly an adverbial postposition (see § 122), when it is put after the predicate verb of a subordinate causal proposition, it characterizes it, as one granting that something is real or possible, whilst the statement thus conceded is limited or revoked by a proposition immediately following it (adversative proposition). The verb dependent on *mo*, as it has been already noticed in § 74, is put in the substantive form with the local termination *ni* or also in the gerund.

Akuru ni mo. *Miru ni mo.* *Yuku ni mo.*
Akete mo. *Mite mo.* *Yukite* (△ *Yuite*) *mo.*

△ *Ika-you ni ndsitte mo*, however it be made. — △ *O kai nasare te mo, O yame nasare te mo, kono uy' wa deki-matalan* ¹), you may buy it or not; I cannot go further. I don't care: take it or leave it.

50. ..tomo, と, also, with a verb preceding in its substantive form. *Akuru-tomo, Miru-tomo, Yuku-tomo. — Idzúré no kóta yóri mairu-tomó* ¹), it does not matter from which side he may come.

51. ..domó, ども, ndomó, contr. from *ni*, Local, and *tomó*. Comp. page 207. Opposed to *Akeba アケバ*, the fusion of *Ake ni va*, is *Akedomo アケドモ*, likewise a fusion of *Aki ni to mo*, and opposed to *Areba* is *Aredomó*, though there is. From *Arandomo*, though there is not, and *Sarandomo*, though it is not so, come *Aradomo* and *Saradomo*. Compare page 258.

52. ..tédōmō, though it is said, though it is called, though... with a previous appositive definition characterized by *to*. See page 209.

忘る≀雖≀ ⎰ 忘る≀雖≀ *Tomi tó tédomó, mádzushiki wo wásurúru koto nakare!*
⎱ *Tóttosi tó tédomó, iyáshiki wo wásurúru koto nakare.*
賎≀勿≀ ⎰ 貧≀勿≀ Though you are rich, do not forget the poor!
⎱ Though you are honorable, do not forget low people!

¹) *Shopping Dialogues*, p. 39   ²) *French-Jap. Treaty.* III. 13

CHAPTER VIII. CONJUNCTIONS. § 131. 345

Sen-riyoo no ko-gane wō tsuma tō iedomo, itsi-nitsi no gaku ni wa sikázu, though gold is heaped up to the amount of a thousand ounces, it is not equal to one day's study. ..*koto wo mō yurusan bési to iedomó*,..*koto wa kesste nazúru bési*¹), though this also be granted, it may not certainly happen that...

53. **Sikare domo**, 然, syncopated **Sare domo**, — though it is so, the concessive form of *Sikar)i*, n. to be so, root *si* (see page 109 n°. 71).

54. **Sore de mo**, also then, the modal of *Sore*, — such, followed by *mo*, antithesis of the conclusive *Sore de wa* (see page 344 n°. 17).

55. **Sika mó**, 尚 , but: abbreviation of *Sikaredomo*. *Hitó no gen-séi naru, sikamó kori ni toyúte, toun-xedrumot* ¹), to oppose men, although they are accomplished and wise, and not allow their advancement.

56. **Somo somo**, 抑 ¹), 亦然, or, explained by the Japanese themselves as concessive ³), concedes the antecedent statement, however introduces an adversative clause. It means properly „so as so as," is a fusion of *Sikâmo*, and this of *Sikâka mo* (just as *Sonte* of *Sikâka nó*, see page 344 n°. 18), and stands with the adversative force of *Tadási* (see page 345 n°. 22) or of *Sikási* (see page 343 n°. 13). Some Japanese etymologists think *Somo somo* an abbreviation of *Sore mo sore mo*, others of *Sate mo sate mo*, which, so far as the meaning goes, approaches our derivation.

In the beginning of a speech it serves to announce that which is to be said, as an opposition of other opinions. In this quality it is stamped as an introductory word (發 語 辭 , *Fat-go no kotoba*), and will approach most nearly to an expression like: „However it may be" ⁴).

Kore wo motomuru ka? Somo somo kore wo atauru (atoeru) ka? ⁵), does he strive for it? or does one give it to him?

---

¹) Neth.-Jap. Treaty. II al. 6. · *Das Galv.* N 14.

ⁿ) „*Yó*, a particle denoting or, either also a commencing particle as moreover." MEDHURST, *Chinese and English Dictionary* ⁴) 發 語 辭

³) The sense we assign to *Somo somo* does not agree with that attributed to it in SIEBEKEWITSCH *Yamato-Kossiki Kwwee*

⁵) *Ron-yu.* I. § 10

346 CHAPTER VIII. CONJUNCTIONS. § 131, 132.

抑モ
而シテ
強ヰ
與ヨ

與ト
北ホク
方ハウ
之ノ
強キヤウ
與ヤ

曰イハク
南ナン
方ハウ
之ノ
強キヤウ

子シ
路ロ
問ト
強キヤウヲ
子シ

Ni-ro kyoo wo tou. Si no no-tamawaku, nan-joo no kyooka? fokn-fau no kyooka? somo somo nandzi ga kyooka? ¹), Tszŭ-lu asked about energy. The Master said, "Do you mean the energy of the South? the energy of the North? or your own energy?"

57. **Mamayo**, — in case it occurs with the meaning attributed to it of „encore que, quoique" ²) for in Japanese writings I have never yet met with this word, it must, to have a concessive force, be reduced to the form of *Mu-ma mo* (see page 337 n°. 31) modified for the sake of euphony, and thus mean „however often," being equivalent to *Toki-toki mo* or *Tabi-tabi mo*. The expression: „However often he tries it, he does not succeed in it," would thus be equivalent to *Kokoro-miru mama yo deki-masa'an*.

Remark. The suffix **mo** gives to all the conjunctions definitive of place and time, or properly words expressive of relation, cited in § 127, a concessive force, i. e. it characterizes the antecedent proposition, which the word expressive of relation governs, as concessive, while the subsequent proposition comes out with an adversative force ³).

The relative comparative of propositions.

§ 132. 58. **Musiro**, 寧ろ, in preference, rather, Lat. *potius*, as an adverb, it is put at the beginning of a subsequent proposition, to the contents of which preference is given above that expressed in the antecedent proposition. As starting point of the comparison the antecedent statement is characterized by *yori wa*. Next to „*Yuku yori wa yukanu ga mashi*, it is better not to go than to go," cited in *Remark* p. 131, is *Yuku* (or *Yukan*, Future) *yori wa musiro yuku na yo!* – rather do not go, than go! Whereas the state or action, to which the preference is given may be represented as one commanded or future, the state or action of the antecedent proposition may be a present, or likewise a future one, as appears from the following saying of K'ung-tsze (*Lun-yu*, Cap. III. *Pa-yi*, § 4), of which we give three Japanese translations, which lie before us.

---

¹) *Tshung-yung*. X. 1, 0.   ²) RODRIGUEZ § 83.

³) According to CONCHARWITSCH Vap.-Russ. sloar, *Mamayo* signifies *Wprotschem* (besides).

CHAPTER VIII. CONJUNCTIONS. § 132.   347

„As to festive ceremonies, be rather sparing than extravagant; as to mourning, be rather grieved than pay attention to observances."

In the translation 1 and 2 the subsequent proposition is taken as Imperative, in 3 as a wish, in the Future, whereas in 1 the antecedent proposition is conceived as Present, in 2 and 3 as Future.

In Mr. J. LEGGE's excellent version of the Chinese text this passage runs: „In festive ceremonies, it is better to be sparing than extravagant; in the ceremonies of mourning, it is better that there be deep sorrow than a minute attention to observances."

Remark. 1. Japanese etymologists see in *Musiro* a variation of *Mosi* (若 し, in case of, see § 129 n°. 46), and explain *ro* as an „auxiliary word" [1]; an explanation that does not prepossess us in its favor. Should not *Musiro* much rather be equivalent to the syncopated form of *Masu-siro* (益 す 代 り), and thus mean „more price" or „higher value" [2]. Used as an adverb, a word with this signification, at least more than any other, would be equivalent to our „by preference." With regard to the so called auxiliary word *ro*, the *Wa-gun Siwori* teaches us, that in the eastern Japan it supersedes the termination *wo*. In Japanese Dictionaries the signification of △ *Sou-si-tai* and *Kou-si-tai*, i. e. to desire to do so or so (see § 105), is given to *Musiro* and 寧 (*ning*, willingly); it is plain that the writer aims at the optative proposition, which is introduced by *Musiro*.

Remark 2. The spoken language supersedes *Musiro* with *Naka-naka ni*, - almost, rather, and *Nengoro ni*, willingly, rather; and makes use of other expedients too. *Ni-sen yori wo naka-naka ni nokorazu sute-oken*, I will rather give up all, than die. *Watakusi wa yuku yori yuki-masetsu hoo ga yorosii to zon-zi-masu* [3], I think, that it is better not to go, than go. I would rather not go. — „*Fito wo gai-suru yori wa futa ni gai-seraruru ga mesi to omoi-masure!* Suffer wrong rather than do it" [4]: literally: think, that it is better to be injured by others, than to injure others!

---

[1] *Wa-gun Siwori*, under *Musiro*.
[2] a. BROWN, Coll. Jap. N°. 419
[3] Compare *Ne ga siro*, worth nothing. § 109, I. 1.
[4] Ibid. N°. 676.

ALPHABETICAL SYNOPSIS OF THE CONJUNCTIONS TREATED.

Aida . . . N°. 32.	Mata ta. . N°. 3.	Site . . . . N°. 18.	Toki ni . . N°. 21.
Anzuru ni . . . 23.	Mase, Maye . . 31.	Site ed . . . . . 19.	Toki ni ro. . . . 24.
Aruita . . . . . 7.	Mai . . . . . . 31.	Sitaa . . . . . . 27.	Tokinra . . . . . 24.
Babo . . . . . . 21.	Migiri . . . . . 25.	Suki mi. . . . . 33.	Tokóro . . . . . 21.
. . domo . . . . 31.	. . mo . . . . . . 1.	Sikaredomo . . . 33.	Tokóro de . . . . 21.
Fodo . . . . . . 42.	. . mo, . . uro. . . 1.	Sikúru ni yotte. 18.	Tokóro ni . . . . 24.
Fodo ni . . . . 42.	. . mo muta . . . 2.	Sikási . . . . . 13.	. . to mo . . . . . 50.
. . ya . . . . . . 19.	Mosi. . . . . . . 16.	Sikósi-nagára . 13.	Toóri ni . . . . 32.
Gutó ni . . . . 21.	Mosikaca . . . . 15.	Sikási-nagáramo 14.	. . to te . . . . . 41.
Gutó)si, ki, ku. 41.	Mottomo . . . . 11.	Somo-somo . . . 36.	. . touite . . . . 41.
Hodo ni . . . . 42.	Musiro . . . . . 32.	Soo-aitá kara . . 16.	Utsi . . . . . . 22.
. . ifdomó . . . 12.	Nagára . . . . . 12.	Soo-aite kara . . 16.	Utsi ni . . . . . 22.
. . ka, . . ka . . 2.	. . nam. . . . . 16.	Soo wo . . . . . 17.	Utsi wo . . . . 22.
Kanete . . . . . 6.	. . narubá . . . . 16.	Sore da kara. 16, 44.	aye . . . . 33.
Kara . . 16, 27, 11.	Nambi ni . . . . 5.	Sore de . . . . 17.	. . ya . . . ya . . 10.
Kóra ya yoi ni. 13.	. . nga . . . . . . 12.	Sore de mo . . . 51.	. . yara . . . . . 10.
Katsu . . . . . 3.	. . ni yirite . 16, 45.	Sore de wa . . . 17.	. . yarun . . . . 10.
Katsu te . . . . 3.	. . ni yote . . 16, 45.	Sore-kara . 16, 44.	Ygu ni . . . . . 40.
Keddsi . . . . . 21.	. . ni yotte. . 16, 45.	Sore ni yotte . . 16.	Yusári . . . . . 11.
Kono yud ni . . 43.	Notsi . . . . . . 42.	Sosite . . . . . 18.	Yoo ni . . . . . 40.
Kore ni yotte . 18.	Ogóbi . . . . . 4.	Sosite kara. 16, 44.	Yori . . . . . . 30.
Ma . . . . 3.	Sin-nayára . . . 14.	Sunaratsi . . . . 20.	Yotte . . . . . . 18.
Mude . . . . . . 39.	Sure domo . . . 53.	Tabi-yoto ni . . 31.	Yad . . . . . . 43.
Ma-ma . . . . . 31.	Siri-nagára . . . 14.	Tabi-tabi ni . . . 31.	Yad ni . . . 16, 42.
Ma-mai ni . . . 31.	Sir-nagára mi. 14.	Tuddsi . . . . . 32.	
Ma-ma yo . . . 62.	Sira-fodo ni . . 42.	Tamé ni . . . . 47.	
Mota . . . . . . 2.	Sára ni yotte . . 16.	Toki . . . . . . 18.	

APPENDIX

The three dialects, those of *Hän*, *U'* and *Tsäny*, mentioned and elucidated at pp. 30 and 31, are, according to a statement, since come to our knowledge, from a Japanese man of letters [1]), the dialect of *Hang-chow* (杭州), capital of the province *Che-kiang*, that of *Fuh-chow* (福州), capital of *Fuh-kien*, and the Official language (官音, *Kwan-yin*), by others, also called *Kwan-hwa* or the Mandarin. A correct instruction in the Official language is extremely rare, the more so, as both the other dialects are generally in use.

As this statement furnishes a satisfactory answer to the question concerning the presumed historical value of the Chinese dialects extant in Japan, we consider ourselves required to quote the original expressions of this statement also.

○本朝ノ傳ヘトヨロ、杭州、福州、官音、三アリ、多クハ杭州福州ナリ、官音ハ至テ精密傳ヘモノアレナリ、

[1]) 四聲解頤, *Si-sei tai-dzun*, = a work to elucidate the four tones, by *Koo-mon Sen-sei*, 1804; reprinted in 1858. Preface, p. 1 verso.

ADDENDA

Page 157. The year-name *Gen-dzi* (1861) is succeeded by 慶を應ず, *Kri-oo* 丑元 1865.

Page 256, § 92, 1. *Remark*. If *ariji*, u, is preceded by a substantief in the Local or by an adverb in *ku*, it stands as a substantive affirmative verb and is a fusion of the particle *zo* and *ariji*, u. Thus *Fána ni zarikeri* stands for *Fána ni zo arikeri*, = a flower has it been; *Sámaku zarikeri*, for *Simuku zo arikeri*, = cold has it been.

ERRATA

Page 294 line 5. *For:* nondeflecting *Read:* deflecting

www.ingramcontent.com/pod-product-compliance
Lightning Source LLC
Chambersburg PA
CBHW032359230426
43672CB00007B/757